I0028035

Cultural Complexes in Europe

What is going on in Europe? The actual conflicts between its nations or states can be traced back to old and revived cultural complexes. In this book, first compiled in 2016, Jungian analysts explore the cultural identities of their European homelands and nations.

This is a new approach to old questions: What makes a people feel at home? How do their traditions and narratives form a cultural Self and identity? How do they differ from one another? Exploring cultural complexes blends knowledge of history, economics, sociology, anthropology, geography, psychology, religious studies, literature, and poetry. But as every complex is built around an emotional core, the study of how cultural complexes live in the psyche is not limited to these disciplines. Each author and reader engages in a confrontation with their emotions, prejudices, and projections. The shape that the ideas and feelings of a cultural complex take in the psyche can be inchoate, rapidly shifting and yet paradoxically long standing, and often quite immune and impermeable to the reason that traditional disciplines of thought would impose on them. These cultural complexes do not necessarily provide a coherent or linear sequencing of facts and events because that is not how they actually exist and function in the psyche of individuals and groups. At the same time, cultural complexes shape what it means to be a citizen of a particular city, region, or country of Europe.

This remarkable book is an important read for Jungian analysts and those interested in Europe's historical and cultural development.

Jörg Rasche, MD, is a Jungian analyst in Berlin. He served for many years as president of the German Jungian Association (DGAP) and was vice-president of IAAP and president of the German Association for Sandplay Therapy (DGST). His books and articles include reflections on creativity, music, politics, and non-violent conflict resolution.

Thomas Singer, MD, is a psychiatrist and Jungian psychoanalyst who trained at Yale Medical School, Dartmouth Medical School, and the C. G. Jung Institute of San Francisco. He is the author of many books and articles that include The Cultural Complexes Series. He serves on the board of ARAS (Archive for Research into Archetypal Symbolism) and has served as co-editor of *ARAS Connections* for many years.

'Qualities of passion and intellectual coherence co-exist in this extraordinary book, itself a product of history, politics, psychology and—often—personal experience and suffering. *But what about the timing?* Europe is in its deepest crisis since the Second World War and, in the absence of any credible solutions from conventional politics, depth psychology and the idea of cultural complexes are entitled to step into the breach. There is more: By assembling authors from so many different nations, Jörg Rasche and Tom Singer have created a special European union before our very eyes. They, and their stellar team of authors, have not only analysed the continental lines of conflict and war, but have also made noteworthy contributions to the achievement of peace-in-diversity.'

Professor Andrew Samuels, *Author of A New Therapy for Politics?*

'This is a remarkable and original book and should be read by all those interested in Europe from historical, personal and cultural perspectives, including the roots of European conflicts and their implications for present-day issues. The authors are Jungian analysts or academics from different parts of Europe, and the book's theoretical underpinning is the concept of cultural complexes, exploring their relevance, dynamics, positive and shadow aspects in individual countries. The editors, Jörg Rasche and Thomas Singer, and the publisher, Spring Journal Books, are to be congratulated for their vision in publishing at this time a book of high quality essays when contemporary Europe is in flux: struggling with its identity; with who belongs and who is excluded; with managing more flexible boundaries, especially challenging with the huge influx of refugees seeking sanctuary in European countries.'

Jan Wiener, *Director of Training, Society of Analytical Psychology, London; Former Co-Chair of the IAAP Education Committee with Responsibility for Eastern Europe*

'This book on Europe and its cultural complexes is both profound and perfectly timed. The individual articles are outstandingly written by authors who have a deep understanding of Jung and analytical psychology, and know how to connect that knowledge with the problems that Europe faces today. The viewpoints represented are essential to understanding the history of the different European countries and helpful in understanding why they are in such turmoil now. I highly recommend it.'

Thomas B. Kirsch, *Former President of the International Association for Analytical Psychology*

Cultural Complexes in Europe

A Jungian Exploration of Soul, Psyche and Identity

Second Edition

Edited by Jörg Rasche and Thomas Singer

Series Editor Thomas Singer

Routledge
Taylor & Francis Group

LONDON AND NEW YORK

Designed cover image: Peter von Hess, Empfang König
Ottos von Griechenland in Athen, 1839, Bayerische
Staatsgemäldesammlungen – Neue Pinakothek München, URL:
https://www.sammlung.pinakothek.de/de/artwork/A9xlnDkGWv

Second edition published 2025
by Routledge
4 Park Square, Milton Park, Abingdon, Oxon, OX14 4RN

and by Routledge
605 Third Avenue, New York, NY 10158

Routledge is an imprint of the Taylor & Francis Group, an informa business

© 2025 selection and editorial matter, Jörg Rasche and Thomas
Singer; individual chapters, the contributors

The right of Jörg Rasche and Thomas Singer to be identified as
the authors of the editorial material, and of the authors for their
individual chapters, has been asserted in accordance with sections
77 and 78 of the Copyright, Designs and Patents Act 1988.

All rights reserved. No part of this book may be reprinted
or reproduced or utilised in any form or by any electronic,
mechanical, or other means, now known or hereafter invented,
including photocopying and recording, or in any information
storage or retrieval system, without permission in writing from the
publishers.

Trademark notice: Product or corporate names may be trademarks
or registered trademarks, and are used only for identification and
explanation without intent to infringe.

First edition published by Spring Journal Books 2016

British Library Cataloguing-in-Publication Data
A catalogue record for this book is available from the British Library

ISBN: 978-1-041-00420-2 (hbk)
ISBN: 978-1-041-00422-6 (pbk)
ISBN: 978-1-003-60974-2 (ebk)

DOI: 10.4324/9781003609742

Typeset in Times New Roman
by Apex CoVantage, LLC

Cultural diversity is a precious heritage that we should treasure and protect. The soul loves variety and the human psyche needs the freedom to imagine, to play, and to create. When globalization and homogenization join forces with militaristic thinking and its unceasing expansionist politics, the soul in all its variations is endangered. This book is dedicated to *Europe's Many Souls*.

About complexes, Jung wrote

Complexes in Person's Life

Certain complexes arise on account of painful or distressing experiences in a person's life, experiences of an emotional nature which leave lasting psychic wounds behind them. A bad experience of this sort often crushes valuable qualities in an individual.

CW 8 § 594

All these produce unconscious complexes of a personal nature. A primitive would rightly speak of a loss of soul, because certain portions of the psyche have indeed disappeared. A great many autonomous complexes arise in this way.

CW 8 § 594

Obscure and Difficult Source

But there are others that come from quite a different source. While the first source is easily understood, since it concerns the outward life everyone can see, this other source is obscure and difficult to understand because it has to do with perceptions or impressions of the collective unconscious. Usually the individual tries to rationalize these inner perceptions in terms of external causes, but that does not get at the root of the matter.

CW 8 § 594

At bottom they are irrational contents of which the individual had never been conscious before, and which he therefore vainly seeks to discover somewhere outside him. The primitive expresses this very aptly when he says that some spirit is interfering with him.

CW 8 § 594

So far as I can judge, these experiences occur either when something so devastating happens to the individual that his whole previous attitude to life breaks down, or when for some reason the contents of the collective unconscious accumulate so much energy that they start influencing the conscious mind.

CW 8 § 594

In my view this happens when the life of a large social group or of a nation undergoes a profound change of a political, social, or religious nature. Such a change always involves an alteration of the psychological attitude. Incisive changes in history are generally attributed exclusively to external causes. It seems to me, however, that external circumstances often serve merely as occasions for a new attitude to life and the world, long prepared in the unconscious, to become manifest.

CW 8 § 594 – C. G. Jung
The Structure and Dynamics of the Psyche

Epigraphs used with permission of Princeton University Press, from *The Collected Works of C. G. Jung, The Structure and Dynamics of the Psyche*, C. G. Jung, vol. 8, 1970; permission conveyed through Copyright Clearance Center, Inc.

Contents

Cover Image

The Entry of King Otto of Greece Into Athens by Peter von Hess (1839)

The cover painting (from the New Pinakothek Munich) shows the reception of King Otto in Athens in 1839. Otto was a Wittelsbach prince from Bavaria, a son of King Ludwig I. After the defeat of the Ottoman Empire the European monarchies were searching for a possible candidate to rule Greece. The royal families of Great Britain, Habsburg-Austria, France, and Russia agreed that the Bavarian prince would fit with their interests and proposed their candidate to the new Greek National Assemblies. Otto was sent to Greece on a British ship, and he brought with him the Bavarian white-blue flag, still the colors of Greece today. The painting by Peter von Hess shows the prince welcomed by Greek priests, patriots, peasants, and many other people in an oriental-Turkish-Greek style, in front of an ancient temple. Otto was not very successful: he was Catholic and rejected the Greek Orthodox religion. When he took the side of Russia against the Ottoman Empire in the Crimean War (1853–1856), the British arranged a revolt against him, and Otto had to leave Greece in 1862. He died in Bavaria/Germany in 1867. The painting shows an episode of the European fantasy of its ancient Greek heritage and of European colonialism in the 19th century. Europe was a fantasy, based on the cultural complex of a common ancient history.

Editors

Thomas Singer, MD, is a Jungian analyst and psychiatrist. After studying religion and European literature at Princeton University, he graduated from Yale Medical School and later trained at Dartmouth Medical Center and the C. G. Jung Institute of San Francisco. Dr. Singer is the editor and co-editor of the Routledge seven-volume series of books on cultural complexes with studies in Europe, the United States, Latin America, Australia, and Southeast Asia. He has also co-edited a series of books on Ancient Greece/Modern Psyche in addition to two volumes of essays with Routledge: *From Vision to Folly in the American Soul* and *Vision, Reality and Complex*. Dr. Singer has served on the board of National ARAS (The Archive for Research into Archetypal Symbolism) for several decades (ARAS.org).

Dr. Jörg Rasche, Jungian analyst, trained in Berlin and Zürich where he studied sandplay therapy with Dora Kalff. Dr. Rasche is a child psychiatrist, working in private practice in Berlin. He served for many years as president of the German Jungian Association (DGAP) and was vice-president of International Association of Analytical Psychology (IAAP) and president of the German Association for Sandplay Therapy (DGST). Also a trained musician, he has published many papers and some books on mythology, music, sandplay therapy, and analytical psychology, as well as serving on the board of various Jungian journals. In 2023, he published a book of essays, *Menetekel: Der Ökozid und das Unbewusste – Was die Klimakrise mit uns macht* (Warning sign: Ecocide and the unconscious: What the climate crisis is doing to us); and in 2024, he published a novel, *Spinozas Freund und die Substanz der Freiheit* (Spinoza's friend and the substance of freedom) (both from Koenigshausen & Neumann). Dr. Rasche has taught in Central European countries for many years and is a training analyst for the IAAP. Dr. Rasche was honored for his work on reconciliation between the Polish and German people by the Polish president who presented him with the Golden Cross of Merit. He gives concerts and lectures around the world. He is married and has three adult children.

Contributors

Henry Abramovitch is founding President and Senior Training Analyst at the Israel Institute of Jungian Psychology in Honor of Erich Neumann, and Professor Emeritus at Tel Aviv University. His books include *Brothers and Sisters: Myth and Reality*; *Why Odysseus Came Home as a Stranger . . .*; and *Panic Attacks in Pistachio: A Psychological Detective Story*. With Murray Stein, he has written plays available on YouTube: *The Analyst and the Rabbi* and *My Lunch with Thomas*.

Olivia del Castillo (Spain) is a clinical psychologist, training analyst, supervisor, and former president of SEPA. She is actively involved in teaching and disseminating analytical psychology in Spain and in writing and publishing articles. Ms. del Castillo is in private practice in Barcelona and Madrid.

Malgorzata Kalinowska is a Jungian analyst (IAAP IM) and a founding member of the Polish Association for Jungian Analysis. She works in private practice in Czeladz, Poland. Malgorzata studies relationships between trauma and culture, especially in the context of Central European history. She focuses on the transcultural dimension of analytical training and translates books on analytical psychology into Polish.

Maria Kendler, originally Austrian, studied German literature at the University of Vienna and worked as a high-school teacher for several years. In 1994, she moved to Switzerland, studied psychology at the University of Lausanne, and today is a psychotherapist in a private practice. Maria Kendler practices and teaches sandplay therapy in several European countries. Currently, she is president of the Swiss Sandplay Society (SGSST) and is editor of *Sandspiel-Therapie*, the Swiss-German journal for sandplay therapy.

Marijana Popović, PhD, is a clinical psychologist, psychotherapist, and supervisor, as well as a member of the International Association for Analytical Psychology. Her PhD dissertation was on the use of fairytales in psychotherapy. She is a member of the European Association of Psychotherapists (EAP) and a member of a Serbian Developing Group. Since 1998, she has worked in the field of psychological assessment and psychotherapy, and she translates Jungian literature from English to Serbian.

Kristina Schellinski, MA, in political science/literature, graduated from the C. G. Jung Institute in Küsnacht, Switzerland. She is a teaching analyst/supervisor with ISAP, Zürich, and a member of the C. G. Jung Institute, and she served as an International Civil Servant for UNICEF from 1983 to 1998. Schellinski has a private practice in Geneva and is a consultant supervisor with the Geneva University Hospital Department of Psychiatry. She has published in international journals and is currently writing a book on the replacement child.

Erel Shalit (1950–2018) was a Jungian psychoanalyst in Israel and past president of the Israel Society of Analytical Psychology. He was the founding director of the Analytical Psychotherapy Program at Bar-Ilan University and chaired the Jung-Neumann Conference in 2015. He authored several books, among them *The Cycle of Life*; *Requiem*; *Enemy, Cripple, Beggar*; and *The Hero and His Shadow*. He edited, with Nancy Swift Furlotti, *The Dream and Its Amplification*, and with Murray Stein, *Turbulent Times, Creative Minds – Erich Neumann and C. G. Jung in Relationship*.

Martin Skála is a Jungian analyst and supervisor who studied psychology at the Charles University in Prague, in the former Czechoslovakia. He is a board member of the Czech Society for Analytical Psychology and a member of the International Association for Analytical Psychology. He also serves as head of Psychopompos, a center of depth psychology in Prague where he lectures and offers workshops.

Pia Skogemann is a Jungian analyst in private practice in Denmark. She has an MA in religion from the University of Copenhagen and is a founding member, teacher, and supervisor at the C. G. Jung Institute Copenhagen. She is the author of numerous articles and books, including *Where the Shadows Lie* (Chiron, 2009) and *The Double Coniunjctio Tales* (Daimon, Schweiz, 2013).

Jelena Sladojević Matić, PhD, is a clinical psychologist, psychotherapist, and supervisor, as well as a member of the International Association for Analytical Psychology. Her PhD dissertation was on "The Shadow and Its Importance in Analytical, Therapeutic and Diagnostic Work." She is a member of the European Association of Psychotherapists (EAP) and a former president of the Serbian Developing Group. Since 2000 she has worked as a psychotherapist in private practice.

Marta Tibaldi is a Jungian analyst of the Associazione Italiana di Psicologia Analitica (AIPA) and of the International Association for Analytical Psychology (IAAP). A training analyst and supervisor in Rome and Hong Kong, she is also Training Supervisor of C. G. Jung Zurich and Liaison Person of the IAAP Developing Group in Hong Kong. She is the author of many articles and essays. Her recent publications include *Oltre il cancro: Trasformare creativamente la malattia che temiamo di più* (Moretti & Vitali, 2010) and *Pratica dell'immaginazione* *attiva* (La Lepre, 2011). She is the author of the blog "C. G. Jung's Analytical Psychology between Italy and China" (martatibaldi.blogspot.com).

Evangelos Tsempelis grew up in Athens, Greece. Co-founder of Stillpoint Spaces (https://medium.com/@stillpointspaces), Evangelos currently lives in Zürich, where he works in private practice as a psychoanalytic counselor.

Caterina Vezzoli is a Jungian analyst in private practice, living and working in Milan. She is a member of CIPA Southern Institute, a training analyst at C. G. Jung Institute Zürich, and a visiting supervisor in Tunisia. She is a teacher and supervisor at different institutions and at the University of Milan.

Acknowledgments

This book would not have been possible without all the friends and colleagues of my old and new European family, especially in Italy, Poland, Latvia, Ukraine, and Russia. Thanks to my parents and to my teachers who opened my mind to the treasures of our cultures and also to the shadow sides of nationalism. I can mention only a few here: Luigi Luisi, Brother David Steindl-Rast, Frieder Staebler, Albrecht and Mechthild Wenck-Ansohn, and Jan Wiener. Thanks to Thomas Singer for his never-ending support and wisdom; to LeeAnn Pickrell and Ann Lammers for their assistance in so many questions; to Jean and Tom Kirsch, Rali and Micha Neumann, and Erel Shalit, who passed away in 2018, for their friendship. Many thanks to all who confronted themselves with the depths of the European cultural unconscious and wrote about this for the book. And thanks to my children and my wife, Beate, for their never-ending support and patience.

— Jörg Rasche

Jörg Rasche has been a wonderful co-editor in the creation of *Cultural Complexes in Europe*. He is filled with a deep knowledge of European history as well as having an intimate wisdom of Europe's rich and varied folkways, mores, and deeper cultural currents and conflicts. This book simply would not exist without his invariably wise guidance, direction, and contributions. Nor would this book or the series of books on cultural complexes exist without both Routledge and Nancy Cater's Spring Journal books supporting this project over a long time. The result of their unwavering support is that more than ninety authors from around the world have now contributed to the exploration of the cultural complex notion in seven separate volumes.

The authors of this volume have been richly creative and uniformly receptive to editorial suggestion. It is a privilege to work with so many thoughtful contributors who have generously shared their unique experiences and perspectives. It is akin to receiving the best tutorials in the most interesting subjects from the most gifted teachers. LeeAnn Pickrell is more than a talented copy editor; her keen sense of value is a steady guide in all things editorial. And, as always, my wife, Jane, and my dachshunds, Lulu and Walter, have put up with my inattention as I focus on European cultural complexes and American baseball.

— Thomas Singer

Map of Europe

Introduction

Jörg Rasche

Mythological Roots of the Old Continent: A Princess From Asia

Deep is the well of history. The dawn of European cultural complexes, their roots and narratives go back to ancient times. It began with the emergence and the definition of a difference: Europe is different from Asia. The early mythology of the Asian princess *Europa* ("the one with bright shining eyes") states the difference as well as the connection. The daughter of Agenor, king of Tyrus in Phoenicia, was playing with her girlfriends in the sunny meadows on the eastern shore of the Mediterranean Sea when a beautiful white bull appeared and invited her to sit on his back. Zeus, master of metamorphosis, had fallen in love with the beautiful Asian girl and carried her away to Crete, the nearest island and the offspring (origin) of what we call European culture. The princess was visited frequently by the Greek god Zeus, and she became the mother of King Minos who resided in his famous palace in Knossos. The Greeks, conquerors and heirs of the ancient Aegean (Minoan) culture, told strange stories about the sacred bulls in Crete; they whispered with horror and fascination about the Minotaur, half man and half bull, who was shamefully hidden in the labyrinth. They praised the Greek hero Theseus who slaughtered the monster with the help of Ariadne's thread. Theseus became king of Crete and Athens as well.

The Asian heritage of early European culture was regarded with respect and suspicion. Already in the oldest mythology, there are traces of projections and complexes regarding Asian cultures, religions, and rituals. The difference is a basic theme in the mythologies of Troy and Carthage. Troy in Asia Minor was the capital of a pre-Hellenic kingdom with the Great Mother Goddess at the top of its religious hierarchy – still in Homer's *Iliad* it was protected by the female goddess Hera and her brother Poseidon. Carthage, capital of the Phoenicians, was an outpost of their Asian empire on the African shore. The Romans destroyed it in the Punic wars because the Phoenicians were their competitors and because, as Cato used to say, Carthage used to sell weapons to the barbarians. Asian culture with its age-old goddesses, traditions, narratives, and cultural mores was always a challenge for Western self-esteem. The idea of a European identity emerged slowly and step by

DOI: 10.4324/9781003609742-1

step. Markers of this emergence were the ancient Greeks, the Roman Empire of Augustus, medieval Christian culture, the Enlightenment with Voltaire and Kant, the French Revolution, and the battle about Napoleon's heritage. The "Europe of Nations," as we call it today, created its own narratives and mythologies, often based on age-old fantasies.

Europe – a Fantasy?

A new vision of Europe emerged again in our own lifetime when the Communist bloc fell apart. The Iron Curtain was opened, and a great release took place in the East as well as in the West. For the first time since two disastrous World Wars and the icy confrontation between the Western and Eastern Blocs, the old glaciers of mutual projections began to melt, and a future of freedom, welfare, peace, and unity throughout Europe, including Russia and the former Soviet Union, seemed to be possible. The inspiration for this book grew out of the hopefulness of those early years after the fall of the Berlin Wall and German Unification.

But human history rarely has a happy ending. I remember a dream I had during the Second European Conference for Analytical Psychology in St. Petersburg in 2012.

I went with a group of people to walk on a melting glacier in the mountains. We and our guide were approaching the cliffs of the glacier. Somehow I knew that it would be possible and not dangerous to walk on the melting ice if we placed our feet carefully. But before we reached the edge of the ice, we came to a torrent of melting water, flowing out from under the glacier. The rushing water washed out a deep bed and took stones and bushes and even trees with it. I saw a tree falling down into the torrent and realized that I should not try to intervene. Otherwise I would fall into the wild water myself.

I understood this to be a social or collective dream, and it became a guide for me to follow carefully and with respect as the raw and melting emotions began to flow in the conference. It gave me pause to reflect on the difficult emotional history of the members of my newly discovered European family. The European Spring of 1989, released by Gorbachev's perestroika, triggered hopes for a better world and the promise of a pan-European code of values: the integrity of the individual person, no gulags, equal rights, economic welfare, free speech, and no humiliation and subjugation of cultures as in the Stalinist system. Many Europeans thought there would not be another war in Europe. But after that euphoric beginning, disillusionment came. The property of the socialist state and its people fell into the hands of oligarchs or was taken over by Western entrepreneurs. The previous guarantees of security in the Soviet system promised everybody a job, a living, and a clear, albeit one-sided, ideology and structure for life, and all of that disappeared overnight. When the government-supported safety net for all people ended, the transition became a nightmare for many. It seemed that the life and guiding principles they had lived by for generations were now meaningless. The heroic Homo Sovieticus lost his role and reputation. New-old national states emerged out of the ruins of the Eastern Soviet Bloc. Age-old fears, projections, and archaic patterns of self-esteem built on tribal and ethnic identities came to life again, fueled by the media and political leaders.

Today, we are witnessing the emergence of a strange European patchwork of formerly repressed collective memories of mutual violations and compensatory grandiosity. This is accompanied by increasing social problems such as unemployment combined with a revival of nationalism. Old spirits are back – evil and good ones. Specters, phantoms, spirits of ambiguous cultural ancestors, and their symbolic *Mana* energy have been revitalized, such as that of the czar in Russia. Increasingly Europe has begun to feel like a dysfunctional family, with its members spread all over the place in both geography and spirit, all of them reacting differently to the increasing number of migrants and refugees. One way to identify the fundamental and disparate elements of this patchwork continent is to think of them as cultural complexes. This book is about the dynamic of such complexes.[1] We can envision with our mind's eye that Europa, the former princess with bright shining eyes, is now an old lady who, as she gazes around her continent, is wondering how best to look after her grandchildren and great-grandchildren, her European offspring. Her family has an impressive cultural history. It is a colorful mix of light and shadow. Europe is the homeland of democracy. Some states have a unique and impressive system of social security; some are suffering from economic misery. Europe is beautiful, and it is much more than just a market or a financial zone; it is a cultural complex itself.

What Is a Cultural Complex?

Complexes are building blocks and working tools of our unconscious psyche. They help us to find orientation in the inner and outer world; they construct a kind of reality; they are emotionally loaded; they have an archetypal core; and sometimes they behave autonomously so that we fall into unconscious projections without hardly being aware of what we are thinking. They are neither good nor bad; they are just what they are. The cultural complex, following Thomas Singer, "is defined as an autonomous, largely unconscious, emotionally charged aggregate of memories, affects, ideas, images, and behaviors that tend to cluster around an archetypal core and are shared by individuals within a group."[2]

A German joke provides a simple illustration of how a cultural complex works:

Nazi Germany during the war: A man on the train is reading a book entitled Mary Stuart. *A Nazi in uniform watches him and asks with a stern voice: "What are you reading? It looks English!"*

The man answers: "This book is written by Friedrich Schiller, one of our greatest poets."

"But then why Mary Stuart?*" asks the Nazi.*

> *The man answers: "Schiller wrote books for all European nations. For the British he wrote* Mary Stuart; *for the Swiss* Wilhelm Tell; *for the French* Jeanne d'Arc; *and for the Italians* Il Fiesco a Genova. *For the Spanish he wrote* Don Carlos. *"*
>
> *"And what did he write for the Germans?" asks the Nazi. The man answers:* "The Robbers. *"*

This kind of joke, told secretly during the Nazi era, reveals something about what a cultural complex looks like: You may laugh at it, even if you don't understand the meaning the joke had or has (in this case) for a German. Of course, the Germans under Hitler behaved like criminals and robbers in Europe. But Schiller's *Robbers* also had another secret meaning for those who told the joke. Schiller, from 1933 to 1945, was a secret hero and code name for those Germans who could not accept Hitler and his criminals to be representatives of German culture. In fact, Schiller had been a revolutionary, a liberal thinker more so than his elder friend Goethe. *The Robbers* (1781) is a theater piece about a group of outcast freedom fighters living in the forest, not unlike Robin Hood. Karl Moor, the leader of the robbers, is a man who was cheated out of his heritage and betrayed in the love of his father by his brother. Karl Moor represents the good one; he finally even rescues his old father who was imprisoned by the bad brother. The character Karl Moor became a symbol for the resistance against the Nazis. Sophie Scholl and her group, White Rose, used to quote Schiller on their leaflets. They were sentenced to death by the Nazis in 1943. Schiller was a true European and admired the 1789 French Revolution against tyranny. Nevertheless, in 1934 (the 175th anniversary of his birth) Schiller was officially praised by Goebbels as a true "German genius." But in 1941, his *Wilhelm Tell* was forbidden by Hitler.

The joke demonstrates that a cultural complex can be hard to understand from outside a culture because it can be so unfamiliar and foreign, just as it can be hard to see it clearly from inside a culture because the intense emotionality of a complex can obscure one's vision and thinking. The *emotional impact* and *reactivity* of a complex – cultural or individual – is usually an identifying hallmark. It can be helpful to have an objective point of view when dealing with a cultural complex. For example, if we touch a cultural complex in therapy with a patient from another culture, awareness of the cultural complexes present in ourselves as therapists and in our patients can help avoid unconscious prejudices and stereotypes. I personally had to confront my own and others' cultural complexes in working with developing Jungian groups in Eastern Europe. I had to discover that people from other cultural backgrounds could experience exactly the same realities in totally different ways than I did. This was the case with Polish, Latvian, Ukrainian, Russian, English, and French colleagues. The differences were not only about the facts of history but also about deep convictions, tastes, fears, and issues of national self-esteem. These complexes seemed to be invariably autonomous in their appearance and functioning.

A personal complex such as an obsessive ego complex or an inferiority complex can lose its energetic charge if one successfully analyzes it in the therapeutic dialogue. This is not an easy job for either the analysand or the analyst. In critical moments, healing symbols can appear out of the unconscious in dreams or active imagination – from the "inner therapist." With activated cultural complexes, however, it is much more difficult because they are collective phenomenon. If open public discussion and real exchange is not possible, the analysis and resolution of complexes possessing an entire society is virtually impossible. Such complexes can continue uninterrupted for centuries. We simply share the complex with most others in our society. This can be a dangerous matter, especially when the complexes involve other groups of people in mutual, unconscious projections. For instance, what feels absolutely clear to a Ukrainian may be absolutely wrong for a Russian, and vice versa. Or what feels familiar to a Catalan may be utterly distasteful to a Castilian. Therefore, cultural complexes are seldom politically correct for members of different cultures, regions, or languages.

160 Types of Cheese

To talk about one's own cultural complex is a bit like a *salto mortale* ("a dangerous leap") or, better yet, a *vitale* ("stimulating" or "crucial"). Self irony is useful in escaping from the energetic field of the complex. In many European countries, this ability is highly developed. Consider these two jokes.

> *A* French *joke*:
> *Charles de Gaulle once said: "How can you govern a people who have at least 160 different kinds of cheese?"*
> *A* Swiss *joke*:
> *A new teacher gives her first class in a school. "Today," she says, "we will talk about a very interesting issue: Where do the babies come from?" One child answers: "They are brought by the stork." Another child says: "The little children are born in the hospital." A third child says: "The babies are born if the father and mother love one another." Then a fourth child stands up and says: "I think, this is different from Canton to Canton" ("es ist unterschiedlich von Kanton zu Kanton").*

Every French and Swiss knows what the joke from their culture is about. If members of another culture laugh about it, there is often a feeling of sympathy and slight superiority along with a mutual understanding of the peculiarities or oddities of the other. What we regard as a neighbor's cultural complex often mirrors our own complex. In the French joke, a German like me hears something about the great French kitchen with its excellent food and wine, the lifestyle of abundance, which is like "God in France," and also the great tradition of liberty and free speech, with the implication that there can be as many differing opinions as there are types of cheese.

France is the country of Voltaire, of the French Revolution, of democracy, the Code Civil, of free thinking and free speech, and it is said that among the most precious things for the French people is the feeling that they can overthrow their government at any time. The humor about Switzerland is also obvious. Among the highest values for the Swiss is the basic democracy inherent in the structure of the different cantons. Both countries are proud of their history and their lifestyle. Voltaire played a role in both. But there are highly sensitive trigger points that one should not touch. Each nation has its own taboos. To give two examples: As a German, I find it quite difficult to talk with the French about the Vichy government, which also shows how cultural complexes exist in the space between two cultures. And a squeamish Swiss cultural complex is surely about the money of dictators from everywhere being in Swiss banks.

Two other jokes regarding cultural complexes:

An Italian told me: In Naples somebody, let's call him Gennaro, is waiting for the bus. After more than one hour the bus arrives. "At least you are here," Gennaro says to the driver. He answers: "Do we have an appointment?"

An Austrian told me: Question: "Vienna is certainly a wonderful city. But why is the suicide rate so high?" Answer: "These are the many German tourists."

When we talk about cultural complexes, we are also talking about identity, at least some of the time. This makes the complexes all the more sensitive because not only are they impersonal and collective, but also they can feel quite personal and intimate to the extent that the cultural complex lives inside the individual. They can be about who and what we are in the framework of our culture, about normality and otherness, about essential and unessential boundaries. If a comment about somebody's culture or nation provokes an *immediate and intense emotional reaction*, you have quite likely stepped on a cultural complex that you may not be able to resolve personally. There is often intense emotion at the core of a complex that can be triggered by words, by associations, by images, by memories of all kinds, by tastes, and by prejudices.

Identity is a quality that one can't put in a question or reduce to something else. Talking about one's identity – both personal and cultural – is like trying to see one's self and one's emotional reactions from outside. Often, the reactions are so strong that we must suppose the underlying structures are not only about the shadow but also about the *Self of the group*. In the Self, the innermost and precious elements of our psychic life are contained and have to be protected. Then we are in the realm of absolute convictions that touch the basic elements of our culture. It is also the home of religious convictions. There are those who are ready to die for these values. This surely makes one blind to the values of the Self of the members from another group.

Cultural complexes are not always so difficult and loaded with violence. They can simply be parts of daily life that we don't think about because they are so automatic. They are like the air we breathe or the water in which we swim. Then they only become apparent when something doesn't feel right. Many cultural complexes express themselves daily: in the language we speak, the ways we cook, the

subtle nuances of everyday relationships, including drinking rituals, family traditions and narratives, family taboos, child rearing, birthday rites, funeral rites, religious beliefs that are inherited from previous generations, projections onto clan or
regional enemies, national identity, things to be proud of or to neglect and forget,
clothing styles, ways to work, ways of structuring the day (siesta) and the week
(Shabbat or Sunday) – all these kinds of carriers of identity and patterns of behavior can be counted among the more benign elements of cultural complexes. If we
neglect them, something feels terribly wrong. Included in these cultural patterns
that form cultural complexes are the rites about mating, sexuality, and love. Young
people osmose the very sensitive cultural language of these basic human needs.

Cultural complexes as carriers of identity can be a bit *like traps*. We step in them
and can't escape. Like personal complexes, they are charged with meaning that is
often stronger than our ego complex. This is the case, for example, in *religious
convictions*. It can easily become impossible to discuss them without triggering
deep-seated reactions. People are at a loss to understand what is going on in such
situations – either in themselves or in those around them. The potent symbols of
deep beliefs, such as those associated with religion, can easily be manipulated and
abused by spiritual, political, and military leaders. European history is full of such
dynamics – from the medieval Islamic invasions and the Christian Crusades to the
religious wars of the sixteenth and seventeenth centuries.

Circumambulation

One way to approach cultural complexes is through *circumambulation* – to study
similar patterns, to amplify, and to create a protected space for communication
and exploration. Academic and scientific approaches – such as sociology and
anthropology – often miss the emotional and energetic charge in the center of the
complex. Unlike the various academic approaches, the cultural complex notion
centralizes the emotional dimension. The neglect of the emotional value in academic disciplines, such as sociology, ethnology, history, and even in the former
Völkerpsychologie (people's psychology) or studies of mass psychology, can be
found in the abuse of pseudoscientific theories during the twentieth century. Cultural complexes abound with values highly influenced by unconscious processes;
and after the devastating experiences of totalitarian regimes with their streamlined
(coordinated, *gleichgeschaltet*) sciences and ideologies, it was appropriate to rid all
social science studies of any kind of prejudices. In Germany, for example, any kind
of emotional statement in a scientific publication was and still is not well accepted.
We learned the awful lessons of the ideological and racist system of the Nazis
and the disastrous consequences of such theories. On the other hand, we have to
observe and study collective emotions. They are powerful and sometimes terribly
destructive, like the rushing water of my glacier dream in St. Petersburg.

The Jungian concept of the cultural complex dates back to the works of Joseph
Henderson, Thomas Singer, and Samuel Kimbles. Today, Jungian theory is one
of the few systems of thinking that includes the emotional side of collective

phenomena. What makes it so difficult is that we are trying to study something that we are also a part of. To study the emotional core of a cultural complex means diving into our own emotions. Like modern field research in sociology, we are not just objective observers; we are also the objects of study. We may think that as Jungian analysts we have learned to manage this paradox in our daily psychoanalytical practice. We use transference and countertransference to establish a therapeutic field and container in which everything can be said, including the most ugly, evil, and shaming material, in the hope that healing symbols may finally appear. In cultural complexes, our countertransference is crucial. We hope to provide an adequate container for the study of cultural complexes as a way to develop the kind of consciousness that can prevent us from slipping into the all-too-frequent negative projections onto an enemy.

Through circumambulation, we can explore the issues and reactions from many different sides. We have to cross the border and study the complex from our neighbor's side, too. Cultural complexes rarely stand alone; they mirror and reinforce one another. To understand cultural complexes, we have to be willing to change our position to get a clearer picture. For instance, what does the Western world look like to a Muslim? This is what Martin Buber and Levinas said: To become "I" you should look through the eyes of the other.[3]

National Complexes

Many of the complexes explored in this book are *national* complexes. The *founding* narrative of each nation plays a pivotal role in the creation of its cultural complexes: mythological ancestors, fantasies about the nation's mission, memories of collective traumas, historic victories over neighbors, and so on. The patterns of this fictive history are often quite similar. Projections are made about neighbors who represent some shadow aspects of their own nation. But not everything is just a complex: For Germans, the Holocaust is both an immeasurable guilt and a guilt complex, and for the Jews, it is a historical fact and a lasting nightmare. In my country, remembering the Holocaust is necessary to prevent it from sinking into the unconscious. It has to be recalled as a historical fact with a lasting sense of responsibility. Some cultural complexes are filled with a reservoir of energy that remains invisible in everyday life until, like an earthquake or volcano, they erupt. The hundredth anniversary of World War I and the collective guilt for the "original catastrophe of the 20th century" stimulated energized discussions among all European nations. Other important pan-European complexes include the loss of former empires in Great Britain, Austria (Habsburg), France, and Russia. Sometimes these complexes combine to create symptoms of a collective depression or explosive dynamics such as in the war between Ukraine and Russia, where we see cultural complexes of inferiority and grandiosity on both sides. We explore these highly reactive cultural complexes in depth in our newest book *Cultural Complexes and Europe's Many Souls: Jungian Perspectives on Brexit and the War in Ukraine.*

Only a few centuries ago, there were only a few "nations" in Europe, and they were all part of greater empires. When J. S. Bach wrote his *Italian Concerto*, *French Overture*, and *English Suites*, he followed cultural rather than national patterns. Modern nations were born in the late eighteenth and nineteenth centuries when the primary religious orientation of most European countries had lost much of its power. The Enlightenment brought forth the idea of individual freedom, modern science, and democracy. Historians see the "Birth of Nations" as a reaction to the 1789 French Revolution and the Napoleonic occupation of the entire European continent. During the wars of national liberation, nationalistic movements emerged in many countries. The economic interests of growing industrial and national markets without tax borders came together with new democratic ideas. Enlightened ideas of freedom combined with the longing for a new spiritual orientation created a different screen for the projection of the Self or a new collective container for this longing. The former *projection of the Self* onto religion and God was replaced by projection onto the earth, the country, and one's own nation state.

L´oubli et je dirai même l´erreur historique, sont un facteur essentiel de la formation d´une nation et c´est ainsi que la progrès des études historiques est souvent pour la nationalité un danger.

In my translation: Forgetfulness or better: False memory is essential for the formation of a nation, and the progress of historical studies can be dangerous for nationalism.[4]

A nation is not a race, nor a special language, nor a special religion, nor a special region or country. In his famous definition, Ernest Renan said the following:

A nation is a soul, a mental principle. Two things, which are in fact one, form this principle. One of them belongs to the past, the other to the present time. One is a common rich heritage of memories, the other is the shared wish to live together . . . A nation therefore is a huge solidarity community, carried on by the feeling for the sacrifices which were brought, and what you are willing to offer in the future.[5]

Essential is the wish to stay and to live together. Later on Renan adds, "*The essence of a nation is that all individuals have a lot in common, and that they all have forgotten a lot.*"[6]

I would add the following: The cultural complex has two sides – one of them structures the inner collective psyche of a culture/nation, and the other side creates a face to show to the outer world, like a *persona* shown to the neighbors. The part of the complex oriented to the outer world does not exist without the other corresponding, reciprocal complex. The interrelatedness of cultural complexes means that if a cultural or national complex is to be transformed this may only be possible in relation to the transformation of the neighbor's complex. After World War II, France under de Gaulle and Germany under Adenauer began their work on reconciliation in the spirit of this mutual interconnectedness. A similar project today is underway in the mutual understanding of Germany and Poland, and prior to Putin's war against Ukraine, there was the tentative project between Poland and Russia. There is no baby without its mother; there is no persona without the other; and there is no nation without its neighbor.

Crypts of Cultural Memories

Europe's history is full of wars and mutual violations. Almost every year since 1500, a war has occurred on European grounds, initially between monarchies that wanted to establish or to save an empire of their own on the Continent. This began with the English, French, Danish, Swedish, Lithuania-Polish, and Russian kings. The Germans came late to the wars of competing empires because their territory was divided into many little principalities and kingdoms and was later hampered after the Thirty Years' War (1618–1648). The first modern "empire" on German soil was built by Prussian kings like Frederick the Great. With the Napoleonic wars, the quantity of mutual killing of the European people began to increase. In 1871, a new "German empire" was founded and began to compete with the French, British, and Russian empires.

The most disastrous levels of destruction occurred with World War I and the following catastrophes. The years of trench warfare, the use of gases as weapons, the Bolshevik Revolution, and later the violent establishment of Stalin's and Hitler's regimes – all led to the apocalypse of World War II and the Holocaust, which took the lives of many millions of people. People as well as cultures were traumatized. Old cities and the former roots of European civilization were destroyed. Many of these traumas are not yet integrated into the collective consciousness; they are still rumbling underground like impending earthquakes.

A psychoanalytical concept to describe what has happened in the collective psyche is the *crypt*. The repressed collective trauma is enclosed like a psychic dead body (in German, we call it *introject*). You cannot speak about it, and it is passed on silently and unconsciously to the next generation. To give one example: In Easter 2013, I was invited to Kyiv, the capital of Ukraine. This old country had suffered enormously under the Germans and the Bolsheviks. The Russian Orthodox Church had its origins in Ukraine, and long ago, Ukraine had been a center of Russian culture (the Kiev Rus were christened in 988). But several times in its history Ukraine has sought to escape the centralized state of the czar in Moscow. When the Bolsheviks destroyed the former regime in 1918, they had to conquer Ukraine. When Stalin's administration ordered a collectivization of agriculture, the mismanagement in Ukraine led to a catastrophe. In the great famine known as the *Holodomor* in 1932–1933, approximately 8 to 10 million people starved to death in Ukraine. This was even before the beginning of World War II when the German troops and the SS came to continue the genocide. The entire country of Ukraine became a battlefield, as it has once again. The suffering of the people is beyond imagination. That suffering has become enshrined in a psychic crypt.

In Kyiv, there is an impressive memorial for the victims of the great patriotic war to free the country from the Nazi invaders (1941–1945). It is a Stalinist memorial. Only 100 meters away is a memorial for the millions who died from starvation during the Stalinist Holodomor (1932–1933). I find it impossible to bring the memories of these two events together in my mind. Another 100 meters away on the next hill is the historical Monastery of the Caves. Beneath the wonderful churches with their golden domes are thousands of meters of narrow medieval crypts and tunnels with the sarcophagi of more than 120 *saints* – the preserved bodies of medieval monks. There, in the narrow underground tunnels, I witnessed many people praying in silence or crying loudly, mourning their lost ancestors and the painful history of their country. I felt this was the only place where they could experience the crypt of their repressed collective trauma. The caves of the monastery and the 120 buried saints provided shelter and the protective containment necessary for confronting the trauma. It was this energy, enclosed and preserved in the stone underground of their collective psyche, which exploded half a year later in the Maidan revolution of 2014.

The "crypt in the ego" contains cumulative trauma.[7] The transgenerational transmission happens through silence, through the unspoken taboo of touching the pain of the parents. This means that the next generation, too, is unable to speak about its own traumas. I think that most Europeans whose parents or grandparents suffered and were traumatized in the last century by war, genocide, expulsion, killing, and bombing – whether they be Poles, Latvians, Russians, Germans, Greeks, Albanians, Serbs, or any other European people – carry such crypts in their souls. The perpetrators also carry similar crypts. They often cannot accept their guilt, and they suffer from the complex of not being able to mourn and having to maintain a false self. The crypts remain in their souls like stones, heavy foreign matter in their bodies. But at any moment the shell can break, and the repressed contents may overflow the psyche.

The collective psyche is unstable, and its lability makes it susceptible to infections. In such moments, cultural complexes may break out, behave autonomously, and flood the psyche. We can see this dynamic at play in the war in Ukraine and Russia. One relatively harmless example of an unsettled psyche is the famous *German angst*: the constant haunting anxiety that something terrible may happen, which, in fact, has occurred often in German history. German angst is a deeply rooted German cultural complex. Today, since 9/11, there is also an *American angst*, and lurking behind this, as with the German angst, there is a big shadow and unconscious guilt complex. Nowadays German angst appears in the form of collective panic attacks, mostly regarding epidemic diseases, viruses, or polluted foodstuffs. Germans are quite sensitive about biogenetics – and this complex can be a useful tool in mobilizing action against the ecological problems caused by profit-oriented international companies. Each complex has two sides: a hammer that can be used not only to nail together a bird's nesting house but also to kill one's neighbor. Recent German angst has a new, yet old focus: antisemitism and anti-Islamism against both foreigners and immigrants that is accompanied by fear of a new war.

Reconciliation Is Possible

In this book some cultures are presented in greater detail; some are not. An encyclopedic study was not attempted and is not possible. Europe is too large and has too many separate people, regions, and nations. This volume touches on a number of cultural complexes, like paradigms, giving a sense of their uniqueness, specificity, and, at times, commonality. But one thing is certain: Europe is in danger, like a dysfunctional family threatened by divorce. The "eternal peace" about which Immanuel Kant dreamed and for which Moses Mendelssohn and his friend Lessing worked is as far away as ever. A new Cold War between the West and Russia has turned into a cruel hot war.

In such circumstances, it is not surprising to see, for example, the old Greek feelings of having suffered under the Germans in World War II resurfacing in their renewed demands for war reparations. The Greek-German cultural complex is just one of many simmering in Europe. As in any war or deep conflict, the first victim is truth. All the information we get is a mixture of opinions, tendencies, and cultural complexes. This makes it all the more urgent to be aware of the power of prejudices, scapegoat projections, crypts of collective traumas, and the power of modern media. C. G. Jung said that the future of humankind lies in its psyche – and that the purpose of human existence is growing consciousness. Everybody should find their own myth.

The original myths of Europe offer a glimmer of hope that at the end peace and reconciliation will be possible. This brings us back to the myth of the Asian princess. Antique Greece was the wellspring of European culture and its original self-concept. It confronted and emancipated itself from the old matriarchal or matrifocal Asian culture. Its founding narratives are preserved in the myth of princess Europa and the great epics of Homer about the Asian city of Troy and the Western Hellenes. Beautiful Helen was abducted by the Trojan prince Paris and taken eastward to Troy at the Asian shore of the Mediterranean Sea. This precipitated a 10-year siege of Troy. It was a bloody war in which each side sacrificed its most honored heroes. Near the end of the war a remarkable event unfolded, which Homer described in the beautiful and psychologically astonishing Book 24 of his *Iliad*. I will tell a slightly abbreviated version of this astounding episode.

One day the Greek hero Achilles killed Hector, the Trojan hero and beloved son of the old Trojan King Priam. Achilles took Hector's corpse into his camp. Achilles was an unhappy man. His name *a-chilleus* means "the non-breast-fed." Achilles did not receive human motherly love. Instead, his divine mother held him by the heel as a baby and dipped him in the cold water of the River Styx to secure his immortality. Achilles may have been the first "early disturbed child" of our cultural history. Old King Priam wanted to recover the corpse of his son Hector. With the help of Hermes, Priam managed to come down from the city and secretly enter the camp of the Greeks and the tent of Achilles. First, the two men stared at one another from a distance. But then something remarkable happened. When Priam asked Achilles for the body of his son, Hector, Achilles thought: *This old man could be my own father; he lost his son as my father will lose me.* And Priam realized: *This young hero is not so different from my own son.* Priam and Achilles approached each other, embraced, and began to sob. "The tent was shaken by the crying of the men."[8] They recognized each other for who they each were: an old father and a son. Priam was allowed to take Hector's corpse. This scene of reconciliation between Hector and Priam is at the heart of the inner development of *The Iliad*. It became a central founding myth of Greek culture, a symbol of reconciliation between old and young, between enemies, and between Asia and Europe. It was an arrangement between men, and the female side was not addressed. The reconciliation of male and female is still open.

Today, this kind of ethic is seldom to be found in military confrontations or even in ordinary business relationships. Our soldiers are not trained in matters that have to do with heartfelt reconciliation. Instead, they learn to bomb the enemy anonymously from a distance. The respect for the "other" was among the central achievements of European culture. For me, it was and remains the hope of the essence of Europe.

Notes

1 I also explored these ideas in "European Cultural Complexes," in Emilija Kiehl (ed.), *Copenhagen 2013: Proceedings of the 19th Congress of the International Association for Analytical Psychology* (Einsiedeln: Daimon, 2014), p. 959.
2 Thomas Singer, "Introduction," in C. San Roque, A. Dowd, and D. Tacey (eds.), *Placing Psyche: Exploring Cultural Complexes in Australia* (New Orleans: Spring Journal Books, 2011), p. xii.
3 Martin Buber, *Ich und Du (1923)* (Stuttgart: Reclam, 2008); Emmanuel Levinas, *Stunde der Nationen* (Paderborn Wilhelm Fink Verlag, 1994).
4 Ernest Renan, "Qu'est-ce qu'une nation? (1882)," in Monika Flacke (ed.), *Mythen der Nationen. Ein Europäisches Panorama* (Berlin: Deutsches Historisches Museum, 1998), p. 17. Translation is mine.
5 Renan, "Qu'est-ce qu'une nation? (1882)."
6 Renan, "Qu'est-ce qu'une nation? (1882)."
7 J. Küchenhoff, "Eine Krypta im Ich," *Forum der Psychoanalyse* 7 (1991, 1): p. 31ff; Uwe Langendorf, "Heimatvertreibung – Das stumme Trauma," *Analytische Psychologie* 136 (2004, 2), p. 35; Jg, Frankfurt/Main: Brandes und Apsel, pp. 207–223.
8 Homer, *The Iliad* (München: Artemis und Winkler, 1962), Book 24, Verse 512.

Introduction

Thomas Singer

Origin of the Project

When Jörg Rasche and I sat down in Montreal in the late summer of 2010 to discuss the possibility of a book on European cultural complexes, Europe was a very different place than it is now, some fifteen years later as we prepare a republished version of this book, which was originally published in 2016. As Jörg sketched a map of Europe on a napkin and talked about the founding myths of several of the European countries, we began to see a possible shape for the book. Jörg was optimistic, both about the book and about Europe. He was filled with the positive spirit of an emerging, vital new Europe that was becoming more whole in the sense of being cohesive and differentiated, honoring both a growing economic and social unity as well as the individuality of its various partner countries. Jörg's optimistic spirit was infectious for good reason. Personally, he had devoted much of his life's work to the pursuit of reconciliation and good relations between former enemies. He had a deep sense of responsibility that his generation of Austrians and Germans needed to step forward in the healing of Europe after World War II.

Jörg did not shy away from the shame and guilt of Germany's Nazi era. It only fueled his humanitarian urge to understand and to repair. Deeply steeped in the classics (he began to speak Latin and Greek with his grandfather when he was eight), a humanist in the finest European tradition, and a passionate musician from a young age, Jörg worked tirelessly with his German neighbors in Latvia, Poland, the Czech Republic, Russia, Ukraine, and elsewhere throughout Europe to realize a vision shared by many of a new, peaceful, and cooperative Europe. Indeed, he was awarded the Golden Cross of Merit by the Polish president Bronisław Komorowski for his healing efforts. At the same time, Jörg had no wish to see a homogenized Europe as he loves the foods, languages, and peoples of varying cultures. He embraces those who differ from himself rather than shunning, excluding, or seeking to do battle with them. He has sought for a Europe that would serve the well-being of all its peoples and countries.

Some six years after that 2010 meeting, when we were putting the finishing touches on the book we first imagined in Montreal, we were already looking at a quite different Europe. There were serious fractures in the dream of European

DOI: 10.4324/9781003609742-2

reconciliation and unity. The grand economic vision of the European Union was in trouble, with dangerous divides between Northern and Southern Europe and, particularly between Germany and Greece. Ukraine and Russia had begun a perilous conflict in 2014 that threatened to break out into full-scale war at any time. Anti-Islamism and antisemitism were on the rise throughout Europe in a way that threatened everyone and signaled a growing sense of fear, insecurity, and urgency among many European populations. To add to the fuel of intra-European conflicts, the swelling tide of refugees from the Middle East and especially Syria only served to increase preexisting tensions around non-European, Muslim immigrants in Europe. The chapters in this book were written prior to the summer of 2015. Yet the fractures and tension have only increased since then.

Many new developments have signaled increasing distress among European nations and touch the souls of all its citizens. Tragic news of bombings in Paris, mass sexual assaults in Cologne, the ongoing debt crisis in Greece, and growing conflict over refugees throughout Europe might have found their way into the chapters of this volume if they were written just months later in 2015. But a book such as this does not aim to be an up-to-the minute bulletin from the BBC, CNN, or Al Jazeera. Rather, we have sought to tease out ongoing fault lines and underlying trends that persist, even as new traumatic events growing out of cultural complexes wax and wane.

It is almost impossible to know how things are going to unfold when living through such events and when cultural complexes take hold of people. It is like living in a permanent fog. I sometimes think of Fordham's formulation about the earliest stages of infant development when I try to understand what is happening in the world today. Obviously, what happens in the development of a single infant and in the life of nations is not comparable, but the notion of integration, deintegration, and disintegration is provocative. Clearly, in 2010 when we first conceived this book, Europe was in a phase of *integration*. Now, in 2024, as we prepare this new edition, it appears to be *deintegrating* at a minimum and perhaps *disintegrating* in the worst-case scenario.

What is the difference between deintegration and disintegration? In Fordham's model, *deintegration* is a normal phase of development when change is essential and the wholeness of a previous moment has to be released in favor of taking in new breath, new life, new possibilities. Are the rise of antisemitism and anti-Islamism and the growing economic divide between Northern and Southern European countries signs of a difficult but normal adjustment to rapid changes in immigration as well as other economic and cultural forces throughout Europe? Or are they just the tip of the iceberg of old rivalries and hatreds resurfacing in a disintegrating climate that will once again lead to a destructive archetypal possession throughout Europe and the rest of the world?

The first major crack in the long-standing but somehow stable structure of Russia and the United States as the two competing world powers after World War II was the fall of the Berlin Wall in 1989. (It seems much longer ago than that – but in historical time, that is not long ago.) Did this usher in an integrative, deintegrative, or disintegrative period – or bits of all three? Not long after the fall of the Berlin

Wall, Jörg had a dream about this massive shift in the structure of the competing superpowers and its potential dangers as well as opportunities.[1] In the dream he found himself walking on a glacier that was melting and causing torrents of water to carry away trees, rocks, and anything else that got in its way. The consequences of the thaw in Europe after the fall of the Berlin Wall have obviously not all been positive, as Jörg's dream anticipated and Russia's invasion of Ukraine has made all too abundantly clear. His dream of the melting glacier and the raging waters brings to mind Jung's essay about Nazi Germany in his 1936 "Wotan."[2]

An archetype is like an old watercourse along which the water of life has flowed for centuries, digging a deep channel for itself. The longer it has flowed in this channel the more likely it is that sooner or later the water will return to its old bed. The life of the individual as a member of society and particularly as part of the State may be regulated like a canal, but the life of nations is a great rushing river that is utterly beyond human control . . . thus the life of nations rolls on unchecked, without guidance, unconscious of where it is going, like a rock crashing down the side of a hill, until it is stopped by an obstacle stronger than itself. Political events move from one impasse to the next, like a torrent caught in gullies, creeks, and marshes. All human control comes to an end when the individual is caught up in a mass movement. Then the archetypes begin to function, as happens also in the lives of individuals when they are confronted with situations that cannot be dealt with in any of the familiar ways.[3]

I remain in awe of Jung's prophetic vision and his formulation of what happens to the collective psyche and nations when they experience an onrush from the archetypal layer of the unconscious. What Jung was not fully aware of in 1936 was the power and influence of the new, modern mass media as it was being so *perfectly* manipulated for the first time in history by Goebbels. The high tide of constellated archetypes in the collective unconsciousness not only provokes the media but also can be triggered by the media.

But over the years I have become increasingly aware that an exclusively archetypal perspective on events between nations can itself become dangerously misleading by generating deep, even irreparable misunderstandings. The failure to speak clearly to and fully recognize the immediate and specific economic, historic, and social causes of upheaval in nations can have its own disastrous consequences. Jung's "Wotan" is a perfect case in point. Wotan didn't just seize Germany. Germany was ripe for a possession because of the terrible aftermath of World War I, the Great Depression, burdensome war reparations, the humiliation of the German people, and profound shifts in economic and political forces. All of these practical and psychological factors contributed to the ripeness of a people and nation to be thrown into fear, disorder, chaos, and a deep yearning for simple answers and clear structures. For the past decades, I have been trying to tease out and give legs to a notion of the cultural complex in which we might better understand what happens to the psyche of a people when unconscious forces stimulated by social, economic, religious, and other disruptive forces reawaken old conflicts and wounds that then give way to the breakthrough of destructive archetypal possessions.

Clearly, what Jung wrote in 1936 resonates with our current crises between Islam and the West; between Jews, Christians, and Muslims; between Russians and Ukrainians; between Israelis and Palestinians. The ancient, archetypal riverbed of rivalrous conflicts between all these groups is once again overflowing with a rushing torrent that threatens to flood the world. This is happening at the archetypal level of the psyche. But it is also happening at the cultural level of the psyche where contemporary forces – religious, economic, political – are shaping the form in which the archetypal contents are expressing themselves. I think of this cultural level of the psyche as existing in the mid-belly or mid-region of the collective psyche – existing part way between the deep collective unconscious and the personal unconscious in a realm that Joseph Henderson called the "cultural unconscious."

Why Do We Need a Theory of Cultural Complexes?

Our old Jungian theory of archetypal possession unleashing destructive forces is good on its own terms. But it has gotten stale in its application when everything unpleasant, whether it be in the individual or the group, is explained away by the "shadow." Once we begin to use the "shadow" to explain every destructive force in the psyche, we stop thinking. We stop asking essential questions that have to do with the specificity of forces at work in a particular place, to a particular people, at a particular time. We need to concern ourselves with basic questions of history, economics, sociology, anthropology, and religious studies to get a sense of what is happening in the world and what is happening in the collective psyche. At the same time, none of these specific disciplines address the question of how these various forces take shape and live in the psyche of individuals and groups. In order to answer questions about where economic and other cultural forces live inside of people, we need to consider the reality of the psyche. The kinds of opinions and emotional reactions that people have to events both close to and far away from home usually have bits and pieces of history, economics, sociology, and so on, in them – but their life in the psyche of the individual or the collective is not organized according to these disciplines. In fact, what order these ideas and feelings have in the psyche can be inchoate, rapidly shifting and yet paradoxically long standing, and often quite immune and impermeable to the reason that traditional disciplines of thought would impose on them.

Our central thesis is that all of these various forces take shape in what we are calling *cultural complexes*. This is how they live in the psyche. We believe a theory of cultural complexes helps us understand how people think and feel about many of the major events and forces that shape their lives. In that sense, this is not sociology, which is descriptive of how these things look from the outside – not how they live inside. I have said before that the study of cultural complexes is more like an inner sociology with a bit of history, psychology, anthropology, economics, mythology, sociology, and even poetry thrown into the stew, everything except perhaps mathematics and physics. Therefore, this is not a book about history, although there is lots of historical information. It is not a book about mythology or religion, but there is a lot of that, too. It is not about economics or anthropology or poetry, but there is a lot of that as well. It is about how all of these things form a living reality of ideas, beliefs, memories, feelings, images, and behavior in the psyche. This living reality does not provide a particularly coherent narrative or linear sequencing of facts and events. At the same time, it shapes what it means to be a European, to be a citizen of a particular country or city or region of Europe. It contributes to the many souls of Europe. If we want to understand something about that, cultural complexes are one way of approaching this most elusive subject. Another way of saying this is that complexes exist in the psyche and history exists in the mind. In this study, we are interested in the many cultural complexes in the psyches of Europe.

What Are the Characteristics of a Cultural Complex?

The republication of this book now makes it one of seven in the Routledge series on the subject of cultural complexes that include studies conducted in Australia, Latin America, the United States, Southeast Asia, two volumes on Europe, and the very first one which was international in content. In a sense, each of these books is an exercise in exploring what a cultural complex is. Early on when Sam Kimbles and I were thinking through basic aspects of the cultural complex notion, I felt it important that we define the characteristics of a cultural complex in simple language that would be easy to understand and apply in a variety of settings for those who found this particular perspective useful. In addition, I thought it was important that we keep our language consistent with what had gone before in our tradition. Because Joe Henderson defined a *cultural unconscious*, it made sense to talk about cultural complexes rather than group complexes, for instance. As a result, I have developed, along with my esteemed colleague Chauncey Irvine, a set of characteristics that allows us to define and recognize a cultural complex. We have made the language of cultural complexes consistent with the theories of analytical psychology that have gone before. Over the past decades that I have worked on this series, the following characteristics have emerged time and again in the **95 separate chapters** contained in these seven volumes about cultural complexes in various parts of the world:

- Cultural complexes are autonomous. They have a life of their own in the psyche that is separate from the everyday ego of an individual or group. Sometimes they are dormant. Sometimes they become active in the psyche and take hold of one's thoughts, feelings, memories, images, and behavior.
- Cultural complexes are repetitive. The ongoing life of a cultural complex goes on uninterrupted in the psyche of an individual or group, sometimes for generations and even millennia. When they are activated, they are surprisingly unchanged, in the sense that they are recurring, repetitive, and expressive of the same emotional and ideological content over and over again.
- Cultural complexes collect experiences and memories that validate their own point of view. Once a cultural complex has established itself, it has a remarkable capacity – like a virus replicating – not only to repeat itself but also to make

sure that whatever happens in the world fits into its preexisting point of view. Cultural complexes are extremely resistant to facts. Everything that happens in the world is understood through their point of view. In this context, for example, one might think of climate change deniers as caught in a cultural complex. Cultural complexes collect experiences and self-affirming memories.

- The thoughts of cultural complexes tend to be simplistic and black and white. Although they form the core cognitive content of a cultural complex, the thoughts themselves are not complex. They are unchanging and without subtlety. They are rigid and impervious to modification. Indeed, they seem to be impermeable to any outside influence.
- Cultural complexes have strong affects or emotions by which one can recognize their presence. Knee-jerk affectivity or emotional reactivity is a sure sign that one has stepped on a cultural complex.
- Not all cultural complexes are destructive; not all cultural complexes are ego-dystonic to the cultural identity of a group or individual. Indeed, some cultural complexes can form the core of a healthy cultural identity, as well demonstrated in this book's chapter on Denmark (Chapter 6).

Another parallel set of criteria that I have developed as a way of identifying a cultural complex involves a series of questions about the various types of mental activity that are recruited when a cultural complex is triggered. A good way to think about a particular cultural complex is to ask the following questions:

- What feelings go along with this complex?
- What images tend to appear with this complex?
- What memories come to mind when this complex is activated?
- What behaviors are triggered by a particular complex?
- What stereotypical thoughts recur with a particular complex?

When you read the various chapters of this book, you will discover that the individual authors do not necessarily describe a cultural complex by listing these characteristics. Careful reading of each chapter, however, will reveal the presence of most of these characteristics. I am convinced that we will be able to identify what we are calling cultural complexes in the neurophysiological laboratories of the future. Areas of the brain associated with memory, affect, image, thought, and behavior will "light up" and be linked when a trigger word activates a cultural complex.

Cultural Complexes: Psychopathological or Normative?

In the course of working on this series of books over the past decades, I have found myself becoming more and more focused on cultural complexes that cause problems in a society or cultural complexes as being the psychopathological land-mines of a culture. Certainly the cultural complexes that catch our attention are the ones that cause disturbances in society. For instance, in *Cultural Complexes in*

Australia: Placing Psyche, considerable attention was given to the various ways indigenous people have been treated by the non-indigenous immigrants to Australia over time. It is not a pretty picture; social attitudes toward the Aboriginal people are clearly in the realm of entrenched cultural complexes that we can say are psychopathological. The same can be said of antisemitism and anti-Islamism in Europe and the West. These are expressions of deep-seated, long-standing cultural complexes that are causing enormous problems today. But it is a mistake – and one that I have fallen into often in my work – to think of cultural complexes only as psychopathological. They can also be normative in the same way that Jung characterized the ego as a complex. Another way of saying this is that one can define a cultural complex with all the characteristics that I have outlined previously, and it does not mean that the cultural complex is necessarily destructive or that it goes against the grain of what is best about a culture.

Cultural Complex, Identity, and Soul

Related to the issue of cultural complexes as normative or psychopathological is the issue of the relationship between cultural complex, cultural identity, and the soul of a culture. In *The Cultural Complex*, I wrote the following:

> Cultural complexes are not the same as cultural identity or what has sometimes been called "national character," although there are times when cultural complexes, cultural identity and national character can seem impossibly intertwined. For instance, those groups emerging out of long periods of oppression through political and economic struggle must define new identities for themselves which are often based on long submerged traditions. This struggle for a new group identity can get all mixed up with underlying potent cultural complexes which have accrued historical experience and memory over centuries of trauma and lie slumbering in the cultural unconscious, waiting to be awakened by the trigger of a new trauma. In the fierce and legitimate protest for group identity freed up from the shackles of oppression, it is very easy for groups and individuals within the group to get caught up in cultural complexes. And, for some people, their complexes – cultural and personal – are their identity. But, for many others, there is a healthy cultural identity (or "cultural ego") that can clearly be seen as separate from the more negative and contaminating aspects of cultural complexes.[4]

It is not always clear if one is talking about a cultural complex, cultural identity, or even the soul of a country as they can all shade into one another, particularly as one gets closer to normative along a spectrum of psychopathological to normative. The more psychopathological a cultural complex appears to be the less likely it is to get confused with cultural identity. Furthermore, a peoples' sense of their group soul can often be forged out of their struggle with their cultural complexes and search for a national identity. Complex, identity, and soul are all intertwined in many chapters in this book: Poland (Kalinowska), Greece (Tsempelis), and Spain (del Castillo) to name a few. The soul part of this entangled triad speaks most clearly in the poetry and literature of a land, such as with Kafka in the Czech Republic (Skála) or in the poets of Greece (Tsempelis). As a result, it is sometimes quite hard to know whether one is talking about soul, complex, or identity as they seem to grow out of one another and into one another. They can also cause great harm to one another.

If we travel just to the east of Europe, to the land from which Europa came, we can see manifestations of how cultural complex and national identity get into real trouble with one another. For instance, remembrances of the Armenian genocide in Türkiye have brought this painfully to the surface for both the Armenian people and as a terrific challenge to Turkish national identity, which has been carefully constructed around denying that such a genocide took place. The headline of an article by Caleb Lauer sums up the conflict perfectly "For Turkey, Denying an Armenian Genocide Is a Question of Identity." Lauer goes on to write: "Turkey's national identity is built on a carefully crafted and tightly controlled version of history."[5] Basically, the Turkish government has long denied – and continues to deny – that there was a genocide of 1.5 million Armenians in 1915. This official denial of the genocide has, in fact, become part of the Turkish national identity and is reinforced by what is and is not taught about history in schools. Most Turks' denial was learned in school and reinforced by various media emphasizing the treachery of those Armenians who backed the invading Russians, foreign powers' manipulation of Ottoman minorities, conspiracy, possible loss of territory to "Greater Armenia," greed for reparations, and the dozens of murdered Turkish diplomats killed by the Armenian Secret Army for the Liberation of Armenia. Lauer states the following:

> Many simply cannot accept that their forefathers may have committed such a crime – a position that becomes more unyielding the more that shaming Turkey becomes the goal and the more that the Turkish government plays this up.[6]

It is easy to see how what is denied as part of national identity becomes the fuel for an unconscious cultural complex of shame, guilt, and denial. And such processes can cause great harm to the soul of a people. A challenge to the reader of this book is to struggle with the complex dynamic of identity, complex, and soul.

Structure of Book

It is a fascinating process to see a book of collected chapters come together. At the outset, it is hard to know what you are going to get. We set out with the idea of exploring cultural complexes in Europe but that can mean many different things to many different authors. Of course, that is what we are hoping for – that different authors will find different ways of talking about the concept in terms of their own personal experience and in terms of their countries' unique experiences. We did provide the authors with the basic description of a cultural complex and its characteristics, which is outlined in this introduction. But it was not until many chapters had been submitted that we began to see various patterns of how we might structure the book. There is no one way to talk about a cultural complex, and there is no one way to structure a collection of chapters on European cultural complexes. Eventually, Jörg and I came up with a structure for organizing this book that seemed "good enough" and true enough to our purposes. We decided to place the chapters in three sections. While preparing *Cultural Complexes in Europe: Jungian Perspectives on Psyche, Soul, and Identity,* the 2025 republication of the original 2016 edition of *Europe's Many Souls,* we had already begun work on a second volume about European cultural complexes, *Cultural Complexes and Europe's Many Souls: Jungian Perspectives on Brexit and the War in Ukraine.* As a result we moved chapters about England, Russia, and Germany from this volume to the second volume focused on Brexit and the War in Ukraine. The remaining chapters now comprise the contents of this republication of the original volume, which are divided into the following sections.

Part 1: Soul, Identity, and Cultural Complexes in Individual European Countries

In the chapters of this section, there is a subtle movement back and forth between soul, identity, and complex as expressed in different countries. As I mentioned earlier, it is not always easy to know which is which as they can easily blend into one another. The reader is advised to allow these distinctions and, at times lack of distinctions, to play in the mind because that is the nature of psyche itself – to be crystal clear in differences at times and to blend without distinctions at other times.

Chapter 1: The Suffering Hero and Messianism in a Polish Cultural Complex, by Malgorzata Kalinowska

This chapter explores the historical roots and manifestations of the Polish cultural complex of the Suffering Messianic Hero. The author explores the question whether or not a cultural complex that is the result of collective psychic struggle with the constant danger of physical, psychological, and spiritual oblivion might serve the function of keeping national identity alive and holding open the hope for renewal.

Chapter 2: The Inner Riddle of "Greek Psychic Debt," by Evangelos Tsempelis

What is the inner fiber of Greek reality? Conversely, what does the possible economic collapse of Greece reveal in terms of a tired European continent finding itself caught up in the demise of its own self-assured intellectual and political machinery? What possibilities for renewal and rediscovery remain dormant within a fossilized/idealized modern Greek cultural heritage?

Chapter 3: The Catalan Vault: The Transformation of a Personal and Cultural Complex, by Olivia del Castillo

This chapter explores an individual's dream that reveals the threat of totalitarianism under the banner of nationalism. It awakens the potent cultural complex of feelings and memories that are part of Spanish history and the deep fears in both the analysand and analyst that accompany opening up this topic for discussion.

Chapter 4: The Forefather Cultural Complex: Between Kafka and Meyrink: Why Didn't Joseph K. Get to the Castle and Why Did Athanasius Pernath Enter a Room Without a Door?, by Martin Skála

The Czech Republic, and particularly Prague, its capital city, exhibits a certain kind of inferiority complex that is characteristic of a small nation at the heart of Europe. Despite this sense of inferiority, there is a hidden and perhaps compensatory feeling of omnipotence that contributes to the secret magic of Prague and its special place in the center of Europe.

Chapter 5: Belgrade: Limes and the City: Hermeneutics of Belgrade's Soul, by Marijana Popović and Jelena Sladojević Matić

The authors trace the history of Belgrade, "the White City," from its prehistoric beginnings as one of the oldest cultures in Europe to its history as a "Portal of Wars" as it changed from Roman to Byzantine to Slav to Ottoman to Habsburg hands. Belgrade's strategic location at the border – the limes – and at the confluence of the Sava and Danube rivers, where the Panonian Plein meets the Balkans, has led to the creation of psychic liminality as well.

Part II: The Feminine and Cultural Complexes in Europe

In this section, the "feminine in Europe" is explored and takes shape in many different ways. These chapters explore wide ranging expressions of the feminine in its movement from royalty to earthy, to mystical and heretical.

Chapter 6: Mother Denmark, by Pia Skogemann

A dominant, feminine, royal shield-maiden figure has been both emotionally important and at the core of the complex (and undefinable) notion of Danishness for close to a thousand years. The shield-maiden image has flourished over the centuries, especially in times of defeat, and has served to rally and rebuild the morale of the Danish people.

Chapter 7: Queens, Saints, Heretics, Prostitutes: Women in Italy, by Caterina Vezzoli

In the course of centuries, from the early Middle Ages to the present day, patriarchal projections on women have constrained them in positions of subjection. Medieval mystics, queens, and nuns were sometimes condemned as heretics only because they used the language of Eros and professed the importance of women in the renewal of the church. They had the courage to speak of love, Eros, and peace in the dark centuries in their constant struggles with the power and supremacy of men.

Chapter 8. Sisi: A Figure of Multiple Projection, by Maria Kendler

The Habsburg Empress Elisabeth, also known as Sisi, was born in 1837, and she was murdered in 1898. The myth of Sisi mirrors the contemporary needs and projections of many Austrian women and the Austrian nation itself in its search for a modern identity. Sisi's myth is paradigmatic of the cultural upheaval that occurred at the Fin de Siècle when Austria and much of Europe was in the throes of a transition from a traditional feudalistic society to a newly emerging modern society.

Chapter 9. The "Small Mother Complex" and the Royal Feminine, by Marta Tibaldi

The author's thesis is the Mediterranean "Great Mother Complex" has now turned into a "small mother complex," that is, in a devalued image of femininity that leads to images of "small men" and "small women," "small feminine" and "small masculine" in both genders – to the detriment of the individual and the collective dynamics of desire.

Part III: The Greater European Family: Cultural Complexes in All European Countries

Some cultural complexes take very different shapes in different European countries and pose problems unique to each country. But some are also common to all the countries of the continent, and it seems best to address them as pan-European cultural complexes.

Chapter 10: The Jewish Anima: About the Christian-Jewish Complex in Europe, by Jörg Rasche

This chapter begins with an exploration of the author's German family relationships with Jewish people. A serious question concerns what happens with the Jewish anima in Europe since a large number of European Jews have returned to live in their homeland. A special focus lies on the Jewish-Christian symbiosis, which was often threatened by pogroms and finally destroyed by the Shoah.

Chapter 11: My European Animus, by Erel Shalit

In the Jewish mind, Europe (mythically founded by the migration of Europa west from her place of birth in Phoenicia) serves as a place of liberty and equality – and persecution; of enlightened reason – and evil darkness; as well as freedom from the bonds of particularism – and loss of roots. The double-edged sword of Europe is compared to the significance of the ancestral soil as a place of possibility and complexity – or sinking into its shadow of despair and fragmentation.

Chapter 12: A Very Narrow Bridge: Israel and Its Cultural Complexes, by Henry Abramovich

In this chapter, the author writes of an Israel that is very different from the one portrayed on TV, in newspapers, or on social media, which focuses on war, conflict, and kidnappings. Israel is a land of polarities and contradictions. It is the realization of a 2000-year-old dream for the people of the Book; it is the *nakba* (the "catastrophe") for Palestinians. It is the land of oppression and terror, yet it is the only democracy in the entire Middle East. Golda Meir told President Biden many decades ago, "Israel has a secret weapon. It has nowhere to go!" The Masada complex highlights an existential anxiety, or *angst*, expressed in the phrase, "When I go to sleep, I don't know if I will wake up to find my country." Such existential anxiety is perhaps unique to Israel and, paradoxically, is also the source of so much of its vitality.

Chapter 13: The Ghosts of Two World Wars: Is the Replacement Child Part of a Cultural Complex in the European Psyche?, by Kristina Schellinski

Many of those born after the two World Wars, which left more than 90 million people dead, are *replacement children*. They are suffering, often unconsciously, from a syndrome that can be passed on transgenerationally. Also, the European Union was conceived on a bed of ruins. What are the chances of a pan-European cultural replacement complex?

Chapter 14: Europe and Islam: A Paradigm of Activated Cultural Complexes, by Jörg Rasche

Christian Europe and Islam have a long shared history. The values of traditional Islam differ from the fascistic "Neo-Islam" of IS and other Islamists. There was once even an intensive interreligious dialogue between the faiths, symbolized by that between St. Francis of Assisi and the Sultan Melek al Kamil, both inspired by a similar mystic faith.

We would hope that the reader will come up with additional ideas for pan-European cultural complexes. For instance, consumerism as a cultural complex in Europe would be most interesting to explore, particularly in inquiring about whether the consumerism of Europe is different in its manifestations from what is undoubtedly a global cultural complex. We chose to focus on the cultural complexes that one cannot ignore at this time in history; surely, there are others as well.

Notes

1 See Jörg Rasche's introduction, p. 1.
2 C. G. Jung, "Wotan (1936)," in Gerhard Adler and R. F. C. Hull (eds. and trans.), *The Collected Works of C. G. Jung*, Vol. 10 (Princeton, NJ: Princeton University Press, 1968).
3 Jung, CW 10, § 395.
4 Thomas Singer and Samuel L. Kimbles, *The Cultural Complex: Contemporary Jungian Perspectives on Psyche and Society* (London: Routledge, 2004), p. 5.
5 Caleb Lauer, "For Turkey, Denying an Armenian Genocide is a Question of Identity," *Aljazeera America*, April 24, 2014. Accessed June 24, 2015, at http://america.aljazeera.com/articles/2015/4/24/for-turks-acknowledging-an-armenian-genocide-undermines-national-identity.html.
6 Lauer, "For Turkey, Denying an Armenian Genocide is a Question of Identity."

Part I

Soul, Identity, and Cultural Complexes in Individual European Countries

Poland

1

The Suffering Hero and Messianism in a Polish Cultural Complex

Malgorzata Kalinowska

Describing a Polish cultural complex that is based on a long history of cumulative trauma is no easy task. Language often fails when one tries to evoke the experience of living in a post-traumatic culture. It is hard to find the right balance between objective analysis and honoring the almost unreachable psychic spaces and affective dimensions of suffering over many generations. Objective analysis alone turns too easily into chilly detachment and unrelatedness. Emotional engagement brings about the danger of identification with the energy of the complex. The distance essential to describing the inner situation of my culture to a reader from another culture and language often leads to a defensive relegation of the complex back into the cultural unconscious. Psychological language itself can become "a stuck semantic differential."[1]

Such dilemmas have played a central, haunting role in my process of studying and writing about the Suffering Hero complex. Experienced in the subjective realm, the complex gave me the feeling of trying to reach the unreachable, beyond any possible means of description. As described in the Polish scientific literature, what I call here the *Suffering Hero complex* left me with the impression that it was something pathological, a relic of old times, and that we should get rid of it for the sake of openness to the future. There is an implicit exhortation to leave behind the national cycle of eternal return to our experience of trauma. Simultaneously, I observed that the polarities of objective description and subjective experience are present in everyday social and political discourse, suggesting, to me, that the complex is quite alive in the cultural unconscious. Such reactions can be seen, for example, in the older generations' conviction that we still do not live in "free Poland" and that current times do not differ much from times of enslavement (that is, during the Communist regime). Right-wing groups often invoke in their slogans the imagery of fight and oppression. An example of this dynamic appeared in the society's reaction to the Smolensk plane crash in 2010 and the years that followed, when the crash victims were sometimes described as "fallen for the nation."[2]

Dale Mathers writes that myth is a form of dialogue, providing a structure that shapes both language and perception.[3] But how can this dialogue be translated from the language and myth of its own culture into another language that, although it refers to the same basic archetypal images, does not have the same grounding in the

DOI: 10.4324/9781003609742-4

historic depths of a very specific group psyche? The notion of a cultural complex as an expression of interweaving historical factors with specific responses to the philosophy, religion, geography, and the psyche of a culture is strongly based on language structure and collective myths. Writing about what was intuitively recognized and known within the language of my own biological birth – Polish – turned out to be difficult to express in the language of my analytical identity – English. The only way I could write the text at all was to first write it in Polish and then translate it into English.

This caused further problems. How, for example, could I describe the widely known and recognized symbol of Christ – the essence of the Suffering Hero complex – to those who haven't experienced Polish Catholicism? How could I express the highly specific emotional meaning of the word *loss* in the Polish language, which turns out to have quite different etymology and emotional nuances than the word *loss* in English? Rebecca Solnit connects the origin of the English word *loss* to the Old Norse *los*, meaning the disbanding of an army.[4] She associates this meaning with the images of soldiers falling out of formation to go home, having made a truce with the wider world and able to enter the unknown. *Loss* in English then would include the experience of meeting with a completely unknown reality, which is possible when defenses are disbanded (falling out of order and formation). This deep, symbolic meaning of the English word *loss* is difficult to apply to or to equate with the Polish word referring to loss: *utrata*. The Polish verb *tracić* (to lose) has its roots in Pre-Slavic *tratiti* (to use, to wear something out) and the Pre-Indo-European meaning "to grate, to grind," which, in older times would be used, for example, to describe grinding the flour in the mill with stones.[5] This etymology of the Polish word for *loss* expresses an unconscious meaning characteristic of my culture when it comes to loss, as evident in the epigraph by Michael Kaufman: "Every Pole feels in their soul that tragedy is not based on the quality of life, it is life itself."

We might say that in the Polish *loss*, we are ground by the hand mill of fate, grated to pieces, transformed into something essentially other than the initial substance. No wonder then that the Polish cultural complex of the Suffering Hero originated during the first of the series of great historical losses in the time of Poland's partitions in the eighteenth century. This first loss of this extent helped create the mythopoetic imagery that carries a deep symbolic meaning for the Polish people of the possibility of transformation in the face of the powerful, indisputable forces of fate and history.

Historical Roots of the Suffering Hero Complex

The independence regained in 1918 at the end of World War I ended in 1939 with World War II and the invasion of Poland by Nazi Germany and the Soviet Union. The Polish complex of the Suffering Hero, however, full of mythopoetic imagery with a strong emotional charge, had been alive in the Polish psyche for at least the last 200 years of our history. A great deal of this time had been spent under foreign domination. By the end of eighteenth century, Poland had lost its independence for 123 years, and its citizens had become targets of repeated persecutions. Our loss of independence occurred as a series of three partitions of Poland's territory, conducted by the Russian Empire, the Kingdom of Prussia, and Habsburg-Austria. Seizing territory, they divided the Polish–Lithuanian Commonwealth lands among themselves progressively. The first partition took place in 1772, the second in 1793, and the third in 1795.

- The Russian Empire took 462,000 square kilometers of Polish territory and 5.5 million citizens.
- The Kingdom of Prussia took 141,000 square kilometers and about 2.5 million citizens.
- Hapsburg Austria took 130,000 square kilometers and about 4.2 million citizens.

After the third partition, Poland – the country that had existed independently since 996 – ceased to exist. The situation of Polish citizens varied in the different partitions. Whereas in Hapsburg Austria, they were allowed representation in parliament and could form their own universities, in the Russian and Prussian partitions, their situation was extremely difficult. Property was confiscated; citizens were forced into military service; and the Polish universities were closed. The situation worsened after the failed Polish uprisings, which were followed by massive repressions.

Poland regained its independence in 1918. This short period of freedom (1918–1939) was soon lost with the outbreak of World War II. After World War II, the Communist regime caused new traumatic experiences, such as the Soviet Union's calculated policy of erasing significant parts of history (for example, the Katyn massacre was covered up for fifty years) along with persecutions.[6]

The emotional atmosphere of the twentieth century in this region of Europe is well portrayed in Marci Schore's book:

Eastern Europe is special. It is Europe only more so. It is a place where people live and die, only more so. In these lands between West and Russia, the past is palpable and heavy. The past is also merciless: by history's caprice, the Second World War and communism were inseparable historical traumas, one bleeding into the other, as Nazi power gave way to Soviet domination.[7]

Such an accumulation of historical traumas creates specific responses in the cultural layer of the psyche and in social patterns. Using Henderson's concept, I could say that they are written in the cultural unconscious – in historical memory – where they contribute to cultural myths and rituals, both in their conscious and unconscious manifestations.[8] They influence the everyday lives of people living within the culture. One of the manifestations of collective trauma on the Polish psyche has been the phenomenon described as Polish Messianism, which here I call the Suffering Hero complex.

The phrase *Suffering Hero* does not appear in Polish literature or its philosophy of history. I choose it for the purpose of this discussion as it contains not only Christian symbolism but also a romantic paradox. It includes both a faithfulness to God's plans as revealed in history as well as a Promethean rebellion against His will. Both attitudes were present in Polish Romanticism, helped to make sense out of defeat in times of partition, and gave hope to the struggles to keep the national identity alive.

This Polish attitude toward difficult historical struggles has been present in every dimension of life during the times of partition or war and has expressed itself in rituals, religious observances, and social myths. It originated in the literature of Romanticism during the time of the partitions.[9] As Mathers notes, "in oral traditions, poets eulogise, satirise, remember, hold and contain the culture."[10] They are "culture carriers." They help create, structure, and contain social myths. The Suffering Hero complex was formed in this era of Romanticism, at a time when the social order was severely challenged and the Polish collective identity was endangered. Writers and poets created a myth of the "Suffering Hero complex" that spoke to and for an individual and collective identity. Accordingly, Polish suffering under the partitions wasn't in vain; it served a higher goal – it was meant to bring salvation to the whole of humanity. The Suffering Hero felt what was happening to him or her was a part of God's plan (*Messianism*), but at the same time, the Suffering Hero struggled against it, fighting for the freedom of his or her nation (*Prometheism*). The polarities of oppressor/sufferer, defeat and death/resurrection, the world of matter and loss/the world of spirit and hope, shape this complex dynamic, and, as such, they have reappeared in difficult historical moments. For example following the Smolensk crash in 2010, President Lech Kaczynski appeared in symbolic imagery as the one who had protected true spiritual and patriotic values, and by dying in the crash, he "gave his life for the nation," which we are obliged to honor by keeping his memory alive as a way of spiritual renewal. Similarly, soldiers who died during World War II (that is, the Katyn or Westerplatte soldiers) are sometimes portrayed as sacrificing themselves in the fight for Poland, and upon entering heaven, their bodies have the shape of "spiritual being" (like the body of the resurrected Christ entering heaven).[11] During the past several years, the presence of the Suffering Hero complex could also be felt in conflicting discussions of films that portrayed soldiers fighting in the Battle of Westerplatte in more human, contradictory ways (I feel that presenting them as having "human bodies" activated the complex). Some felt this presentation as a betrayal of "national memory" and national identity.

The birth of the cultural complex of Suffering Hero, as mentioned previously, dates from the eighteenth century in the times of loss of national independence during three consecutive partitions. The Polish literary historian Maria Janion compares the influence of the partitions on the Polish psyche to the influence of the Lisbon earthquake on the Western collective psyche.[12] According to Zygmunt Bauman, the Lisbon earthquake awakened Western civilization once and for all to the danger to humanity that can come from Nature.[13]

The Polish experience was of a different character. Unbelievable and overwhelming loss came from the hands of other human beings, rather than Nature.

A country that used to be important in Europe disappeared from the map. This experience was both individual and collective; it touched everyday life through the changed social order. The collective reaction to the disappearance of Poland was shaped by romantic Messianism that challenged the reality of partition and loss. Messianic imagery can be found in Adam Mickiewicz's drama *Dziady*, in which Poland is portrayed as the "Christ of nations":

> Now my soul is incarnate in my country,
> My body has swallowed her soul,
> And I and my country are one.
> Million is my name, for I love
> And I suffer for millions.[14]
> A tyrant hath arisen, Herod! – Lord, the youth of Poland
> Is all delivered into Herod's hands.
> What do I see? Long snowy ways, with many crossroads,
> White roads that stretch through wastes too distant to descry!
> All running to the north, that far, far country,
> As rivers flow; . . .
> The cross has arms that shadow all of Europe,
> Made of three withered peoples, like dead trees.
> Now is my nation on the martyr's throne.[15]

Polish Messianism was not an escape from the world of facts, as some believe now, but rather a struggle to soften and transform the everyday reality of bondage. The Suffering Hero refused to submit to the "empirical" reality of partition by creating his or her own spiritual order. With a huge intellectual and emotional investment, Polish Messianism preserved an imaginal existence of Poland as a whole, as a spiritual community, and saved the Polish people as individuals rooted in it.[16]

This Messianic attitude toward the influence of history on individual and collective life allowed the people of Poland to make sense out of the repeated defeats and suffering generated by subsequent bloody national uprisings. The repressions that followed each defeated uprising (especially the November uprising in 1830 and the January uprising in 1863) were felt to be an essential sacrifice according to God's will. Suffering was understood not only as a road to freedom but also as an indispensable condition; it was meant not only to redeem national identity and sovereignty but also to bring a spiritual renewal to all of humanity.[17] In this way, the meaning of Polish history was merged with the meaning of the Christ myth – a repeated story of agony, death, and resurrection. According to this parallel, Poland's suffering was to usher in a new age in the world, an age of freedom.

Wojciech Dzieduszycki, Lviv University professor, writer, and philosopher, wrote in the second half of nineteenth century:

> I remember how in the childhood years the nation believed in the great fate, that our bards sang us. It was ready to offer itself for burnt offering to save

humanity . . . it believed as a lunatic, that Poland's resurrection is inevitable, as inevitable as a sunrise is when a night ends.[18]

In this way, Polish romantic literature re-created a lost homeland "in thought and yearning," which allowed the preservation of a collective identity endangered by partition. A similar function was served by a myth of Slavic origin that connected in one story a primordial age of the Slavic people with biblical times.[19]

To assume that these stories were simply an abstract or theoretical position attempting to express a symbolic or spiritual attitude to reality would be a mistake. Rather these "myths" had dramatic and tangible effects, displaying the uniqueness of Polish expressions of romanticism. In comparison with other cultures of that time, the Polish embrace of romantic stories of its fate as a nation was one of the most striking examples of nineteenth-century European ideals. Andrzej Kijowski observes

> In the history of different literatures romantic revolution was usually related to a kind of literary work, as for example "The Robbers" of Schiller, or to events where literary ideas were confronted, as for instance in Comedie-Française at the famous premiere of "Hernani" by Victor Hugo. Poland is the only country, in which the romantic revolution was an armed fight. At the premiere of "Hernani" young poets, painters, journalists appeared in fantasy dresses, armed with sticks, which they used to beat the audience that was hissing and booing at their beloved master. In Poland young poets, painters, journalists came to their premiere armed with guns and daggers, and they wanted to kill the Russian duke, the Tsar's brother.[20]

How can we understand the underlying motivations for such a powerful expression of national yearnings that led to continued violent struggles?

In the course of its history, Polish national identity was based on fundamental Catholic beliefs, originating in the creation and baptism of Poland as a country in the year 966. This image was reinforced in the seventeenth century by two important historical events: the Siege of Jasna Gora and the repulsion of the Turks attacking Vienna by Jan III Sobieski.[21] These events strengthened Poland's earlier status as an *antemurale christianitis* – an outpost of Christianity.[22]

The threat to national identity that resulted from the partitions and lost independence led many to turn to those deeply embedded Christian cultural symbols, which affirmed the previously stable Polish identity with its mythical roots in biblical imagery. These myths had enormous psychological importance for the way in which the Polish people subsequently dealt with traumatic events. Although rationalized and criticized in the age of Positivism (dating from the failure of the January uprising in 1863 to the 1890s), the Messianic myth became an integral part of the Polish psyche's landscape, imagery, and language. For instance, the Reconstruction of Poland in 1918 was interpreted as a rebirth; World War II was described as "the fourth partition" and "the suffering of a new cross"; the Communist times

(1945–1989) were identified as the "fifth partition" and the next crucifixion. These descriptions served to connect two myths in the Polish psyche: Catholicism as the heart of Polish identity and Messianism as the essential fate of that identity. Suffering was understood as central to the Polish experience. Poland's agony in partitions and its loss of independence intensified the symbolic role of the Church in the nation's survival, linking that role with the Polish people as being "chosen" – "the Polish people are God's people."[23]

After the end of the Communist era, many assumed the influence of the Polish Romantic tradition on Poland's myth of itself as a country had waned.[24] But this was not true, as evidenced by the social reaction to the Smolensk crash in 2010. The reawakening of the Romantic ideas about Poland (suffering and loss, endangered patriotic ideals, the fear that the memory of the plane crash victims would be erased like the memory of the Katyn soldiers in the times of Communism) has become even stronger since then, easily aroused by social and political tensions between the state and the Catholic Church or by supercharged issues such as abortion, sexual orientation, and other gender issues (the defensive function of the complex that allows some to avoid difficult current social issues).

I describe elsewhere the dynamic of the cultural reaction to the Smolensk crash. It started with shared mourning, which was quickly amplified by the memories and recounting of other difficult historical moments.[25] The Smolensk crash was associated with the Katyn massacre. In 1940 in Katyn Forest near Smolensk, on Stalin's orders, the NKVD shot and buried over 4,000 Polish service personnel who had been taken prisoner when the Soviet Union invaded Poland in September 1939 in support of the Nazis. Katyn then became the symbol of the mass killing by the NKVD of at least 22,000 Polish officers and representatives of Polish intelligentsia in the Katyn Forest in Russia, the Kalinin and Kharkiv prisons, and elsewhere. When the mass graves were discovered in 1943, Stalin claimed the victims had been murdered by the Nazis. The Soviet Union and its leaders continued to deny responsibility for the massacres until 1990, when it officially acknowledged and condemned the perpetration of the killings by the NKVD. In Communist times, the memory of the murders was repressed, and investigating the victims' fates could prove dangerous for their families. As a result, the Katyn massacre became a highly charged content in the cultural unconscious. The Smolensk crash took place in the location historically associated with the Katyn massacre and on its anniversary. In response to this association, the emotional social reaction identified the murdered Katyn soldiers and intelligentsia with the crash victims (as Polish ex-president Walesa said after the crash: "The elite of this nation was for the second time taken away from us").[26]

Polish people split into two camps in their reaction to the crash. There were those who were tired of the endless mourning that they felt was fueled by the irrational myth of Poland as a Suffering Hero. Others felt the catastrophe was a repetition of previous Soviet crimes, or even suspected the Polish government of taking part in a plot to kill the president. The latter belief revived the old Messianic symbolism. The grief triggered an emotional complex made up of fear, anger, and

sadness. Symbols of national suffering started to appear, as a result of an unconscious identification between the Smolensk crash victims and the murdered Katyn
soldiers. One example was the wooden cross placed in front of the Presidential Palace in Warsaw, where thousands of people gathered to pray and sing together, the
idea that the cross could be removed activated strong protests and people gathering
there received the name "defenders of the cross." On the second anniversary of the
crash, the names of the victims were read out during the calling of the Roll of Honor
in the same way as the names of those who died fighting in wartime. They were
described as "giants of spirit," and Katyn was mentioned as the Polish Dolorosa
of the East. The bodies of the presidential couple were buried in the Wawel Castle
in Kraków, the traditional burial place of Polish kings, heroes, and great writers.
Burial in Wawel Castle has always been the sign of the highest respect. I believe
it also served the unconscious purpose of honoring the unmourned Katyn soldiers.

Paradoxically, this complicated social response to the Smolensk crash and its
powerful emotional link to the Katyn massacre revealed the contents of the cultural
unconscious that had remained hidden after the fall of communism. Perhaps their
manifestations could have been observed before in collective interactions, commu-
nications, and rituals, but their meaning remained unconscious.

Individual and Collective, Realistic and Mythical: Polarities as a Field of Complex Activation

Social and cultural reactions to the Messianic motif in the Polish psyche oscillate
between identification with its emotional truth and denial of its importance. Both
reactions fail to grasp the symbolic meaning. They treat the Messianic idea as "as
literally real, or irreal/unreal – 'mythic.'"[27] There is no "as if" position that could
enable a deeper understanding of symbol, in which myth is understood as embodied in people, places, and time, and in their relationship to history. Such concrete,
polarized reactions to the Messianic idea indicate a cultural complex is at work.
They seem to give a specificity to the Polish cultural complex related to Poland's
unique geographic position between East and West. Geography itself contributes
to Poland's being divided between a spiritual/mystical attitude to history and a
rationalistic/scientific attitude that takes away from history its subjective meaning.
Both the literal embrace and rejection of the Messianic fate of Poland fail to consider the consequences of historical processes psychologically; they do not allow for
the internalization of historic events as experiences that have symbolic meaning.[28]

In my previous writing about how such processes manifest themselves in collective memory, I emphasized their defensive function as a result of long-term
reactions to cumulative trauma.[29] We need to be careful though, when applying this
same conclusion to the complex of the Suffering Hero.

In Poland, I've frequently heard the opinion expressed that Polish Messianism is a symptom of our immaturity and our narcissism, that we look obstinately
to the past and "pride ourselves with our dead bodies." As a corollary, a "mature
reaction" is described as "belonging to oneself," free of "national collectivism."[30]

This attitude toward the Suffering Hero complex places it among relics of the past, treating it as something we should discard. Again, little space is left for the "third position," where, as Jung says, we can see the individual is intimately connected to the collective and looks for a way to relate to it as to a meaningful part of him- or herself in the process of individuation.

Todorov takes a stand similar to the third position in relation to history:

> The choice that we have is not between remembering and forgetting; because forgetting can't be done by an act of will, it is not something we can chose to do. The choice is between different ways of remembering. . . . Memories do not always bear fruit and may even lead us astray. If we treat the past as holy, we exclude it from the world of meaning and prevent it teaching lessons that might apply to other times and places, to other agents of history. But we do just as much damage through the opposite approach: making the past trivial by likening present events to past ones too easily, trawling it for facile solutions to current issues, betrays history, distorts the present, and opens the door to injustice.[31]

The psychologist also struggles to find a third position between a faithfulness to old myths in which memory and history are reified, which closes the door on experience in the here and now, and a rationalistic attitude in which the old myths are seen as defensive or a way to avoid current conflicts. If, as Todorov says, both ways of social remembering of history do not bear fruit, is there another way, allowing us to embrace both the dimensions of the individual and the collective and of reality and myth?

Trauma and Obliteration of Distinctions

Joseph Henderson in his essay "Cultural Unconscious," which is a foundation of cultural complex theory, defines this concept as

> an area of historical memory that lies between the collective unconscious and the manifest pattern of the culture. It may include both these modalities, conscious and unconscious, but it has some kind of identity arising from the archetypes of the collective unconscious, which assists in the formation of myth and ritual and also promotes the process of development in individuals. This process is not final.[32]

It is of note that he describes the cultural unconscious as an area of historical memory. This Jungian formulation went unnoticed in the memory studies boom at the end of twentieth century, although it points to an important paradox – the cultural unconscious embraces both a conscious and an unconscious modality. This definition is quite important in the context of the Polish cultural complex because of our specific attitude toward collective memory. Collective memory is sometimes described here as "carrying an excess of memory," or that we are "obliged to remember" and be faithful to the memories of the past. It is expressed, for example, in the following paraphrase of the quotation from Adam Mickiewicz:[33] "If we forget about them, Thou, God forget about us," which is inscribed on the symbolic grave of the soldiers murdered in Katyn at Powazki Cemetery in Warsaw. Writing about memory in a country where memory itself became a relic of religious mystery is a challenging task. Usual definitions that describe the dynamics of memory seem to fail to grasp its essence. Instead they perpetuate the splits between faithfulness and unfaithfulness, remembering and forgetting, victim and persecutor.

The cultural unconscious as an area of historical memory is the field where cultural complexes are activated, "autonomous, mainly unconscious, emotionally charged aggregates of memories, ideas, and images that cluster around an archetypal core and are shared by individuals within an identified collective."[34] They shape collective *meta-narration* – stories that are building blocks of collective identify. This meta-narration allows difficult historical experiences to be contained within a known set of symbols, rituals, and images.[35] "The Great Story" often contains unexpressed fragments of traumatic memories that manifest themselves in a symbolic way. Unconnected, they tend to reappear, activated in the context of new situations that carry similar meaning. Traumatic memories that express themselves through cultural complexes influence our current interpretation of events in the context of past trauma, and sometimes they even participate in its reoccurrence. As Edkins notes, "trauma always implicates relationships to community, language, and symbolic order in which it is set."[36] Erikson notices another feature of trauma on the group level; "it destroys social tissues, the ability of a culture to serve as a cushion for pain, a context for intimacy, and a repository for binding traditions."[37]

Edkins makes one more important observation: trauma is often seen as an injury. Initially, the word implied an injury to the body, but now it is commonly taken to mean an injury to the psyche or even the community or the environment. But what happens if we consider this differently, as Edkins proposes? She suggests that rather than seeing trauma as involved with an injury to the object, we consider trauma as having something to do with a crossing of distinctions we take for granted, for instance, the distinctions between psyche and body, body and environment, individual and collective. She hypothesizes that the obliteration of distinctions itself can be horrific, prompting us to describe an event as traumatic. The very idea of separateness, which is the basis of Western development, is endangered; traumatic events "tear us from ourselves, bind us to others, transport us, undo us, implicate us in lives that are not our own, irreversibly, if not fatally."[38]

This obliteration of distinction between the individual and the collective as a result of trauma is of interest in relationship to the numinous symbolism present in romantic literary works expressing the Suffering Hero complex. Typically, we see numinous symbolism as a sign of the activation of archetypal energy, but Rosemary Gordon observes another possibility: "Numinosity which is usually regarded as accompanying the experience of an archetype may perhaps be more likely to result from simultaneous presentations of collective and personal features."[39]

Similarly Mogenson sees the traumatized soul as "a soul that stopped mediating events and making differences between itself and everything else" – the obliteration of distinction.[40] A traumatic event is not pushed out of awareness; rather it is too big to register in awareness. A distinctive characteristic of trauma is that it occurs outside the already known parameters of experience, a perspective confirmed by contemporary neuroscience. As Wilkinson posits, because of lack of adequate neuronal processing, traumatic experience remains unavailable to recall but may come to govern ways of being and behaving in relation to others.[41] Unprocessed traumatic experience lacks analogy.[42] Overwhelming events for which we cannot find fields of comparison and, therefore, cannot be fully experienced and integrated polarize "consciousness into opposites – black and white, male and female, pleasure and pain, guilty and not-guilty."[43]

A Cultural Complex as a Bridge Between the Individual and Collective Traumatic Experience

Mogenson outlines one more dimension connected with a reaction to trauma that seems to explain the religious symbolism of Poland – Christ coming through the cycles of death and resurrection:

> Whatever we cannot imagine, we reify and deify. Whatever we cannot inhabit psychologically we propitiate with religious responses. It is not just that God is unknowable and unimaginable; it is that we reach for "God" most earnestly when imagination fails us. . . . To stand before an event for which we have no metaphors is to stand in the tabernacle of the Lord.[44]

When we look at trauma from this point of view, our attention is directed to its inherent religiousness. Just as God is described as transcendent and unknowable, trauma is an event that transcends our ability to experience it or to reflect on it psychologically.

Having this conceptual frame in mind we can now see the Polish cultural complex of the Suffering Hero came into being as a result of repetitive trauma on the collective and individual level. Violent changes in Polish life at times of loss of independence (partitions of the country) caused a reawakening and return to old myths of a Christian national identity. The repeated experience of national and individual trauma resulted in a continual obliteration of the distinction between the individual and collective. This resulted in a kind of *spiritual emigration* or retreat to the metaphoric, symbolic narrative where trauma and the national myth become one. Linking trauma with the national myth at the level of the group psyche can be seen in the poetry of Adam Mickiewicz ("Ksiegi narodu polskiego i pielgrzymstwa polskiego"):

> and they crucified the Polish nation, and laid it in its grave, crying out "We have slain and buried freedom," but they cried out foolishly.

For the Polish nation did not die. Its body lieth in the grave; but its spirit has descended into the abyss, that is into the private lives of people who suffer slavery in their own country. . . . For on the Third Day the soul shall return again to the Body, and the Nation shall arise and free all the peoples of Europe from slavery.[45]

Mickiewicz's metaphor solves the problem of the loss of the Polish state: the country is lost (the body lies in the grave), but its spirit is incarnated in the private lives of individuals who each day bear witness to the suffering of the nation. The symbolic identification between the suffering of the nation, the suffering of Christ, and the suffering of individual citizens makes everyday struggles sacred and, at the same time, reifies the nation through connection to the archetypal image of agony, death, and resurrection. Defeats are transformed; hope for change is sustained; and polarities in the image of Christ as Self are contained. All contribute to the creation of a deep field of meaning for individual and collective existence.

This formulation shows how a cultural complex compensates for the functions that a fragmented culture cannot provide. It creates the territory of collective identity and binding traditions; it provides the culture with a space that can contain the suffering of the individual, which can be recognized by the nation, and forms its unifying spirit. The cultural complex actually serves as a bridge between the individual and the collective at a time when the culture has been radically damaged by repeated trauma.

The Cultural Complex as a Defense Against Denied Mourning

Over time, however, the unifying symbols of suffering hero, martyred state, and crucified Christ came to provide not only a containing function but also a defensive function. Analyzing the religious dimension of trauma, Mogenson comments that when we look at trauma from this angle, we will see that

any metaphor that offers itself as the ultimate metaphor is no metaphor at all. The soul's mediating function, knocked around by events it cannot relativize into images, is completely knocked out when "saved" by the metaphor that ends all metaphors.[46]

The ultimate image of Poland as Christ existing through endless cycles of agony, death, and resurrection in the course of its history has paradoxically contributed to the Polish people's inability to mourn overwhelming losses. Not long ago after the Smolensk crash, Wojciech Wencel commented:

National tragedy threw us starboard out of our comfortable existence. We went down, to the bottom, where we would surely have drowned if the huge fish hadn't swallowed us, the symbol of Christianity. The biblical three days and three nights are going on. Out of the belly of the big fish, Polish people pray together to the Lord. . . . They see, that God writes our national history, and our individual histories. They realize that only being faithful to His will can make us happy.[47]

This fragment of mediocre poetic prose would not be treated seriously in any Polish social or cultural analysis of our history, most likely being attributed to immaturity and reverting to the past. But if we analyze its symbolism, we will see it presents perfectly both the defensive and transformative functions of the complex. According to this image, we are all in the role of Suffering Hero after 2010, the year of the Smolensk crash. We were thrown out of the "boat" of security into the sea where we could easily drown. In a way, the "big fish" itself served as a national defense against mourning by our being held in its belly waiting for the transformation of resurrection. In this sense, the "group ego" can be seen as being held in the energetic field of the complex.

I focus attention on the image of being swallowed by a big fish as it corresponds precisely to the personal, emotional impression I had after the Smolensk crash. I had started my studies on collective memory as an expression of the inability to mourn two years earlier.[48] Prior to the Smolensk crash nobody paid much attention to this subject. Working on the topic, I had the impression that I was writing about something that was implicit everywhere in the cultural unconscious but not explicit in the national consciousness. In 2010, the situation changed overnight. Instantaneously, the public space was filled with grief that very quickly was defensively covered with the symbolism of martyrdom, which flooded political and social discourse. At the time, I remember thinking that something had "swallowed us" whole on the group level – the "big fish."

The image of being swallowed by a big fish is similar to that described by Jung: "The night sea journey is a kind of descensus ad inferos – a descent into Hades and a journey to the land of ghosts somewhere beyond this world, beyond consciousness, hence immersion in the unconscious."[49] In "On Psychic Energy," Jung observes that "just as adaptation to the environment may fail, so adaptation to the inner world may fail because of the one-sidedness of the function in question."[50] Both seem to be true in the conditions of severe trauma. Jung continues:

Thus the complete orientation towards the inner world becomes necessary until such time as inner adaptation is attained. . . .
    [Hero's] entry into the dragon is the regressive direction and the journey to the East (the "night sea journey") with its attendant events symbolizes the effort to adapt to the conditions of psychic inner world. The complete swallowing up and disappearance of the hero in the belly of the dragon represents the complete withdrawal of interest from the outer world.[51]

I can translate Wencel's metaphor to a statement that the group ego has been captured by the unconscious complex, which has potentially transformative meaning but also serves as a protection against a deeper diving into the unconscious contents of unmourned previous trauma activated by the current event.[52] The symbolic imagery signals a regression in the psyche of a culture that lacks the tools to work psychologically on the mourning of previous trauma. Jung describes such a situation as an involution or degeneration – when an individual going through the night sea journey is stuck in regressed condition.[53]

At the same time, we can see that the recurrence of the exact same images from previous traumas signals a cultural complex is at work. In a way, the metaphor has trapped collective consciousness in the complex, which is perpetuated, while, at the same time, presenting the possibility of working through it. According to Mogenson, "Like the festering action that removes the sliver from a wound, the traumatized imagination works and re-works its metaphors until the events which have 'pierced' it can be viewed in more adaptive fashion."[54]

From this perspective, we can understand the reappearance of the affects and images of the cultural complex in moments of collective traumas as a struggle to organize what is outside the normal parameters of experience and what is beyond the capacity of the individual and collective psyche to contain and integrate it. In the cases of massive losses when collective ways of containing painful experiences fail, activation of the complex structures the experience and makes sense of the everyday struggle with loss.

The reappearance of a complex also has its darker side. Like individual complexes, cultural complexes tend to behave autonomously and collect experiences that confirm their historical points of view.[55] Their protective function is served no matter whether they are really needed, and the activated energy of archetypal defenses can distort perceptions of current events and shape responses that suit the old patterns.[56] This dynamic can be observed in the current reactivation of the Suffering Hero complex in Polish social life. As Singer comments, identifying with the simplified vision of the world offered by the complex is much easier than confronting the ambiguity of everyday experience.[57] Similarly, identifying with the Suffering Hero complex is easier than experiencing complicated issues that come from transgenerational transmission of primitive affects and ideas that refer not only to loss but also to the aggression and crimes done by one's own people to others. For instance, in observing the right-wing demonstrations on Polish Independence Day in November 2013 in Warsaw, many of the partisans were young people who have experienced profound uncertainty in changed social and economic conditions. They struggle with unemployment issues and lack a sense of group belonging. In such conditions, identification with old historical "truths" provides them with a feeling of purpose and helps them deal with shame and a lack of security.

A resilient culture can serve as a container for deeply conflicted feelings arising out of cultural complexes when the level of dialogue between opposing opinions and beliefs can be trusted and is perceived as safe. But historical trauma in a country or region often results in a lack of trust in the official narration.[58] It drives citizens back into the defensive and protective function of the complex with its cyclical return of affects and stereotypical ideas that rely on well-known symbols of past historical conflicts to shape perceptions of the world.

This vicious cycle – withdrawal into identification with the cultural complex energy as a defensive reaction to trauma combined with a lack of any other viable cultural tools to manage pain, struggle, and conflict creatively – results in a collective imagination shaped by trauma that pours forth its images of martyrdom.

How do we escape from such a vicious cycle? It seems the Polish psyche and imagination lacks the ability to relate to any potential national symbols that might heal or carry meaning. This could well be a post-traumatic reaction to trauma in the Polish people. At the same time, slowly, some early hints at change can be glimpsed in literature, art, and film. These pieces tackle difficult questions, bringing them into collective consciousness. A good example is the film *Aftermath*, which caused a violent social reaction, even leading to an attack on one of main actors.[59] His character lives in a village that took part in a Jewish pogrom during World War II, and he discovers that his father was the main leader of the attack on the Jews. In the final scene, he is crucified on the doors of a barn as a punishment for trying to reveal the old secret. This plays on and reverses the old myth in which the Jewish people are held responsible for murdering Christ. In this case, the inhabitants of the village are in the role attributed to "a mythical Jew," and the member of the community who tries to make amends for the past crime ends up in the role of Christ – the Suffering Hero.[60] The actual public reaction to the film re-created this scene: the actor who played the Suffering Hero was symbolically "crucified" for playing the role. The film ends with the brother of the Suffering Hero returning to the village years after emigrating to the United States, making the crime known, and finding public atonement. A similar motif is repeated in the book *Winter Journey*, in which the main character returns to Poland from Australia after many years.[61] She helps reveal old secrets and faces a difficult truth about herself.

When the capacity for change is not available within the culture, the old pattern – the cultural complex – repeats itself. In that case, a transformative shift in the collective psyche, which would reduce the autonomous, repetitive acting out of the complex, needs to come from outside the culture and its current set of cultural attitudes. Such an outside perspective helps the culture return to its own roots outside of a cultural narrative possessed by the complex.

Conclusion

Writing about the cultural complex requires entering its energetic field and struggling with the polarities it evokes. If we don't do that work, we end up with a cold scientific analysis that accumulates information but does not bring us closer to the complex's transformative energy.

In the case of the Suffering Hero complex, the Polish people need to find a way to move beyond the sense of shame that accompanies the repetitive cycle that leads nowhere and results in the feeling that nothing can be done. The *nowhere* and *nothingness* of the ever-recurring cultural complex needs to be approached differently – as a kind of a borderland, even a field of possible transformation. This is my experience of working with the contents of the cultural unconscious and teaching about trauma and culture – the theory and experience of depth psychology provides tools that enable us to hold in ourselves the grief coming from the level of the cultural unconscious, allowing us to experience a cultural complex in a different way. It is no longer a trap for the ego; on the contrary, it allows us to have a new self-image on the individual and group level. I experienced a similar process while working on this chapter. What at first felt shameful, and then overwhelming and too complicated to express, in the process of writing became a new understanding and curiosity that influenced my perception of the individual and group phenomena I observed and participated in.

Jung posits that "you deprive a man of his best resource when you help him to get rid of his complexes. You can only help him to become sufficiently aware of them and to start a conscious conflict within himself."[62] We should embrace the opposing poles of conflicted complexes, make them a center of our interest and provide new tools with which old conflicts can be reevaluated. Depth psychology can provide understanding to traumatized cultures, especially if it succeeds in finding new ways to create dialogue between the individual and the collective psyche. It offers the hope of creating a space where old conflicts can be addressed and reformulated in a symbolic, containing way that is digestible for people living in cultures in which the psyches of both individuals and the collective have been traumatized for generations.

Notes

1 D. Mathers, *An Introduction to Meaning and Purpose in Analytical Psychology* (London: Routledge, 2001), p. 172.
2 The *Smolensk crash*, most often described in Poland as the "Smolensk Catastrophe," occurred on April 10, 2010. The plane crashed in Smolensk (Russia), 1 km short of the runway in foggy weather conditions, killing ninety-six people on board, including President Lech Kaczyński and his wife, Maria; former president Ryszard Kaczorowski; the chief of the Polish General Staff and other senior Polish military officers; the president of the National Bank of Poland; Poland's deputy foreign minister; Polish government officials; eighteen members of the Polish parliament; senior members of the Polish clergy; and relatives of victims of the Katyn massacre (a series of mass executions of Polish nationals carried out by the People's Commissariat for Internal Affairs [NKVD], the Soviet secret police, in April and May 1940). Passengers of the plane were en route from Warsaw to attend an event marking the seventieth anniversary of the massacre; the site is approximately 19 kilometers (12 miles) west of Smolensk. The mourning that followed the crash associated it with Katyn massacre activated imagery connected with past persecutions caused by Soviet Russia. Right-wing groups have described it as "the worst national disaster to befall Poland since World War II." M. Kalinowska, "Monuments of Memory: Defensive Mechanisms of the Collective Psyche and Their Manifestation in the Memorialization Process," *Journal of Analytical Psychology* 57 (2012, 4): pp. 425–444.
3 Mathers, *An Introduction to Meaning*, p. 172.
4 Rebecca Solnit, *A Field Guide to Getting Lost* (New York: Viking, Penguin Group, 2005), Ch, "Open Door," Kindle Edition.

5 A. Bruckner, *Słownik etymologiczny jezyka polskiego* (Krakow: Krakowska Spolka Wydawnicza, 1927).

6 A mass execution of Polish nationals carried out by the People's Commissariat for Internal Affairs (NKVD), the Soviet secret police, in April and May 1940.

7 Marci Schore, *The Taste of Ashes: The Afterlife of Totalitarianism in Eastern Europe* (London: William Heineman, 2013), Ch. "Preface."

8 Joseph Henderson, "The Cultural Unconscious," in J. Henderson (ed.), *Shadow and Self* (Wilmette, IL: Chiron, 1990), p. 103.

9 The publication by Adam Mickiewicz's *Poetries Part I* in 1822 is regarded as a beginning of Polish Romanticism.

10 Mathers, *An Introduction to Meaning*, p. 196.

11 The *Battle of Westerplatte* was the first battle in the Invasion of Poland, the beginning of World War II in Europe. The defense of Westerplatte served as an inspiration for the Polish Army and people in the face of successful German advances elsewhere, and today it is still regarded as a symbol of resistance to the invasion.

12 The Lisbon earthquake, also known as the Great Lisbon Earthquake, occurred in the Kingdom of Portugal on November 1, 1755. M. Janion, *Gorączka romantyczna* (Krakow: Universitas, 2000).

13 Z. Bauman, *Płynny lek* (Kraków: Wydawnictwo Literackie, 2008).

14 Adam Mickiewicz, *The Great Improvisation*, trans. Louise Varèse (New York: Voyages, 1956). Adam Mickiewicz, "Dziady. Czesc III," in *Dziady* (Warszawa: Czytelnik, 1956/1980). Open Edition Books. Accessed December 28, 2013, at http://books.openedition.org/ceup/2369.

15 Dziady, Scene V., "The Vision of Father Peter," in George Rapall Noyes (ed.), *Poems by Adam Mickiewicz*, trans. Dorothea Prall Radin (New York: Polish Institute of Arts and Sciences in America, 1944), pp. 291–294. Open Edition Books. Accessed December 28, 2013, at http://books.openedition.org/ceup/2369.

16 M. Janion and M. Zmigrodzka, *Romantyzm i historia* (Warszawa: Panstwowy Instytut Wydawniczy, 1978).

17 Janion and Zmigrodzka, *Romantyzm i historia*; M. Janion, *Niesamowita Slowianszczyzna* (Krakow: Wydawnictwo Literackie, 2006).

18 W. Dzieduszycki, *Messyanizm polski a prawda dziejow* (Krakow: Drukarnia Czasu, 1901), pp. 6–7. Repozytorium Cyfrowe Instytutów Naukowych. Accessed December 28, 2013, at http://rcin.org.pl/dlibra/docmetadata?id=17882. Translation is mine.

19 Janion and Zmigrodzka, *Romantyzm i historia*.

20 A. Kijowski, *Listopadowy wieczor* (Warszawa: Panstwowy Instytut Wydawniczy, 1972), p. 16. Translation is mine.

21 The Siege of Jasna Gora took place in the winter of 1655 during the Swedish invasion of the Polish-Lithuanian Commonwealth.

22 G. Zubrzycki and A. Arbor, "Odczuwając naród: estetyka martyrologii mesjanistycznej w Polsce," *Sensus Historiae. Studia interdyscyplinarne* VI (2012, 1): pp. 49–77.

23 Zubrzycki and Arbor, "Odczuwając naród"; Janion, *Niesamowita Slowianszczyzna*; and M. Janion, *Placz generala. Eseje o wojnie* (Warszawa: Wydawnictwo Sic! s. c, 2007). There are striking parallels between this description of the Polish people and that of the Jewish tradition, further complicating the history of Polish-Jewish relationships.

24 M. Janion, *Czy bedziesz wiedzial, co przezyles* (Warszawa: Wydawnictwo Sic! s. c., 1996).

25 Kalinowska, "Monuments of History."

26 "Rz: 'Zginęła elita naszego kraju,'" *Polskie Radio*, April 10, 2010. Accessed December 29, 2013, at http://www.polskieradio.pl/5/115/Artykul/198738,Rz-Zginela-elita-naszego-kraju.

27 James Hillman, *Healing Fiction* (Putnam, CT: Spring Publications, 1983), Ch. 3, Section Title "Jung Daimones."

28 G. Mogenson, *A Most Accursed Religion: When a Trauma Becomes God* (Putman, CT: Spring Publications, Inc., 2005).
29 Kalinowska, "Monuments of History."
30 Janion, *Czy bedziesz wiedzial*, p. 4.
31 T. Todorov, *Hope and Memory: Lessons From the Twentieth Century* (Princeton, NJ: Princeton University Press, 2003), as quoted in Duncan Bell (ed.), *Memory, Trauma and World Politics: Reflections on the Relationship Between Past and Present* (New York: Palgrave Macmillan, 2006), p. v.
32 Henderson, "The Cultural Unconscious," p. 103.
33 Mickiewicz, *Dziady*, part III, scene 1. This is a paraphrase of Mickiewicz's quotation. The original is "If I forget about them, you, God in Heaven, forget about me." The plural form is often used in cultural references, and this is the meaning I am using in the text.
34 Thomas Singer and C. Kaplinsky, "Cultural Complexes in Analysis," in Murray Stein (ed.), *Jungian Psychoanalysis: Working in the Spirit of C. G. Jung* (Chicago and La Salle, IL: Open Court, 2010).
35 P. Czaplinski, *Polska do wymiany: Pozna nowoczesnosc i nasze wielkie historie* (Warszawa: Wydawnictwo W. A. B., 2009).
36 Jenny Edkins, "Remembering Relationality: Trauma Time and Politics," in Bell, ed., *Memory, Trauma and World Politics*.
37 K. Erikson, "Notes on Trauma and Community," in C. Caruth (ed.), *Trauma: Explorations in Memory* (Baltimore, MD: The Johns Hopkins University Press, 1995), pp. 183–189.
38 J. Butler, *Precarious Life: The Powers of Mourning and Violence* (London: Verso, 2004), as quoted in Edkins, "Remembering Relationality," p. 110.
39 Rosemary Gordon, "The Symbolic Experience as Bridge Between the Personal and the Collective," *Journal of Analytical Psychology* 22 (1977, 4): pp. 331–342.
40 Mogenson, *A Most Accursed Religion*, p. 15.
41 M. Wilkinson, *Changing Minds in Therapy: Emotion, Attachment, Trauma & Neurobiology* (London, New York: W. W. Norton & Company, 2010), p. xx.
42 Mogenson, *A Most Accursed Religion*, p. 161.
43 Mogenson, *A Most Accursed Religion*, p. 161.
44 Mogenson, *A Most Accursed Religion*, p. 14.
45 Quoted in N. Davis, *Heart of Europe: A Short History of Poland* (Oxford: Oxford University Press, 1984), p. 202; A. Mickiewicz, "Ksiegi narodu polskiego i pielgrzymstwa polskiego," in *Wirtualna Biblioteka Literatury Polskiej* (Gdansk: Instytut Filologii Polskiej Uniwersytetu Gdanskiego).
46 Mogenson, *A Most Accursed Religion*, p. 16.
47 W. Wencel, "Prawda jest gdzie indziej," *Rzeczypospolita*, 2011, at http://www.rp.pl/artykul/695905-Prawda--jest-gdzie-indziej.html. Translations are mine.
48 M. Kalinowska and A. Rozycka, "The Shot Memory: Reflections Over the Influence of the Second World War Trauma on the Contemporary Polish Psyche" (Presented at The First European Conference of Analytical Psychology, Vilnius, Lithuania, June 25–27, 2009).
49 C. G. Jung, "The Psychology of the Transference (1946)," in G. Adler and R. F. C. Hull (eds. and trans.), *The Collected Works of C. G. Jung*, Vol. 16 (Princeton, NJ: Princeton University Press, 1966), § 455.
50 C. G. Jung, "On Psychic Energy (1928)," in G. Adler and R. F. C. Hull (eds. and trans.), *The Collected Works of C. G. Jung*, Vol. 8 (Princeton, NJ: Princeton University Press, 1969), § 68.
51 Jung, "On Psychic Energy," §§ 67–68.
52 Wencel, *Prawda jest gdzie indziej*.
53 Jung, CW 8 § 69.

54 Mogenson, *A Most Accursed Religion*, p. 141.
55 Thomas Singer, "The Cultural Complex and Archetypal Defenses of the Group Spirit: Baby Zeus, Elian Gonzales, Constantine's Sword, and Other Holy Wars (With Special Attention to 'The Axis of Evil')," in T. Singer and S. Kimbles (eds.), *The Cultural Complex: Contemporary Jungian Perspectives on Psyche and Society* (Hove and New York: Routledge, 2004); Thomas Singer and Samuel L. Kimbles, "The Emerging Theory of Cultural Complexes," in J. Cambray and L. Carter (eds.), *Analytical Psychology: Contemporary Perspectives in Jungian Analysis* (Hove & New York: Brunner-Routledge, 2004).
56 Donald Kalsched, *The Inner World of Trauma: Archetypal Defenses of the Personal Spirit* (London and New York: Routledge, 1996); Singer, "The Cultural Complex and Archetypal Defenses of the Group Spirit"; E. Weisstub and E. Galili-Weisstub, "Collective Trauma and Cultural Complexes," in T. Singer and S. Kimbles (eds.), *The Cultural Complex: Contemporary Jungian Perspectives on Psyche and Society* (Hove and New York: Routledge).
57 Singer, "The Cultural Complex and Archetypal Defenses of the Group Spirit," p. 21.
58 Kalinowska, "Monuments of History."
59 Wladyslaw Pasikowski, *Aftermath*, directed by Wladyslaw Pasikowski (Apple Film Production, 2012).
60 Janion, *Placz generala*.
61 Diane Armstrong, *Winter Journey* (New York: Harper Collins, Fourth Estate, 2012).
62 C. G. Jung, "The Fight with the Shadow (1946)," in Gerhard Adler and R. F. C. Hull (eds. and trans.), *The Collected Works of C. G. Jung*, Vol. 10 (Princeton, NJ: Princeton University Press, 1969), § 456.

Greece

Greece

The Inner Riddle of "Greek Psychic Debt"

Evangelos Tsempelis

Ivo Andríc, the Bosnian literature laureate, in his wonderful novel the *Bridge on the Drina*, tells the story of a young Christian boy who was abducted according to the infamous institution of παιδομάζωμα (devshirme), the summoning and abduction of Christian children by the Ottoman authorities. The children were then raised as Muslims to eventually serve its infamous Janissary corps.[1] The boy rose to the highest echelons of the Ottoman Empire, eventually becoming a grand vizier of the Porte. In this wonderful tale, Ivo Andríc tells the quintessential Balkan story of an impossible return, the central focus of which is an old bridge. The boy who became a vizier, as so many others who fell victim to that cruel practice, would be raised in and assimilated to the beliefs and institutions of a foreign consciousness. His return to who he was, or who he might have become had he not crossed that bridge, is not a tenable option to be entertained. Rather, it is a barred possibility. And yet today still, in that same part of the world, which is called the Balkans, by an inextricable and indiscernible alliance between objective geographical language and value-laden pejorative speech, there are demurring signs that point to a trace from some such initial trauma: the trauma of being raised according to the trappings of a foreign consciousness. Moreover, this element, this trace, is not a positive sign of something concrete that can be seized and turned into a foothold or a demonstrable object that can then be clearly captured and spoken of in intelligible language. Rather this trace takes the negative form of an absence. As such, this absence is also indicative of a certain state of mind, or to be more precise, this trace speaks of a way of being that exerts its mysterious presence on anyone who grew up in this little corner of the world. This way of being is experienced in the various pulls that it exerts on one's life, mysteriously, elusively, and often so preemptively, yet unmistakably as to constitute a certain reality of a different sort – a reality that begs to be recognized and acknowledged by its very elusiveness. It is a reality that can as easily be ignored or tripped over at one's own peril.

I remember a few years ago visiting a remote village in the north of Greece, close to the border with Albania. There, I met an old woman dressed in black, as women, in what seems a perpetual gesture of mourning running across unaccounted millennia, are customarily dressed in rural parts of Greece. She spoke to me and my wife about a different world: hers. She told us about a different kind of

DOI: 10.4324/9781003609742-5

παιδομάζωμα, which had taken place during the civil war in Greece in the 1940s. She, like the young boy in Andrić's novel, belonged to a generation of children who had been abducted to be raised away from their families, away from their country, according to the trappings and the demands of a foreign consciousness. This time the bridge that had been irrevocably crossed was not one separating a Muslim world from a Christian one. Rather, the separating line was now one between the East and the West as a new Cold World era was taking form and being defined in the aftermath of World War II. During the time of the civil war in Greece, which had pitted communist and republican forces in deadly, fratricidal confrontation over the future place and status of a liberated, hemorrhaged, and emaciated country in a new world era, children, such as that old lady in black, had been summoned by the withdrawing and defeated communist forces and taken away to the other side of the border, where the Eastern Bloc had already been defined and erected. These children were first taken to Albania and from there were divided and spread, according to who knows what arbitrary and expedient logic, all across the entire Eastern Bloc.

Today, seventy-some years later, it can be said with a certain precision that most of these children, belonging to our parents' generation, never found their way back across the bridge over which they had been abducted. Nor has their fate been anyone's serious concern. As such, they remain lost and unaccounted for in our cloudy memory. I once met an old man in the Macedonian city of *Bitola*, a city which is still called *Μοναστήρι* on the other side of the Greek border where I belong. And on my side of the border, one could refer to that city with the adjective *Macedonian* only at one's own risk in the early 1990s. This old man came up to me out of nowhere and spoke Greek with a sense of discernible nostalgia that I could not quite understand in my youthful ignorance. He asked if he could give me his address and if I would send him a postcard once "I arrived back in Greece." "Of course I said." Shamefully, that postcard was never sent, as if that man had not existed, as if he had been some dream-like image whose request had no status in the waking life of my state of consciousness, as if his existence had been as dubious as that "Macedonian city," which had some intelligible status in my world only so long as it was called "*Μοναστήρι*," a name that in its turn referred to another world that no longer existed *stricto sensu*. And as I remember this man, and the old lady before recounting her story of abduction, I can't help but think of that initial moment of summoning: the very moment when men in unkempt uniforms and scruffy beards and a frantic look of defeat in their eyes, as their aspirations had been forever dashed and their war and cause were declared lost and betrayed, "intervene" so resolutely, so irrevocably in little children's lives. Is there a word or a term capable of reflecting with some dignity, even so remotely, something of that violence and its corollary in terms of pain and despair, which is here implied? I think of a certain word: *ξεριζωμός*, usually deployed to describe another human tragedy recorded in collective memory: the "uprooting" of Greek communities from their perennial lands after the national disaster of an offensive expedition gone wrong, so terribly wrong, in Asia Minor, following the defeat of the Ottoman Empire in World War I.

What is it like to be uprooted? To be torn from the root that nourishes? To be taken away from the warm maternal embrace at the most tender time in one's life before one even has a proper chance to be who *one* properly *is*, as to even be able to begin to trace a loss retrospectively at some future point in time? What is it like to be carried away at the other side of a border to another world that speaks another language according to another peoples' experiences and according to another peoples' sensibilities? What is it to live an alienated life of yearning for some impossible return? Or worse: what is it like to discard how *yearning secretly yearns* as one forgets in powerless resignation?[2] And how dangerous it is, in pure and simple human terms, to believe that one knows what the answers to these awful questions are simply because they can be subsumed under the abstract notion of *exile*. And, once again, I wonder if we have a word that can capture and communicate the gist of a misunderstanding and the consequences that arise from the act of *hubris* from which it springs and of which it speaks – defining a whole other way of existing: sovereignly, comfortably, knowingly. One surrenders the possibility of a fundamental basic *act* of human empathy and understanding – which concerns and entails and draws from a primary and unmediated relationship with the very core of the fragility of "being" – for the *fact* of having an abstract command over some field of human life and experience by means of a vantage point delivered in vague and disembodied terms that are divorced and removed from *their* own roots. After all, it is ξερίζωμα (*uprooting*) that we are still trying to trace and reenact here, isn't it?

Years before the financial crisis had announced itself, there had been an underlying sense that something had gone terribly wrong in Greece. Yet what has been also remarkable, almost eerie, about this predicament is how long a certain ambience of normality has persevered, accompanying the unfolding of a drama with catastrophic consequences for peoples' lives. The acute, dispassionate outside observer would have had to look carefully at the edges to discern how the old décor showed signs of wear and tear long before its actual collapse. And that hypothetical observer would have had to be even more acute in her observation if she were to ever deduce and infer from these hardly visible signs of tear in an old décor, still subsisting in the background, the existence of human realities of an order that does not readily register in the prevailing sensualist-laden attitudes of our time. True, there are no emaciated children in Athens today, though there have been stories in the press alluding to children fainting at school as a result of malnourishment. Greece still today, at the time of this writing, betokens the appearances of a developed European country – even as its economy is de facto bankrupt, even as its society is worn and torn after years of anguish, disillusionment, and strain. Ironically, in the midst of its fall, Greece has oddly found itself in yet another disorienting predicament. Namely, that of acting as a gatekeeper country for the thousands of migrants and refugees fleeing war and destitution in Northern Africa and Asia in the hope of entering the safe haven of European Union countries. In that vein, today, one can see in the streets of Athens, in the squares and in the parks, scores of destitute people waiting in transit for a better future in Europe. The tragedy of our times has been captured in the stories and the images of people drowning at the very sites – the Aegean shores – that also comprise the points of attraction for the only remaining, burgeoning Greek industry, selling nice views and sandy beaches to the tired workforces of northern Europe looking for some careless respite from their busy lives.

Though there has been a marked increase in armed robberies and house break-ins, there is no shooting between warring parties in Greece; the kind of peace that European institutions were built to safeguard against the past horrors of two World Wars in the twentieth century still looms here.[3] But what if an increasing number of law-abiding, democratically blessed European citizens decide to support the idea of punishing Greece for its inability to reform by drying up the financial assistance that keeps its economy solvent? What if, after sixty years of integration, built on a discourse of solidarity among Europeans, an increasing number of politicians and citizens in Europe address the financially renegade south as if the euro and Europe altogether is some technical project that *they* own? A project from which the inferior parties can be expelled with no serious consequences? Who cares to notice that while everything is still seemingly and largely in place something of enormous proportions has already occurred and the world that we have known, as we have known it (or imagined it), no longer exists?

In 2009, as the Greek prime minister was turning in humiliation to the European Union and the IMF in order to safeguard the necessary financial assistance, which would have allowed the national economy to avoid a catastrophic collapse, curiously the story that was on the front pages of most newspapers in Greece was a different one. It concerned the supposedly leaked sex tape of a certain blond and voluptuous young starlet. Hundreds of thousands of copies of the story about this sought-after archetype were sold; the entire nation seemed to have been hypnotized by the itch that this new scandal had provoked: a young girl in her twenties, who had been raised by a middle-class family in Athens, with piano and ballet lessons and all the trappings of a certain respectable Athenian living, turned into a voluptuous TV starlet, then turned into a porn star and performer of the hit song "Money Is the Goal." The metaphor for what had been happening to the country is almost too obvious to risk redundancy or vulgarity by attempting any further analysis by means of simple inductions from this individual to the collective or in terms of depth psychology's terminology about the feminine element in the collective layer of the psyche.

A few years earlier, the customary summer fires, which slowly and methodically swallow entire areas of green rural landscape in Greece, took on even more menacing proportions. In the summer of 2007, sixty-three people were burned when a village was surrounded by the blaze and the residents failed to evacuate. Then the fire consumed a great part of the forest of Mount Parnitha. In a gray moon-like landscape, ashes had replaced ancient trees – belonging to the Gods and faeries of another era – and carcasses of wild animals lay charcoaled while another symbol of the times found expression in the proud rescue of the casino hotel at the summit of the mountain. And then another fire preemptively made itself present on the ancient site of *Olympia* as if everyone were caught in the hypnotized itch of that previously referred-to sex tape. The flames reached all the way down to the old site of the Olympic games; the museum where the statue of *Hermes of Prax-iteles* in dazzling serendipitous beauty still stands unperturbed was caught in the fire defenseless. The signs of an imminent collapse and of a deep decadence were there already. At the danger of a certain *esoteric* line of thought, one could even claim that these signs and a whole number of other such undetected signs were not really signs but already the effects by which a certain catastrophe, which had already occurred at some other deeper level long ago, was now announcing itself to desensitized, or somewhat complacent and dulled by force of habit, sense/perception human apparatuses. I see this as somewhat like another phenomenon of sense-perception fallacy with which we are familiar when we look up at a starry sky cognizant of the great distances that light has to travel to traverse the space separating a celestial object from the surface of an observing retina.

And as I think of this catastrophe, I once again find myself wondering back to that actual moment when something of enormous proportions in terms of its significance for peoples' individual lives as well as a collective culture first occurred. Was there such a "first precipitating moment" – an ultimate and foundational point of reference, some sort of a *first principle* in terms of which the present crisis can be understood through hindsight? Or is, rather, the cumulative result of an infinite number of small undetected acts suffered and perpetrated by individual psyche(s) across great segments of time only capable of being rendered intelligible retrospectively from some later vantage point when one has already crossed, irrevocably, some bridge to another state of consciousness? As I ponder these questions, I have begun to realize that there is something about the soul's ability to absorb enormous amounts of violence so tacitly, something about its ability to enclose events of such vast and cataclysmic significance, that I have not even started to understand.

Whereas *humanitarianism* concerns itself with humanmade or natural disasters of great volume and scale, we still lack the means to address and to speak of harm of vast proportion and scope yet not necessarily of an enormous scale. What is a catastrophe for the abstracted notion of a "humanity" calling for an organized humanitarian response finds its corollary here in *ontological destruction* for the individual human being – though here our civilization does not recognize an interpellation to act correctively. And although the former may also imply the latter as a consequence, the reverse does not appear to be necessary. The terms are not mutually inclusive. Moreover, whereas *humanitarianism* points to an imperative to act to attenuate human suffering in great numbers, here we lack the terms that make it possible to account for a reality of a different sort and to speak of destruction in the realm of "being." This realm is arguably way too fragile, way too elusive to permit clear-cut definitions and corresponding interventions. Arguably, its fragility is directly proportional to its capacity to be obliterated. So the notion of *ontological destruction* in its vagueness is the outcome of an incomplete attempt to capture something of that phenomenon sustained by the individual soul, in its infinitesimally minute and unexplored texture, when a certain violence diminishes the possibilities for meaning and where spirit, as a quality of discernment and relationship, is injuriously violated.

In that vein, the signs referring to a violence perpetrated in the realm of "being" and *that* deeper destruction to which they elusively allude are obviously of an order foreign to the one that institutions such as the IMF and the World Bank – created by the Allies in the aftermath of World War II to safeguard not only the peace, as previously mentioned, but also the financial stability of a newly erected post-war world – were designed to address.[4] And so, from the low point of national decadence, where I find myself coining these words, I wonder if there will be a day in some distant future of acme when Europeans, inhabitants of this old and tired continent, inhabitants of this fallen country, might recognize the need to set up institutions to protect endangered ways of life, or forgotten qualities and sensibilities, or dashed hopes and expectations, or charcoaled ancient forests and blackened ancient marbles and unperturbed statues – tokens of an ancient culture's tribute to peace and beauty – from the multiple menaces that threaten them, not so much as "objects" in the economy of a palpable and concrete world, but rather as signs of an unintelligible world, which they can only vaguely represent to us and which can so easily be forgotten or discarded at our own peril? Will there be a time when such un-noteworthy signs will be considered seriously by some institutionally supported "early warning system" I wonder?

But all of this talk is as self-indulgent as what it attempts to condemn and to castigate. It is talk about others not about one's own self. It speaks of the hook and not of the projection that always looks for a hook to attach itself to. And as I begin to think of the psychology, which underpins and makes this projection possible, I start to realize that a whole new *psychology of decadence* might be needed in order to somehow account for the feeling that lays heavy in the heart and conditions the mind. Or the challenge is perhaps this: once this psychology of national decadence is developed and cultivated, as to render its contents intelligible to the dispassionate observer, to then go deeper to inquire what conditions it and what makes it possible. What is it that determines the feeling that something has gone so terribly wrong in this country, way beyond the current crisis of finances and way before scarcity, the founding principle of economics, became a lived experience once again? Is it the fact that this relatively young national culture has been built upon the premise of a certain organic continuity with ancient Greece – itself an unattainable expectation, for who can live up to such a heritage? Is it perhaps that this very national myth and its construed heritage was in its turn built on a certain reinvention of ancient Greece by the Age of European Enlightenment? An enlightenment that reached Greece as a ricochet in the form of an epiphenomenon largely influenced and conditioned by another European cultural counter-movement to the Age of Reason: nineteenth-century Romanticism? Is it that the sovereign rights of the new national Greek culture were at that time asserted and articulated in counter-distinction to the *Sick Man of Europe* – the Ottoman Empire?

Apparently, the political argument that won the day in the nineteenth century and earned the nascent Greek state the international support it needed to achieve its national aspirations was that Greeks were not revolutionaries who aspired to subvert the international order but rather an oppressed people living under the Ottoman's barbarous rule. Not only that, the Greeks, defined according to widely variable circumstances as individuals belonging to Christian Orthodox faith and/or speaking (notions of) Greek language, were an ancient people who had been trapped in the forced bondage of four long centuries of darkness. In Western Europe, Kant would famously say that "enlightenment is exit from the darkness which man is responsible for," a copious work of (pure) reason pitting man against himself.[5] In Greece, that responsibility for self-emancipation was interpreted and applied as a mandate to emancipate against the imposed darkness of the outside (Ottoman) oppressor. And then? What would happen once the oppressor was overthrown and a new independent order founded? Once liberated, how would this "ancient people" with a heroic past, which had brought the lights to the rest of European civilization some 2000 years ago, now account for the deficit in its own brightness? How else than in terms of an "Ottoman legacy," which would later become a perpetual attributing cause – a sort of "first principle" in the account of every future malaise? *If so, then this foundational argument, as a pan-ultimate explanation for all that seemed to be backward in Greece, would inevitably point to the existence of a permanent gap, a structural psychic deficit between that country and the rest of Europe. A deficit separating Greece not merely from the rest of Europe – whose historical trajectory is often turned into a developmental norm in terms of which degrees of deviation are then attributed to Greek historical experience up to the present – but, paradoxically, from the image of its very own (imagined) self.*

Was this argument then, namely, that a Greek nation had existed in a lineage of three thousand years and that, at the beginning of the nineteenth century, after four hundred years of oppressive and barbarous Ottoman rule, it had finally managed to revolt and to assert its sovereign rights as an independent nation state, the threshold to a state of (sponsored) consciousness that truncated aspects of being that still lie irretrievable and unmourned today and that continue unconsciously to condition life? Or to put it differently, was this winning argument perhaps the bridge that once crossed severed any possibility of going back to recover who one was, or might have been, or could become in relation to some other form and in some deeper congruence of experience of which today we have only a remote and vague trace? Or is this indeed a barred possibility?

Perhaps it is worth considering that it is only in terms of such a trace that we can begin to come to terms with a strange modern Greek predicament whereby one lives distraught by a formative experience of unattainable luring promises lying ahead, part of a forever-elusive horizon of anticipation, on the one hand, and a broken bridge of nostalgic yearning for some impossible return to a no-man's land lying behind, on the other. And perhaps the current crisis confronting Greece will continue to remain unresolved, like the riddle of the Sphinx in Thebes, waiting for an Oedipus to finally answer it (with its own share of tragic consequences), as long as some way out of this curious conundrum is not found.

As I think of this conundrum, I wonder if we do have in the myths of our collective history an image or a story that captures this dynamic. Is there an image that describes what takes place in the intimate core of "being" as one is ushered all too early, all too prematurely into a foreign world? This is not a story of rape; neither is it a story of some God devouring his children. As a story of false consciousness it inevitably takes me back to the opening theme of "abduction." Once again, I find reasons to acknowledge Jung's contribution, which has allowed us to uncover the rich relevance of myth to our psyche, way beyond another pan-ultimate explanatory cause: sexuality. Now we can talk of an *Oedipus complex* in an entirely different light – namely, as the complex of a false consciousness faced with the tragedy of its own constitutive falsity. From this point of view, the story of Oedipus is the appalling story of awakening to a tragic, unfathomable truth. Not the literal truth that one has actually slept with one's mother – rather the deeper truth that one-is-not-who-one-is and that, curiously, and as a consequence of *that*, one is called to face one's true destiny. It is only in terms of the simple fact of "(not) being who he 'is,'" by a prehistory of renunciation, abduction, and fostered parenting, that Oedipus killed his father and *actually* slept with his true mother. *The gold lies in the fact that falsity is the higher truth of one's own true destiny.* Could that be an answer to the Greek riddle of the Sphinx today?

The slow awakening to the constitutive fact of falsity is recorded by Sophocles in the most daunting and shattering manner as Oedipus slowly puts together the fragmented pieces, which terrifyingly, one after the other, coalesce and which, at one awe-full moment, release in blinding insight the image of a uniform truth. An insight that strikes the proud king down with an abysmal force that supersedes and reveals at once something bigger than any man can contain or attribute to himself. Here, individual enlightenment is confronted with the structural element that makes it possible and conditions it: the realm of abysmal darkness. Blind Oedipus is the man who has seen the truth. This could be the opening sentence, in the form of an acknowledgment, in that hypothetical *psychology of decadence*, a descriptive psychology referred to previously and whose founding mandate would be to disclose the myriad aspects in daily living that condition the heart and bind the mind in my home country. And perhaps the closing sentence of that psychology would similarly attempt to capture something of the gist of that experience of an impossible return that seems to be so constitutive of what it means to be a subject of this "Greece." As if Greece is not an actual place, as if it is not even a country but some unfulfilled promise that is either always deferred for some later time or crushingly betrayed every time, or actually both: deferred and betrayed at the same time, every time.

As I write these words, for the first time, I'm beginning to understand another riddle – namely, what Greeks mean when we say that "*Greece never dies . . .*" whenever our country is confronted with some menacing crisis. I'm beginning to understand that behind this proverbial statement lies unaddressed a deeper truth, which, when considered, actually discloses the reverse of what it purports to claim. You see, this statement is not a statement that asserts a country's ability to persevere against the odds as it first seems to be doing. Quite inversely, the statement reveals that Greece is not capable of dying. It does not possess that prized ability. It is sadly not *die-able*. Perhaps because it has not yet entirely entered time, perhaps because it has actually not yet properly fully materialized as a country (in our consciousness) in order to be perishable, or perhaps because we who comprise it can at will always keep her in our minds and hearts in the nonperishable, uncorruptable no-man's land status at the price of a perpetual, unaccounted, and still unaddressed individual inner death. To think of it, indeed, Greece is not a country. It is a blood-thirsty, life-crashing, vampire-of-an-animal. It is an idea or an ideal, I am not exactly sure which, attached for life-support to individual lungs and hearts sucking oxygen and blood out of them only to stay alive forever in intensive care: her postponed death is our (mode of) life; our (individual psychic) death is her way of existing. Yet this strange and ominous *psychobiological formula* cannot be even momentarily pondered here without immediately digressing to some form of tacit confession of love. I would even use the term *incestuous love* to capture something of the dynamic of a not-wanting-to-be-born-kind-of-love-for-one's-country if I knew for certain that in a Jungian fashion we had by now steered clear from the literal readings of Oedipus's story.

And so, from this revealed vista, the whole body of this *psychology of decadence* would be deployed to offer some insight into a series of other remarkable riddles, such as, for instance, how a country of a mere ten million people could amass such a staggering public debt – three hundred billion euro – without anybody seriously noticing? Without anybody blowing a whistle? How could an entire country find itself so unprepared to acknowledge and to deal with the consequences of its own making? How could so many people live for so long so self-forgetfully and so self-indulgently? And mostly, how is it possible that even today, when that catastrophe has been acknowledged by the entire world and the country hangs from a single thread over the brink of some unexplored abyss, that an increasing number of its citizens can still pretend that this calamity can be wished away or denied or attributed to someone else? And how can so many people believe that, as easily as this catastrophe can be denied and responsibility for it ascribed to someone else (the Germans, the capitalists, the politicians – the list is long), that there is some way out of it by means of some outside intervention?

So it would fall to this descriptive psychology of decadence to display the various aspects of the just-mentioned state of mind in its widest possible variety and permutations so as to increase the chances and the probabilities of a confrontation with some revealed image in individual consciousness, hoping to thus reawaken a sense of awe, to mobilize insight, and to resuscitate some life-forward-striving dynamism: an immense unexplored individual potential that still seems to lie at large, dormant, or in a state of suspended animation and inner bondage. This unlived potential seems to lay hostage to a perverse, debt-incurring inner economy of (self-denying) retention and (frivolous, carefree) release in repeating unconscious circles of endless yearning and timeless deferring. That life silently follows a rigid rule, known in colloquial Greek as ελληνική πραγματικότητα (*Greek reality*). It can be unmistakably recognized by the kind of gravitational pull that it exerts on existence and that binds and reduces the complexity of life by subjecting it to the double bind of individual denial and collective forgetfulness: the individual denial of responsibility toward the constitutive "other" facing one and in relationship to whom one stands reflected, and the collective forgetfulness of one's obligations toward revealed "being" in the face of imminent darkness and personal death. So one is constantly confronted, almost vengefully, in every facet of private and public life, by the two sides of the same siren-infested dire strait leading to the *Scylla* of egotistical *hubris* and the *Harivdis* of group fatalism. A kind of lose-lose situation that can produce lost generations, failed economies, hubristic escapades, and when *they* go wrong, terribly wrong, corresponding disasters – just as it can produce "nihilistic national cultures" and a grotesque form of cynical individualism that is often a caricature of its own self. The kind of situation, that is, to whom a nascent descriptive *psychology of decadence* is hereby wholeheartedly – lamentably – dedicated.

And yet the intention was to go deeper. To inquire into the background of this feeling of demise and to ask what conditions it. Is it the actual catastrophe of Greece's national economy that produces a sense of pessimism for the decadence of its national culture? Or is it the reverse? Namely, the operation of some deeper psychic force ingrained in the fabric of this writing, as a self-indulgent attitude of pessimism and defeat, which as a specimen of a collective psychology of decadence is encountered, in turn, in the very fabric of Greek society, and in relation to which actual events can be subsequently analyzed? By way of recapitulating, I earlier pointed to a certain winning argument deployed in the nineteenth century, according to which Greeks were an oppressed people with direct lineage to a classical era so idealized by Enlightenment Europe. And I have claimed that the identification with such an ideal as an origin, as an *arche* for a nascent modern national culture inevitably would create a problem of measuring up and living with an almost impossible cultural heritage. As I have also claimed that, once liberated, Greeks seem to have found ourselves in a situation of "psychic debt" toward our (impossible) past as we have also felt at some level structurally unfit to fully attain integration in a European future.

According to varying contingent circumstances, at any point in time Greeks seem to oscillate between one-sided euphoric aspirations of success and equally one-sided self-indulgent feelings of defeatist pessimism. On a different axis, this oscillation registers its movement between two poles: one recognized by feelings of superiority associated with a well-documented historical proclivity going back all the way to Byzantium to view one's self as the *Chosen Christian Orthodox people* (περιούσιος λαός). And a second pole characterized by a sense of inferiority to the West and to Europe. Here, every shortcoming is immediately interpreted in terms of a structural deficit in the Greek psyche as a consequence of "having suffered four centuries of Ottoman subjugation" or "having not properly experienced a Renaissance or a Reformation, or our very own home-grown Enlightenment." Against this background, the matrix of available choices of action follows, in turn, this inner oscillation. Here, the scope is determined by those, on one end, who proclaim the importance of modernizing and adapting to the requirements of a globalizing world and by those, on the other, who disdainfully reject that idea and who counteract the importance of finding "national dignity" by means of asserting the right to exist according to one's own terms. Sadly, both of these tendencies are one-sided and maladapted. Modernizers have turned Greece, without scruples, first into an endless lucrative – and now cheap and defunct – development project with little respect for its traditions, its old ways of being, its unique landscape and beautiful nature, as well as the idiosyncrasies of its people and culture. Similarly, at the other end, populists and left-wing ersatz revolutionaries of various sorts display once again an astonishing proclivity in cultivating a national predisposition toward a mixed breed of isolationism and escapism that blunts and misdirects those individual and group resources necessary to push the country forward and to overcome this crisis.

Within the course of the one-hundred and eighty years from the founding of their modern state, Greeks have managed to consolidate national borders, which includes a significant geographical area in one of the most pivotal corners of the Eurasian continent. They have fought successfully wars of liberation against the Ottoman Empire; they have fought two Balkan wars and two World Wars; they have suffered the consequences of a disastrous offensive expedition against the fallen Ottoman Empire at the end of World War I and of a civil war at the end of World War II. They have endured dictatorships, the last one only forty years ago. They have survived the harsh realities of exile, poverty, and immigration. And despite all of this, they have remarkably consolidated a European-style democracy and partaken in a long and unprecedented era of affluence and stability. And yet the financial crisis that began in 2008 seems to have exposed symptoms of deeper ailments present in the collective national psyche long before the crisis erupted.

Like every crisis, collective or individual, this one that has befallen us is unique. Like every breakdown, this crisis summons our vital energies and demands our concentrated attention. It confronts us with challenges that threaten established ways of being and calls for a response. Nobody can prescribe how that call can or should be answered by each one of us. One thing is certain, however: we are now being addressed. Each one of us is called to define the jump necessary to reach his or her own earth. This may very well be our ushering in of a new era, a new mode of existence, a new stage of development reminiscent perhaps of what Jung associates with "obeying the law of one's being."[6] Just as no outside criterion or definition exists for a true self, similarly the inner principle underpinning the historical development of a culture can only be sought in its own history.[7] *The crises of a culture form the history of its truth coming to terms with its self.* Every crisis is an interpellation to renew and redefine notions of integrity, authenticity, and autonomy. It is an opportunity to further deepen and cultivate individual and collective identity by adding layers of further differentiation and by integrating aspects of the past within new modes of existence. As there is no precipitating cause in terms of which the ailments of the present can be reductively explained, there is similarly no certainty that history follows a path of evolution leading to higher and more creative forms of psychic integration for a collective of people. Yet the opportunity to renew, redefine, differentiate, and integrate is certainly present for individual consciousness in history. The flourishing or demise of cultures and traditions is a function of how this opportunity folds and unfolds across segments of time; it is a function of how this individual opportunity is used and/or misused.

In concluding, I would like to offer some additional thoughts relating to an earlier remark according to which a hypothesized answer to the riddle of the Sphinx today was understood as *"The gold lies in the fact that falsity is the higher truth of one's own true destiny."*[8] In an era that has put so much emphasis on the "social construction" of reality, an era from which we have not yet fully recovered, this statement can be easily misinterpreted. According to such a misinterpretation, the falsity of the modern Greek national narrative, or the "Greek psychic debt" to which I have previously alluded, would be construed as categories belonging to an attempt aimed at exposing a fallacy: a lie. Social constructivists like to show how every phenomenon presented as a fact or every identity, which refers to some core essence, is, in fact, a construct that if carefully studied and examined will reveal not only the various aspects of its constructiveness but also those strategies that attempt to conceal it. This act of concealment that they undertake to expose reflects, they claim, strategies of power and dominance that assert themselves by means of presenting as natural and essential some artifact that is only manmade. Along this line of thought, emancipation is inextricably related to deconstruction: the copious and serious work of exposing strategies of concealment, uncovering the constructiveness of constructs fallibly presenting themselves as permanent natural essences. Against that background, my previous statement can be posited as an attempt to expose the constructiveness of modern Greek identity and to reveal an oppressive fallacy that wants to pass as a natural fact some manmade invention – which the individual psyche cannot and will not swallow. This is a tortuous path, not the one I chose to take here.

Suffice it to say that the falsity of identity is invoked as a structural element. Every identity, every act, every object arises in relationship to a vacuum. At times of crisis, we are often, like Oedipus, momentarily confronted by a frightful image of its abysmal darkness; sometimes we are fortunate to experience how benevolently and miraculously it supports us. The falsity that it exposes is an invitation to face the vacuity and the gratuity of human endeavors. To dispel this or that identity simply because one can demonstrate that at its core there lies a strategy of concealment and to thus call every identity, disdainfully, rejectfully, a "construct" and to treat it as if it could be interchangeable with any other equally arbitrary "construct" is to remain blind both to the mystery of what is concealed and to the wonder of what is disclosed: always in relationship to a vacuum, always (in a certain way) arbitrarily, unexpectedly. And how dangerous it is, in pure, simple human terms, to believe that one knows what that vacuum is: that one can somehow overcome and sublate the debt that it incurs simply because the essence of some lived falsity may point, negatively and abstractly, to a possible field of knowledge waiting to be acquired and – alas(!) once so often – exhaustively imposed in (total) systematic fashion![9]

And so the question remains and perseveres as to how *we* modern Greeks are to confront today – in our falsity – the higher essence of our true destiny. As we find ourselves at this dismal crossroad, we might perhaps learn something useful or draw some courage by remembering an article published some sixty years ago under circumstances quite different to our own, on the front page of *Kathimerini*, a daily newspaper still published today.[10] In that article, which had the form of an open letter to Adolph Hitler and which can perhaps be read as a prized counter-example to today's withered and discredited public discourse, a respected journalist – Angelos Vlachos – offered an account of Greece's entry into the war against Italy and described the various episodes of its confrontation with the harsh military and diplomatic realities of the time. As Germany was now at the brink of entering the war against Greece with devastating consequences, Vlachos asked Hitler what he would do if, instead of an infantry or an artillery to meet the victorious and robust army of the Wehrmacht, Greece sent to the front "twenty thousand injured soldiers, young men without hands, with no legs, wrapped in bandages stained in blood" (from the previous confrontation with Italy). "Will there be an army to strike such soldier-guardians?" Vlachos asks Hitler. Only to retort immediately that no this will not happen.

The remaining Greek army that is still free will stand, if called, in Trace as it stood in Ipirus. And what will it do? It will battle. There too. It will fight. There too. It will die. There too. And it will wait for the return from Berlin of the runner who had carried the Olympic light as to convert the torch into a flame and to bring the fire back to this small in size but otherwise immense topos (place) which after having taught the whole wide world how to live now it has to also teach it how to die.[11]

Notes

1 Ivo Andríc, *Bridge on the Drina*, trans. Lovett F. Edwards (Chicago, IL: University of Chicago Press, 1977).

2 *"nothing nothings,"* says Heidegger. Martin Heidegger, *Introduction to Metaphysics* (New Haven, CT, and London: Yale University Press, 1935).

3 Institutions from the European Community of Coal and Steel in the 1950s to the Common Market and the European Union to the European Monetary Union.

4 The United Nations Monetary and Financial Conference, where these agreements were reached, was held in Bretton Woods, New Hampshire, in 1944.

5 Immanuel Kant (1724–1804), *An Answer to the Question: "What is Enlightenment?"* (London: Cambridge University Press, 1991).

6 C. G. Jung, "The Development of Personality (1934)," in G. Adler and R. F. C. Hull (eds. and trans.), *The Collected Works of C. G. Jung*, Vol. 17 (Princeton, NJ: Princeton University Press, 1954), § 314.

7 Here, I am also thinking of the phenomenologist's dictum: "to the things themselves!" Edmund Husserl, *Logical Investigations (1900/1901)*, ed. Dermot Moran, 2nd ed., 2 Vols (London: Routledge, 2001), p. 168.

8 The original riddle is known to have been: "Which animal stands in the morning on four feet, at noon on two, and at evening on three?" Oedipus correctly answered, "It is man

who starts life crawling on four feet, grows to stand on two, and walks with the help of a cane at old age." Today, that riddle could be reread as: "What presents as natural and self-assured lying horizontally on earth, to then appear standing as a reflection of its superior image, to finally become the measure of its own support? Truth" (Essence).

9 My though drifts to F. W. J. Schelling, *The Grounding of Positive Philosophy, The Berlin Lectures (1842)* (Albany: State University of New York Press, 2007).

10 *Ανοικτή επιστολή προς την Α.Ε. τον κ. Α. Χίτλερ, Αρχικαγκελλάριον του Γερμανικού Κράτους, Καθημερινή* Μάρτιος 8, 1941.

11 (translation mine) Διότι τί θὰ κάμη ὁ Στρατὸς αὐτός, Ἐξοχώτατε, ἂν ἀντὶ πεζικοῦ, πυροβολικοῦ καὶ μεραρχιῶν, στείλη ἡ Ἑλλὰς φύλακας εἰς τὰ σύνορά της εἴκοσι χιλιάδας τραυματιῶν, χωρὶς πόδια, χωρὶς χέρια, μὲ τὰ αἵματα καὶ τοὺς ἐπιδέσμους, διὰ νὰ τὸν ὑποδεχθοῦν; . . . Αὐτοὺς τοὺς στρατιώτας φύλακας θὰ ὑπάρξη στρατὸς διὰ νὰ τοὺς κτυπήση;

Ἀλλ᾽ ὄχι, δὲν πρόκειται νὰ γίνη αὐτό. Ὁ ὀλίγος ἢ πολὺς στρατὸς τῶν Ἑλλήνων ποὺ εἶναι ἐλεύθερος, ὅπως ἐστάθη εἰς τὴν Ἤπειρον, θὰ σταθῆ, ἂν κληθῆ, εἰς τὴν Θράκην. Καὶ τί νὰ κάμη; . . .Θὰ πολεμήση. Καὶ ἐκεῖ.

Καὶ θὰ ἀγωνισθῆ. Καὶ ἐκεῖ. Καὶ θ᾽ ἀποθάνη. Καὶ ἐκεῖ. Καὶ θ᾽ ἀναμείνη τὴν ἐκ Βερολίνου ἐπιστροφὴν τοῦ δρομέως, ὁ ὁποῖος ἦλθε πρὸ πέντε ἐτῶν καὶ ἔλαβε ἀπὸ τὴν Ὀλυμπίαν τὸ φῶς, διὰ νὰ μεταβάλη εἰς δαυλὸν τὴν λαμπάδα καὶ φέρη τὴν πυρκαϊὰν εἰς τὸν μικρόν, τὴν ἔκτασιν, ἀλλὰ μέγιστον αὐτὸν τόπον, ὁ ὁποῖος, ἀφοῦ ἔμαθε τὸν κόσμον ὅλον νὰ ζῆ, πρέπει τώρα νὰ τὸν μάθη καὶ ν᾽ ἀποθνήσκη.

Spain

おそらく

The Catalan Vault
The Transformation of a Personal and Cultural Complex

Olivia del Castillo

> Anyone who can read Freud's Interpretation of Dreams . . . will not fail to be deeply impressed at that point where Freud reminds us that an individual conflict, which he calls the incest fantasy, lies at the root of that monumental drama of the ancient world, the Oedipus legend. The impression made by this simple remark may be likened to the uncanny feeling which would steal over us if, amid the noise and bustle of a modern city street, we were suddenly to come upon an ancient relic – say the Corinthian capital of a long-immured column, or fragment of an inscription. A moment ago we were completely absorbed in the hectic, ephemeral life of the present; then, the next moment, something very remote and strange flashes upon us, which directs our gaze to a different order of things. We turn away from the vast confusion of the present to glimpse the higher connection with the historic.
>
> – C. G. Jung, *Symbols of Transformation*

This chapter seeks to demonstrate the unexpected and uncanny connections between extreme nationalism, psychic incest, and dissociation. By *dissociation*, I mean what can happen to the psyche when it has to defend itself in the midst of unbearable pain.[1] *Actual incest*, for example, is a profoundly dehumanizing primitive experience, resulting in intolerable suffering and the need to wall off parts of the psyche to go on living. As Jung said, the so-called incest barrier "is a product of culture which nobody invented and which grew up naturally in the basis of complex biological necessities . . . facing the endogamy social danger."[2] *Psychic incest* (as differentiated from actual incest) is a kind of assault on the infantile ego, which still identifies projectively with the mother and has not yet come into its own separate being. This kind of union is characteristic of the early stages of development and can result in pathological states if the developmental steps of differentiation between conscious and unconscious are interrupted.[3] In those cases, the ego's identity is swallowed by the unconscious.

The term *psychic incest* correlates with *participation mystique* in Jung, *ouroboric incest* in Neumann, *ouroboric omnipotence* in Samuels, and *incestual* in Racamier, the psychoanalyst who distinguished between the Oedipus complex's psychic incest, which is individual and *intra-psychic*, and the *incestual* or *familiar*, which is *trans-psychic*.[4] The terms *incestual* and *trans-psychic* are terms coined by

DOI: 10.4324/9781003609742-6

Racamier to describe psychic incest as a dynamic that penetrates the psyches of the different persons belonging to a family, agglutinating them against socialization.[5] In choosing among these various overlapping terms, I have decided to refer primarily to *psychic incest*, following in the footsteps of León Febres-Cordero who describes incest and sacrifice in Greek tragedy as follows:

> [T]he incest referred to here is not the physical incest, but a much more perverse one because it is natural, invisible and difficult to detect, is extended, tolerated and stimulated, a form of incest which precedes the physical incest: psychic incest, understood as identification with the way of life of the members of the family, tribe, clan. Established in our homes, the homes of the families, imposed in an atavistic way from prehistoric times, and before the times of Greek tragedy, in clans and tribes, psychic incest makes us fall into the trap of the living and the dead, so that we can never mentally move through hunches that emerge from the center of our personality; preventing us from thinking about what we have to deprive ourselves of, sacrificing it for the purpose of our own destiny; a destiny that would make us face the challenge of being ourselves above being part of familiar ethnic, religious, ideological affiliations, after having been exiled, as Orestes, from the house in which we shed the blood of the psychic incest.[6]

Failure in individuals with a psychic incest problem occurs in the relationship between their ego and the unconscious. The fragile ego remains undifferentiated from the unconscious and is flooded by the archaic, omnipotent, and archetypal psyche. When the ego is not mature enough to establish a spontaneous, more differentiated relationship with the unconscious, it is easily overwhelmed, and there is no room or ground for humanization. Conflict between the conscious and the unconscious is continuously triggered, leading to various psychopathologies with their corresponding defensive responses.

As an extension of the idea of psychic incest in individuals, *extreme nationalism* is a condition characterized by an all-encompassing state body that has coupled with its citizens in a suffocating way, heightening an unconscious yearning for belonging and identification to a larger corporate order. I differentiate this state of being from the less fervent, more "normal" nationalist feelings toward earth, culture, country, or the nation in which one was born and feels at home. If the ego of an individual and his or her group lacks a natural connection with healthy national feeling, there is the danger of rootlessness. Simultaneously, underlying archaic impulses toward merger and fusion can overwhelm the ego of the individual and the group. Under such circumstances, the "ism" of nationalism can gain in strength, and both individuals and groups can become possessed by collective ideology. As Jung points out:

> Alienation from the unconscious and from historical conditions spells rootlessness. That is the danger that lies in wait for the conqueror of foreign lands, and

for every individual who, through one-sided allegiance to any kind of -ism, loses touch with the dark, maternal, earthy ground of his being.[7]

Nowhere do we know for sure about these matters, but least of all where "isms" flourish, for they are only a sophisticated substitute for the lost link with psychic reality. The mass psyche that infallibly results destroys the meaning of the individual.[8]

Again, the feeling of national identity can be a natural, healthy feeling that arises among citizens who don't need to be indoctrinated or intoxicated by the state. Such citizens are freer to tolerate differences and nuances in the depth of national feeling among fellow citizens and are less prone to need to impose their beliefs on others. When identification with the nation intensifies, however, it can easily acquire the character of a defensive dogmatism in which recurring paranoid fantasies of being endangered by other nations or enemies from within can find fertile ground.

As the twentieth century's history has shown repeatedly, the effects of extreme nationalism can be enormously destructive, including the dehumanization of the individual by the collective ideology. Such ideological intrusion, even invasion, can result in dissociative disease. John Hill writes of this phenomenon in the history of his homeland, Ireland:

> The extremists of both sides have perpetuated opposing mythological concepts of their land. . . . The Protestants rely on patriarchal structure and tradition; the Catholics on the other, enduring myth of "Mother Ireland," for whom her sons die. . . . As long as individuals identify with one or the other pole, with the archetypal father or mother of a nationalized mythology, there is little hope that a unity between civic order and ancestral heritage can be achieved.[9]

In this chapter, I highlight the influence of psychic incest in the pathological dissociation that occurs both at the individual level, when consciousness is overtaken by certain unconscious complexes, as well as at the collective level, when consciousness is overtaken by extreme nationalism, which I think of as a cultural complex. I approach these issues by exploring the similarities between three apparently unrelated subjects in the psyche of Spain: the deep emotion surrounding death in Greek tragedy, the structure of a specific Spanish architectural form – the Catalan vault – as an archetypal container, and the syntonic countertransference experience of horror and shadow I had with a patient's dream imagery.

The Spanish Case

As a Spaniard, the issue of extreme nationalism has affected me throughout my life. I was born in a little town in the Aragon region of Spain sixteen years after the Spanish Civil War had ended (1936–1939). My parents were both children during the war and were married at a young age. When I was four years old, my parents, as many young couples did at that time, settled in one of the big cities of Spain, where there were opportunities for jobs or developing their own businesses, as was the case for my parents. They chose the city of Barcelona. Those were times of great enthusiasm. The postwar period, filled with the difficulties of rebuilding the country, was beginning to pass, and people were energized, almost caught in heroic nationalistic attitudes.

For thirty-six years, until 1975 when Francisco Franco died, Spain was governed by a dictator. During that period, heroic nationalistic values were not discussed as there was no room for criticism. As a young woman, I fought this suffocating pressure that gave us no freedom to think and to live. At times, I was literally afraid that I would be killed for speaking out about issues in the Spanish psyche related to politics and to nationalism. I was afraid that someone might "steal my own death" from me. I came across this phrase – "to steal your own death" – during a seminar with León Febres-Cordero who examined the phrase in the context of Greek tragedy. He helped me understand what it meant "to steal your own death" in terms of the terrible traumatic difficulties of living under a totalitarian regime.[10]

Febres-Cordero focused on a character from Euripides' *Hecuba*, who meets her own death by accepting it, not as a victim of someone else but as a responsible agent for her own sacrifice. Hecuba's daughter, Polyxena, is being taken to be sacrificed by Neoptolemus. Hecuba, wanting to stop the killing of her daughter, clings to her. Polyxena prefers to go to her death rather than live her life as a slave. It is as if Hecuba and Polyxena are two branches of an intertwined and entangled plant whose connection needs to be severed so each can experience her own life and destiny. Both the audience and the play's main characters share in the experience of this tortured separation of mother and daughter – which is both an intra-psychic and interpersonal phenomena. The daughter has to separate from the "otherness" of the mother who dwells within her own psyche. Paradoxically, this rupture can be interpreted as a step forward in consciousness both on the personal and cultural level. The incest fantasy that the mother and daughter are one and the same is broken, and it is the breaking of this incest fantasy that Jung saw as a "product of culture."[11] An undifferentiated state becomes differentiated. The individual moves from being a victim of an unconscious oneness to being a conscious participant in the creation of her own fate. She is able to elaborate her own life and choose her own fate. This choice to separate from oneness with the mother or, in the case of extreme nationalism, oneness with the state, puts one at grave risk. This is no easy choice for even the most heroic. But those who choose to break from the oneness of psychic incest – whether with the mother, the clan, or the nation – do not see death as the most precious good. Rather, they place the highest value on living life freely, fully, and responsibly. When the state controls every aspect of living – as in cases of extreme nationalism – there is little room for individual consciousness or destiny. This is why I use the word *suffocating* to describe the experience of those living within the psychic incest of too close a relationship with the mother or the state.

Although he lived and painted more than a century before the rise of Franco's dictatorship, the Aragonese artist Francisco de Goya lived under the tyranny of the Napoleonic wars and witnessed the horrors of its state-imposed destructiveness. He allowed it to penetrate his psyche, and through his work, he revealed it to the Spanish people. Among the results of his fierce refusal to turn away from the horrors of his times was the series known as the *Black Paintings*, which emerged from Goya's inner experience during a critical phase of his life.[12] At the time of his illness and psychological crisis, the artist felt the need to grapple in his art with the frightful, suffocating atmosphere of vaulted spaces.

Goya locates his scenes in an urban space that is clearly defined by architectural elements, described by a scholar in the following way:

> The building is only suggested in the drawing by means of soft outlines of reddish-purple tincture to represent the stones in contrast to a more intense trait of parallel lines to indicate the opening in the wall of entry surely of a church. . . . As we have seen repeatedly, the use of vaulted architecture to locate scenes provided a special dramatic quality that is another of his visual constants.[13]

Later, I return to the experience of horror represented by Goya through the architectural imagery of the vaulted space (Figure 3.1) and its relationship to being suffocated by extreme nationalist feeling. The Goya paintings helped me understand my strong countertransference reaction to a patient's dream, which follows.

Figure 3.1 Francisco de Goya, *Not for those* (© artehistoria)

The Experience in the Analytic Space

To demonstrate the link between extreme nationalism and dissociation, I will describe a clinical vignette that took place in my practice some time ago. The patient was a young woman approaching her thirties. When she came to me for the first time, she told me she was "blocked and lost." She felt quite vulnerable and unable to remain alone at home. When she was a child, she had suffered night terrors, and as a girl she had never been able to be alone in her parents' house. In her own house, away from her parents' house, she was afraid of having visions or seeing "presences," and she also suffered some episodes of panic attacks. At those moments, she did not feel secure in differentiating between reality and fantasy. Sometimes she heard noises and felt as if she might be assaulted by somebody who terrified her.

Her father had been a depressed and frustrated civil servant who suffered from a severe narcissistic disorder. He made his daughter feel that her behavior was important to him, yet he always felt dissatisfied and frustrated by her. He saw her as having the potential of being capable but also as being hopeless. Although he lacked expression and was uncommunicative, the father was a persecutor. He never stopped observing and negatively "seducing" the daughter, under the pretense of taking care of her but, at the same time, accusing her of being the cause of his pain and discontent. This generated arguments between the father and daughter that spilled over into the family. The mother was apparently a friendly and liberal woman, but actually she had abandoned her daughter to the narcissistic whims of her husband, totally ignoring the continuing disputes between father and daughter, saying "It is up to you – you have to solve the problems between you; I do not want to get involved in your problems." Thus, the patient was trapped in a psychic incestuous relationship with the father, from whom, on one hand, she had tried to escape, while, on the other hand, remaining unconditionally loyal to him and also to her mother and the family as an entity that she couldn't abandon.

She also had a sister who was ten years younger and who did not create conflicts with her parents; she was proud of her parents and seemed to be the perfect daughter. She had studied at the university and had a boyfriend with whom she had been in a long-term relationship since she was an adolescent. The younger sister's only trouble was the continuous conflict with her older sister because of her "desire for prominence." This family was a frustrated clan in which the patient, who felt as if she were the leading cause of the conflict, was the first daughter and the first grandchild. This was a relationship of intense bonds and binds that often resulted in dissociative feelings. Her family destroyed her internally; at the same time, their affective loyalty to her was unquestioned. Thus, her self-punishment for not satisfying them had been ongoing since her earliest childhood.

After school, the patient had not gone to the university. She thought that her father was right on a certain level when he reproached her for that. Such a reproach implied that she had the capacity and could have had a career if she had not been such a "disaster." Her disaster was, however, nothing more than being confused and disoriented with regard to her individuality and her own personal identity. She tended to psychic dissociation and was overwhelmed by unconscious perceptual distortions when she was alone. She had friends and also certain creative outlets; these two qualities allowed her to subsist. When she could, she moved overseas with a young man with whom she lived for some time until she broke it off because she was feeling unsatisfied and frustrated emotionally. Then, she returned to her parents' home at which time we initiated the analysis. After a little time, she began a new loving relationship with a companion, which ended when dissatisfaction was again aroused – and also mutual reproach and conflict. She tormented him, demanding affection from him, and he tormented her by refusing her constant demands.

The relationship ended when a third person became involved – a young woman who began an intimate relationship with the young man. During this time, my patient was extremely anxious because of the young man's infidelity; I had to be quite close to her, demonstrating my loyalty while she was being obliged to accept the presence of this *third* person and to tolerate separation from the companion on whom she had projected her demanding relationship with her father. In the midst of her deep grief caused by this separation, the patient told me about a dream. In that session, I was touched by a sensation that Jung said, "may be likened . . . to the uncanny feeling which would steal over us if . . . we were suddenly to come upon an ancient relic."[14] The dream contained the image of just such an ancient relic – the Catalan vault:

> *I arrived at our house in Sant Feliu for a visit. It had changed on the outside. Now the exterior wall was white and not green, and it was more integrated into the façade of the entire estate, which is white. A poetic graffiti protest was painted on the wall. I walked in. The space with a vault, the Catalan vault* [the patient emphasized this, looking at me as if seeking my agreement, as if she were testing me], *was divided into two areas with a medium height wall in the middle. The entire hall was full of pictures painted by "him" . . . the whole house was very warm, except a wall at the end that was untidy and had to be ordered, but that didn't bother me. It was rich but not crowded, full but not suffocating. "He" was there. I liked the richness that the paintings gave to the space. We looked at each other and gave each other a very delicate kiss. There was a spectacular feeling of purity, of loving him, of falling in love again, feeling him within me. It was a powerful scene. After kissing, we hugged; we merged, giving breath to the other, feeling deep love and respect for each other. Then we talked about what we wanted from each other, and it seemed that he was not yet ready for that.*

As I said, the dream took place at a time when my patient had just ended a relationship with her partner after he became involved with another woman.

At the deepest level, the dream announced the resolution of the psychic incestuous aspect of her personality. Eros could be experienced between two differentiated parts. On the one hand, the unconscious revealed this to me, if not immediately to the patient. On the other hand, when the patient emphasized the characteristic of the vault as being Catalan, looking at me as if seeking my agreement, I experienced the opposite: the presence of a negative cultural complex, with its mixture of national-istic and familial incestuous feelings that, in my view, validated my earlier intuitive perception of this kind of problem in my patient and her family. In that moment, I remembered that in one of our sessions at the beginning of the analysis she had said that the solution for the difficult times we were living in was "to recover tradi-tions." She said this with a confident attitude; at the same time, she seemed to be asking for my agreement or perhaps testing me and my ideology, as I am not from Catalonia, and it is not my personal heritage.

It is important to understand that, under Franco, it was illegal to speak Catalan or to have any connection with Catalan traditions. After Franco's death, this policy was reversed, and since then the newer generations from Catalonia have been raised speak-ing Catalan, not only at home but also in schools, in stores, everywhere. A national-ist Catalan government has now been in power for more than thirty years – years spent immersed in the Catalan language, culture, and history. As a result, my patient's attitude was typical of the nationalist narrative in Catalonia. Many young people searching for an identity and the resolution of difficult social and personal issues have gotten trapped in these intense, Catalan, nationalist, ideological reactions, which can be as suffocating to individuality as life under Franco's Spanish totalitarianism.

In that early analytic moment, I had thought that, although my patient's life had been devastated in so many respects, recovering her Catalan traditions was not the answer to her problems. Now, after long work in analysis and many emotional crises with mixed results, it was important for her – at the conscious level – to emphasize that the vault was Catalan, from Catalonia, from the clan, from nation-alist feelings of identity. That little detail scared and horrified me. A huge shadow appeared in my mind. On the one hand, she was testing me in regard to my own ideology about the Catalan renewal to see if I agreed with her point of view about its positive value. On the other hand, I was concerned that her attitude could rep-resent a psychic regression to nationalist values as a defense against the Eros that flooded the dream. She had been far too angry with her ex-boyfriend to see him as a partner with her in a beautiful coniunctio under the vault. It was much easier for her to see this as the magical embrace of nationalism than as an embrace with her ex-boyfriend with whom she remained furious. My own countertransference reaction assaulted me and stimulated my imagination, suggesting that a cultural complex simultaneous with a personal complex was manifesting itself, making me feel the suffocating psychic incest within her. I felt like the hidden darkness in the image of the Catalan vault needed to be experienced consciously in some way, in this case, through my countertransference.

The Vault

The *Catalan vault* is a thin-walled brick vault related to the original tiled vaults, also called *lightweight vaults* or *timbrel vaults*. The Catalan vault is unique to the Iberian Peninsula and has Middle Eastern origins. These tiled vaults are made with bricks placed close to each other, along the vault's curvature, like a very thin wall.

The brick, among the oldest of building materials, is one of the elements that characterizes the Catalan vault. These bricks were manufactured with clay that was simply kneaded and dried in the sun. Muslim architects in Syria have used them since the end of the Umayyad period (661–750 CE). The growth of Islam resulted in the spread of this brick-construction technique.[15]

But two more essential elements also characterize the tiled vault: plaster and construction without *cimbra* (formwork). These elements originated with cultures located in places with warm, dry weather (Mesopotamia, the Mediterranean, and North Africa). *Plaster* is a hydrated calcium sulfate that is cooked and crushed to form a powder that hardens when mixed with water and that softens in cold and wet climates. In Spain, plaster is abundant in the Levante region (the southeastern part of Spain), and the more refined use of it can be found in the historically Muslim areas of Spain, such as the Alhambra of Granada. Cimbra, or formwork, is a timber structure used to hold the weight of an arch or a vault temporarily during its construction; tiled vaults can be built without cimbra. The culture of construction without cimbra reached Spain before the Arabs, however. The Emperor Justinian, and with him the Byzantines, spread the knowledge of how to construct vaults without cimbra, beginning with the central dome of what was then Santa Sofia Cathedral in ancient Constantinople (now known as the Hagia Sophia in Istanbul, Türkiye), and extending to Gibraltar and Denia (the extreme south to the east of the Iberian Peninsula).[16]

Archaeologists have since concluded that the tiled vault appeared in Spain, especially in Al-Andalus with its Spanish Muslim architecture. It appears that the tiled vault evolved in three distinct stylistic directions. Today, the oldest, original type of tiled vaults can be found in Extremadura, the region above northwest Andalucía, near Portugal. The second and simpler type of vault was so popular in the seventeenth century that Madrilenian Fray Lorenzo de San Nicolas ordered that many of them be built in the Old City of Madrid. The Catalan *alarifes* (builders) were the best at this style of construction, which was distinguished by the masters of the Court in Madrid with the name *Catalan vault*. Its most important examples in Catalonia are the Monastery of Pedralbes, Santa Maria del Mar, the Pinos Church, the Royal Chapel of Barcelona's Cathedral, and in the work of Antoni Gaudí. The third style of tiled vault can be found in Valencia, where builders developed a high degree of technical complexity. An example of this style can be found in New York City in the central dome of the Cathedral of Saint John the Divine, built in 1909 by the Valencian Rafael Guastavino.[17]

It is interesting to read what twentieth-century architects have to say about the building technique of this light, tough, and economic vault. The architect and builder Rafael Guastavino introduced the style in the United States with great success. According to Bassegoda Musté, Guastavino lamented that this kind of vault had to be constructed "by rule of the thumb," as making accurate measurements was difficult. Accordingly, Bassegoda Musté explains in a 1952 conference that the timbrel vault was highly praised at the School of Architecture of Barcelona for having "the vice of holding together,"[18] meaning that, despite its simplicity, it has the strength to hold together. Its refined technology and primal vaulted system allow for the swiftness of its construction. Bassegoda Musté points out that there is need neither of "cimbra" nor of any kind of "supporting wood" to act as a structure or frame. Select materials and expert craftsmanship are the only necessary ingredients. Catalan ceramic brick is very thin and light, making it easier to "turn on a table" with a firm and free hand. For the freehand construction of the tiled vault, the first sheet of thin brick must hold up almost on its own. Two other ceramic bricks are then matched in the joints in both directions, walling them up with "staggered joints," so that the space where one brick joins another in each row does not coincide with that of the upper and lower rows. Bassegoda Musté explains that "experience teaches that in the deformations the vault acquires during its construction, a trend to compensation and propping manifests, which results in an '*estereodia-grama* of efforts,'" which I understand as a kind of design or schema that develops in two directions – in stereo – with mechanical properties that the construction is able to sustain. The stability of such an airy vault is due "to the good eye, to the skilled hand, to the knack and intuition of the worker." "No shame," said Bassegoda, "to accept this bare and naked empiricism." He goes on to say this:

> Things were taken out of proportion by an obsession to do too much theorizing. If only for mental economy, we introduce in the "static calculation simplifying assumptions" "in an attempt to make it approachable." It is unfair to demand that reality be unfailingly accurate to our image, whose arbitrariness is only justified by the elimination of danger and by keeping calm the architect's nervous system in view of the ten years of civil and criminal responsibility that he risks.[19]

The Commitment of the Analyst

I surprised myself by delving into such a detailed architectural inquiry, but immersion in the subject began to suggest to me an underling archetypal psychology, as well as architectural structure, in the dream's use of the Catalan vault as an image. The architectural terms I use in this chapter were unfamiliar to me prior to becoming curious about the dream imagery and are most likely unknown to the reader as well, but they are where the amplification of the dream symbol of the Catalan vault led me.

We can think of the dream as an empirical fact like the tiled vault. Neither can be measured nor counted with precision. In fact, the lack of precision – "the rule of thumb" – distinguishes its uniqueness. Like the "Corinthian capital" in the epigraph from Jung, the dream and the tiled vault surprise us and speak for themselves. What does the Catalan vault with its partial wall defining two separate areas symbolize in the dream? By delving into the origin of the Catalan vault and by trying to decipher Bassegoda's 1952 conference proceeding as if it were a hermetic text of hidden meanings, I stepped out of the boundaries of the everyday analytic space. In my attempt to understand the powerful dream image of the Catalan vault, something was being forged within myself, something that would influence the analytical process with my patient.

The dream compelled me to understand more about the history, structure, and unique cultural context of the Catalan vault, and although it may appear

idiosyncratic or arbitrary for me to have explored the esoteric meaning of the architects' conference, I felt that somehow I was staying with the objective facts of the
dream imagery, not forcing "static calculations of simplifying assumptions" in an
attempt "to make approachable" the issues presented by my patient.[20] She came to
me because she suffered a severe dissociative tendency in her personality. My aim
was to come to grips with the living image of the patient's dream without demanding that it conform to a preconceived idea that I might have of its meaning. In this
case, the Catalan vault, as I perceived it when the patient emphasized its condition
as *Catalan*, triggered my own personal and cultural complex: at the same time that
I was perceiving the shadow of this nationalist commentary, I felt the fear of being
killed if I spoke out about an authoritarian government that demanded extreme
nationalist fervor and loyalty, just as I had felt when I was young during the time
of Franco's nationalist government and as I have felt many times in relation to the
current nationalist ideology in Catalonia. The heroic exaltation of the condition of
being Spanish or of being Catalan, each inflated with the intoxication of an "ism,"
made me feel the same danger of an unconscious, undifferentiated identification
with the collective, with the clan, or with the family.

It is at this point that I can now return to the symbolic imagery of Francisco
de Goya's use of vaulted spaces. Goya's vaulted dark paintings awakened in my
mind the shadow's presence under the vault, and by allowing it into consciousness I saw the opposite of the idealized, unilateral perception of nationalism.
In this sense, Goya's vaulted spaces gave me the opportunity to see clearly the
incestuous illusion of safety and wholeness under the "ism" of the Catalan vault
that was my patient's regressive wish. The vault of Catalan nationalism did not
provide the security for which she yearned. Her dream vault suggested what I felt
was its real meaning, which through the dazzling erotic relationship offered the
possibility of a real transformation into two separate but related areas under it.
To apply Bassegoda's advice to the architect who would design a Catalan vault,
it was my job to "to keep calm in view of the . . . civil and criminal responsibility." If I were completely taken over by the complex of being afraid of being
killed, I could have found rationalizations and strategies to justify my reflexive
response, which was to shut up and resist exploring the meaning of the vault as a
symbol beyond seeing the rather empty, one-dimensional nature of the apparent
meaning of the vault that existed in the mind of my patient and myself. Instead
the dream demanded that I explore its meaning in greater depth. I learned from
the architects' conference how one goes about building a solid structure that can
hold together the weight and structural tensions of the building in all its complexity. And I began to realize that the dream architecture pointed to a potential
psychological construct in the patient that might be able to bear the weight, hold
together, and support a differentiated space that was previously impossible to
sustain in her psyche.

It is interesting to note that, owing to the pain my patient had experienced
throughout her life when faced with the rupture of significant emotional bonds, this
vaulted space had now been divided into two distinct, mutually accessible areas,
limited by a half height wall.

The Vault in Goya

To understand the Catalan vault in greater depth, I found myself turning to Goya's *Black Paintings* because they open a view to the shadow side of the vault. Goya's *Black Paintings* reveal the inevitable shadow that lurks behind idealistic nationalism. The similarity between Goya's paintings and my patient's symbolic vault in her dream allowed me to see the shadow side of her nationalism and opened the possibility for transformative consciousness in both of us. The vault in her dream showed the transformation of the internal space when a third element appeared, and the patient integrated that third with the help of the analytical relationship. She had passed a terrible crisis lasting some months. In a sense, my imaginings about the similarity between Goya's vaults and her dream vault also acted as the third.

As José Manuel Matilla points out:

[Goya] uses vaulted architecture, of unquestionable symbolic value, under whose darkness abuses take place. This use of the architecture, vaulted space of violence, oppression and injustice, is one of the constants of the Goya's work.[21]

The image [following] intensifies the visualization of this architectural space, showing a solid building with an arched element that leaves a group of men carrying more bodies [Figure 3.2]. . . . the use of vaulted architecture to locate scenes of a special drama is another visual constant [in Goya].[22]

Figure 3.2 Francisco de Goya, *Cartloads to the cemetery* (© artehistoria)

Goya's symbolic use of the vault suggests an all-engulfing horror that is created by the oppression of a totalitarian state. Like Goya's vault, the state swallows everything in its monolithic being. The vault is not a nurturing container; rather it is a container of terrible suffering that the artist forces his viewer to face directly and see consciously. Through his direct portrayal of such horrors, Goya challenges the veil of unconsciousness that a suffocating, extreme nationalism forces on all of its citizens.

My fear of the Catalan vault – triggered by my patient's reference to Catalan nationalism when she explained the dream – had been the fear of being suffocated by the oppression of extreme nationalism. It could not only steal my own voice; it could also "steal my own death." In this context, it is worth looking at Goya's *Los fusilamientos del 3 de mayo en Madrid*, which portrays the killing of Spanish men who resisted Napoleon's army during its occupation of 1808 in the so-called Peninsular war (Figure 3.3). Seen through the lens of "stealing one's own death" versus "living one's own death," the man in the white shirt with outstretched arms can be seen as accepting his sacrifice, openly showing both his rebellion and his embrace of his own death.

In a less final way, I found the energy to avoid the hidden, incestuous trap of embracing extreme Catalanism that threatened to force me into thinking one way

Figure 3.3 Francisco de Goya, *Los fusilamientos del 3 de mayo en Madrid (The Third of May 1808) (detail)* (© Madrid, Museo Nacional del Prado)

in the face of the threat of being criticized as a person against Catalan nationalism. Denying my negative countertransference reaction to the extremes of nationalism could mean that my fear would steal my own death. Accepting the sacrifice openly showed both my rebellion and my embrace of my own death and destiny and probably helped my patient to respect the vault of her dream, which was to free her inner individual energy.

Contemplation of this image suggests that sometimes identity springs from "renunciation," whereas loss of identity accompanies passive victimhood.

Case Analysis

The image of the vault in the patient's dream provided the differentiation between two areas, conveying a sense of a living vault with a capacity to hold and embrace the transformation of what it contained. The initial psychic space of being "under the vault" symbolized an undifferentiated identity. Lack of differentiation between the parties reigned. Maintaining the tension caused by the pain and wrenching emotion experienced by the patient during the months after her partner took on another lover and broke off his relationship with my patient was met by my encounter with the suffocating shadow, heartbreak, and horrible feelings of living "under the vault." My growing ability to imagine the way in which the Catalan vault could be suffocating in the same way that totalitarianism could be suffocating in a cultural complex (Goya) and an incestuous identification with the father could be suffocating in a personal complex helped make her transformation possible. The "medium height" wall that divided the single, open vaulted space created both a connection and a separation, generating a creative tension between the two spaces. We can think of this as Eros intervening, both connecting and separating. Eros creates an essential breathing space that allowed my patient and her lover to be both together and separate.

If we think of the dream as a symbolic representation of the analytic space, I would first point to the unifying color of the house. The all-white facade acquired the character of an "outer" vessel that contained the entire property, on whose walls a *graffiti protest was painted* – a beautiful metaphor of the *poetic protest* and transformation that took place inside the house. Inside the house, the analytic space was symbolized by the way in which we both experienced the vault. My patient made a point of identifying it to me as a "Catalan vault," and through my subsequent research, I saw it as a tiled vault from the Middle East. My presence in the analytic container helped affirm the inner identity of the patient and also brought the inclusion of a new element, a new cultural perspective, that allowed us both to see the horror that goes along with nationalist extremism (Goya's paintings) and the beauty that goes along with a differentiated love. The vault of my patient's dream was built as a result of holding the tension of heartbreaking pain during an almost one-year period; after this, the actual space under the vault could be divided, opening two separate areas that allowed a true coniunctio to generate creative energy.

I believe that what was most important in this dream was the emergence of a differentiated space that, at the personal level of the psyche, allowed real communication between her and her inner and outer partners. The possibility for real communication replaced her older, stormier, and more problematic style of relationships, modeled particularly by the incestuous relationship to her father and family. Her own inner process, the analytic process, and the process of her relationships with others began to reflect the wealth of her dream house and its paintings: *the whole house was very warm. . . . It was rich but not crowded, full but not suffocating.* The dream and its new dynamic of relating reflected a change in the patient's internal world, a new order that was no longer based on a lack of differentiation and dissociation as a primary defense.

The Archaeological and the Archetypal

The Catalan vault in the patient's dream had the value of holding together in an intra-psychic space personal conscious and unconscious elements that were undifferentiated, as well as conscious and unconscious elements of her family, society, and culture that grew out of a specific historical period in which a strong regression to "recuperate traditions" was promoted by the nationalist political interests in Catalonia. The patient's dissociated psyche had been confined to a suffocating, internal environment that only opened up with the appearance of the gracious, differentiated psychic space contained by the Catalan vault.

As I became acquainted with the historical origin of the tiled vault, the all-too-familiar unbearable tone of my patient's dissociation resonated within me when she said, "The space with a vault, with the *Catalan vault.*" Her unconscious was pointing at something, something that might have gone unnoticed if I had not stopped to feel and experience the image. I have come to believe that psychic incest, whether personal as in my patient's early enmeshed relationships or impersonal as with dogmatic extreme nationalism, disconnects the individual from the richness of the inner and outer world, including the history of her own and other cultures. This internal and external disconnection explained the enormous suffering and disorientation my patient had experienced since her early childhood, when she could not be alone at night because the phantasms within assaulted and harassed her.

Conclusion

In this chapter I have highlighted the connection between the undifferentiated and dissociative psychological state of an individual who was living in the shadow of a suffocating psychic incest of a family and of a nationalist ideology that did not allow the freedom to feel, to think, or to utter thoughts other than in a stereotypical language and way of thought established by the prevailing ideology. In working with this patient, my own psyche experienced a threat. The internal threat of "living under the vault" activated my own fear and regressive wish to remain within a psychological world that was predictable, safe, conventional, and measurable. If I had let myself be governed by that suffocating psychic incestuous, nationalist mentality, unwilling and unable to face my own historic and personal horror, my patient might also have been trapped endlessly and unable to live her life freely . . . and I would have remained trapped with her.

The symbolic image of the Catalan vault that emerged from a dream prompted me to explore the relationship between the psyche of a patient and my own reactions to the suffocating "isms" of intense nationalism. This same vaulted space became a healing symbol that catalyzed a transformation from a dissociative condition brought about by both personal and cultural incest – a too-close connection with both the family and the state. At the cultural level, the *psychic incest* brought on by extreme nationalism prevents the possibility of a more open and flexible connection to the history of one's own society. I believe this can be the case whether the suffocating vault, as it appears in Goya's paintings, originates in Spain, China, Germany, the United States, Venezuela, with ISIS, or anywhere else. As we have seen, the vault can be devouring, as in Goya's paintings, or it can be positively containing and even liberating, as in my patient's dream. The suffocating vault encloses an incestuous psychic space, whereas the differentiated vault supports freedom and a breathing connection to one's own cultural history.

The experience in the analysis with my patient forced me to break down my own mental barriers, my fear of being killed for thinking and speaking out, that is, for analyzing the ideology imposed by nationalism – both the present one in Catalonia and the one under which I lived in my infancy. I believe this allowed the image to arise in my mind in order to see, think, and feel my life and my death, which is the only way in which analysis makes sense. It is hard to imagine what an analysis would have been like if I had avoided the encounter of the horror we had both experienced in the face of extreme nationalism. Most likely, it would hardly have been an analysis at all. The analysis required that I recognize my own misery and confront my own fear of death. It has been essential for me as an analyst to look directly at the consequences for individuals and groups living in a country seized by the monotheistic monster of extreme nationalism. It creates a cultural complex of living in constant fear of saying the wrong thing and being branded an enemy of the state (see Figure 3.4).

The image of the vault in the patient's dream, together with the shadow of the cultural complex experienced by me in my associations with Goya's vaulted dark spaces in his paintings, which surfaced in the analysis, catalyzed the emergence of a coniunctio characterized by two separate but related psychic spaces. Under this new space of the Catalan vault, speech and thought could flow without the fear of losing our warmth and our respect for one other.

Figure 3.4 Francisco de Goya, *Because he moved his tongue in a different way*
(© Madrid, Museo Nacional del Prado)

Notes

1 Michael Fordham, "Defenses of the Self," *Journal of Analytical Psychology* 19 (1974): pp. 192–199; Donald Kalsched, *The Inner World of Trauma* (London: Routledge, 1996).
2 C. G. Jung, "Symbols of Transformation (1952)," in G. Adler and R. F. C. Hull (eds.), *The Collected Works of C. G. Jung*, Vol. 5 (London: Routledge Chapman & Hall, 1967), § 652.
3 Donald Kalsched, *Trauma and the Soul: A Psycho-Spiritual Approach to Human Development and Its Interruption* (New York: Routledge, 2013).
4 C. G. Jung, "Psychological Types (1921)," in G. Adler and R. F. C. Hull (eds. and trans.), *The Collected Works of C. G. Jung*, Vol. 6 (London: Routledge Chapman & Hall, 1971), § 781; Erich Neumann, *The Origins and History of Consciousness* (Princeton, NJ: Bolligen, 1993), p. 16; Andrew Samuels, "Incest and Omnipotence in the Internal Family," *Journal of Analytical Psychology* 25 (1980, 1): pp. 35–57; Paul Claude Racamier, *L'incest et l'incestuel* (Paris: Dunod, 2010).
5 Racamier, *L'incest et l'incestuel*.
6 My translation of León Febres-Cordero, *En torno a la tragedia y otros seminarios* (Madrid: Verbum, 2010), pp. 111–113.
7 C. G. Jung, "Mind and Earth (1927/1931)," in G. Adler and R. F. C. Hull (eds. and trans.), *The Collected Works of C. G. Jung*, Vol. 10 (London: Routledge Chapman & Hall, 1964), § 103.
8 C. G. Jung, "On the Nature of the Psyche (1947/1954)," in G. Adler and R. F. C. Hull (eds. and trans.), *The Collected Works of C. G. Jung*, Vol. 8 (London: Routledge Chapman & Hall, 1970), § 427.
9 John Hill, *At Home in the World: Sounds and Symmetries of Belonging* (New Orleans: Spring Journal Books, 2010), p. 196.
10 During the time in which Spain was governed by a dictatorial regime, and as a student at the university, I was warned by my grandmother not to say things that could put me in danger. She said "they" could "kill me." My grandmother had lived through the war and knew that people could be killed for what they thought or said.
11 Jung, CW 5, § 652.
12 Spain, during the period between 1808 and 1814, was dominated by turbulent events. Carlos IV was forced to abdicate. Napoleon wanted to install his brother Joseph Bonaparte on the Spanish throne. After Napoleonic forces repressed the Mutiny of Aranjuez, a popular protest against the political instability, a wave of proclamations of outrage and public calls for armed insurrection spread across the country. This lead to the May 2 popular protest in Madrid and the executions of protesters on May 3 and, with that, to the War of Independence.

 Goya, a court painter, never lost his job with the new governors, but he no longer had concerns because its relations with the Francophile illustrated that "His heart certainly favored the rebels, and he did his best not to go against that conviction. Obviously, this was not heroic behavior, but it is far from a slavish attitude or an interested and unconditional submission." Javier de Prada Pareja, *Goya y las pinturas negras desde la psicología de Jung* (Madrid: Editores Asociados para la Divulgación Literaria, 2008), p. 194. In Goya's work in *Los Desastres de la guerra* and in the *Black Paintings* we can see how the artist captures the conditions and horrors suffered in any war, at any time and place, in which both polarities in conflict are involved.
13 Goya en el Prado, "Comentario sobre el desastre 64," *Museo Nacional del Prado*. Accessed January 19, at https://www.museodelprado.es/goya-en-el-prado/obras/ficha/goya/carretadas-al-cementerio-1/. My translation and italics.
14 Jung, CW 5, § 1.

15 Manuel Fortea Luna, *Origen de la Bóveda Tabicada* (Zafra: Centro de Oficios de Zafra, 2008), vi, p. 7.

16 Luna, *Origen de la Bóveda Tabicada*, xi, p. 7.

17 Rafael Guastavino, *Essay on the Theory and History of Cohesive Construction Applied Specially to the Trimbel Vault* (Boston: Ticknor and Co, 1893).

18 Bassegoda Musté, "Bóvedas Tabicadas" (lecture, Curso Superior de Materiales Cerámicos Instituto Técnico de la Construcción y del Cemento Consejo Superior de Investigaciones Científicas, Madrid, November 1952).

19 Musté, "Bóvedas Tabicadas." If the vault were to fail, the architect would risk civil and criminal liability.

20 Musté, "Bóvedas Tabicadas."

21 José Manuel Matilla, *Gola: Luces y Sombras* (Barcelona: Fundación "la Caixa," 2012), p. 206.

22 Matilla, *Gola: Luces y Sombras*, p. 210.

Czech Republic

Czech
Republic

The Forefather Cultural Complex

Between Kafka and Meyrink: Why Didn't Josef K. Get to the Castle and Why Did Athanasius Pernath Enter a Room Without a Door?

Martin Skála

Introduction: The Story of My Cultural Complex

My interest in the cultural complex began in Copenhagen at the International Jungian Congress 2013, with an invitation by Jörg Rasche and – obviously – a positive stimulation of my personal father complex. After a solitary evening walk, I bumped into Jörg Rasche of Berlin in the foyer, who, in some unnamable manner, had already caught my attention. I went over to him, but I didn't know what to say. I don't know how he awoke such emotion in me – perhaps by his silent presence, his profound gaze, his modest manners, or his radiant kindness.

As people from various locales in the world arrived, Jörg showed them to one of the rooms. There it seemed as if a society of devotees to secret deliberations were meeting. Later I was invited by Jörg into that room where everyone sat in a circle. The deep caverns of my soul now seemed to reverberate with the silent echo of an ancient secret initiation. The participants began to talk about their lands of origin, and, just as knights with their swords, they laid down their *cultural complexes* in a circle.

And now I had a bee in my bonnet. What is a *cultural complex*? Why is this man involved in it? What are these feelings that have been awakened in me? These and similar questions engaged my mind, but the following evening, when I heard Jörg Rasche play the piano I felt emotion that humbly dissolved a sense that I carried of the father's wrongs.

So a positive *father complex* constellated in me as a counterweight to my own often despotic father, who had little understanding of my desire for freedom. Now, however, I'd been invited to talk about the *Czech cultural complex* to this group of devotees! A voice of authority emerged in me from the evening's discussion in that enigmatic room and gave promise of a summons to *The Castle* to write an article about the *Czech cultural complex*. But Kafka's hero, K., who was also summoned to the Castle for service, was never admitted.

So far, I'd been convinced that as a Czech I didn't have a *cultural complex*. Patriotism or national pride didn't play a major role for us (or for me?). A colleague

DOI: 10.4324/9781003609742-7

from America jovially remarked, "Yes, you Czechs only know pubs and beer." And once again it touched on my *complex*, probably *cultural*. Or *father*? Did it actually awaken a number of associations closer to my negative *father complex* – non-acceptance, estrangement, lack of understanding, mute anger, shame, helplessness – or closer to the *Czech cultural complex* – or both? Now my *father cultural complex* straddled acceptance and devaluation, depth and superficiality.

"What do you know about the depth of the Czech soul, when you yourself skate over the surface," I quietly thought to myself, as is customary in the Czech Republic.

"You Czechs don't do anything openly; you never intervene or take initiative," my colleague from Belarus, who has been living in the Czech Republic for a long time, told me. "If you're dissatisfied, you only moan amongst yourselves."

"And why be active? What could we do? No one has ever made himself heard at the Castle, no one from the village below the Castle has entered the Castle; it has a life of its own," I replied.[1]

But now the important thing is that a secret buried deep in my soul was brought back to life when I was called on by Jörg to write an article about the Czech cultural complex, which meant, among other things, taking Kafka into account. But K. didn't get to the Castle – at least on first sight. As if he lacked a mystical dimension, about which my personal favorite, Gustav Meyrink, wrote so engagingly. So why didn't Kafka's K. get to the Castle and why did the hero of Meyrink's *Golem*, Athanasius Pernath, enter a room without a door and spend the rest of his life as a hermaphrodite in *The House at the Last Lantern*?[2]

About the Castle and the Golem

Prague is certainly one of Europe's most beautiful cities, with the Vltava River, the medieval bridge, the towers and churches, and the huge Hradcany Castle like a crown above the many houses. It is also the hometown of famous literature revealing a dark shadow and mysticism behind the splendor. Kafka's *Das Schloss* (*The Castle*) and Meyrink's *The Golem* are icons of Czech culture and literature, even if written in the German language. Kafka's novel has many levels, and we will see how deeply the modern experience of estrangement and Kafka's personal individuation process are intertwined through the overcoming of his father complex and its transformation in his unique language. *The Castle* is about the land surveyor K. who, following a secret task, again and again tries to get to the "Castle," the anonymous and ever-present symbol of power that we can speculate is somehow connected to a cultural complex. Gustav Meyrink's novel about the "Golem" develops and mystifies the atmosphere of the medieval city and the haunted Ghetto of Prague. It is a breathtaking fantasy about secrets and hidden meanings; the room without a door, where the Golem is said to dwell until his return, is an inexhaustible symbol of the crypts of collective memory and nightmares. Another Czech writer, Jaroslav Hašek (1883–1923), created the famous Good Soldier Švejk who, in contrast to K. of *The Castle* and to Athanasius Pernath of *The Golem*, was able to survive the foggy old world and the war by his courage, humor, and irony. The fourth author I will refer to in my chapter is Václav Havel, the writer and first president of the former Czechoslovakia after the collapse of the Soviet system. His motto "To live in truth" became a guide for many in my country – and for me as well. Somehow, he, too, was struggling with the collective psyche of the Czech and Slovak people. But what is the Czech cultural complex?

Motherland or Fatherland

Although Czechs definitely suffer from many undesirable social characteristics associated with the country's national character, such as racism and the primitive nationalism of skinheads, chauvinism, the tendency to project its shadow onto neighbors, and so on, it cannot be said that these phenomena are focused around some sort of positive national pride, but rather around an ever-present sense of threat. In my opinion, national consciousness and patriotism aren't strong components of the *Czech cultural complex*. More often we meet a negative Czech *national* (a possible synonym for *cultural*?) complex rather than a positive one; more often than not Czechs suffer from feelings of inferiority and injustice rather than excessive grandeur. Can this be explained by the fact that we are a small nation that has rarely been entered into the annals of world history? Or is it because of the long-term domination of the nation by foreign powers? Or is it because of the rupture and abuse of national traditions by propaganda during the socialist era?

The phrase most used in 1938, when foreign powers signed the Munich Agreement handing over part of Czech territory to Nazi Germany, thus creating the Protectorate of Bohemia and Moravia, was "About us and without us." Only a few brave souls in the resistance took up arms. What, for instance, was the point of the assassination of Reinhard Heydrich, the head of security services of Nazi Germany and Reichsprotektor of the Protectorate of Bohemia and Moravia? So many innocents paid for it when the towns mistakenly linked to the assassination – Lidice and Ležáky – were destroyed? Many of the brave resistance fighters who didn't fall in the war were eliminated by the socialist elite in the trumped-up show trials of the 1950s. And, once again, we lived for decades in a foreign system that held "sway over a huge power bloc controlled by one of the two superpowers."[3] Our fathers became passive members of the Communist Party; others even cooperated with the Secret Police – often out of fear rather than conviction. Thus, the systematic liquidation of patriotic heroes continued. Only a handful of our fathers refused to take part in this socialist "game" or even actively engaged in "dissent," making personal sacrifices to keep "living in truth," which could only work in the famous *underground*. But isn't there something to this passive approach? Let's recall Tibet's position regarding its Chinese occupiers – strength expressed through introverted patience rather than extroverted demonstrations. Who are the greater heroes for the Czechs: the Mašín Brothers, who blazed a trail to the West at the cost of human life, or Jan Palach, who immolated himself in 1968 in order to voice his inability to "live a lie"? Personally, I'm more inclined to Jan Palach.

The Mythical Origins of the Czech Nation

Truth be told, I find it hard to talk about a typical Czech soil out of which a specific Czech culture can grow. Czech mythology does, indeed, date back to Forefather Czech, who led the Czech people of Slavic origin on his Moses-like journey from the ruins of the tower of Babel to a country surrounded by mountains, lying in the very heart of Europe. Forefather Czech climbed the slightly rounded Mount Říp, rising from the flat landscape of the Czech tableland, where he saw "a land of milk and honey belonging to no one," and he promised it to his people. The people named their country after their forefather – Czech.

Historically, however, the Slavs came to our territory in about the sixth century after Christ, when the country was far from virgin. Since the fourth century BCE, a Celtic tribe called the *Bój* dwelt here; they lent their name to the alternate name for the Czech Republic – *Bojohemum, Bohemia*. Germanic tribes were here before Forefather Czech and his people finally wandered in. So from the start, the Czech Republic has been more of a crossroads, and sometimes a battlefield, of European cultures, rather than "the land belonging to no one." Not even the best-known Czech characters are purely Czech: the "Father of the Nation," His Majesty King Charles IV, the Crown of the Land of Bohemia from 1347, had a Czech mother named Přemyslovna, but he was the son of John of Luxembourg, who occupied Bohemia by force in 1310; Saint John of Nepomuk, the Bohemian and Bavarian patron, was the descendant of German colonists who settled the Czech monastic estates in the thirteenth century, among them Pomuk; the *Golem* was brought to life for protection in the Prague Jewish Town by Rabbi Löw; *the Infant Jesus of Prague, Jesulus Pragensis*, is a statue originating from Spain. Even the two main protagonists of this chapter, Franz Kafka and Gustav Meyrink, cannot be considered typically Czech. Or, because they're not, they've become so.

Czechs don't put much stock in their national mythology. I remember the Czech language lessons when I was a child and having to read the overly complicated and archaic *Old Czech Legends* by Alois Jirásek without a comprehensible interpretation.[4] A few names and some vague stories emerge from my memory about the mythology of the "Golden Age" of Forefather Czech and the following "Silver Age."

The "Silver Age" began with another mythical Czech ruler, perhaps the son of Forefather Czech, Prince Krok, who, according to legend, began building Vyšehrad, the first residence in what is now the territory of Prague. The youngest of Krok's daughters was the oracle Libuše who made famous prophecies. One was that a ploughman called Přemysl and his clan would rule the country:

> Behold, beyond those mountains in Lemuz is a small river called Bělina. Near the river is a hamlet, in it the Stadic clan dwells. Not far from the hamlet a fallow one hundred and twenty paces wide and long, *a strange fallow lying among many fields yet belonging to none*. There ploughs your lord with two dappled oxen . . . Přemysl is his name.[5]

"A strange fallow lying among many fields yet belonging to none." Thus the sun hero of the Czech cultural complex was born from such a strange crack, "a strange fallow belonging to none" (in accordance with Forefather Czech). And it is Přemysl the Ploughman with two oxen yoked to his chariot, the mythical original founder and one of the few purely Czech ruling dynasties, which arose as a vision from the bottom-up as the ploughman became a prince.

The Prague Cultural Complex

Another tale from Jirásek's book details the judge Libuše's vision of the future city of Prague:

> Libuše, ecstatic, held out her hands to the blue slope across the river, and gazing at the long crest, spoke with a prophetic spirit:
> "I see a great city, its fame will touch the stars.
> "There is a place in the forest, thirty paces distant from here, the River Vltava orbits it.
> "This is enclosed at midnight by Brusnice stream in a deep ravine, on the noon side a rocky mountain next to the forest of Strahov.
> "Walking there you'll find a man in the middle of the woods cutting the threshold of a house.
> "And call the castle you build Praha (it means threshold). And as princes and dukes will bow toward Prague, so they will bow toward my city.
> "It will be honored and praised and esteemed by the world."[6]

Of course, Czech's have long been accustomed to living under the dominion of more or less benevolent foreign powers. The Habsburgs ruled us for a long time, and we gradually became part of the Austro-Hungarian monarchy. Three Habsburg emperors resided in Prague's castle. After a brief experience with our own sovereignty during the First Republic, Hitler's Reich Protectorate of Bohemia and Moravia followed, and subsequently came Soviet Union domination.

After the collapse of the Soviet system, hope in the creation of a European nation emerged. However, after all of these experiences with alien dominion, we are also skeptical of the European Union. The Euroscepticism of former President Václav Klaus is very strong, even for the people of the Czech Republic, but generally some skepticism throughout the population is not uncommon. Many people believe that "the Czech state was sold to foreign capital." Recently, we saw a drunken President Miloš Zeman teetering in front of the coronation jewels during his inauguration. Even the president of the Republic may not retain his respect.

The state of Czech politics does not inspire much confidence in the long term, but rather feelings of insignificance and injustice. To escape the shadow of *Foolish Jack* and *The Good Soldier Švejk*, we use a typically Czech self-deprecating sense of humor.[7] People comment that in the elections they "will vote for the Communists, but they don't know from which party."

In a different place, as paraphrased in a Czech fairy tale, a giant named Cimrman points out that he "stands there, where you, you and you are sitting" – they are all sitting on the giant's leg, and no one sees him. Jung saw the giant Izdubar and differentiated the "inner truth" of Izdubar's priests and the "external truth" of our science. But what if only one is true, however, and we don't see it for its size, even though we are sitting on its leg? Could Cimrman, like many other genii, have even surpassed Jung, but again remained misunderstood and unappreciated?

Another favourite Czech escape from the system's domination is the weekend passion – the country cottage. Each weekend many Czechs, especially from Prague, travel to our cottages, places of privacy and freedom that we build and fix up over our entire lives, where we live our dreams and where, if possible, we want to live out our pension. How is it that we hardly realize that here again we sit on the leg of a giant and that every other Czech builds his own "Bollingen Tower," as Jung did, and that it is completely ordinary and normal? And is it really a Bollingen Tower when there is no consciousness of a Bollingen Tower? Or is the cottage a purer fact of unconsciousness than Jung's Bollingen Tower simply for this lack of consciousness? Do the cottage, Bollingen Tower, the Castle, and the House at the Last Lantern have something in common?

My family has a cottage under the sacred Mount Blaník. According to legend there is an army of sleeping knights inside the mountain who will awaken when the Czech nation most needs them and will fight under the leadership of Saint Wenceslas.[8] And other Czech saints had something in common with this underworld. Saint John of Nepomuk didn't betray the queen's secrets, which is why he was thrown from the Charles' Bridge into the Vltava. The place is marked by a magical cross that everybody wants to touch. Then he visited the underworld and was subsequently taken into heaven. Thus he forms an invisible, third vertical arm of a cross, whose horizontal arms are the river and the bridge. These are other models of the bottom-up path.

Behind this, there is a *threshold* experience. Deep down in our hearts, we hold secrets, secrets about the predestination and the great mission of Prague and Bohemia. The cultures that have come and gone in our territory sowed magic seeds that sprouted at the right time. According to another legend, which Gustav Meyrink enjoyed, Prague was founded by an "order of Asian brethren" as the foundation of the house that man-hermaphrodite will inhabit at the end of the world.[9] The name Prague points to a *threshold* (*Prah* is "threshold" in Czech, *Praha* is "Prague" in Czech) – a *threshold* between two worlds.

We believe there is a spiritual energy concentrated in Prague, which manifests itself on the thresholds of two historical epochs. Once in a while

as quick as a flash there was a kind of spiritual epidemic lightning, empowering human souls for a specific (hidden) purpose . . . and its effects gave rise to . . . the outlines of a characteristic being (Golem), which perhaps lived here centuries ago and thirsts after shape and form. . . . And the Unknown, which walks here, must be an image of fantasy or thought . . . (which) now returns at regular periods – during the same astrological constellation of the stars as when it was created – driven by a desire for materialization.[10]

Did this idea enter into the realm of action in 1989 during the Velvet Revolution in the figure of Václav Havel, who came from the underground to become the Czech president? Havel wrote the following:

> The singular, explosive, incalculable political power of "living within the truth" resides in the fact that living openly within the truth has an ally, invisible to be sure, but omnipresent: this hidden sphere. It is from this sphere that life lived openly in the truth grows; it is to this sphere that it speaks, and in it that it finds understanding. This is where the potential for communication exists. But this place is hidden and therefore, from the perspective of power, very dangerous. The complex ferment that takes place within it goes on in semidarkness, and by the time it finally surfaces into the light of day as an assortment of shocking surprises to the system, it is usually too late to cover them up in the usual fashion. Thus they create a situation in which the regime is confounded, invariably causing panic and driving it to react in inappropriate ways.[11]

So says Václav Havel, who is, of course, the most current Czech hero, who on his way up from the bottom, came from the "velvet underground" via the "Velvet Revolution" to Prague Castle. Havel completed his journey to the Castle. It's as if Václav Havel, like the president of the First Republic – "father" Masaryk – entered the *crack between histories*, between two epochs. Tomáš G. Masaryk stepped out of the *crack* between the Austro-Hungarian empire and the Reich Protectorate, between the two World Wars; and Václav Havel stepped out of the *crack* between socialism and the market economy, during the collapse of the "Iron Curtain" separating East and West. Masaryk and Havel "saw the only starting point for a more dignified national destiny in man; for them the starting point for the metamorphosis of the nation's position was the transformation of man."[12] "Slavs focus on the person," noted the famous Czech Cardinal Špidlík, and not on the system, I add.[13]

In the cases of Masaryk and Havel, ploughmen ploughing like Přemysl on the *"strange fallow, lying* [between] . . . *fields yet belonging to none,"* we are again reminded of that threshold experience. Were these individuals Meyrink's "unknown, which walks here" the "image of fantasy or thought . . . [which] is driven by a desire for materialization to return here at regular intervals of time"? Is it here, in magical Prague, that the "internal" and "external truth" intertwine and thus create an *imaginary* world linking the internal and external worlds?[14] Is it here that the "hidden sphere with complex movements taking place in the shadows to the light of a life in truth" leaks out, as recorded by Václav Havel? Does Jung's "spirit of the depth" speak in the *crack between histories, between two "spirits of the age"*?[15] Even Jung's experience and the time in which he lived were thresholds. Is this crack between histories a collective image of the hole that arises in the human soul after a trauma? Speaking unbearable veracity and waking uncertainty, do these openings lead to re-traumatization?

Czech history is full of traumas and disappointments. A deep trauma resulted from the brutal suppression of the "Prague Spring" in 1968 by Soviet and even east-German troops. The last occurred during the Velvet Revolution, the "revolution of students and artists" in which we believed that "truth and love [would] prevail over lies and hatred" and that this slogan would even dominate the politics and administration of the Czech lands and "people [would] return to governing their matters."[16] Nevertheless, such a faith buckled under the "invisible hand of the market," which soon ruled here and whose actions must now be revealed by Swiss courts.[17] And in the Czech Republic there is once again a feeling of threat and mistrust in both state institutions and the world, in the form of Euroskeptic restraint, fear of the validity of the Beneš decrees, or rejection of U.S. radar, and so on.[18] Now we are living in another system that devalues and humiliates Havel's threshold experience and labels ex-president Václav Klaus's supporters as naïve dreamers (or "Luna Lovegoods," referring to a character of this name in the Harry Potter books). Our contemporary President Zeman denigrates "the hidden sphere" as *Prague Café*."

The Greengrocer-Dissident Complex

In 1978, Václav Havel wrote a treatise with a title symptomatic of the Czech cultural complex: *The Power of the Powerless*.[19] In this philosophical reflection, he analyzes the specifics of socialist power: "An ideology, which in its complexity and closeness assumes the nature of a kind of secularized religion" in which reason and conscience are delegated to the "hands of the superiors," and the "center of power" is identical with the "center of truth." This ideology promises

> in the epoch of a crisis in metaphysical and existential certainties, in the epoch of human uprooting, alienation and loss of meaning in the world . . . a special hypnotic attraction is offered to mankind by an easily accessible "home."

This "home" can be understood by what Jung called the "spirit of the age." For us in the Czech Republic, however, the "spirit of the age," or "home," is a priori perceived of as a foreign and unfriendly one. Certainly, at least in my *cultural complex*, it does not create an image of a welcome home; it is more likely seen as a necessary evil. This enforced system presents itself as a "home" from which it is impossible to escape. One cannot imagine it possible to grow freely, to stand on one's own two feet, or to find and build one's *own* home. The impossibility of holding such a vision of freedom, autonomy, and a positive home or homeland is rooted in the specifically Czech constellation of the father *and* cultural complex. The combination of these two negative complexes strengthens the wish to escape from the system, from the "spirit of the age," toward individual meaning.

The "spirit of the age" creates what Havel termed the "panorama of everyday life." He ruminates over the example of the greengrocer who puts up the slogan: "Workers of the world unite!" in his shop window:

> Slogans are also found in other shop windows, on lampposts, bulletin boards, in apartment windows, and on buildings; they are everywhere, in fact. They

form part of the panorama of everyday life. . . . This panorama, of course, has a subliminal meaning as well: it reminds people where they are living and what is expected of them. It tells them what everyone else is doing, and indicates to them what they must do as well, if they don't want to be excluded, to fall into isolation, alienate themselves from society, break the rules of the game, and risk the loss of their peace and tranquility and security.[20]

Living the truth is thus woven directly into the texture of living a lie. It is the repressed alternative. . . . Under the orderly surface of the life of lies, therefore, the hidden sphere of life in its real aims slumbers, of its hidden openness to truth.[21]

When Havel's greengrocer's "living within truth" becomes dissatisfied with "merely" ignoring "living a lie," and he begins, in a certain manner, to articulate creatively, this is the place where something begins to be born, something that might be termed the "independent spiritual, social, and political life of society." In this way then, Havel's greengrocer may become a "dissident," creating the "second culture" that we often associated with the *underground*. Great leaders, the nation's elite, could therefore not go through the system's machinery and naturally did not rise; rather they fell down to the underground. Here, "in obscurity," a belief could be found, a belief in freedom, life within truth, honesty, friendship, and so on. This "semidarkness," this "hidden sphere" described by Havel is like *"the strange fallow belonging to none"* from the Forefather Czech and Přemysl the Ploughman stories.

These "pre-political processes," this "second culture" is, of course, often concocted in pubs. Thus, when someone wants to penetrate below the surface of the Czech love of beer and pubs, they must realize that here the pub is also the place for initiation into the secret and hidden laws of the underground. It was the same already for the Good Soldier Švejk. Next door to the grammar school I attended during the socialist period was a pub called the *Haus* ("house" in German). Here, as it happens, was where the local underground scene met. At the time these people showed me a far more cordial, interesting, wiser, and happier world than the one taught in the building next door – in grammar school. It was a secret no one was supposed to have learned about.

Of course, when this kind of "hidden life" in Bohemia entered "into the light" following the "Velvet Revolution," it immediately doubted itself and was unsure, soon bowing down to the lies of another "spirit of the age," in this case, market economics. Is it because the "external" and "inner truth" may amalgamate for just a moment, only during a turning point, in the *crack* between histories and the strange fallow, *belonging to none*? Otherwise might not the "spirit of the depth" live separately from the "spirit of the age," in the underground and in hiding, so that during the next turning point, just like the Golem, it might come out "into the light"? To ride as the mythic Blaník Knights from the mountain's depths at the moment when the nation most needs them? Isn't this the *threshold* experience, like the magical seed that again and again drops into the furrow, to again and again bring another crop? After all, Havel's "pre-political sphere" remains, albeit in a changed form – a

"pre-political sphere" even after "real political shifts" leading to a change in relationships and the "spirit of the age" have been born from it.

The Kafka Complex

When I was invited to participate in the discussion of the cultural complex in
Copenhagen, I found myself feeling like the personality created by Franz Kafka.
I wandered, like the surveyor Josef K. in Kafka's *The Castle*, from one culture to
another, with none accepting my Czech soul. In this sense, Franz Kafka's alienation and futility may make him a representative of the *Czech* or *Prague cultural
complex*. Just like Bohemia, Kafka's soul was also a crossroads and battleground
between the various cultures. We can say that even Kafka suffered the typically
Czech constellation of the father and mother complex. Kafka is rooted in our souls,
even though he speaks to readers from all over the world. *Kafkaesque* means a
special type of strange and uncertain world we all know.

Kafka is also inspiring as a person. In Prague, one encounters many
"Kafkas" – dark, sickly, young intellectuals, solitarily burrowing into the shad-
owed, twisting lanes of old Prague and its soul, strange bugs engrossed in themselves, alienated from and misunderstood by the world, hopeless sleuths of
existential questions. Today, with democracy, it is true that there are fewer of them
than under socialism. Just as there are fewer dark alleys, flaking walls, and cheap
cafes in old Prague.

Václav Havel speaks of the adaptive function of the system, in which some
circles may try to integrate values of people from the "parallel world" into the
official structures, to appropriate them, to become a little like them while trying
to make them a little like themselves, and thus to adjust an obvious and unten-
able imbalance.[22] Similarly *The Castle* and its offices accepted the services of surveyor K., although it didn't have a place for him and found him a hostile element.
May I reveal another secret? Kafka's work shouldn't be interpreted. It is the same
with him as with ancient, illuminated manuscripts, which, in Jung's words, one
should not explain. Instead the reader must find his or her own path within them.[23]
So even today the "Kafkas" hide, even as the "system" has absorbed Kafka, making him toothless in issuing a prospectus and information booklet about him, thus
destroying an individual path toward him. Even this *threshold*, this *strange fallow*,
belonging to none, this "spirit of the depths" has been defined and entered into the
coordinates of the "spirit of the age." This awakens in our hearts a nostalgia similar
to the one we feel for Prague's lost "shadow lands," dissolved in the light of the
lamps and advertisements.

Even before Kafka becomes Kafkaesque and lights up like a banner in neon,
permanently becoming a part of the "system," I'd like to convey a certain sense
for the supernatural, which I see as characteristic not only of Kafka but also of my
Czech or Prague soul. In addition to Kafka, I mean magical Prague; the alchemists
of Rudolf II; Master Kelly, a renowned alchemist from England; Gustav Meyrink; *underground* pubs; and so on. Writing this, I once again feel that familiar

uncertainty and fear of a lack of understanding and judgment. But the "promise from the Castle," which I felt in the "castle" foyer of the Copenhagen conference hall, when I was invited "behind the counter" into the room (which the surveyor Josef K. never had the pleasure of!), this invitation for a discussion on the cultural complex was so encouraging and kind, I couldn't reject it. But even Josef K. was encouraged by the Castle. This hope, however, was always relativized or led to nothing. How shall I get to the *castle* of the *cultural complex* if I can't define exactly my own *cultural complex* and its practical impact? In my confusion I feel like the surveyor K. below the Castle. He had no job, as everything was already well-defined, like in psychoanalytical theory today: "The boundary markings of our little farms are all established, everything has been duly recorded. Property hardly ever changes hands, and we settle any little arguments about the boundaries ourselves."[24] But, because the aforementioned "*crack* in history" has appeared before me, it has a purpose in the Czech soul. So where is the *strange fallow* in which surveyor Josef K. could plough when all the holdings below the Castle are defined? What is the way forward? The path to the Castle? Why didn't Josef K. ever get there? Is the path more important than the destination?

Franz Kafka (1883–1924) is ranked among the Czech authors writing in German from the turn of the twentieth century. Other representatives of this group include, for instance, Alfred Kubín and Gustav Meyrink. Sonu Shamdasáni states that Jung read Alfred Kubín and Gustav Meyrink before his Nekyia. Jung even stressed that Gustav Meyrink's *The White Dominican* directly corresponds with some of his personal experiences and that the "Vermilion Book" of *The White Dominican* inspired Jung to write his own *Red Book*.[25] Unfortunately, I don't know if Jung also read Kafka's work. I would be interested to know what he would say about him. In any case, all these authors ploughed the "*strange fallow. . .* belonging to none." Like Jung, he captures the oppressive, ossified, and outdated atmosphere of the pre-war "spirit of the age" and turns to his inner world of fantasy. Kubín leaves for "The Other Side;" Josef K. roams beneath the Castle.

Perhaps it is only Meyrink's Athanasius Pernath who finds a way into a room without a door and becomes a hermaphrodite living in the House at the Last Lantern. His fantasy world is laid out according to mystical and hermetic laws. Thus, it can be said that Meyrink is the key to Kafka and Kubín. But is this really so? As already mentioned, Jung separated the *internal* and *external* truth. Didn't Kafka speak about an internal and invisible giant? Didn't Meyrink make him visible, externalize him, and name the terms of a mystical system? But let's not get ahead of ourselves.

Kafka's *Castle* is often seen as a parody of the ossified Austro-Hungarian bureaucratic apparatus, which was the Kafkaesque "spirit of Kafka's age." Nonetheless, the bureaucracy of Kafka's *Castle* transcends the metaphor of the monarchy's bureaucracy. Bureaucracy can then represent any "system" and Zeitgeist – "spirit of the age" – in which we live. This is doubly true for the Czech cultural complex as the "spirit of the age" was not an abstract concept for the Czech citizen, as it was for Jung. Remember that in Bohemia various foreign cultures have settled like pigeons in a dovecote. Josef K. makes a distinction: "we have to distinguish between two things here: first . . . can be taken as official; and second, my own person."[26] For a person under the influence of the *cultural complex between Kafka and Meyrink*, individuation doesn't happen in direct contact with the world and the "spirit of the age," but in contact with the world in *hiding*. Contact with the outside world and its "living a lie" is only a cover, enabling the hidden "life within truth," whether in the pub, in the resistance, in the underground, or on the weekend at the cottage, to be attained.

Forgotten Religion

One important thread in the Czech cultural complex is or was the existence of Jewish culture. Kafka came from a Jewish family, but his religious education ended with the Bar Mitzvah when he was age thirteen. Even though Franz Kafka and his father only went to the synagogue four times a year, Franz's father reproached his son's lax approach to Judaism. According to Franz Kafka, however, his father was equally as indifferent and formal in his approach to faith.

In *Letter to His Father*, he writes this:

> You really had brought some traces of Judaism with you from the ghetto-like village community; it was not much and it dwindled a little more in the city and during your military service; but still, the impressions and memories of your youth did just about suffice for some sort of Jewish life, especially since you did not need much help of that kind, but came of robust stock and could personally scarcely be shaken by religious scruples unless they were strongly mixed with social scruples. . . . You did, in fact, believe in yourself. Even in this there was still Judaism enough, but it was too little to be handed on to the child; it all dribbled away while you were passing it on.[27]

"It was much the same with a large section of this transitional generation of Jews, which had migrated from the still comparatively devout countryside to the cities," Kafka adds. At the age of fifteen he claimed to be an atheist and several times even visited the Club of Young Czech Anarchists.

Only at age twenty-eight, around the year 1911, after having visited the Yiddish theatre, did he begin to study Jewish issues, language, and literature written in Yiddish. At the end of his life, he wanted to live with his friend Hugo Bergman in Tel Aviv, in what was then Palestine. Bergman, however, refused Kafka's request for fear of Kafka's tuberculosis. Is it possible to see in this desire for an unrequited promised land the surveyor Josef K.'s desire to get to the Castle?

The Father Complex of Franz Kafka

Even in the case of Franz Kafka, when analyzing the *cultural complex*, we are drawn to consider the *father complex*. Kafka certainly suffered from a strong negative *father complex*. According to many critics, all the feelings of alienation, intangible guilt, and inconclusiveness originating in the negative father complex were reflected in his work.

Kafka's father, Hermann Kafka (1852–1931), was a relatively successful Jewish haberdashery wholesaler. He was described as a big man and a go-getting, over-bearing trader. Franz Kafka characterizes his complicated relationship with his father in the famous *Letter to His Father*, dated 1919. On the one hand, he perceives him as "a true Kafka":

> You, by contrast, a true Kafka in strength, health, appetite, loudness of voice, eloquence, self-satisfaction, worldly superiority, stamina, presence of mind, understanding of human nature, a certain generosity, of course with all the faults and weaknesses that go with these advantages, in which you are driven by your natural disposition and sometimes your hot temper.[28]

On the other hand, although his father "doesn't reproach him for anything directly improper or bad," Franz attributes "uncomprehending, grumbling, threatening, ironic, despotic and tyrannical" attributes to him. Franz Kafka, in contrast with his father, sees himself as a "sickly man, anxious, hesitant, nervous." He sees his father as "too strong" for him. Franz Kafka has a feeling that his father "simply stamps on the ground and there will be not even a memory of Franz . . . maybe something worse." Because of his father's influence, a feeling of guilt and of "being nothing, which often dominates him (a feeling that, in another respect, is also noble and fruitful)" remains in Franz. He feels that he means nothing to his father, but his father was a great authority for him.[29]

Kafka describes his experience with his father as follows:

> Hence there were for me three worlds, one where I lived, a slave under laws that had been invented solely for me and, moreover, with which I could never fully comply (I did not know why), then another world, infinitely distant from mine, in which you dwelt, busy with ruling, issuing orders and being angry when they were not obeyed, and finally a third realm where everybody else lived happily, free from orders and obligation. I was forever in disgrace.[30]

This feeling, which can be observed in a number of Kafka's works, is also an experience characteristic of the Czech cultural complex, which is deeply sensitized to suffering under dictatorial domination and harbors envy toward those other neighbors who are seen as happy, free, and rich.

Kafka's Nekyia

An important period in Kafka's life was 1912 when Kafka turned twenty-nine. Was it then that his individuation process associated with *Nekyia* – descent to the underworld – began? As mentioned, this was the year that Franz Kafka encountered Jewish culture through the Yiddish theatre and also met the greatest love of his life,

Felice Bauer. At the end of the year, he also seriously considered suicide. He began to write his seminal story *The Metamorphosis*, which was first published in 1915 in Leipzig. Critics consider this novella to be one of the major fictional works of the twentieth century. *The Metamorphosis* is about a traveling salesman who, overnight, turns into a "monstrous vermin," "an enormous vermin," a "beetle."[31] Does this feeling of being a "strange beetle" correspond to Kafka's cultural complex? Does Kafka feel this in his relationships with his partners or work? And why does he change into a "beetle"? For readers familiar with Jung's *Red Book*, this image may invoke a memory of the picture of the Underworld in which Jung saw the corpse of a man, a beetle, and a red sun.[32] In this Jungian vision, however, the beetle was identified as a *Scarab* symbolizing the *sun*. In one Gustav Meyrink story, an old professor spends his whole life seeking a *Scarab* under sheep dung. His students laugh at him and purposefully scatter sheep dung in front of him to get the old professor to pick it up. They are all the more surprised when the old professor really does find a *Scarab* under a piece of their dung. Why isn't Kafka's "beetle" interpreted as a *Scarab*? Is it because of a ruptured cultural tradition? Or because of Kafka's feeling of inferiority? Or does the reader have to find this interpretation alone? Or are Jung's and Meyrink's interpretations too benign, romantic, and grand?

Franz K.'s Journey to the Celestial Castle

In the autumn of 1917, Kafka began to suffer from tuberculosis. A few years later, in 1922, he began writing his last great novel, *The Castle*. At the same time, he stopped work at the insurance company because of his illness, and two years later, on June 3, 1924, he died. His friend Max Brod published the unfinished manuscript posthumously. The hero of the story, K. wants, for unknown reasons, to gain access to the mysterious authority located in the Castle that somehow controls the village below. Kafka's intention for the ending of the book was that the authority at the Castle would tell K. on his death bed that his "legal claim to live in the village was not valid, yet, taking certain auxiliary circumstances into account, he was permitted to live and work there."[33] K. will be redeemed by mercy.

For K. the Castle is the only destination and the path to it is a mystical pilgrimage. The dying clerk Kafka sees *The Castle* as an illuminated office where, behind the partitions, there are other partitions and other partitions and other partitions . . . in silence, the officials behind the partition are working continuously, those at the top give silent commands to servants below, and they willingly carry them out and sometimes they'll call a messenger to take a report to the village below – back down on earth.

As already mentioned, many see in *The Castle* a metaphor for a bureaucratic system in which the person as an individual is lost. In the days of socialism, Kafka's work reminded us of the depersonalized bureaucratic state apparatus of the Communist Party, often unfairly persecuting citizens' free speech. Today, however, we might think of the market economy as embodying the spirit of *The Castle*. This system constantly imposes a feeling that there's something one needs and something one wants to buy. And don't humans mostly desire what we can't attain, rather than what we can?

This plays more to the views espoused by, for example, Thomas Mann, who sees in Kafka's work a metaphysical path seeking nature and God. So perhaps *The Castle* is an image of the Kingdom of Heaven? In *The Red Book*, Jung includes a mandala depicting a castle with a temple in the middle.[34] He likened it to the archetype of the Self. Is it true that K. didn't get to the Castle?

The Meyrink Complex

Unlike Kafka, Gustav Meyrink is clearly and explicitly mystical. In his novels, the external plot intertwines with dreams, with mystical symbolism, and with their interpretation. Maybe that's why Meyrink fascinated Jung, but to Kafka and Max Brod, Meyrink seemed too ornamental. Here, too, we can ascertain the tendency of the Czech cultural complex to implicitness, mystery, and hermetism, or, in Havel's words, to the truth hidden in the sphere of semidarkness.[35] Kafka is far more that *strange fallow*, which "lies among fields . . . belonging to none." Meyrink's field is far clearer, albeit mystically measured and staked out.

Gustav Meyrink (1868–1932) is even less of a Czech author than Franz Kafka. His years in Prague left a profound impression on him; however, and, like Kafka, he was able to distill the Prague spirit – or Prague awoke a similar *cultural complex* in him. For financial trickeries Meyrink was sentenced in 1902 in Prague. His time in prison partly inspired him to write the novel *The Golem*, which was published in 1915.

Because of the financial affair, Meyrink moved from Prague to a house in Starnberg, Germany, and gave it the same name as the house of the hermaphrodite in *The Golem – The House at the Last Lantern*. In his novel, Athanasius Pernath, in a mad quest to rescue Angelina, takes underground passages to a room without a door and a barred window, where he sees his folly – tarot arcana, *the fool* – wrapped in the Golem's cloak.

The Golem as well as the Blaník Knights symbolize spiritual power that, in times of crises, should help us (Prague's Jews in terms of the Golem or the Czech in terms of the Blaník Knights). For this, Rabbi Löw made the Golem out of clay at the end of the sixteenth century, and in Meyrink's case, the Golem is seen as a spiritual creation that emerges on the "threshold of histories" at times of social and historic changes. In both of these occurrences, we can again see the opening of vertical dimension in which transpersonal energy flows on the "strange fallow belonging to none," which is typical for the Czech cultural complex. The Golem is known in Prague and is encountered by everyone.

Havel to the Castle!

On December 17, 2013, on the second anniversary of Václav Havel's death, the Polish sociologist Slawomir Sierakowski wrote "Václav Havel's Fairy-tale" for the *New York Times*:[36]

> Many years later, this wonderful land would become the subject of yet another fairy tale. After defeating the dark forces of Communism, a humble sage, Vaclav Havel, found himself its leader, ensconced in Hradcany Castle, in 1990.

Havel, in his treatise *The Power of the Powerless*, compares socialist identity to the identity of Western democracy. "This is much more than a simple conflict between two identities. It is something far worse: it is a challenge to the very notion of identity itself."[37] Havel, on the basis of the historic meeting of a dictatorship with the consumer society, asked provocative questions, even in 1978:

> Is it not true that the far-reaching adaptability to living a lie and the effortless spread of social auto-totality have some connection with the general unwillingness of consumption-oriented people to sacrifice some material certainties for the sake of their own spiritual and moral integrity? With their willingness to surrender higher values when faced with the trivializing temptations of modern civilization? With their vulnerability to the attractions of mass indifference? And in the end, is not the grayness and the emptiness of life in the post-totalitarian system only an inflated caricature of modern life in general? And do we not in fact stand (although in the external measures of civilization, we are far behind) as a kind of warning to the West, revealing to its own latent tendencies?[38]

After experiencing nearly twenty-five years of democracy in the Czech Republic, I ask whether today we can talk about democracy at all. Of course, we have free elections and a far greater measure of freedom in all senses. But does it concern the real world in which we live? Haven't our lives inconspicuously brought us to the "virtual world" of our civilization, which, existing under the domination of the "market economy," ever distances actual reality and our environment, and, with its promises of "*castles* in the air," controls the covetousness of politicians and every single person? So as with socialism, we can see the market economy as the reigning "spirit of the age." If socialism bets on censorship and shortage, the market economy bets on excess and overload. Both systems then remove the person from "life in the truth": What is the difference, when the socialist greengrocer must hang the slogan: "Workers of the world unite" in his window, and the market-economy greengrocer has in his window the logo of the multinational corporation: "You need me unconditionally, buy me!" Both slogans are lies. The difference is that what was called socialism was a lie leading to restriction and shortage, whereas today, in a market economy, we live in a lie leading to unlimited hedonism. But hedonism has reached unbearable levels, and in the economic, environmental, social, and political crises, it threatens to destroy almost the entire planet. Hedonism now requires constraints. And so, for instance, Václav Klaus, the second president of the Czech Republic and an orthodox defender of the market economy, speaks of the threat of a "green dictatorship" that wants to limit the market in favor of the environment. The economies of many countries have had to limit their budgets due to the economic crisis, which leads to growing unrest. In the framework of the "War on Terror," the restriction and control of people is taking on unprecedented dimensions. The European Union's standards also limit a number of locally acceptable specificities. Is one epoch transforming into another? Have we again passed the zenith of the "spirit of the age"? Due to the various crises we now face, when will a new idea arise, one that will seek to find realization so the Golem will once again appear in the streets of Prague?

Conclusions

To conclude, let's return to the question, what is typical of the *Czech cultural complex*? It is a sort of mistrust of the surrounding world, of one's own doctrines and institutions, as well as of the external world or reality overall. It is the double life we lead – the external one for appearances, the internal candid one. It is our *strange fallow*, on which we plough and which belongs to none. Shame, a lack of confidence, and perhaps some sort of a self-indulgence, which keeps us focused on our internal, private world and retards us in external assertion, are characteristic. But sometimes the external pressure becomes intense enough to open the *crack* between histories and the Golem steps out. Another characteristic of our cultural complex is the third, vertical dimension of the cross of John of Nepomuk – the direction from the top down, to the *underground*, where figures fall in dark times, and the direction *bottom-up*, where they can once again ascend, if that aforementioned crack between histories opens. If someone wants to understand the Czech soul, he or she must look to what isn't visible, rather than to what is. Politics are created in the pub, wisdom is handed over by jokes, individuation takes place at the weekend house.

Personally, I have to admit that *my* cultural complex (still blending and interweaving with my father complex) can spring into action, accompanied by a feeling of helpless anger and shame, when someone bounces off the surface of "my culture" far too quickly and overlooks a certain depth below it. Likewise I admit that this deliberation about the cultural complex has enriched me in the sense of a probe into Czech history and culture, a reminder of long-forgotten stories and myths, as well as in formulating my feelings, which involves an emphasis not on separating the "internal" and "external" truth, as Jung does when meeting with Izdubar, but on their junction, at "life in the truth," which is only possible if we plough the *fallow* belonging to none and if the *crack* between histories opens. Then we live in a dream and imagination unfolds in front of us.

Of course I'm not at all sure how the Czech cultural complex, or the Prague cultural complex, or the cultural complex between Kafka and Meyrink, or my personal cultural complex relate to the notion of the cultural complex in general. I still have difficulties in finding the sense and practicality of an otherwise intellectually inspiring elaboration of the cultural complex. I am open to it. The adventure began in the foyer of the International Jungian Congress "Castle," when I was shown the way to the secret room (albeit with a door) and invited to meet people initiating themselves into the idea of the cultural complex. And perhaps it is in this meeting in a room with doors that I have begun to discover *my* cultural complex.

Notes

1 See Franz Kafka, *The Castle* (New York: Alfred A. Knopf, 1968).
2 Gustav Meyrink, *Golem* (New York: Dover Publications, 1985).
3 Václav Havel, *The Power of the Powerless* (New York: Routledge, 2009), p. 11. Also see Václav Havel, "The Power of the Powerless," *vaclavhavel.cz*. Accessed December 29, 2014, at http://www.vaclavhavel.cz/showtrans.php?cat=eseje&val=2_aj_eseje.html&typ=HTML.
4 Alois Jirásek, *Staré pověsti české* (Praha: Státní nakladatelství dětské knihy, 1951).
5 Jirásek, *Staré pověsti české*, p. 32.
6 Jirásek, *Staré pověsti české*, p. 32. "The noon side" is a literal translation, meaning south, or the side where the sun is at noon.
7 These characters were depicted as naive, stupid, or very simple, but persistant and stubborn, leading to forcing their way or not being punished. Švejk especially is considered either very intelligent and playing stupid or just plain stupid.
8 St. Wenceslas (907–935) was the first historically documented Czech prince from the Přemyslid family.
9 G. Meyrink, *The Golem* (Prague: Argo, 1993), p. 138.
10 Meyrink, *The Golem*, pp. 35–37.
11 Havel, *The Power of the Powerless*, p. 22.
12 Havel, *The Power of the Powerless*, p. 36.
13 Audio interview with Cardinal T. Špidlík, *Czech National Radio*. Accessed December 30, 2014, at http://www.radio.cz/cz/rubrika/krajane/o-jeho-budouci-draze-rozhodl-pry-pohlavek-rika-kardinal-tomas-spidlik.
14 Henry Corbin, "Mundus Imaginalis," Originally published in *Cahiers internationaux de symbolisme* 6 (1964): pp. 3–26.
15 C. G. Jung, *The Red Book: Liber Novus*, ed. Sonu Shamdasani, trans. Sonu Shamdasani, Mark Kyburz, and John Peck (New York: W. W. Norton & Co., 2009).
16 Václav Havel said this during the Velvet Revolution, and it stuck with people; they wrote it on walls, shouted it at police, and so on.
17 "Such a faith," from M. Kubišová, from "Prayer for Marta," sung during the Velvet Revolution. "Invisible hand of the market" is one of Vaclav Klaus' favorite slogans.
    Land, factories, and so on, that were forcefully acquired by the state in the era of communism, were given to rightful owners when democracy was established. Unclaimed real estate was sold at auction, sometimes with dubious prices or under other illicit circumstances. Some of these cases, regarding mostly mines and steel mills, were brought to the courts, going to higher and higher institutions until they finally reached the EU courts in Switzerland.
18 The Benešov decrees gave up a part of Czechoslovak land to Germany in negotiations with Hitler (land on the borders, where many people were of German descent and spoke German). The decrees were considered unlawful, and the land was given back to Czechoslovakia after WWII. To this day, there are discussions and political talks about the rightful ownership of this land.
    The Czech people were mostly opposed to building a NATO radar station in the Czech Republic, fearing the republic would again be of interest to Russia, fearing Russian transgressions, not wanting to give up newly acquired sovereignty from one superpower (Russia) to another (United States) – the main impetus behind building the radar station.
19 Havel, *The Power of the Powerless*.
20 Havel, *The Power of the Powerless*, p. 18.
21 Havel, *The Power of the Powerless*, p. 22.
22 Havel, *The Power of the Powerless*, p. 51.

23 Sonu Shamdasani, *C. G. Jung, A Biography in Books* (New York: W. W. Norton & Co., 2012).
24 Kafka, *The Castle*, p. 55.
25 Shamdasani, *Jung: A Biography in Books*. Also see Sonu Shamdasani, *Jung: Život v knihách* (Praha: Portál, 2013), p. 142.
26 Kafka, *The Castle*, p. 61.
27 Franz Kafka, *Letter to His Father* (London: Oneworld Classics Limited, 2008), p. 59.
28 Kafka, *Letter to His Father*, p. 20.
29 Kafka, *Letter to His Father*, p. 26.
30 Kafka, *Letter to His Father*, p. 29.
31 Franz Kafka, *The Metamorphosis* (New York: Bantam Books, 1972).
32 Jung, *The Red Book*, manuscript Cap. V.
33 Kafka, *The Castle*, p. vi, Publisher's note.
34 An analogy to Corbin's, *Mundus Imaginalis*; Jung, *Red Book*, manuscript, p. 163.
35 Havel, *The Power of the Powerless*, p. 22.
36 Slawomir Sierakowski, "Václav Havel's Fairy-tale," *New York Times*, December 17, 2013. Accessed December 16, 2014, at http://www.nytimes.com/2013/12/18/opinion/sierakowski-vaclav-havels-fairy-tale.html?_r=0.
37 Havel, *The Power of the Powerless*, p. 20.
38 Havel, *The Power of the Powerless*, p. 20.

Serbia

Belgrade: Limes and the City

Hermeneutics of Belgrade's Soul

Marijana Popović and Jelena Sladojević Matić

A *borderland* is usually defined as a "district near a border" or "an area of overlap between two things."[1] This term could easily be used as a second name or nickname for our native hometown Belgrade, Serbia's capital and largest city. Belgrade's geographical and historical position predestined its borderline or liminal fate and determined its soul; it is a city full of contradictions, difficulties, positive and negative surprises, and peculiar ways of being and surviving. To know Belgrade in all its complexity, to come close to the richly textured, historically multilayered aspects of its soul, would require a long life spent in detailed observation and investigation. The focus of our interest is limited to what is *liminal* in Belgrade's soul and identity and how this liminality has been created through history.

As a term of discourse, *liminality* comes to analytical psychology by way of anthropology, especially by way of van Gennep's and Turner's research on *rites de passage*.[2] It appeared first in Arnold van Gennep's famous work *Rites of Passage*, where he described rites of primitive initiation ceremonies.[3] He observed that most initiatory rites of passage go through three stages: 1) *separation*, 2) *liminality* or transition, and 3) *incorporation* or aggregation. These rites provide and prescribe how a person is separated from one status in society (*separation*), placed in an intermediate state of liminality "betwixt and between," and finally returned, after initiation, into the social structure in a newly achieved role status (*incorporation*).[4] *Liminality* is the quality of ambiguity or disorientation that occurs in the middle stage of rituals, when participants no longer hold their pre-ritual status but have not yet begun the transition to the status they will hold when the ritual is complete. During a ritual's *liminal* stage, participants "stand at the threshold" between their previous way of structuring their identity, time, or community, and a new way, which the ritual establishes.[5]

During liminal periods of all kinds, according to anthropologist Victor Turner, social hierarchies may be reversed or temporarily dissolved; the continuity of tradition may become uncertain; and future outcomes once taken for granted may be thrown into doubt. The dissolution of order during liminality creates a malleable situation that is imaged as a "place that is not a place and a time that is not a time."[6]

DOI: 10.4324/9781003609742-8

Being in liminality is like being in a tunnel between the entrance and the exit, says Turner.[7] In such a liminal situation

> the initiands live outside their normal environment and are brought to question their self and the existing social order through a series of rituals that often involve acts of pain: the initiands come to feel nameless, spatio-temporally dislocated and socially unstructured. In those states of mind the initiand progresses from the normal space-time world across a threshold (*limen*) into a realm of experience normally repressed and unapproachable to everyday consciousness. The neophyte then returns to normalcy and temporality with the experience obtained through access to this [atemporal realm].[8]

It is not hard to infer that liminal experiences are those that host powerful archetypal energies. Turner also suggested "a liminal state may become 'fixed,' referring to a situation in which the suspended character of social life takes on a more permanent character."[9] A liminal state then is not so much constituted by defined boundaries of time and space as it is pure being on the boundary itself.

But let us speak of the liminality of Belgrade and how this affects its soul. Belgrade (which, translated into English, means "the White City") boasts a tumultuous history that is several millennia long. The first human settlements on Belgrade soil developed nearly 7000 years ago, which makes the city among the oldest in Europe. The oldest Belgrade we know of, a settlement that did not yet bear this name and to us remains nameless, began with one of the largest prehistoric cultures of Europe – the *Vinca culture*, a Neolithic archeological culture that prospered in the sixth millennium BCE in Southeastern Europe. The area was held by Thraco-Dacian tribes afterward and then Celts who gave it the name *Singidun* in 279 BCE. The first part of the word *singi* means "round" and the second part, *dun(um)*, means "enclosure, fortress," or "town." Another possibility is that it is a composite name, the first part of which (*Sin-gi*) means "old prayer" (*seangui* in Gaelic), implying this was originally a site of Celtic religious significance, in addition to becoming a fortress (*dun*). The Romans conquered Singidun during the reign of Octavian Augustus somewhere between 29 BCE and 6 CE, and it was under their rule for a full four centuries. Singidun was then Romanized to *Singidunum*. The Romans fortified the city, making it one of the largest and most important strongholds on the *limes* (border) whose role was to protect the civilized Roman world from barbarian intrusions. The *Roman limes* was utilized by Latin writers to denote a marked or fortified imperial frontier. This is probably the oldest known historical fact about the city that hints at its future borderland or liminal character. Singidunum soon became one of the most important Roman crossroads to the provinces of Moesia, Dacia, Pannonia, and Dalmatia.

A *crossroad* is a *locus* where roads and paths converge and diverge, where routes multiply and intersect. Belgrade or *White City-on-limes* is an urban metaphor for *coincidentia oppositorum* (Heraclitus' "the unity of opposites"). Since Roman times Singidunum/Belgrade has symbolized and represented a place of unification and integration (which is indicated in its Celtic name – *singi* [round] and *dunum* [enclosure, fortress, or town], both of which represent well-known symbols of the Self). Being at the border that limits one area in relation to another and being a crossroad where roads separate, however, Belgrade also symbolizes departures and a parting of the ways. It can be seen as standing for separation, splitting, abandonment, fragmentation, disintegration, or disunity. Belgrade personifies our psychological junctions, meeting points, crossroads, as well as boundaries and confines. *White City-on-limes* indicates our psychological borders and frontiers and marks the place where, in our soul, the alien and the foreign touch the familiar and common. Finally, our city is the traveler who wanders from here to yonder, between the known and unknown.

In the centuries to come, the liminal character of the city would be confirmed on many occasions. For example, after the division of the Roman Empire into western and eastern halves in 395 CE, Singidunum once again became a border town, now a threshold *within* Christianity (that is, between two Christian empires, or Eastern and Western Christendom). This new position of the town determined its later fate, for it became not only a linking point of various cultural influences but also a demarcation line and constant battleground in wars to come between various civilizations, religions, nations, or ideologies. The disintegration of the Roman Empire was followed by the invasion of barbarian tribes: Eastern Goths, Sarmatians, Avars, Slavs, and others. Because of its forward position at the border – *limes* – Belgrade suffered frequent attacks and destruction. The attacks that came from the north, across Pannonia, the Danube, and Sava, were so fierce that even Singidunum, an important military stronghold, could not resist them. Attila – "The Scourge of God," as he was called – besieged Singidunum and completely destroyed it in 441 CE. Singidunum lost all of its Roman inhabitants then. After the fall of the Huns, the town became a part of the Byzantine Empire in 454 CE, but soon it was conquered by the Sarmatians and changed hands several times, although mostly staying in the Byzantine Empire. At the end of the sixth century, however, while the Byzantines were occupied with wars in Africa and Asia, the Avars and Slavs conquered the town after two sieges. Once again, the city was exposed to a complete change of identity. The name *Singidunum* disappeared after the barbarian invasion and destruction of the town, never to appear in the town's history again. Around 630, the Serbian (the south-Slav tribe) settlers came to this area. After the arrival of the Serbs, there are no records about the town for more than two and half centuries. The Avars and Slavs no longer cared about the town as it had lost its status as a border stronghold. It was then within the wider region of the Balkan Peninsula, which had been conquered already by the Slavs.

The town was not mentioned again until the ninth century, under the Slavic name *Beograd* (White City), not only because the city walls were made of white limestone but also due to the famous Košava northern wind. For the Slavonic tribes, Belgrade was in the northernmost reaches of the populated world and therefore constituted a boundary of what was known. Subsequent to the first mention of Belgrade as a Slavic town, various armies and conquerors controlled it over time.

The Franks were the first to reach Belgrade and destroy the Avars under the command of Charles the Great (788–792). Bulgarians replaced the Franks' rule in 827, and they, in turn, gave way to the Hungarians in 896. By the end of the tenth century, Belgrade had already changed rulers a countless number of times. By 1018, it once again became a border stronghold for the Byzantine Empire. During the eleventh and twelfth centuries, the rival forces of Hungary, the Byzantine Empire, and Bulgaria fought for it.

During that period, the town was also a transit point for numerous Crusades heading to the east, which left their own destructive mark by slaughtering its habitants and demolishing the city itself. After the Crusades of 1096 and 1147, Belgrade was again in ruins. Serbian rule over Belgrade began in the thirteenth century – a period of intensive settling by the Serbian population as well as increasing influence of the Serbian Orthodox Church. Serbian King Dragutin's court was in Belgrade. Yet Serbian rule didn't last long. At the beginning of the fourteenth century, in 1319, the Hungarians captured and totally destroyed Belgrade. The demolished and abandoned town then became a border foothold of Hungarian resistance to the expansion of the Serbian state from the south. It was in that condition that Belgrade entered the fifteenth century, when the Ottoman Turks, a new conquering force, appeared on the historical stage of Europe.

With a strong desire to be as prepared as possible to resist the Turkish invasion and needing a powerful stronghold on the Sava and Danube, the Hungarians were forced to hand over Belgrade to the Serbian Despot Stefan Lazarevic, who ruled Belgrade from 1403 to 1427. His rule was a time of great prosperity, and the town became the most important economic, cultural, and religious center in this part of the Europe. Despot Stefan Lazarevic said the following about Belgrade: "I have found the most beautiful site since ancient times, the most spacious town of Belgrade which was by chance destroyed and neglected. I built it and dedicated it to the blessed Our Lady."[10]

The despot's successor to the throne, however, was forced to surrender the town to the Hungarians. During the hundred years of Hungarian rule from the fifteenth to the sixteenth centuries, the entire population changed as did the very shape of the town. The town abruptly stagnated, and the expelled Serbian population, forced into the outlying districts, was not allowed access to the town itself.

The Turks of the Ottoman Empire's rising military knew that Belgrade was the greatest obstacle in their campaign toward Central Europe. By 1440, the Belgrade fortress was under siege by the Turkish army with its over 100,000 soldiers, led by Sultan Murat II. Remarkably, Belgrade and its Serbian and Hungarian citizens resisted Turkish attacks for almost a century. Finally, under the command of Sultan Suleiman the Magnificent, the Turks managed to conquer Belgrade on August 28, 1521. Belgrade had been the very rampart of Christianity and a key defense for the whole of Hungary. The town was demolished and burned down. The way to Western Europe for the Turks was open. "The bastion of Christianity," as Europe called Belgrade in those days, had been defeated. The whole of its Serbian population went into slavery, most of whom were sold in the marketplaces of Istanbul. The Ottoman Empire reigned for nearly five centuries.

By moving the border north of Belgrade, the city's strategic position changed. For the next hundred years, Belgrade was a relatively peaceful town, with a more significant commercial and communication function. Crafts and trade prospered in the newly reconstructed town, which took on an oriental look. It was the meeting point and the crossroads of merchants and craftsmen from Dubrovnik, Venice, Greece, and Austria. The Turks, Armenians, Jews, Gypsies, and Serbs all helped to develop well-known trade routes connecting the East with Europe via Belgrade.

The Turks proved to quite inventive when it came to giving nicknames to Belgrade. Belgrade was referred to as *Sultan's Girl, Stone Foundation, House of Wars for Faith, Heavenly Settlement*, and *Portal of Wars*. Kalemegdan, the famous Belgrade fortress with an exceptionally magnificent view overlooking the confluence of the Sava River into the Danube, was called *šaćir-bajir*, or the "Hill for Contemplation." Keeping in mind the town's turbulent history, perhaps the most fitting nickname would have been the "Hill for Contemplation above the Portal of Wars." Quite a liminal image! Just imagine yourself in the midst of contemplation while a war is waging below you or trying to fight while meditating. Imagining doing both simultaneously is hard, yet aren't we doing this from time to time in analysis when confronted with such contradictory states of mind?

After some years of relatively peaceful development, the town again became a place of war. "An eye for an eye" way of negotiating between conflicting military powers once again took a heavy toll on Belgrade. After the Turkish defeat at the walls of Vienna in September 1688, the Austrians conquered Belgrade, completely destroying its oriental look. Two years later, the Turks regained control (1690), but these conflicts left Belgrade destroyed once again and its population killed, persecuted, and robbed because of their cooperation with the Austrians. After these events, Belgrade resumed its role as a Turkish border town, and it remained so until 1717, when it was again conquered by the Austrians. Their brief rule over Belgrade (1717–1739) was marked by the town's real transformation, for it lost its Turkish and Middle Eastern outlines and gained the characteristics of a European baroque city. When recaptured by the Turks in 1739, it was exposed to heavy destruction. Again, Belgrade became a Turkish *Casbah* with Middle Eastern characteristics and a border position. Many documents written by contemporaries witness that during those days, whenever somebody passed through Belgrade, it was in somebody else's hands: Serbian, Hungarian, Austrian, Turkish, and in between those times, it seemed to belong to no one. And yet Belgrade was always another city, with different houses, churches, people, and customs. Even the name of the city was subject to frequent change: *Alba Gracea, Griechisch Weissenburg, Nandor Alba, Nandor Fejervar, Castelbianco, Alba Bulgarica, Belgraduk* – so many names, so many identities depending on the conqueror.

The identity of our city over the centuries and even now resembles alchemical Mercury; like him it is shifty, erratic, unstable, capricious, fickle, protean, moody, and ever changing. Travelers would visit on one occasion and find hundreds of churches; upon returning all the churches were gone and replaced by mosques. At the end, they would say there were no longer any churches or mosques or people.

To live in Belgrade in the past – as well as now – is to think constantly about the people who are ruining and demolishing it. As a result, both in the past and in the present, Belgrade is always "a new city," "a city in the making, becoming." It never stays the same. Every generation from the distant past until now knows a different city. Belgrade is a place of constant battle between demolishing and replacing, between destroying and flourishing. Alas, amid all of these destructions and demolitions we have never had enough time for proper psychological reparation. As a consequence, traumatic events engraved on Belgrade's soul and not worked through have led to future retraumatizations over the course of its history and have created a cultural complex of Belgrade's liminality unique to it throughout Europe.

The awakening of national consciousness around the slaughter of a major part of Belgrade's population during Turkish rule led to the First (1804) and Second (1815) Serbian Insurrections against the Turks. After several years of fighting with the town in ruins, Belgrade was finally liberated. The Turks left Belgrade for good in 1867 after being there for nearly five centuries. And in 1882, Serbia became a kingdom and Belgrade its capital. The Turks' departure was the stimulus for faster economic and cultural development of the town. In the second half of the nineteenth century, the city was brought closer to Western Europe and the intensive development of Belgrade continued during the first years of the twentieth century. As so many times before, however, the peaceful period did not last for long.

As Belgrade has always been a border city caught between opposing forces, it again found itself in the path of foreign power interests. The continuing Austrian expansionistic policy against the Balkans doomed Belgrade to further destruction. Indeed, World War I started with the Austrian ultimatum to Serbia on July 23, 1914, and the Austrian attack (July 30, 1914) on Serbia. Belgrade's agony lasted four years this time.

The years between the two World Wars were quite prosperous. Belgrade, built from the ashes of a ruined city, became the new shape of a European city. Alas not for too long! In the spring of 1941, during the early part of World War II, Belgrade became the target of terrible bombing and destruction. After all the persecutions and sufferings caused by the German occupying forces, the citizens of Belgrade also had to endure considerable losses from the Allies' bombing, especially in the spring and autumn of 1944 (see Figure 5.1). Many buildings were demolished, including hospitals, churches, and residential homes, as well as all the bridges on the Sava and Danube. During World War II, the population of Belgrade dropped ten times over between 1941 and 1945.[11]

So as not to forget its fate of perpetually recurrent destruction, let us recall that Belgrade was again bombed nearly day and night for 78 days by NATO forces in 1999. Eighteen nations in Western Europe and the United States, under the cloak of NATO in an action named "Merciful Angel," unleashed on Belgrade and other towns in Serbia explosive forces greater than were dropped on Hiroshima at the end of World War II.[12] (More than 40 tons of explosives were dropped on the whole of Serbia and more than 40,000 kilos of explosives containing depleted uranium.) Life became hard in Belgrade; there were no air links with the outer world and no

Figure 5.1 Bombardment of Belgrade by Nazi forces in April 1941. (This work is in the public domain in the United States and other countries.)

electricity or tap water. Foreign diplomats had long since departed, and Belgraders, revolted by the bombing, demolished the cultural centers of countries taking part in the air strikes. These ruined sites, side by side with those reduced to rubble by NATO aircraft, gaped with their open wounds. Another bloody page in Belgrade's history was written. Another traumatic experience was carved upon its soul.

After this brief history of one of the oldest and most battered cities in the world, it is not easy to write about its soul. One needs imaginal vision and a subtle, delicate eye to *see* Belgrade on the level of the soul since these cruel historical facts are neither very soulful nor nourishing. The great Serbian poetess Desanka Maksimović described it in these words:

Belgrade, city of Illyric and Celts, dear Balkan and Slavic city, generous citizen of the world, live on and resist every power. You opened your door wide to everyone, but your heart remains unseen, your Soul undiscovered, ancient lock with seven seals in the shade of towers, linden trees and plane trees.[13]

In a city called the "Portal of Wars" by the Turks and "the Bastion of Christianity" by the Christians, how did the soul manage to survive? The specific location of the city itself and its important strategic location – at the border and at the confluence of the Sava and Danube rivers where the Panonian Plain meets the Balkans – have led to the city being fought over in more than 115 wars and razed to the ground more than 44 times! This rich and painful history as well as its geo-strategic position have placed Belgrade at the crossroads of the East and the West, of Europe and the Middle East. The confluence of the Sava and Danube rivers defined the geographic limit between the "civilized" and "barbarian" worlds and led to the creation of psychic liminality as well. The Celts, Romans, Avars, Huns, Byzantines, Goths, Bulgars, Ugrians, Crusaders, Turks, Austrians, Germans, and Russians all passed through this "Portal of Wars," leaving behind traces of their power, their rage, and their cultures. All the civilizations that marched through the *White City-on-limes* were confronted with its unique transitional or liminal phe-nomenology and responded by exhibiting various primitive mental states over the city and its population. For example, during Turkish rule, the Serbian population was considered to be *not* human; they were "nobody" in the sense that one could kill, harm, or rob them without being held responsible; also during World War II, the German soldiers had a rule that for each German killed 100 Serbs should be killed, and for each German wounded 50 Serbs should be killed.

In the myths and traditions of various cultures, as well as in life, the *limes*, the *threshold*, or the *border* represents the spot where action of the utmost importance takes place. The border symbolizes separating, parting, or bifurcation, yet, at the same time, it is a space for union, a meeting place, a spot where formerly broken alliances are once again forged. It is the fate of Belgrade to exist at the crossroads or limes as well. We understand the limes not as a connection between two defi-nite points on the earth's surface but as *a particular world*. The limes is a place or container that can or has to hold all sorts of powerful events. Place is a matter of containment; therefore, to be in a place is to be enclosed within a containing boundary, to be held there. This is why being at the limes is a matter of holding, embracing, enclosing, or encapsulating – and also why images of Belgrade, such as the crossroad, the junction, the confluence of two rivers, and its bridges, capture what is most crucial in the notion of limes. Martin Heidegger gives us a positive definition of boundary or liminality: "A boundary is not that at which something stops but, as the Greeks recognized, the boundary is that from which something *begins its presenting*."[14] In fact, a place is that for which somebody makes room; a place allows a dwelling within its boundaries. Things for which we make a place are, at the same time, things that are bound together – embraced by the very place they occupy.

Belgrade-as-liminality is a place where phenomena come into being. Essen-tially, the limes/border/crossroad is an archetypal image of exceptional importance, a *locus* where conscious and unconscious, ego and psyche, I and Thou, spirit and matter, body and soul, health and illness, personal and archetypal, touch each other and unfold each other.

Keeping in mind that each city embodies distinctive psychological qualities, the question we are addressing is how being on the borders for centuries, living on limes, affects the soul of the city and its citizens and how that is experienced in the bright lights and dark shadows of its everyday life and its recurring historical patterns. The history of Belgrade is all about attacks, sieges, destruction, liberation, construction, abandonment, forgetting, and renewal. And it always seems to hover on the scales between two opposites – surviving and being demolished. In Belgrade, there has never been a generation who has escaped the experience of war!

It is not hard to understand then how extraordinarily traumatized the soul of Belgrade is! The most visible (and invisible) signs of this ever-present trauma are in the dissociation and denial of vast parts of its history. Belgrade has an extremely short memory and easily forgets its enemies, its painful life, and the centuries of destruction. Belgrade has learned how to live and survive in the "present moment," easily losing sight of the past and the future. An ever-present "compulsion to repeat" is inseparable from its being. Somehow Belgrade is inextricably drawn into situations that replicate the endless cycles of demolishing and reconstructing. The presence of denial of and dissociation from these experiences prevents the soul of the city from achieving a healthier position in processing inner and outer challenges. We dare to say that because these specific traumatic experiences have happened regularly throughout Belgrade's history, it has never been possible to integrate them into conscious functioning, and, therefore, they are left in the unconscious shadow, which lives on its own and is nourished by itself. This shadow provokes the shadow of the perpetrators, and the vicious circle is closed. Belgrade's history is all about shadow – its own shadow and the shadow of its conquerors. Repeated trauma, repressed memory, endless destruction and reconstruction: all of these factors contribute to the unconscious cultural complex that sits at the heart and liminal edge of Belgrade.

On the one hand, this traumatic experience triggers a sense of vulnerability and fragility both on the individual and on the collective level; on the other hand, the positive aspects of the shadow refer to the possibility of "enduring" and "surviving" trauma. For example, during the NATO bombing in 1999, people sat in the city's squares, in its restaurants and cafes; life continued more or less normally in completely abnormal conditions. Certainly on the individual and on the collective level, strong defense mechanisms were in place, primarily splitting and negation, but somewhere between them, the survival instinct was activated, which exists in the collective experience of Belgrade.

Tolerating uncertainty is ingrained in the soul of Belgrade. It carries much less fear and apprehension and much more acceptance of things as they are. Today there are thousands of refugees from Syria, Afghanistan, and Libya passing through Belgrade. While our neighbors' shadows have been triggered and they defend themselves by building walls and wire fences, Belgrade and its citizens can feel empathy and simply accept and integrate this experience. We are not overwhelmed by the horror and panic like those in other cities. Only through lived experience can one develop true empathy, which Belgrade has, and that is the positive aspect of its shadow, and it is why foreigners who pass through Belgrade feel accepted and safe and often come back again.

Across from the city's most elite hotel, the Hyatt Regency, is a cardboard settlement where the gypsy population lives. They work in the basement clubs of some buildings, for it is in the night that Belgrade opens the door to the shadow that temporarily "releases" its guests and residents from the responsibility of the persona. Parallel with that, there is a feeling of security and safety, so that in the midst of all this commotion, one can walk freely on the streets of Belgrade, even after midnight, and most likely, nothing bad will happen. We experience this shadow side of the soul of the city more as a "safe space" for living differently rather than as a place for self-destruction. There is still a lot of suffering, of course, but our accumulated collective traumatic experience has developed our capacity to understand and recognize suffering and to live with a clearer awareness of uncertainty.

When one steps onto the streets of Belgrade, with just a quick glance, it is obvious that Belgrade is a city of shadows. Shadows are everywhere! Higgledy-piggledy streets full of garbage; houses with no style, or perhaps better to say, many styles mixed together without any unifying vision; evidence of destruction everywhere combined with Levantine neglect. Everything appears shabby, with a completely undeveloped sense of aesthetics, perhaps because there was never time to develop a coherent or beautiful look as survival was always the first order of business. Belgrade is only partly aware of being identified with its shadow. And nowadays tourists from abroad are coming in great numbers just to enjoy this shadow – to see the bombed and ruined houses, to enjoy the wild nightlife and get drunk in the bars and restaurants, which are open until the early morning hours even on workdays. It seems that the shadow is so present and lived out in the open that it has become part of the city's persona.

When Le Corbusier said that Belgrade was the ugliest city in the most beautiful location, he was witnessing the results of centuries of destruction that has marked the city with its shadow.[15] Those who love and know the city today understand it not from what they have actually seen since its finest parts have long since disappeared without leaving a trace and cannot be touched or photographed. But that which is gone, that which can never be reconstructed, belongs to its history and identity. Perhaps what people love is how these vanished times somehow remain in the ineffable soul of the city. Through much of history, Le Corbusier's ugliest city in the most beautiful location was often the most beautiful city in the most awful location. To paraphrase a *New York Times* article from 1876: "Had the Turkish march on Europe not come up against Serbia and Belgrade (which was razed to the ground), Germany and France, Vienna, Munich and Marseille would assuredly look like Belgrade."[16]

In that same year of 1876, the famous French writer Victor Hugo, who was quite knowledgeable about Belgrade and Serbian history, penned his essay "For Serbia," in which he wrote: "A nation is being killed. Where? In Europe. Are there many witnesses to this act? Only one – the whole world. Do the European governments see it? No."[17] Unbelievable how true his words still are today!

The history, geography, and psyche of the city's past and current inhabitants unite to create Belgrade's special identity, which in its positive and its shadow qualities can be thought of as a *liminal identity*. Liminal identity is a kind of oxymoron – but it points to something profound, abysmally deep and unfathomable, while, at the same time, being shallow, hollow, and highly erratic. Belgrade's liminal identity is dual in nature. If we internalize the benevolent side of the "White City's Soul," then it would be "she" who encourages us to befriend different complexes and archetypes. Or, shall we say, it is her amiable and benevolent nature that promotes our individuation or psychological wholeness. On the other hand, Belgrade as a meeting point, junction, or crossroad is not only the place where *coincidentia oppositorum* can happen but also the place where separation, division, disunion, or severance can begin. In its negative aspect Belgrade personifies psychological separation, fragmentation, and splitting.

How it feels to live on the boundary that is Belgrade is best expressed by the words of the great Dušan Radović, Serbian novelist, poet, and aphorist, who embodies the city's liminal identity: "Whoever was lucky enough to wake up in Belgrade this morning, should ask nothing more from life. Wishing for more than that would be immodest."[18]

Settling and being in the liminal space that is Belgrade means so many things and raises so many questions: Does the town have one coherent, accepted history or does every generation write the history anew regardless of what has happened before? Is this history a glorious one to be proud of or should it be forgotten as soon as possible? And when exactly did this history begin? Which dates are important and which are not?

Nearly every Belgrade street has between three to five formal names, and officials argue endlessly over which one is best! Belgrade is always in transition and never knows when this transition started and where it will lead. Although history is everywhere, Belgraders are frequently ashamed of it because it includes so many experiences of loss and destruction. At the same time, they are ignorant of their own disorientation, which is caused by the lost connection with their historical identity. This loss of connection to the past leads to vague and uncertain aims and goals for the future – a prominent part of Belgrade's liminality. For Belgrade, the forgotten past is still the present and the future. One often feels as if time stopped long ago and that now Belgraders participate in a time without time or outside of time. On the other hand, it may be that Belgrade's very survival has depended on its being stuck in the liminal. Otherwise it might have been buried and forgotten long ago! For millennia, Singidunum/Belgrade/White City has been "betwixt and between"; its threshold geography suits its edgy psychology. Belgrade is still stuck in its in-between liminal identity. Is it located in the East or in the West? Does it belong to the Middle East or to Europe? Is it predominantly Orthodox Christian or atheist despite the endless clashes between the Muslim, Catholic, and Orthodox religions?

Belgrade has never managed to hold together all the opposite and conflicting sides of its history, to transcend the polarity between construction and destruction. During its whole history, it has been desperately sought after, under siege, battled for, defended, hated, loved, despised, destroyed, and abandoned only to be rebuilt and renewed. Belgrade is a city in constant self-renewal, forever under construction and reconstruction and deconstruction, changing constantly but seeming to never change at all.

Belgrade reminds us of the Jungian archetype of the *Puer*. Its eternal youth, spirit of cheerfulness, spontaneity, and the fact that it does not fit into any set formulas or models of what a city should be is part of the city's allure and character. The Belgrade mentality with its charm of being carefree even in the most difficult situations has been well-known for centuries. This surely must derive partly from perpetually living with what we might term "liminal insecurity and instability." It is a city whose worries seem to be constantly drained by its two rivers, leaving it paradoxically carefree. Is it surprising that in a country and a city beset with problems that are among the gravest in Europe, the two most frequently spoken words are "*Nema problema*" ("No problem")? Japanese tourists have concluded that "no problem" is a local greeting!

Being at a major physical crossroads, Belgrade has seduced many to cross great waters, transgress all kinds of boundaries, and move through multiple time zones in order to conquer the fortress on the "Hill for Contemplation above the Portal of Wars." But whoever wants to conquer the fortress must first conquer its soul. And this is precisely what has never been destroyed in Belgrade despite the scars of its tempestuous historical fate. The ever-present beauty of Belgrade lies precisely in its untamable liminal nature. This quality is beautifully expressed in the words of Belgrade's well-known journalist Bogdan Tirnanić, in his aphoristic book *Belgrade for Beginners*: "Belgrade is destiny. And yet, there are those who believe that it is merely a choice. People like that [play] dice with destiny."[19] Belgrade's true essence will always manifest itself in a light and friendly aspect and in a dark and frightening one. Whenever we overestimate one side or deny the other, we are not acknowledging its dual and liminal nature. So, as a famous Belgrade graffiti puts it, "If you are lost in Belgrade, do not despair. You are in Belgrade."

Notes

1 According to the Thesaurus Dictionary.
2 *Liminality* comes from the Latin word *limen* meaning "a threshold," also "beginning," "border," "frontier," and "entrance." Latin *liminalis* is derived from *limen* (threshold) + *-alis*, (adj. ending). The Latin noun *limes* had a number of different meanings: a path or balk delimiting fields, a boundary line or marker, any road or path, any channel, such as a stream channel, or any distinction or difference. Arnold van Gennep, *Rites of Passage* (Chicago, IL: University of Chicago Press, 1960); Victor Turner, *The Ritual Process: Structure and Anti-Structure* (Chicago, IL: Aldine, 1969). Quoted in Robert L. Moore, "Ritual, Sacred Space and Healing: The Psychoanalyst as Ritual Elder," in Nathan Schwartz-Salant and Murray Stein (eds.), *Liminality and Transitional Phenomena* (Asheville, NC: Chiron Publications, 1991), p. 15.
3 van Gennep, *Rites of Passage*, p. 15.
4 James A. Hall, "The Watcher at the Gates of Dawn: The Transformation of Self in Liminality and by the Transcendent Function," in Nathan Schwartz-Salant and Murray Stein (eds.), *Liminality and Transitional Phenomena* (Asheville, NC: Chiron Publications, 1991), p. 34.
5 Hall, "The Watcher at the Gates of Dawn," p. 35.
6 Victor Turner, *Dramas, Fields and Metaphors: Symbolic Action in Human Society* (Ithaca, NY: Cornell University Press, 1974), p. 239, quoted in Hall, "The Watcher at the Gates of Dawn," p. 35.

8

7 Turner, *Dramas, Fields and Metaphors*.
8 Turner, *Dramas, Fields and Metaphors*.
9 Turner, *Dramas, Fields and Metaphors*.
10 Milorad Pavic, *A Short History of Belgrade* (Belgrade: Dereta, 2011), p. 22.
11 It is impossible to give precise numbers because there is no agreement about how many people were killed. The various sources have different data. For example, Belgrade was bombed 11 times in 1944 by "friendly" Anglo-American allies and more than 4,000 people were killed; Nazi Germany bombed Belgrade four times in April 1941 (and many times during the war) and that was at the beginning of the Second World War and the invasion of Serbia as well. According to German data, around 4,000 people were killed. One of the greatest losses was the total destruction of the National Library, which contained pre-medieval and medieval manuscripts of innumerable value and importance.
12 Pavic, *A Short History of Belgrade*, p. 71. For additional information, see Coordinamento Nazionale per la Jugoslavia-onlus (www.cnj.it), Siete nella sezione dedicata alla aggression della NATO contro la RF di Jugoslavia 1999, especially the papers of Mrs. Mirjana Andjelkovic-Lukic. She has a PhD in the field of technology applied to explosives and is a research assistant at the Institute of Military Technology for research and processing explosives.
13 Desanka Maksimović, "Poem of Belgrade (Fragment) (1969)," in Slobodan Šorgić (ed.), *I Love Belgrade* (Belgrade: Valera, 2007), p. 39.
14 M. Heidegger, *Poetry, Language, Thought* (New York: Harper & Row, 1975), p. 154.
15 Le Corbusier (1876), quoted in Pavic, *A Short History of Belgrade*, p. 60.
16 Pavic, *A Short History of Belgrade*, p. 60.
17 Victor Hugo, "For Serbia," speech given on August 29, 1876, in Paris. In Pavic, *A Short History of Belgrade*, p. 60.
18 Dušan Radović, aphorism given on the daily radio program "Good Morning, Belgrade!" in the 1970s and early 80s on Belgrade Radio Station "Studio B".
19 Bogdan Tirnanić, "Belgrade for Beginners," in Šorgić (ed.), *I love Belgrade*, p. 21; *Beograd za pocetnike (Belgrade for Beginners)* (Beograd: Dereta, 2012).

Part II

The Feminine and Cultural Complexes in Europe

Denmark

Denmark

Mother Denmark

Pia Skogemann

Denmark is often at the top of world rankings of happiness. In the *World Happiness Report 2013*, Denmark was once again named the world's happiest country.[1] Why? According to a new report, the eight most important factors to happiness are trust, feelings of safety, prosperity, freedom, work, democracy, cohesion in civil society, and a good balance between working and family life.[2]

Many Danes react with suspiciousness rather than pride, however, when confronted with the country's high happiness ratings: given the suicide rate and high prescription numbers for Prozac, they believe the ratings must arise from a misunderstanding of "happiness." Another reaction is an ironic attitude: Danes are just superficially satisfied with themselves; they don't expect much of themselves and don't care much about others.

Perhaps such reactions are based on a cultural complex: modesty is extremely important, whereas boastfulness, even merely calling attention to oneself, can result in raised eyebrows among one's social group. After a novel from 1933, *En flygtning krydser sit spor*, by Aksel Sandemose, this modesty complex is also called the "Jante Law."[3] The novel depicts the provincial town Jante. All the repression and pettiness that dominates society is summarized in the Jante Law, modeled on Moses' Ten Commandments. The central commandment is "You shall not think that you are something (or more or better than us)." The frequent use of the term *Jante Law* in Denmark suggests that it is an integral part of the Danish ironic self-image. It is often cited as an expression of collective pressure that restricts the individual. On the other hand, those not as successful as they believe they deserve may also blame the Jante Law, turning it upside down.

The modesty complex may also have origins in Luke: "For whosoever exalteth himself shall be abased; and he that humbleth himself shall be exalted" (14:11). To take an anthropological approach to the Jante Law, however, would be to look to its origins in a general (historic) Nordic caution when it comes to highlighting one's own happiness or praising the happiness of others. Its roots can be traced to the ancient Nordic notion that happiness is protected through certain precautions: through modest behavior, the envy of others may be averted, along with this notion: "pride goes . . . before a fall" (Proverbs 16:18). Clearly, all this focus on modesty aims at establishing a narcissistic balance between inferiority and grandiosity.

DOI: 10.4324/9781003609742-10

Perhaps this modesty is typical for small countries in general, although the focus of this chapter is on Denmark in particular.

The Little Mermaid

When the statue *The Little Mermaid* (Figure 6.1) was sent to Shanghai for the world exposition in 2010 (Expo 2010 Shanghai, China), many protested against the statue leaving Denmark at all as it was a national symbol like the Statue of Liberty.

Figure 6.1 *The Little Mermaid*, by Edvard Eriksen (Photographer: Rasmus Flindt Pedersen)

Others felt the sculpture was more a "symbol of our worst inferiority complex," and that "it is a mystery how this trifle of a sculpture can become a national issue."[4]

The Little Mermaid was not meant to be a national symbol at all; it was a tribute to ballerina Ellen Price (1878–1968), who danced the title role in the ballet *The Little Mermaid* in 1909. Edvard Eriksen (1876–1959) created the sculpture, which was displayed in Copenhagen harbor in 1913. The sculpture led a quiet life for many years, until 1935 when the Tourist Association discovered *The Little Mermaid* was more popular among foreigners than the National Museum. The tourists came to see the sculpture because they knew of Hans Christian Andersen's tale. The Tourist Association was surprised to realize the importance of Andersen for Denmark. After Danny Kaye played the role of Hans Christian Andersen in a 1952 Hollywood musical of the same name, the *Mermaid*'s fame virtually exploded. The musical is not a biographical film of Andersen's real life: "The Moss Hart-Myles Connolly screenplay largely disregards the facts concerning Denmark's great storyteller, opting for a fanciful blend of comedy, fantasy, romance and music."[5] Much of the story is told through song and ballet and includes many of Andersen's most famous tales such as *The Ugly Duckling, Thumbelina, The Emperor's New Clothes,* and *The Little Mermaid.* The phrase "Wonderful Copenhagen" comes from a song in the film.

From then on, *The Little Mermaid* became an icon of Danish tourism, branding Denmark as a fairytale country. Like a star in a reality TV show, the *Mermaid* became famous for being so terrific. Not all Danes could or would recognize Danish values in the tourist tale of *The Little Mermaid.* The sculpture was first vandalized in 1964, when her head was cut off to protest the national self-understanding of Denmark as a fairytale country, which the *Mermaid* had come to represent. An artist later took responsibility for the "beheading." The statue was vandalized on other occasions in 1984 and 1998. The sculpture has also been used for political demonstrations. She has been dressed in a burka; she has been painted pink; she even had a dildo placed in her hand. The latest vandalism occurred in 2003 when she was pushed off her stone pedestal.

Do these stories somehow qualify *The Little Mermaid* to be thought of as constellating a cultural complex? If so, it would be by means of a kind of projective identification since the imagery around the sculpture comes from outside the country. Or, taking the vandalism into account, does she perhaps connect to a wider process taking place in Denmark from the sixties? I will return to that question later in this chapter.

The drama of *The Little Mermaid* statue is, in any case, only about eighty years old compared to the story of another feminine figure whose roots go back for at least a thousand years.

Thyra Danebod

If cultures have complexes like people, we must also think of a culture as a kind of personality, where some complexes are more stable than others and not always traumatic or negative. Viewed from a certain perspective, Denmark as a nation has had an unusually stable history. The Viking king, Gorm the Old, who died in 958, is considered the first Danish king. The current ruling Danish royal family is still of his dynasty and is the only royal house in Europe that has maintained continuity for more than a thousand years. Gorm was buried in the town Jelling in Jutland under a big rune stone, raised by his son and successor, King Harald, in memory of his parents, Gorm and Thyra. Another smaller stone beside it was, according to the inscription, raised by King Gorm himself over his wife, Queen Thyra.

Little is known of her as a historical person, but already by 1200 BCE, when Saxo Grammaticus wrote the history of the Danes, *Gesta Danorum*, she had acquired mythical traits. Saxo tells that Thyra demanded all of Denmark as her morning present at her wedding, meaning that even then (in Saxo's time) she personified Denmark. Another historian, Svend Aggesen, wrote about Thyra at the same time. Although the two stories are not identical, both historians agreed on the essential narrative – that she was beautiful and smart and that she wrought the construction of a protective wall around the kingdom's former southern border, *Danevirke*, as a defense against the German King Otto because her husband had become old and tired. (The archaeologists, however, inform us that Danevirke, in reality, was built long before Thyra's time; the earliest walls date from around 500 BCE.) Furthermore, Saxo and Aggesen agree that her courageous determination and wise leadership gave the queen her epithet: *Danebod*, meaning "the ornament of Denmark."

Saxo's *Gesta Danorum* is composed of sixteen "books" written in learned Latin.[6] The first nine books deal with ancient legendary material; Saxo clearly wished to present the Danes as an ancient culture of people who were a natural and important part of the Western European culture group. The last seven books are historical and about events closer to Saxo's time. In the previous century, Denmark had been ravaged by civil war, but Saxo established a picture of his king, Valdemar 1, as the righteous victor.

Thyra, as an idealized strong royal figure, appears, I suggest, as a compensation for the loss of dominion over large areas of land, such as England, after the glorious Viking era came to an end – symbolized by the old and tired King Gorm. Thyra's image inspired courage and a common feeling of identity, at least in the circles of King Valdemar and his allies. But Thyra was alive among common people, too.[7] A local legend from the area around Danevirke tells about a war against the Germans in which the Danish army was about to lose. Suddenly a female rider on a white horse appeared. She grabbed the flag from the flag bearer, exclaiming "Shame on those who do not follow." As she rode on to lead the army, great courage returned to the Danes, and they were victorious in the battle. Afterward, the woman disappeared, but they all believed it had been Thyra herself returning to save her people from destruction.

Queen Margaret I

Another era of worldly greatness began under the Valdemar kings, culminating in the Kalmar Union in 1397, during the rule of Queen Margaret, a daughter of

Valdemar IV.[8] This union included Denmark, Norway, Sweden, Finland, Iceland, Greenland, the Faroe Islands, and the Orkney and Shetland Islands. Without parallel, Margaret was the most powerful Danish woman during the Middle Ages.

After her death, she, too, took on mythological traits. Before the Viking ships in Roskilde Fjord were examined by archeologists, the local fishermen had "always" known that Margaret had let a ship sink there to prevent the enemies from entering Roskilde.[9] But as with Thyra and Danevirke, the ships were, in fact, much older. A tale from the island Læsø in the northern Kattegat tells that Queen Margaret once suffered a shipwreck there. The people of Læsø rescued her, and gratefully she granted them the privilege to own their land. In addition, she gave the women their richly silver-decorated Læsø dresses.[10] Læsø was not the only place where the queen was shipwrecked. In Reersø, a small peninsula on the northwest Zealand coast, she was helped by the locals who did not know who she was. In gratitude, Margaret granted the inhabitants tax exemption.[11]

She was also cunning. One day Queen Margaret was hard pressed by an enemy who pursued her near Schleswig. The queen found a hiding place on a hill. She put shoes on her horses in reverse (so the tracks would seem to run backward) and rode away. This trick saved the queen, and the hill has since carried the name The Horse Mountain.[12] A number of similar stories have been told about her in different locations throughout Denmark.

The End of Worldly Power

The Kalmar Union held together until 1523 when Sweden left the union. Since that time, Denmark has been losing external power. During the seventeenth century, Denmark and Sweden went to war repeatedly, and Denmark lost her old territories – the whole southern part of present-day Sweden – Skåne, Halland, and Blekinge. Many territories in northern Germany were also lost. In addition, the great Danish fleet was destroyed in 1803 by the English because Denmark had taken sides with Napoleon. Furthermore, the Danish state went bankrupt in 1813, and Norway left the union in 1814.

These national, economic, and military disasters initiated, paradoxically, a Danish cultural Golden Age in which writers such as Grundtvig, Oehlenschläger, Ingemann, and, of course, Hans Christian Andersen conjured up the legendary past and sang its praise to Denmark. (The world famous philosopher Søren Kirkegaard lived about the same time, also in Copenhagen, but his interests were totally different.) The ancient idea of Denmark personified as a female royal figure was strongly enhanced through images, poetry, and also by the Danish language itself.

First and foremost, Denmark's relationship with Germany, its big neighbor to the south, has been subject to symbolization. All the other (in reality much bigger) losses were repressed. It is with Germany that Denmark has its only mainland border, and it is primarily the changing boundary conditions in Jutland that live in the collective memory. In particular, Denmark's humiliating defeat in 1864, when

Denmark lost all Schleswig to Germany – and with it, alas, Thyra's Danevirke – was particularly hard.

Interestingly, Danevirke, until approximately 1800, was located at the southern boundary of the Danish language – the Danish *heart language*, its mother tongue – which from then on became an important component of the anima figure.

The Princess in the Underground Palace

A fairy tale from Jutland illustrates this anima figure:[13] There was a king in Northern Jutland whose youngest daughter always thought of climbing trees. The king, believing he was going to die, said he would grant the wishes of his five children. Four of them just wanted to stay at home, but the youngest daughter wanted to go out into the world. So traveling to Southern Jutland, she came to a large forest with tall trees to climb. There, she built a castle. Soon a German prince came to propose to her, but she rejected him. On the way home, he met a traveler and complained of his misfortune. The traveler gave him a serpent to throw in the princess's face as he said: "Now you will be like dead until someone speaks to you in your mother's tongue." No sooner was that said than done than the princess fell to the ground, the castle sank, and a dense forest grew up around it. A long time passed. A poor widow in Northern Jutland had a son who heard about the castle. He went off with the intention of finding the princess, and he managed to get through all the obstacles, including climbing from tree to tree. He went into the palace and found the princess. "You look pale," he said, "I wish I could save you!" But as he had talked in her mother tongue, she woke. The castle and its people were freed from the curse. Now the young couple married and went home to her father, who was so happy that he decided they should inherit the kingdom after him.

In the old days, Northern Jutland designated the peninsula of Jutland down to Kongeåen. Southern Jutland covered the area from there down to the river Eider, which is connected by Danevirke to the east coast (see Figure 6.2). Fairy tales seldom have any interest in geography or nationality, but this one, collected in the mid-nineteenth century, picks up themes that had become quite heated. Denmark's hostility toward Germany is personified in the rejected suitor who takes revenge in a way similar to the better-known thirteenth-century fairytale *Briar Rose* by the Brothers Grimm. The princess exhibits nonconformist female behavior in her love of climbing trees and wanting to travel the world and build her own castle. Her savior, who speaks the Danish folk language and who can climb trees as easily as the princess herself, actually had to be of lowly birth in order to use Danish. He personified Denmark, too. In the early nineteenth century, Denmark really was a poor, undeveloped peasant country. Among the upper classes, the court language was French, the administration language was German, and the scholarly language was still Latin.

Figure 6.2 Map of Denmark

The Shield-Maiden – Mother Denmark

This painting from 1851 by Elisabeth Jerichau-Baumann (Figure 6.3) illustrates perfectly the shield-maiden image. The young blonde woman is walking in a Danish corn field with the sea at the horizon; she carries the Danish flag over her shoulder and a Bronze Age sword in her hand and wears a heavy ancient gold ring around her neck. This could have been a portrait of the Viking Queen Thyra, a thousand years before. The painting was never accepted in the world of fine arts, but it became immensely popular, even iconic, and to this day, any Dane would immediately know what it means.

Figure 6.3 Havfrue, 1863, by Elisabeth Jerichau-Baumann (1819–1881). Brandts Museum. (By permission of Ny Carlsberg Glyptotek, København. Photographer: Ole Haupt.)

The image is called *Mother Denmark*, but this kind of motherhood is far from what Jungians associate with the mother archetype. I refer to such a figure as a representation of the *daughter archetype*.[14] I define the daughter archetype as a basic concept for the woman as a subject for herself, a concept for female agency that otherwise is lacking in analytical psychology. I've chosen the term to differentiate it from the mother archetype. The phenomenology of the daughter archetype is represented at all levels of psychic functioning. The images range from ego-representations to goddess-like Self representations. The notion of the daughter archetype addresses the female psyche, but it does not define the feminine as such. In masculine psychology, the daughter archetype appears as the anima.

Historical examples of this archetype go quite far back: The Sumerian Inanna was a goddess of both love and war. Originally, she was the special goddess of the city-state Uruk. The armed Valkyries, Diser and Fylger, have been known since Scandinavian pagan times. The Norse Freya was also a love and war goddess.

The Singing

A new custom of singing together began in the mid-nineteenth century; national songs in Danish spread across the country, both as part of public education as well as in public meetings.[15] In my own school days in the 1950s, the whole school gathered every morning to sing from a rich repertoire of national songs. Moreover, we heard about the Nordic myths and the legendary kings of Denmark's prehistory. In this way, we realized that, although we were only a small country, we had a rich and noble common past.

Denmark was typically portrayed in such songs as a beautiful, young noble shield-maiden, who now guarded a spiritual Danevirke, as in the song "Our Mother's Tongue Is Wonderful" by Edvard Lembcke (1859):

If in the east and west we have raved and sought
The wisdom of bygone days, the distant countries wit,
She lures, and she draws, we follow her bid,
Because she is so young and so lovely to behold.

Her enemies, they thought to cause her grief,
they offered her bondage in her own castle,
but just as they thought she was bound and chained,
she laughed so hearty that all chains burst.

And the bards, whom she bestowed the power of words,
they formed around her throne a strong and loyal guard.
Every song that people knew and listened to with pleasure,
became a ring of armor covering her breast.[16]

Inge Adriansen differentiates between the official symbols of the State and, what she calls, "unofficial symbols"[17]: "The unofficial symbols reflect the ideal of a harmonic national community, while there is barely any reference to the state and, in such manner, they present themselves as being apolitical and unchanging."[18] They have "prepared the ground for a largely non-aggressive internalized nationalism."[19] The *official symbols* are what Jung would call "signs" because their exact meaning is known and well-defined, whereas the *unofficial symbols* are "symbols" in the Jungian vocabulary.

In more psychological terms, this dominant feminine figure has been emotionally important for the majority of the population and is at the core of the complex (and undefinable) notion of *Danishness*. Other European countries have feminine personifications, too, but I believe none of those have had quite the same importance to their populations.

As mentioned earlier, the shield-maiden image flourished especially strongly in times of defeat, and so it did once again during the Second World War occupation by Germany from 1940 to 1945. Many poets of left-wing persuasion with an international attitude, who prior to the war had despised national symbols, now wrote glowing poems about Denmark as a subjugated, maybe raped, yet deeply loved woman.

Post-war Western Europe experienced an economic boom during the 1950s and 1960s that had not ever been experienced previously. The socialist governments that dominated the period began the construction of the modern welfare state, and broad sections of the population gradually accumulated considerable material wealth. This increased prosperity made leisure, vacation, consumer goods, and entertainment essential elements in the lives of ordinary people.

The Great Change: Youth Rebellion and Women's Movement

Part of the late 1960s so-called youth rebellion was against what was seen as a spiritless materialism in their parents' generation. But the rebellion went much further: several groups attempted a break with traditional policy forms, social structures, and family patterns. In short, down with all the authorities – down with the old boring traditions. Participants in the youth rebellion experimented with forms of family, sexuality, religion, dress, and narcotics. Gradually the youth rebellion changed character, in the sense that more serious political organizations came to dominate it – often with declared Marxist positions. This added momentum to the effort to abolish what was seen as bourgeois norms and traditions in general.

Different groups of women also increasingly rebelled against the traditional view of women. The revolt came partly because of several phenomena that emerged during the postwar period and especially in the 1960s: women coming into the labor market, the pill, and access to abortion. The Danish feminist movement was inspired by an international development, formulating a theoretical basis for the notion that gender differences are not only biologically but also socially and culturally determined.

Figure 6.4 The Mermaid, 1863, by Elisabeth Jerichau-Baumann (1819–1881). Fyen Museum

I believe the political and artistic actions against *The Little Mermaid* can be seen in this light. Famous with and visited by the capitalists from the United States, as a small, inward-looking figure, she deserved to be decapitated!

Interestingly, the same Jerichau-Baumann who painted the iconic *Mother Denmark* also did several little-known paintings of *The Mermaid*; the one in Figure 6.4 from 1863 is the first. She was a personal friend of Hans Christian Andersen, and he wrote a small poem to thank her "for putting soul in the eyes of the mermaid." Soul is, however, not the first thing you might notice about this pin-up mermaid!

Political Upheaval

When Denmark joined the European common market (now called the European Union, or EU) in 1972, it was in many ways the major postwar epoch-making event. From then on, Denmark was economically as well as politically a part of a wider Europe.

Contrary to expectations, a deterioration of the economic situation soon followed, and this had its political counterpart in the so-called landslide election in December 1973. One-third of the members of the parliament were replaced, and the number of parties represented in parliament doubled from five to ten. Three of them were brand new parties; one of these was an ultra-liberal protest party, *Fremskridtspartiet*, with a political program that looked like a joke. Among other things, the party called for abolishing the income tax, reducing the public sector significantly, monthly elections of a greatly reduced parliament, and abolishing defense and replacing it with an answering machine saying "We surrender" in Russian. Nevertheless, the leader, Mogens Glistrup, and his party appealed broadly to Danish society. In 1973, the party stormed into the parliament after the elections as the country's second largest party. Ten years later, Mogens Glistrup ended up in prison for tax fraud. By then his party – significantly reduced and suffering from a number of splits – had taken up another concern, unnamable by the other parties: worries about immigration.

Net migration had started to change the country's cultural profile. Guest workers from Türkiye and Yugoslavia had been in the country since the 1960s, and they stayed. The number of foreign-born grew, therefore, and ghetto-like concentrations of immigrants in the major cities began to arise.

Between 1989 and 1992, the Iron Curtain fell and the Cold War ended; the EEC became the European Union through the Treaty of Maastricht, or The Treaty on European Union (TEU), which represented a new stage in European integration because it opened the way to political integration. The treaty introduced the concept of European citizenship, reinforced the powers of the European Parliament, and launched the economic and monetary union (EMU). Opposition to the European Union idea among the Danish population proved to be much more extensive than politicians had imagined, and in the referendum held on June 2, 1992, the Treaty of Maastricht was rejected, sending shock waves all over Europe. A number of exceptions for Denmark were negotiated, however, and another referendum passed in 1993.

The Splitting of the Cultural Complex

What happens to a cultural complex that used to be a uniting factor in the collective consciousness when its content, over a relatively short time, seems to be devalued? Clearly, the nation had become deeply divided on several issues concerning its own identity – relations with Europe and immigration. From the last decades of the twentieth century, any serious use of the Mother Denmark imagery has automatically stigmatized the user as a backward nationalist or even a racist person or party. This strong, negative emotional reaction was a sure sign of the activated cultural complex, only it was now polarizing the population instead of uniting it.

Dansk Folkeparti, DF (The Danish Folk party) was founded in 1995 by Pia Kjærsgaard. In a cartoon by Roald Als from 2007 in the Danish newspaper *Politiken*, Pia Kjærsgaard was shown dressed in a soiled and torn Danish flag with a satirical reference to the Mother Denmark figure. Clearly, her way of thinking "Danishness" did not please the cartoonist, who himself is left-wing. The DF's political program places a strong emphasis on national emotional values – "Danishness" – a restrictive and tight immigration policy, opposition to the development of a multiethnic and multicultural society, and strong criticism toward greater political integration in the EU.

When the DF first sent MPs to the Danish parliament, *all* the other political parties agreed to keep them from having any influence. They were simply seen as unfit to join a respectable company. But as the party steadily grew after each election and as it became the parliamentarian support party to the "blue" (liberal) right-wing government from 2001 to 2011, securing its absolute majority, contempt and even hatred of the DF was expressed by the "red" (socialist) left-wing parties. After that, polls automatically count the DF votes as a part the "blue" block, which is, in a way, contradictory because most of their voters are former social democrats, belonging to the "red" left-wing block. The last election in June 2015 came out with DF as the second largest party.

The Queen

While all these changes were occurring for the last half century, one symbol remained a positive, unifying force of the cultural complex, incarnated in Queen Margrethe II herself. She was born in April 1940, just a week after the Nazi invasion, and as the royal couple's first child, she became a symbol of hope in the dark years.

Margrethe became queen in 1972 when her father died, and so she ruled the country though all the upheavals described previously. In 2024 she abdicated, and her son became King Frederik X. Formally, monarchs appoint the prime minister and are the head of the Lutheran church, but they have no political power. Instead, Margrethe, and now her son, incarnate deep emotional and symbolic meaning. Every year on New Year's Eve, she would speak to the nation on national TV, and the nation actually watched her address and discussed it. Being above politics, she embraced the entire population. Every year on her birthday, thousands of people assembled at the royal castle, shouting for her to appear on the balcony; and when she did, they cheered and waved small flags. This symbolic quality may explain why the otherwise fanatically equalitarian Danes just wouldn't dream of changing the monarchy for a republic – and also why Queen Margrethe II not only was extremely popular but also even frequently appeared in the dreams of clients in my analytical practice, usually with positive associations relating to her independence and intellectual and creative interests, which included painting and a serious interest in archeology and history.

Conclusion

A strong cultural complex has existed in Denmark for at least a thousand years, based on an image of a royal shield-maiden protecting the Danes. Interestingly, her imagery was about protecting not only borders but also, especially in later times, spiritual, cultural, and emotional values as well as language (since the gradual loss of worldly power left "core" Denmark with one language only). The imagery helped Denmark come to terms with defeat, verbally expressed in the phrase, "Every man should build a Danevirke in his own breast."

Although the Danish queen still symbolizes a united Denmark, the population has become polarized since the second half of the twentieth century. Opinion leaders tend to look down on the threats to traditional values that are felt by a large part of the population. Serious use of Mother Denmark imagery now brands groups as right-wing, whereas the left-wing only uses the image for satirical purposes. But the strong emotions around the issues involved show that the cultural complex is still quite active.

Notes

1 *World Happiness Report 2013*, Sustainable Development Solutions Network, September 9, 2013. Accessed September 23, 2014, at http://unsdsn.org/resources/publications/world-happiness-report-2013/.
2 Institute for Happiness Research: Meik Wiking, *Der er et lykkeligt land*, September 2013. Accessed September 23, 2014, at https://www.danicapension.dk/da-dk/Documents/Medarbejdere%20-%20private/Presse/Der-Er-Et-Lykkeligt-Land.pdf.
3 "Aksel Sandemose," Den Store Danske, *Gyldendals åbne Encyklopædi*. Accessed September 23, 2014, at http://www.denstoredanske.dk/Kunst_og_kultur/Litteratur/Norsk_litteratur/Efter_1914/Aksel_Sandemose.
4 Mikael Frausing, "Myte: Er Den Lille Havfrue et dansk nationalsymbol?" *danmarks.historien.dk, Aarhus Universitet*, August 18, 2011. Accessed September 23, 2014, at http://danmarkshistorien.dk/leksikon-og-kilder/vis/materiale/myte-er-den-lille-havfrue-et-dansk-nationalsymbol/.
5 Hal Erickson, quoted in *Hans Christian Andersen* (1952), Rotten Tomatoes. Accessed September 23, 2014, at http://www.rottentomatoes.com/m/hans_christian_andersen/.
6 Saxo Grammaticus, "The Danish History of Saxo Grammaticus," in Oliver Elton (ed.), *The Nine Books of the Danish History of Saxo Grammaticus* (New York: Norroena Society, 1905). Accessed September 23, 2014, at http://www.sacred-texts.com/neu/saxo/.
7 Inge Adriansen, *Nationale Symboler I det danske rige 1830–2000*, Vol. II (Copenhagen: Museum Tusculanums Forlag, 2003), p. 200.
8 Anders Bøgh, "Margrethe 1. 1353–1412," *danmarks.historien.dk, Aarhus Universitet*, June 6, 2012. Accessed September 23 2014, at http://danmarkshistorien.dk/leksikon-og-kilder/vis/materiale/margrethe-1 -1353-1412/.
9 Vikingeskibsmuseet, DKonline. Accessed September 23, 2014, at http://www.dkonline.dk/Vikingeskibsmuseet_Roskilde___museum_-81960.html.
10 Inger Maria Larsdatter Kiil. Accessed September 23, 2014, at http://www.vaeversted.com/a/per01264.htm.
11 Thorkild Gravlund, "Rids af Reersoes Historie." Accessed September 23, 2014, at http://nordvestsjaelland.dk/artikler/1908/1908%20048-075%20Gravlund,%20Thorkild%20%20-%20Rids%20af%20Reersoes%20Historie.pdf.
12 Helge Noe-Nygaard (ed.), *Dronning Margretes flugt* (København K: Grænseforeningens årbog, 1986).
13 Carsten Høgh, *Prinsessen der blev en mand og andre trylleeventyr* (Copenhagen: Haase, 1993).
14 Pia Skogemann, "The Daughter Archetype," in Pramila Bennett (ed.), *Montreal 2010: Facing Multiplicity: Psyche, Nature, Culture* (Zürich: Daimon Verlag, 2011).
15 Adriansen, *Nationale symboler i Det Danske Rige*, p. 570.
16 Author's translation.
17 Adriansen, *Nationale symboler i Det Danske Rige*, p. 570.
18 Adriansen, *Nationale symboler i Det Danske Rige*, p. 575.
19 Adriansen, *Nationale symboler i Det Danske Rige*, p. 576.

Italy

Queens, Saints, Heretics, Prostitutes

Women in Italy

Caterina Vezzoli

In this chapter, I will consider Saint Clare, the heretic movement of the Gug-liemites, the figure of a prostitute, and two medieval Italian queens: Theodelinda, Queen of the Lombards, and Constance of Hauteville, Queen of Sicily. I will start with the queens. Their political and spiritual heritage has remained alive in the collective psyche of the Italian people and has served as a model for Italian women through the generations in spite of the patriarchal power structure that dominated medieval and later Italian society.

The forceful personalities of these noble women have remained with me since my early school days. Theodelinda and Constance were highly intelligent women with incredible political intuition. Each, in their own time, was able to fill in the momentary void of masculine royal power and to soften conflicts and unify opposing factions. The nuns in my elementary school introduced us seven-year-old girls to the queens' historical importance as well as their championship of female virtues, especially Theodelinda.

In the early 1970s, when I was student at Milan University in the Philosophy Department, I prepared a monograph on medieval queens, saints, and swashbuck-ling women.[1] Not unsurprisingly, it became clear that there was little place in Italian and European history for descriptions of the lives and actions of outstanding women. Those histories were written by clerics, and their vision of women was strongly influenced by their religious beliefs, which included powerful gender preferences. The role of women during the medieval era has thus remained an untold story, even today, and there are few reliable sources.

In 1977, Joan Kelly, Professor of History at City College of New York, was the first to question the academic establishment with her famous question, "Did women have a Renaissance?" Her answer to that question was "No."[2] Kelly's work inspired my own research into the history of women, which I hoped to reconsider from a nonclerical and gender-conditioned perspective. Since the 1980s, thanks to a generation of both female and male academics who have studied historical documents with an eye toward the influence of gender prejudices, a new history of women in the medieval era has emerged that is not only quite different from the old "official history," but which has also gained wide academic acceptance. These more recent studies inspired and facilitated my current work, which is aimed at understanding the cultural inheritance in the psyche of Italian women.

DOI: 10.4324/9781003609742-11

I believe that the embedding of culture into the personal psyche is directly connected to the formation of complexes that, in turn, are grounded in innate archetypal potentials. Complexes are the structuring units of psyche, and they develop from the interactions that take place between the developing child, caregivers, and the affective social environment. Specific cultural aspects and beliefs are metaphorically and emotionally passed on with the "mother's milk" and the first interactions between the infant and the environment. Culture and nurture, present from the beginning of infant development, are interconnected elements that aggregate into complexes. In this sense, culture and nurture are part of a whole.

Associating Freely

Before going to the hairdresser, I found myself sitting on a bench in the Church of San Giorgio al Palazzo in Milan, looking at the Magdalene in Bernardino Luini's painting of the *Deposition from the Cross* and listening to a Gregorian chant, "*Ave Mundi Spes Maria*," well-known to me since my school days when the nuns sang it at morning prayers. Gregorian chants were a continuous presence during my childhood and teenage life as I used to stop at church on my way to school every morning – especially as a teenager when my school was next to a cloistered convent where the nuns' angelic voices had the power to create a peaceful oasis in the midst of my rages, confusions, and distress. Unfortunately that morning in San Giorgio the chants were recorded! What remained unchanged, however, was the smell.

Italian churches have a familiar smell; it is like entering a home I have known since my infancy and in which I have grown up. It is the smell of wax, candles and incense, wood, old painting, marbles, and cleaning soap. As smells go directly to the oldest and most emotional part of our brain, I could say it is like the smell of my mother with whom I went to church since childhood. To be enveloped in the church smell is to be deeply moved and peaceful at the same time.

In the empty church built on the Roman Imperial Palace, where in 312 Emperor Constantine signed the Edict of Milan recognizing the Christian religion and putting an end to the persecutions of the Christians, I let my thoughts wander through the seventeen centuries since that time. They drifted to the Milan of Roman times and the reasons why the emperor had transferred his court to the north of Italy. Not far from here is the Basilica of Saint Ambrose, an important Romanesque basilica in the history of Milan and Christianity. It was initially built during the time of Saint Ambrose who was the Bishop of Milan from 374 to 386, and it was rebuilt in the ninth century by Archbishop Angilberto II.[3] Saint Ambrose had evangelized the region of *Mediolanum* (the Latin name for Milan) in the fourth century. Ambrose's father was the powerful Roman Prefect of Gaul, and therefore his family was from the highest Roman nobility. He received the best Roman education in literature, law, and rhetoric, and he knew Greek, which was rare at the time. When his father died prematurely, Ambrose was appointed consul of the region by Emperor Valentinian I, and after two years, he became the bishop of Milan. Ambrose was Catholic and did not accept the Pagans or the Arians. The *Pagans* were Roman subjects who believed in the Roman gods, derived from the Greek pantheon; the *Arians* were Christians who were considered heretics because they followed the teaching of the Alexandrian presbyter Arius (250 CE–336 CE), who considered the Son of God a demigod.[4]

Ambrose's relations with the Roman emperors were not always easy, but he treated them as equals while defending his own creed. He died in 397, and the church of Milan was at the center of the new Christian faith. To give a sense of the enormous influence of Ambrose and his church, it should be sufficient to say that St. Agustin converted from the Mani religion to the Christian religion after meeting Ambrose. After teaching in his native Roman province of North Africa, Augustine moved to Milan to be near the Roman court. He greatly admired Saint Ambrose for his rhetorical abilities and teaching and for his political aptitude. It seems that he was even shy toward Ambrose. He felt Ambrose was superior to him by birth, as he came from Roman nobility, had the best education, and knew Greek. Also Ambrose was skilled in the administration of power from all his dealings with the Roman government. Furthermore, having been in the highest ranks of the Roman Army, Ambrose was experienced in military campaigns and strategy, which had proven useful in the Christianization of Northern Italy.

That same day I decided to stop at the Church of Saint Satyrus on my way home from the hairdresser. It is not far from San Giorgio, and I wanted to see the newly restored, fifteenth-century, polychrome terra-cotta *Deposition from the Cross* by Agostino De' Fondulis. Saint Satyrus was Saint Ambrose's brother. This little church dating from the ninth century was enlarged by Duke Gian Galeazzo Maria Sforza in the fifteenth century. Close to Piazza Duomo, it is one of my favorite churches, with its beautiful stucco perspective created by Bramante. In what was the mortuary chapel of Saint Satyrus, from Carolingian time, there's a sculpture representing the deposition of Christ, containing a Magdalene with long red-brown hair that covers her.[5] The position of the saint at the feet of Jesus shows her great piety and concentration at the same time. This part of the church had been reopened after a thorough restoration. It was the first time I had seen it since my childhood, and I didn't remember it at all.

The Magdalene is frequently represented in Milanese and Italian churches. With her beauty and long hair, to me, she resembles some of the Hollywood stars I saw in American films as a young girl. She has always been one of my favorite female saints, the other being Saint Catherine of Alexandria. Her story, too, with all the shadow aspects that the nuns tried to conceal, fascinated me. How was it that a "lost" woman like the Magdalene had become a saint?

The Magdalene is a composite saint. The construction of her sainthood began in the seventh century with Pope Gregory the Great in the church of Saint Clement in Rome. He proclaimed that Mary Magdalene, who was called a sinner in the Gospel of Luke (Luke 7:36–50) and whom John called Mary (John 11:2), was the same Mary from the Gospel of Mark (Mark 16:9) from whom seven demons were cast out. Gregory had several reasons for combining the identity of the women mentioned in the Gospels of Luke, John, and Mark. The Magdalene hagiography, created by Pope Gregory I, was aimed at giving women the possibility of being in the grace of God. The Church Fathers of the first centuries created the Magdalene because women, especially married women, presented a constant contradiction for them. The men of the Church considered women to be inferior, and they were required to be submissive to and obey their husbands. This was in clear contradiction to Jesus's message that considered men and women to be equal. The revolutionary principle of the Gospel was that all human beings were equal in the eyes of God. This principle was well-known to the popes, who only partially respected it but also couldn't ignore it altogether. Even more importantly, the Roman Catholic Church had adopted the system of laws of the late Roman Empire that gave women the right to inheritance and of being free subjects. These laws, although often neglected, were never abrogated. Married women presented an additional problem that assigned to them important functions.

Wives were important because they had to contain the libidinal temptations of their husbands; the institution of marriage had been created for this reason. Ecclesiastic power entered into all aspects of the sexual life of a couple, and chastity in a marriage was considered a virtue equivalent to virginity before marriage. The good wife had to take care of the husband and of the husband's father and mother. She had to keep the love of God alive in her husband and take care of the children, the servants, and so on. Demands placed on the wife were impossible. Conjugal fidelity, in theory imposed on both the husband and the wife, was only strictly enforced for women. Many other prohibitions and restrictions prescribed how women were to dress, speak, and act. At the same time, as the centuries passed during the Middle Ages, the importance of women had to be recognized. The Church could not ignore the fact that women often became Christians before their husbands, assuring that children would be baptized and educated in the Catholic religion.

The men of the Church and the men of arms exercised control over society and over women. The sin of Eve was projected onto women in opposition to the virginity of Mary. The figure of the Magdalene emerged as the penitent saint, mediating between the sins of Eve and the virginity of Mary. Jesus first appeared to Magdalene on the day of his resurrection, and the fact that Jesus preferred a woman to the male apostles was a direct threat to masculine supremacy. With the development of the mendicant order and the renewal of the Church during the first centuries, the cult of the Magdalene was widespread in the first millennium. And, significantly, the same Pope Gregory I who created the Magdalene had an important relationship with Queen Theodelinda of Lombard, whom he addressed as *Gregorius Theodelinda Reginae*.[6]

Theodelinda, the First Queen of Italy

Theodelinda was the first queen I came to know. As a child, what I liked about her was her ability to solve conflicts and assure peace. The history taught at my elementary school was strongly influenced by the nuns' hubris. My teachers stressed that the Queen of the Lombards was on good terms with the papacy, and they always pointed to her pious life. Nevertheless the dignity of the queen resisted my further studies. Daughter of the Frank Duke Garibold I of Bavaria, Theodelinda became Queen of the Lombards with her first marriage to Authari, son of King Cleph of the Lombards.[7] Her first marriage lasted only one year, and when Authari died, she was allowed to choose her second husband, Agilulf, in 591 when she was twenty-one years old.[8]

The Lombards were a Scandinavian tribe that arrived from Austria in the sixth century, when the north of Italy was terribly impoverished, and only a few soldiers were left from the Roman garrisons to defend a territory constantly under siege by the Barbarian tribes.[9]

Cultural Trauma

In the late sixth century, the Lombards of Agilulf and Theodelinda had settled in a territory that had once been a rich Roman province but was by then losing its splendor. The Lombards, like the other Barbarian tribes, were not used to the elite Roman lifestyle. The richness of the Roman villas and palaces was foreign to them. They had a nomadic background and were used to living in tents, huts, or in the open.

The Roman population was simultaneously witnessing the decline of their quality of life as the Roman Empire collapsed in the middle of the fifth century. There were killings, famine, and ransacking because of the wars. The population of northern Italy had lived for decades under the umbrella of the *Pax Romana* (Roman Peace) and were used for economic stability and protection. Roman subjects were used to receiving grains at low prices during times of economic difficulty; they had appreciated the thermal bath houses, roads, and aqueducts – services provided to the population by the emperor. These were now abandoned and left to deteriorate. The administration of the law, a prerogative of the Praetorian garrisons and available to Roman subjects and freedmen, had disappeared, and there was a growing sense of insecurity. The new conquerors ignored the Roman laws of the late empire as well as its previously efficient administrative organization. Those who had lived and inherited the Roman way of life were shocked by the cultural differences and the loss of their familiar points of reference (no laws, no road maintenance, no security). Many fled their houses in the cities and tried to find other places to live.[10] The decades of the Roman Empire's fall and the early centuries of the Middle Ages were filled with wars, invasions, cultural differences, and loss of identity. Today, we would speak of the collective trauma. There was also religious conflict as the descendants of the population who had lived under Roman jurisdiction were Christian Catholics, whereas the Lombards were Christian Arians. These religious differences, as explained previously, were a source of conflict between the new rulers and the local population before the Barbarian tribes settled and mixed with the local population and submitted to the Christian religion and the Church.

Theodelinda's attitude was aimed at maintaining a balance as she considered both the Lombards and the local population who had lived or inherited the traditions of Roman civilization as her subjects. She sought to create an integration of the differences in the name of the common good. Being herself a representative of a new identity as both Lombard and Catholic, she hinted at the possibility of resolving trauma. For the local population, the Queen's closeness to the Pope offered further reassurance because the Church represented continuity with the Roman Empire and its rules as well as with their ancestry. The Christian message of hope for a better life after death also had a reassuring value. In fact, the Church of Pope Gregory became the real successor of the Roman Empire. In a time of continuous war, the good relations between the queen and the pope offered hope for peace.

Theodelinda and the Administration of Power

Amid the turmoil of the collapsed Roman Empire and the construction of a new world, Theodelinda was a different kind of Lombard. She was Catholic, not Arian; she had an education; she knew written Latin, the language of official transactions and what remained of Roman culture. She used Latin in her dealings with Pope Gregorio Magnus. From her personal treasures, left to the Church of Saint John the Baptist in Monza, which she had built near her summer residence, we can tell even today that she liked Roman artifacts, jewels, and art works. Her political position was one of religious tolerance. Most of the pagan altars had already disappeared under those who vehemently disapproved of them, including Ambrose. As for the Arian faith, there was even less tolerance on the part of the Church.[11] The Arians were Theodelinda's people, however, and were protected by the Lombard dukes. She did her best to keep the religious conflicts at bay. Respected by both the Lombards and the Christian population, on good terms with the papacy, Theodelinda became the reigning queen at the death of Agilulf. Her reign ushered in an era of prosperity and peace in which a kind of integration between the cultures took place.

Theodelinda's Heritage

Centuries later, during the early Renaissance, the Visconti dynasty ruled Milan. Taking the title of duke, the dynasty needed recognition of their nobility. To ensure the authenticity of their noble blood, which was important to their plans of expansion, they tried to establish an idealized, ancestral link to Queen Theodelinda. They commissioned two painters – the brothers Zavattari – to paint the frescos in the Monza's Duomo to illustrate their Theodelinda lineage. So more than eight hundred years after her death, Theodelinda was portrayed as the oldest ancestor of nobility. These frescos and the angelic beauty of the queen, with her blond hair and golden dresses, fascinated me when, as a seven-year-old little girl, I went with my schoolmates on a cultural visit to see the frescos and the treasure.

The myth of Theodelinda as an enlightened queen remained active throughout the Middle Ages. The most precious object of her treasure was the *Corona Ferrea*, or the *Iron Crown*. Tradition says that Theodelinda had the crown built around an iron ringlet that was obtained by fusing one of the nails from the Cross. It is the highest symbol of royalty for the kings of Italy, and for Napoleon as well who used it at his coronation in 1805.

What is surprising in the story of Theodelinda is that she was allowed to choose her second husband, which was highly improbable for the time. Fiction or not, this is what Paolo Diacono, a cleric living in the Monte Cassino Monastery and a Lombard himself, wrote about her well after her death and wanted to transmit to posterity.[12] What he wrote was probably commissioned as a way of maintaining the queen's memory. One certain fact is that what he transmitted was useful for the policy of the emerging temporal power of the papacy. The papacy wanted to use the memory of the queen to control not only the Lombards but also the other Barbarian tribes that were following each other in an attempt to be the new rulers. Among the opposing powers, the dignity conferred to Theodelinda went well beyond the conscious intention of the clerics. The myth that built up around her celebrated her spirituality, her womanhood, and her nobility and became a part of the culture's conscious and unconscious inheritance that could be called on by women in the future.

Some centuries later, Constance, Queen of Sicily, was equally loved by her people and demonstrated herself perfectly capable of dealing with the manipulations of the men of power around her. She was able to maintain her spiritual and political capabilities relatively independent of the ongoing struggles between the Church and the emperor.

Constance d'Hautville, Queen of Sicily

My reason for choosing Constance of Sicily as the second Queen to illustrate the medieval heritage transmitted through the centuries to women is related to her ability to function well in both the spiritual and political worlds. The story of her spirituality will help me to introduce the importance of women's mysticism.

Posthumous daughter to Roger II, the Norman king of Sicily, and his third wife, Constance of Sicily was born in 1154. She spent her infancy in Sicily at the Palermo court with her mother, where she was brought up in the traditions and habits of her natal land. Dynastically, Constance's position was important. During her lifetime, there was an ongoing conflict between the papacy and the emperor, and her marriage to the emperor's son had important political significance. The world had had no news of her before 1184 when she was betrothed to the emperor's son. To allow her marriage to the future emperor, the pope dispensed her from her vows as a nun. The historic record of Constance's monastic life is uncertain. The Monastery of San Salvatore in Palermo was able to show proof of her presence in the form of a precious New Testament with Constance's handwritten notes in Greek and a book of prayer belonging to her.[13] During her life, the popes counted on Constance's loyalty toward the Church as their conflict with the German Emperor Frederick I grew for possession of the lands of southern Italy. Favoring Constance as queen of Sicily, the papacy's intention was to maintain a feudal obligation on Sicily by sustaining the priority of her inheritance rights by "paternal succession," which were previous to Emperor Frederick's rights of *antiquum ius imperii*. The pope wanted to challenge Emperor Frederick I of Hohenstaufen, and he intended to use Constance's rights against the emperor. The emperor had the same intention. Constance was no puppet, however, as we will see.

Constance's Marriage and the Political Conflict Between the Emperor and the Pope

William II, son of Roger II and half-brother to Constance, accepted the marriage of Constance to the emperor's son. Constance moved to Milan, the most anti-imperial of the Italian cities, for her marriage to the emperor's son Henry VI. The Emperor Frederick Barbarossa wanted the marriage to take place in Milan, in the Basilica of Saint Ambrose. The citizens of Milan, loyal to the pope, had been in conflict with the emperor and had defeated him in several battles before being defeated by the emperor and his allies. In 1162, Frederick I Barbarossa ordered that the city, which had dared to rebel against him, be destroyed by fire to demonstrate his power. Having the wedding in Milan was a way to show to the world and to the pope that the old conflicts were over. By sanctioning a marriage of his son to a bride dear to the pope in a city politically on the side of the papacy, Frederick wanted to demonstrate a change of policy. In fact he wanted his son to be the Holy Roman emperor, and only the pope could ensure that.

Constance's Heritage

Dante encounters Constance in Paradise and calls her "*la grand Costanza.*" "*Quest'è la luce de la grand Costanza/che del secondo vento di Soave/generò 'l terzo e l'ultima possanza.*"[14] He mentions the birth of Constance's son who will become the third Holy Roman emperor, Frederick II. Dante greatly admired Frederick II's cultural and political courage as he writes in his "*De Vulgari eloquentia*" and in the "*Convivio.*"[15] Dante was a White Guelph, then a mild supporter of the papacy – or to put it another way, he supported a distinction between the State (the political power) and Religion (the spiritual power).[16] This is a long, well-known conflict in Italy; even today we see aspects of it.

What is interesting about Dante's encounter with Constance's soul in Paradise is that she is introduced by Piccarda's soul. Piccarda was from a prestigious Florentine family well-known to Dante, the Donati.[17] She had chosen the life of the convent against the will of her brother who wanted her to marry into a noble family. She was obliged to leave the convent and had to marry. Dante's Piccarda speaks of the perfect life of the women with the veil, of religiosity, of charity, of the beauty of life in the convent. She indicates Constance as a soul who had to renounce the life of the convent to obey her family and the pope.

Here, Dante shows that for women the real sacrifice was not to renounce the secular life, but to renounce the spiritual life in the convent. To live in the world was not the best of choices for women, not even for a queen. The seclusion of the convent, a life of prayer and poverty, could be a much better place than life in the world.

Many noble as well as poor women were obliged to marry; when widowed or with the permission of their husbands, they would then retire to the convent, especially to Cluny, which at that time was one of the few convents to accept women. The Abbot of Cluny, Peter the Venerable (died in 1156), refers to the fact that his mother had in horror undertaken the duties of marriage. She had to become like a new Magdalene, throwing herself at the feet of all venerable men and asking for forgiveness and protection.

Whether historical reality or legend, the fact that Constance of Hautville was remembered as a woman who lived in the convent before taking on the position of consort to the emperor's son points to the development of an ideal femininity and the desire to follow the path of a spiritual life, defying the impositions of the masculine world. In a world dominated by ferocious and cruel masculine powers, a world in which women had no voice, the road to mysticism was a path to salvation and freedom. More importantly, the life of the convent gave women like Constance the freedom to think in their own way and to overcome the destructiveness of clashing political powers.

Saint Clare of Assisi

Saint Clare was one of the first followers of Saint Francis of Assisi. Born in 1194 into a noble family, her destiny was to marry a young man who was also a wealthy noble. After hearing Francis preach, however, she left home to follow his teachings, resisting every attempt by her father to bring her home. Her mother, Ortolana, was a devoted lady who had undertaken pilgrimages to Rome, Santiago of Compostela, and the Holy Land. Clare's destiny and interests differed from that of her mother; instead, she had to become the "new woman" herself, following the preaching of the *homo novus*: Francis.

Clare's Mysticism of Love

Even if Clare took the vows of the order of Francis, she interpreted them according to the principles of joy and freedom. Obedience for her was to take the initiative of obtaining from the pope recognition of her Order of the Poor Sisters, the canon laws that would later become those of the Order of the Clarisse. Chastity was seen as a positive choice for life, not as a restrictive rule negating life. Virginity was viewed as a state of freedom. For women to live in poverty like men was bold for the time. Even more so for Clare, poverty was the discovery of things and nature in its freshness as gifts newly created.[18]

Clare took care of the Poor Sisters who had joined her and expressed her love to them as we read in a letter to Agnes of Prague, in which she expresses the benediction and the joy of being sisters in God:

> To the other half of her soul and repository of the special love of her deepest heart, illustrious queen, spouse of the Lamb of the eternal King, the Lady Agnes,

her own dearest mother and, among all the others, her special daughter, Clare, unworthy servant of Christ and useless handmaid of his handmaids who live in the Monastery of San Damiano in Assisi, sends greetings and her prayer that Agnes, together with the other most holy virgins, will sing a new song before the throne of God and of the Lamb, and will follow the Lamb wherever he goes.[19]

Agnes was the daughter of the king of Bohemia and had been engaged to Henry, the son of Emperor Frederick II, who was the grandson of Constance of Hautville. When, because of political intrigues, the betrothal was canceled, Agnes, with the help of Pope Gregory IX, refused to marry and found a convent that followed the canon law of the Order of Clarisse. A nun and abbess herself, she took care of the lepers and paupers before retiring in cloister. The letters from Saint Clare were meant to support her in her effort to spread the Order of the Poor Sisters. Clare's empathy for Agnes, her sister in God, gives her language a warmth that reveals a deep understanding even within the limitations and restrictions of official formality.

Following Clare's path, Agnes could, in obedience to the Church, refuse to be a pawn on the chessboard in the game of the emperor and the pope. She could follow a life in which she could express her spirituality by embracing a life of poverty and prayer with the freedom of loving in her own way. The only way in which women could express Eros or love was in their relation in God and to God; in this way, they could give value to their feelings.

Mystical Marriage

The mystical marriage with Christ was seen as the highest union of souls. Love coming from the heart was the greatest enrichment. It overcame all limits of the world and that of the enclosure. The nuns lived in seclusion and dedicated their payers and thoughts to God and to his creatures that lived in the world. The salvation of the world included taking care of the poor and the sick. In the convents those nuns living in cloisters were, in a way, the elected spirits. The care of people living in the world was the task of the sisters of lower rank. As we read in the hagiography of Saint Clare and in her letter to Agnes of Bohemia, however, she embraced both the material as well as the spiritual world. A good example of the integration of the love of God and respect for the world is Saint Francis' *Canticle of the Creatures*, in which he praises God for the creation of the world. The *Canticle* starts praising Brother Sun and Sister Moon and ends with a praise to Sister Death. The marriage of souls includes the world in which humans live. The nuns refused power in favor of poverty and sought to include all beings in the spirit of love.

The mysticism of Saint Clare and her Order of the Poor Sisters altered what women could become and, from them, came a message of spiritualized Eros. In the language of the prayers, letters, and confessions of the female mystics emerged a new perspective that gave love a place in the world. They were the brides in a mystical marriage and could express their feelings of love and passion in God's love. In the mystical marriage, the union of the soul with God created ecstasy and joy, the greatest fulfillment of life.

Psychology and Mysticism

Moving from the historical to the psychological level, Jung in *Psychological Types* writes about the Christian religion of the first centuries and the psychological, primitive regression to an unconscious form of the representation of God:

> The relativity of God in medieval mysticism is, therefore, a regression to a primitive condition . . . the regression to the primitive is not surprising, in view of the fact that every vital form of religion organizes one or the other primitive tendency in its ceremonials or its ethics, thereby securing for itself those secret instinctive forces that conduce to the perfecting of human nature in the religious process.[20]

What I found interesting in Jung's approach is that the relativity of God is found in the necessity of regression to unconsciousness. Jung is saying that in the part of the unconscious that is in relation to the instinctual forces, that is, to matter, we find the possibility of *perfection*. Perfecting human nature in the religious process means that through religion we can transcend the limits of the conscious mind and access the forces of the archetype that are related to matter. In medieval times, the mystics regressed to the images of the collective unconscious to find the perfection of their humanity in God. In the same chapter, "The Relativity of the God-concept in Meister Eckhart," Jung reflects on the unanswered question of medieval psychology:[21] "the Worship of Woman and the Worship of the Soul."[22] For him, medieval mysticism, as in the Gnostic tradition, gives value to individual revelation and individual knowledge. Through visions, women developed in their mysticism the only possibility left open to them by the Church, which secluded them in convents and prohibited them from elaborating on theological matters. The phenomena of women's mysticism and their visionary love freed the religious function from the intellectual limitations of intellectual criticism.[23]

For women, it was difficult to escape masculine projections that attributed so many wrongdoings to them; even more difficult for women was to express their feelings and thoughts. In an attempt to realize an inner stance to a life in which they could find expression for their spirituality, medieval women projected into *religion* their unconscious need for Eros and liberation of the constraints imposed by their society and its forms of power.

We can think of their quest for union with God as the kind of regression to perfection mentioned by Jung that allowed women to explore their soul. God became the other half of their soul. In and with the mystical marriage, the most precious and spiritual part of the soul would survive all evils and dangers. The power that medieval men had over them did not allow women much freedom, but the unconscious need to self-realization allowed some of the more fortunate women to express themselves and have their voices heard. They were able to recognize that love was a need in itself, and through meditation and the development of spiritualized thinking around God, they could overcome the limitations imposed by a religion supercharged with power and political issues.

In spite of the widespread brutality against them, women of the medieval period did convey feelings of compassion and understanding that changed visions of life and created the possibility of a peaceful world. Women's mysticism was not enough to change or convert the addiction to war and power of the masculine world, but at least it contributed to the establishment of values like peace, respect for the other, and love for all creatures and nature. Women' spirituality offered Eros as the opposite of Scholastic Logos.

Clare and the other woman mystics were profoundly embedded in their religious creed and devoted their lives to the realization of the perfect life they wanted. Today I don't see this as a limitation but rather as a potential; they had no other choice than to refuse violence, materialism, and power struggles. In other words, they were trying to be themselves.

Feminine mysticism flourished in the Middle Ages, particularly in conjunction with the development of the mendicant orders along with the cult of the Magdalene. Clare's liberal mysticism changed the relationship with God, who was seen more as a father than as the judge of previous centuries. The female mystics created a new vision of humanity, and in this context, Clare was the new expression of femininity.

Guglielma and the Function of Women as Redeeming Factor

The Gugliemites were considered a heretic sect by the Inquisition. Small in number, their influence was limited to a restricted Milanese area. Their movement is interesting to study, however, for its connections to the Milanese church and the Cistercian Abbey of Chiaravalle.

Guglielma, the presumed founder of the Gugliemites, was of the order of the Humiliati.[24] The Humiliati were a mainly male order that was dissolved by the papacy in 1576. The Humiliati nuns, however, remained active in northern Italy until the twentieth century. The Humiliati were one of the many penitent orders that stemmed from the repentant movements and the creation of the Mary Magdalene cult. The Gugliemites of the thirteenth century preached that the only hope for the salvation of humanity was the advent of a woman in the papacy.[25] Not only did they proclaim that Guglielma of Milan was the incarnation of the feminine Holy Spirit, but they also preached that the pope of the new Church, as well as the Cardinals, should be women. Only with the advent of a Church with feminine ministers and values could there be salvation for the entire world. The perfect ecclesia had to be governed by women. Even if this heresy sounds absurd to our ears, it was not so new, as many proposed a new *ecclesia spiritualis*. Feminine mysticism, the cult of the Magdalene, the development of the mendicant orders, all increased the number of women who looked toward religion as a possibility for a better life. The majority of Gugliemites were women; many were widows, which is important because the hereditary laws of the late Roman Empire, which gave women the right to inheritance, had been better accepted by that time. After they were widowed, women went to live in monasteries with their inheritance intact, and, of course, they were most welcomed and respected for their choice. The economic power of women increased their value as they brought not only their rich spirituality to the convent but also their increasing material wealth and its power. The solidity of Roman jurisprudence, which after centuries of neglect was integrated into the laws of the Church and the States, contributed to a stable and lawful environment. To be in a place that accepted and protected their legal rights and their spirituality, intelligence, and love made women feel protected and accepted. Being socially reassured and accepted gave them daring: their spiritual boldness brought the development of many new orders. Some of them, like that of the Gugliemites, were later declared heretical by the Inquisition.

In the Milanese church of the time, there were many conflicts and there was great need for renewal. In a way, the Gugliemites were in alignment with the part of the church that saw the Magdalene as the preferred apostle, *Apostola Apostolorum* as proclaimed by the Church. The reasoning was that Jesus had chosen to appear first to Magdalene so he privileged women over his men apostles.[26]

Bernard of Clairvaux, the Cistercian Abbot who founded many monasteries, including Chiaravalle (translation of *Clairvaux*) near Milan, was devoted to the Virgin Mary and an advocate of feminine mysticism. He was much in favor of the vision of salvation through the feminine spirit and was favorably inclined to the Gugliemites' movement.

The Cistercian Abbey was an important center of religious and economic development. Beginning in the eleventh century, the monks of the mendicant orders accumulated large tracts of lands that they cultivated and where they introduced agricultural innovations that increased the production of crops. They farmed and raised poultry and pigs; they learned to store and preserve meats and grains.[27] Their apothecaries knew the secrets of the use of herbs for medicinal and agricultural purposes. They used their knowledge to improve the conditions of life. The years 1000 to 1350 saw an economic revolution that changed the condition of life for men and women. The Church and the monasteries transmitted values favorable to technical and economic development. Usury was condemned but lending money at reasonable rates accepted. Florentine and Italian banks developed all over Europe. The liberal arts were greatly favored and depicted as valuable in the churches as well.

With the improvement of economic conditions, there also came a renewal of religious movements. The mendicant orders stayed out of the power struggles between the emperors and the papacy. The Gugliemites movement was part of this renewal until the Inquisition targeted them and killed mostly the women. The Chiaravalle Cistercian monks had the body of Gugliemita, who died in 1279, transferred to their abbey where she was venerated until the Inquisition arrived to destroy it. Saint Bernard of Clairvaux had always had a more positive view of the feminine and of women than most other clerics. His voice, not without some ambiguity, was always in favor of the dignity of women. Other voices, like that of Dante, had no ambiguity, and he chose a woman, Beatrice, as his guide to Paradise.

The Inquisition argued, however, that the women of the Gugliemites had committed adultery and all sorts of sexual sins including *meretricium*, or prostitution.

Prostitutes: Cabiria and Her Sisters

I will conclude this chapter with a reflection on Federico Fellini's 1957 masterpiece *Le notti di Cabiria* (*The Nights of Cabiria*). I had already decided to write about this film when I came across an article in an Italian newspaper noting that the new Pope Francis had spoken fondly of Fellini's films from the mid-1950s, *The Nights of Cabiria* and *La Strada*. The two protagonists, Gelsomina of *La Strada* and Cabiria from *The Nights of Cabiria*, represent two aspects of women who are sacrificed to the cruelty of men and society.

The most famous scene from *The Nights of Cabiria* is when Cabiria, a prostitute, goes on a pilgrimage to the Sanctuary of Divino Amore to ask for a miracle. In the crowded sanctuary, Cabiria repeats, together with hundreds of other women and men, a sort of obsessional litany: "*Madonna fammi la grazia . . . la grazia*" ("Madonna grant me the grace . . . the grace"). The cacophony of sound and voices creates a suffocating anxiety, and Cabiria is near to collapsing. It's not clear what miracle Cabiria is asking of the Madonna until she says: "*Madonna fammi cambiare vita*" ("Madonna grant me to change my life"). Cabiria's basic value remains that of a woman who would like to have respectable love and maybe a family. Cabiria lacks common sense; she believes in love, and we know from the first scene that a man who she thought was her lover was instead after the money she earned and saved in her profession. The man had pushed her into a lake with the intention of killing and robbing her. In the later scene of her visit to the sanctuary, we witness a procession that reminds one of religious pilgrimages from the Middle Ages.

Cabiria is an ingenuous woman who has many illusions. She has lived a life of deprivation in search of somebody who could compensate for the lack of love in her life. She is an uneducated woman with a huge heart who is ready to believe in love. She comes from the working or peasant class and is used to scratching out an existence. Her friend Wanda, a beautiful corpulent prostitute, tells her in an affectionate way to wake up and invites her to open her eyes to the world of men who would betray her trust and take her money. The pimp, the cocaine pusher, the famous actor, the illusionist, the accountant, all these men use Cabiria for their own purposes and then get rid of her. She tries to please them all without any perception of her own value. We can recognize in her desire to please, in her desire to love, in her generosity, in her need for relationship, in her joy of dancing, in her appreciation of food, in her simplicity, in her courage, that she is much superior to the petty men who think of using her for their immediate needs. Cabiria is unaware of her positive qualities: she has had no love, but she believes in love; she can feel empathy for the poorest; she wants a better life for herself. But she is condemned by being a poor orphan to live without hope. With all her being, Cabiria refuses to live without hope; she wants to believe in charity, rights, and good deeds.

After another disillusioning experience, when once more she is wandering alone at night in the countryside, she meets a company of young people who surround her with music and dance, and playfully they walk in a merry way along the road together. Does this last scene represent the possibility of a new beginning? The young people remind one of the *Commedia dell'arte*, which, unlike the *Commedia Erudite*, performed outside on the roads. The actors were people of the lower classes. They were tricksterish and knew quite well the difference between morality and ethics. The *moral code* concerns rules related to the social code; *ethical consciousness* is autonomous and subject to unconscious aspects.[28] With their dirty jokes and crazy antics, the performers questioned the contemporary morality of power, of church rules, of nobility and gentry. In this last scene from the film, the comedians are young people, even teenagers, representing the new generation born after the Second World War. Will they embrace the values of liberty and equality between men and women that emerged after the war? Cabiria and Gelsomina believed in a better world and dreamed about it. In *La Strada*, Gelsomina died for it; in *The Nights of Cabiria*, Cabiria might survive the violence of men and a society dominated by the greedy thirst for power.

In the 1950s, the Catholic Church's religious *integralism*, the belief that one's religious convictions should dictate one's political and social actions strongly impacted Fellini and challenged his ethical capacity to integrate how the new and old exploitations of men and women operated in a changing Italy. After the devastation of the Second World War, the Church was afraid of the new Barbarians – the Communists. As a result, free thinking was forbidden to men, but especially to women. In those years, the impact of traditional Catholicism on women had not changed significantly since the Middle Ages, although there were some important differences as access to education was becoming equal for boys and girls. And even if the expectations regarding the role of housewives were unchanged, Italian women had started to work in offices and factories after the war and were becoming economically more independent.

Nearly sixty years passed before a pope could recognize Fellini's ethical values and that so many had suffered from the integralism of the Church. The Church had condemned the film as immoral. The undercurrent of a male-dominated society that could only see women as saints or prostitutes was not able to accept the humanity of Cabiria and her sisters. Fellini's visionary message, believing both in the humanity of Cabiria and the inventiveness and joie de vivre of a new generation, survived censorship, however; and his work of art was recognized worldwide.

Cultural Complex

Culture and nurture are interconnected elements that help form the personal complexes. At the core of the complex we find the archetype with its potentially structuring energy. The potential of the archetype interacting with the developmental events in the life of the individual shapes the transmission of culture. Growing up in the 1950s in post-war Italy, I received from my extended family and social environment the values that were important to them: love, dignity, the Catholic religion, spirituality, respect for knowledge and culture, but, most importantly, liberty. I use the word *liberty* and not *freedom* because the Latin word *libertas* implies something that requires the effort of will. Indeed, the *Libertos* were the Roman slaves who were legally freed because of their abilities and good will. For me, the word *freedom* does not require the human effort that is a precondition of obtaining "liberty."[29] After the devastation of Europe by Nazism and Fascism, *liberty* was a condition that we would fight to maintain. For previous centuries, the Catholic religion was the glue that had held the community together. This was especially true for women, as their daily and overall life pattern was regulated and sustained through religious rituals and landmarks. The deep spirituality of the medieval mystics was well-known to women, and the dignity and respect accorded to the saints reflected positively on those women who behaved in accordance with the religious rules.

When I was a child, I wanted my mother to tell me the story of Saint Catherine of Alexandria over and over again. What I liked about the hagiography of Saint Catherine was that she rebelled against her father, the king. He had forbidden her to be a Christian, and ultimately, he executed her. The images of the beautiful Saint Catherine in the paintings that I saw in churches and museums intensified the spell of this woman saint on my mind. My experience taught me that adults could be wrong on occasion. Together with fairy tales in which children were able to survive the malevolence of trolls, I found confidence in myself through the stories of women and children who found an inner voice to follow. I loved my parents, and the fact that the women of my family were strong, determined, kind, and spiritual gave me the ability to trust in my thoughts and beliefs. It also provided me with the strength to be a rebel, questioning conventional wisdom. The independence of mind that Saint Catherine professed was my childhood inspiration. My youthful religiosity found in the marvelous stories of the women saints a foundation for free thinking. I'm not sure this is exactly what the nuns and the priests of my childhood wanted, but I learned to follow what I valued.

I spent most of my time as a child with my mother, her sisters, and other women cousins. I learned from them that women were different but equal or even superior to men. From my uncles and father, I experienced firsthand men who respected their wives, daughters, and sons. I also learned that there was a very different world beyond my own extended family. In that world, men beat women and children. When I saw the film *The Nights of Cabiria* as an adult, the poverty on the outskirts of Rome portrayed by Fellini reminded me of the poverty of the maids who worked in the house where I grew up. Their gratitude toward my mother who was kind to them stands out in my memory. *Prostitution* was not a word that was spoken in our families when I was a child. Fellini's compassion toward Cabiria reminded me of the compassion I heard in my mother's voice when speaking about some poor women who had lost their way. The warm feelings that flow from Fellini's Cabiria include her being sympathetic to others, even if she is too ready to believe in untruthful men. Her generosity toward the suffering of others remains her best quality.

The name *Cabiria* comes from *Cabiri*. In *The Red Book*, Jung meets the Cabiri in Chapter XXI of "Liber Secundus: The Magician." The Cabiri say, "*We carry what is not to be carried from below to above. We are the juices that rise secretly, not by force, but sucked out of inertia and affixed to what is growing.*"[30] The Cabiri are the mysterious creative powers that work below the threshold of consciousness.[31] They are the emanation of unconscious powers.

In the film, Cabiria is abandoned at night on a deserted road in the countryside by one of her clients. She is trying to find her way back to Rome when she meets a young man who takes care of the poor and ill living in caverns that are little more than holes in the earth. In her night journey among the poorest, Cabiria meets a prostitute who she once knew and who is now dying in one of the caves. The woman gives her good advice about what she obtained and lost in life. When the young man leaves Cabiria at a bus stop in Rome to go to her house, she has regained hope. The encounter with a lost soul with deep human understanding helps Cabiria to recover her trust in life. Symbolically, the encounter with the poor living underneath the earth represents a meeting with the resources of the unconscious, bringing renewal of life. Cabiria is grounded in her big, forgiving heart and the inexhaustible resources that come from the depths of the feminine.

Thanks to the visionary strength and confidence in love of the women of the Middle Ages, an independence of mind was transmitted unconsciously through the generations until, in the second half of the twentieth century, the establishment of truly equal rights and education for women allowed them to develop liberty in all aspects of life. I do not idealize the Middle Ages, as I am well aware that the Inquisition and its witch hunts killed many more women than childbirth and famine. The Middle Ages did, however, give a spark of dignity and spirituality to women. Today, that same spark remains strong, with the important difference being that women have the liberty of trusting their own subjectivity and spirituality independently from any professed religion.

Conclusion

Medieval society was a misogynist, male-dominated society. Nevertheless the best poetry of the period was written by women and particularly the female mystics such as Saint Clare who found in the convents a space to discover a philosophy of love. They used their Eros in the ways that the world allowed them at that time, when women were considered inferior and were not allowed to speak for themselves.

The Middle Age mystics did not know the term *unconscious*, but they had visions; they were not aware of their *projections*, but they had poetry, music, hymns, and the Gregorian chants to the Virgin Mary. Their visions were represented in paintings, poems, and tapestries that hung in churches, convents, and castles. The female mystics used dreams and visions to express freely their feelings and knowledge without relying on theology, which was in the masculine domain.

Clare was no exception in that she used her dreams to reflect on the future development of her order as well as that of the Franciscan order. Clare dreamed that St. Francis invited her to suck from his breast. When she placed in her hands the remains of what she had sucked, she found that it was like pure gold, so clear and brilliant that she could see herself as in a mirror. The dream has been explained as a symbolic fellatio of the spirit of the Franciscan order. The Franciscan spiritual fluid was likened to the milk of the mother that nourished the children.[32] In this sense, the symbolic image mirrored the teachings of Francis that did not ask for obedience but for love that was given as freely as a mother would give love to her child. Clare transcended her condition of being a woman only and identified with that of being a human being, understanding humanity through her feminine love inspired by the Spirit.[33]

Today, we are quite far from a world in which women could only express their spirituality by going to the convent. The history of women was rewritten at the turn of the twentieth century.[34] Since then, much has been done to restore women to their dignity and worth. Still, much remains to be done. Discrimination influences the minds of those who are discriminated against, and the influence of patriarchal power on women's development remains a huge factor for women, both individually and socially. Many of us who attended the nun's schools as girls in the 1970s continued our studies at universities and abroad; we learned to be free thinkers and were encouraged by our mothers and fathers who saw the potential in us. Paradoxically, the nuns helped us to become feminists, women in our own right who could be proud of our culture. We could leave the formal religious teaching and find our spiritual expression in other ways that expressed our humanity and our full maturity as women. We have been able to interpret values and ethics in our own way and have recovered the dignity of being citizens with full rights.

I wish to conclude by mentioning a fact that may indicate the way in which the Church has changed its attitude toward women in recent times. In 2012, a few months before his retirement, Pope Benedict XVI recalled the importance of Queen Theodelinda in the history of the Church of her time and thanked her for being an enlightened queen and for her "friendship" toward the Church of the first centuries. To remember the Queen of the Lombards in this way, after so many centuries, is to acknowledge her value and that of the other women who, far ahead of their time, tried to live in peace in a period of wars and repeated trauma.

Notes

1   S. Wessley, *Sante Regine avventuriere nell'occidente medievale*, ed. Derek Baker (Florence: Santoni Editore, 1983). The original title was *Medieval Women*, published by the Ecclesiatical History Society, 1978.
2   J. Kelly, "Did Women Have a Renaissance?," in Joan Kelly (ed.), *Women, History, and Theory: The Essays of Joan Kelly* (Chicago, IL: University of Chicago Press, 1984).
3   Romanesque architecture was an architectural style in medieval Europe.
4   Arius' view concerning the eternal deity of Christ and his equality to the Father and his questioning of the Trinity of the Divinity of God was considered the first heresy of

Christianity. The Synod of Alexandria condemned it in 320. The controversy continued and found followers among Egyptian clergy and bishops. The Arian creed was definitively considered as heresy and therefore banished at the Constantinople Council in 381. At that time, however, the early church's legislation was confined to the borders of the Roman Empire. The Barbarian tribes maintained their belief in the Arian creed until the seventh or eighth century. The first tribe to refute Arianism was the Franks in 534.

5 Charlemagne, King of the Franks, became king of Italy in 774 and from 800 became the first emperor of the Holy Roman Empire. The time of his reign and empire is known as *Carolingian Empire*.

6 Gregorio Magno – Epistole (From the Epistles of St. Gregory the Great).

7 Teodolinda da Principessa a Regina, Comune di Monza, XXXI rievocazione Storica.

8 Whether legend or historical fact, choosing a husband was not the custom at that time.

9 I wish to specify that the Greeks and Romans defined Barbarians as those who did not speak their language. I maintain this definition for two reasons: first, because it's the point of view from which I learned history, and second, for the reference to language that conveys the idea of the clash of cultures.

10 I. M. Ferris, *Enemies of Rome: Barbarians Through Roman Eyes* (Stroud, Gloucestershire: Sutton Publisher Limited, 2000).

11 For the problem of Arian heresy, see endnote 4.

12 The fact that Paolo Diacono was allowed to mention Thoedelinda's freedom of choice reveals the great consideration given by the Medieval Church to the Queen of the Lombards. Paolo Diacono, *Storia dei Longobardi* (Cinisello Balsamo: San Paolo edizioni, 2008).

13 Knowing Greek meant that Constance was highly educated as Latin was more commonly learned in the courts and convents, and only very few knew Greek. Greek language and Greek philosophy were reintroduced to Europe by the Arab philosophers. Sicily had been an Arab emirate, and it was only after the first Crusade against the Moors that it returned to Christianity. The fact that Constance knew Greek, or was believed to know it, indicates that at the Royal Court the influence of Arab culture and teaching had remained important. The Holy Roman Emperor, Frederick II, Constance's son, also became King of Jerusalem after the Sixth Crusade, maintaining the link between the two worlds, especially from the point of view of science and poetry.

14 Dante Alighieri, *Paradiso*, Canto III, 118–120: This is the luminary of mighty Constance/Which blew the second over Saubia realm,/That power produced, which was the third and last.

15 Dante Alighieri, "De vulgari eloquentia," in *Opere Minori di Dante Alighieri*, Vol. II (Torino: UTET, 1998); "Convivio," in *Opere Minori di Dante Alighieri*.

16 In the long struggles between the opposing factions of the Guelph party, favorable to the papacy, and the Ghibelline party, favorable to the emperor in thirteenth-century Florence, the Guelphs split into the White and Black Guelphs.

17 Even today it's still possible to visit the Donati's beautiful palace in Florence. Dante's wife was also from a branch of the Donati family. The leader of the Black Guelphs, who opposed Dante and definitely decided on his exile from Florence, was a Donati and brother to Picarda.

18 Audrey Fella (ed.), *Le Femmes Mystiques* (Paris: Édition Robert Laffont, 2013).

19 Letters of Saint Clare to Agnes of Prague, letter 3.

20 C. G. Jung, "Psychological Types," in G. Adler and R. F. C. Hull (eds. and trans.), *The Collected Works of C. G. Jung*, Vol. 6 (Princeton, NJ: Princeton University Press, 1971), § 415.

21 Jung, "Psychological Types," § 407.

22 Jung, "Psychological Types," § 375.

23 Jung, "Psychological Types," § 411.

24 F. Andrews, *The Early Humiliati* (New York: Cambridge University Press, 2000).
25 S. Wessley, "I Guglielmiti del XIII secolo: La salvezza tramite le donne," in Derek Baker (ed.), *Sante Regine avventuriere nell'occidente medievale* (Florence: Santoni Editore, 1983).
26 J. Dalarun, *Dieu changea de sexe, pour ainsi dire: La religion faite femme XI–XV siècle* (Paris: Fayard, 2008).
27 Even today, in 2013, the Chiaravalle Abbey represents the vestiges of Cistercian world. On Sundays, there's a market of agricultural products produced by the monks and the farms nearby.
28 C. Proulx, "On Jung's Theory of Ethics," *Journal of Analytical Psychology* 34 (1994): p. 101.
29 B. Cassin, *Vocabulaire Européen des Philosophies* (Paris: Edition du Seuil, 2004).
30 C. G. Jung, *The Red Book: Liber Novus, A Reader's Edition*, ed. Sonu Shamdasani, trans. John Peck, Mark Kyburz, and Sonu Shamdasani (New York: W. W. Norton & Co., 2012), p. 426. Italics are mine.
31 Jung, *The Red Book*, p. 425, n. 310.
32 Jacques Dalarun, *Gouverner c'est servir. Essai de démocratie médiévale* (Paris: Alma, 2012).
33 B. Forthomme, *Le Femmes Mystiques*, p. 254.
34 G. Duby and M. Perrot, *Storia delle donne in Occidente*, 5 Vols., eds. Georges Duby and Michelle Perrot (Rome: Laterza, 1990).

Austria

Sisi

A Figure of Multiple Projections

Maria Kendler

Sisi: The Dream of a Princess

The Austrian Empress Elisabeth, whose pet name was "Sisi," was and still is a most fascinating figure for Europe's women and girls. Born in 1837, she was not only the admired and loved empress of the whole Habsburg Empire; she also had a kind of love affair with death. Nearly everyone has seen the famous movie trilogy *Sissi*, with Romy Schneider from the 1950s. And the musical *Elisabeth* was performed around the world from 1992 to 2014. From all corners of the globe, people flocked to see the moving story of the happy Bavarian princess. The musical has been shown in eleven countries, been translated into seven languages, and is the most successful German musical of all time. So far it has been seen by ten million people.

Sisi is obviously a figure of great interest and multiple projections. Girls today still collect pictures and figurines of the admired heroine. They read stories about her. But many of their fantasies have almost nothing to do with the real Sisi, the Habsburg empress from 1854 to 1898, the wife of Emperor Franz Josef I. My grandmother was born in a rural village 100 km to the west of Vienna in 1899, one year after Empress Sisi was murdered. Never in her life did my grandmother make the journey to the big city of Vienna. Tears came to her eyes, however, when I asked her in her seventies about the Empress Elisabeth. She uttered her name with a kind of reverence; she seemed to adore her like a saint. But I never fully understood why she was so profoundly touched by the figure of Sisi.

Sisi is an especially prominent symbol in Austria. When you arrive at an airport in a foreign country, that country tends to reveal itself and its preferred identity. In Switzerland, for example, the national icons are Swiss watches and banks. When I arrived at the airport in Vienna in February 2015, it was Sisi who welcomed me with her sweet smile and her impressive white robe covered with pearls and rubies. The other Austrian hero, little Mozart with his chocolate confections (*Mozartkugeln*), looks like a dwarf beside mighty Snow White. Sisi has become a myth that the nation identifies with, even more than her big and famous motherly predecessor Maria Theresa. In my hometown of Wieselburg in Lower Austria, I recently discovered a new mosaic showing Sisi with diamond stars in her hair. It was made

DOI: 10.4324/9781003609742-12

during a competition between the best Austrian tilers in 1998 to commemorate the hundredth anniversary of Sisi's death.

The figure of Austria's Empress Elisabeth echoes in the most prestigious musical theaters around the world, in the hearts of little girls and old country women, and even as a motif on a mosaic created by Austria's best tilers. When we look more closely at these representations of Sisi, what emerges is not only a historical figure but also one that evokes intense personal reactions. In conversations about her, I have encountered fascination, dismissal, criticism, pity, incomprehension, and curiosity, to name just a few of the reactions to her life story. Some know about her tragic death; many know about her anorexia-like behavior and her struggle with the expectations of being a royal personage and her longing for freedom. But the myth of Sisi seems to be deeper than any historical facts. It represents a European cultural complex of the first order.

Europe and Its Royalties

The importance of royal figures is certainly not easy to understand for Americans, even if they are familiar with the kings and queens of the German fairy tales written by the Brothers Grimm. On the old European continent, noble families were and still provide projection fields for private family dynamics and for archetypal values. During the centuries preceding World War I, each European country was a monarchy, and the king and/or the queen was the supreme authority, connecting in his or her person heaven and earth. The democratic movement that spread throughout Europe gradually brought to a close the traditional patriarchal order of the world that defined everything from the cosmos to political systems. The crucial break came with the French Revolution in 1789. When Louis XVI and his wife, Marie Antoinette (daughter of the Austrian Maria Theresa), were sent to the guillotine two years later in 1791, the patriarchal identity between the real king and the archetype of royalty suffered a fatal blow. Europe was upset and deeply shocked. Even Napoleon, the revolution's heir, tried to reestablish a monarchist system and crowned himself French emperor. In 1871, a second German Empire was established by Bismarck, and the Prussian king was crowned as Emperor Wilhelm I. The Habsburg monarchy of Austria and Hungary did not become part of the German Empire. The era of empires ended abruptly in 1918 when the Ottoman, the German, the Habsburgian, and the Russian empires all collapsed. Only in Great Britain and the northern European states were constitutional monarchies preserved. These monarchies seemed to contribute to the stability of those nations; the people loved their royals, even if they sometimes hated them. The British model of a shared representation of irrational (the king) and rational politics (the prime minister) seems to be a clever structure for managing a country. In France, the missing king is still an object of grief and nostalgia for some people (the Royalist party), and the heritage of the revolution of 1789 is often regarded with ambivalence. In Germany, Emperor Wilhelm II fled in 1918 to the Netherlands, leaving the empire without a head of state. The new Weimar democracy was not strong enough to cope with the longing for an absolute authority. With the Nazi Empire, the irrational drive broke through in a disastrous way. The Habsburg monarchy ended, and twenty-one years later Austria joined or was captured by the Third Reich.

In this chapter, we will look at Sisi's myth against the background of this history. Like Princess Diana in Great Britain, the Habsburg/Austrian Sisi plays a part in the collective symbolic drama around the *Archetype of the Royal*, the king and the queen who carry the Self of a Nation. Or still better, the royal person can be seen as the projected head of the Ego-Self axis that symbolizes everyone's inner "Royal family." One big difference between Great Britain and Austria is that the royal family in Austria has been banned since 1919. As long as some of the Habsburgs still made a claim to get their crown and title back, they were not even allowed to cross the border into Austria until recently. What happened to the more than 600 years of projected archetypal contents onto Austria's royals after the abrupt and categorical break with the Habsburgs? We can imagine that Sisi's popularity is still being nourished by those old patterns of historical projection that continue in the cultural unconscious to be active in each Austrian's collective psyche, especially as royalty, with all its potent meaning for the population, was radically banned and forbidden. The contents of those long-standing royal projections were abruptly cut off and could be neither integrated nor transformed in the psyche of the people. In that sense, Sisi could still be the carrier of those old projections.

Sisi's Real Life

When I think about Sisi, two scenes from her life come to mind.

The first is of the sixteen-year-old Bavarian princess arriving in Vienna on April 22, 1854. The journey from her home along the Danube River had taken two days, as she had been obliged to make many dutiful stops, presenting herself to the country that would crown her its queen. The king's bride-to-be entered Vienna in a resplendent carriage, accompanied by the boom of canons and the chimes of the church bells ringing out across the city in her honor. The eighteen-year-old King Franz Josef welcomed her, as did tens of thousands of adoring citizens who lined the streets hoping to catch a glimpse of their future queen. Amid the jubilation, the triumphal procession of clerks, military and political dignitaries, and representatives of foreign countries led Sisi to the Schönbrunn Palace. There, she received a diamond crown, among other bridal gifts, and was presented to her new royal court.

The wedding took place the following day. Eight horses pulled Elisabeth's carriage, leading the cortege. Once again, the public came out in support of the alliance, thousands crowding the decorated streets. Tremendous hope was projected onto the new queen. Only five years had passed since the young Franz Josef had quashed a revolution in his country and strengthened his absolute power. Messages from the public honoring Sisi's arrival testified to the fact that the people were looking to her to mediate between them and the king. In words reminiscent of Christian prayers appealing to the Virgin Mary, the mother of God, to intercede on behalf of the supplicant, Sisi was entreated to help unite a suffering people with

their king. Suppressed freedom of expression, unemployment, and hunger following bad harvests the previous year, and the threat of war in the Crimea – these were
the heavy burdens on the population of Vienna and the whole multinational state.

How would the unassuming Elisabeth, raised without any aristocratic pomp or
exposure to politics, live up to these expectations? A few months of preparation had
not given this sixteen year-old girl the resources to cope with such an overwhelming
responsibility. Almost overnight she became the nation's most important political
and social hope. Today, it seems surprising that a young woman such as Princess
Sisi could embody the hopes of a whole nation, but perhaps this simply shows the
reverence and the demigod-like status that people had extended to their rulers.
Inside the glass state carriage that moved through the cheering crowd, Sisi buckled
under the pressure and wept. Although she was in love with her husband-to-be and
desirous of marriage, her dearest wish was that he had been a "simple dressmaker"
and not the emperor.[1]

The second scene that comes to my mind is the one that marks the end of
Sisi's life, forty-four years later. A mile-long funeral procession moves slowly and
silently from the train station Westbahnhof toward the center of Vienna. Murdered
by an anarchist in Geneva a few days previously, the body of the empress had
been transported by special train to her hometown, arriving just before midnight,
September 15, 1898. The crowds lined the streets to pay their final respects as the
hearse transported her to the Hofburg, accompanied by the empire's whole morbid
neobaroque pomp.

Between these two scenes, Sisi lived her life. What kind of life was possible
for her?

From Abundance to Anorexia – the Suffering Heroine

In the aftermath of her death, the Austrian people again showed their support for the
empress by flocking to the streets of Vienna. Public perception of her had changed
dramatically, however, since the time of her coronation. Toward the end of her life,
Empress Sisi had become a veritable stranger to the Viennese people, a far cry from
the once exalted figure of hope and glory for the nation. Her prolonged and frequent
stays abroad coupled with her consistent refusal to participate in life at the royal
court meant that over time she had effectively disappeared from the public eye.

The start of this withdrawal had begun with the queen's intolerance for the conservative and stifling Habsburg court-life in Vienna. Her indignation at the imposi-
tion of this lifestyle on her fueled her sympathies for the Hungarian people who, at
the time, were fighting for a level of independence from Austria. At the beginning
of her reign, Elisabeth used her newfound power and influence over the king to
instigate political changes in favor of Hungarian independence. Indeed, the accord
between Austria and Hungary in 1867, in which the former Hungarian constitution
was reestablished and Hungary was granted its own government and capital, was a
fruit of Elisabeth's commitment to this cause. Sisi was crowned queen of Hungary
in 1867.

Soon after her marriage, however, Sisi's health began to suffer. Doctors spoke of lung disease, anemia, nervous symptoms, and dropsy. To the distress of everyone around her, she began to impose radical starvation diets upon herself, a practice she would have recourse to throughout the rest of her life. She was incredibly slim, 172 cm tall (5 ft, 6 in), and between 47 and 52 kilo (103 to 114 pounds); her waist was only 51 centimeters (20 inches)! Today her eating behavior would be seen as a tendency toward anorexia, although we cannot be sure exactly what Sisi was really suffering from as her symptoms clearly extended beyond this. Whatever her illness, it seems it was alleviated when she left Vienna.

Sisi had three children. Her mother-in-law demanded that the children stay in the palace for a rigid "royal" education. Sisi had to fight for her motherly rights to spend time with them. In 1857, she revolted, taking her two little daughters with her on a trip to Hungary. Unfortunately the girls became ill in Hungary, and little Sophie died from diarrhea at the age of two. From then on, Sisi gave up being a mother for her children. She began to travel obsessively throughout Europe; she did sports and became a passionate horse rider, often risking her life on fox hunts. In order to improve her health she spent most of her time abroad, staying many months in Madeira, Corfu, Hungary, and, during her last years, the French part of Switzerland. Due to her absence, the image of the formerly celebrated Queen faded almost entirely from Austria's public life. Officially, her absences were excused and understood as being due to ill-health and a subsequent need for convalescence. But knowing what we know about her today, it seems more likely that the empress had found a way to live a life that was bearable for her, moving undetected and anonymously in the world. Thus, Vienna forgot her empress. A few months before her death, Sisi turned sixty years old – a fact that almost went unnoticed by the Viennese press.

The Dawn of an Empire

It was not until her assassination on September 10, 1898, that Sisi dramatically reappeared in the spotlight. The twenty-five-year-old avowed anarchist, Luigi Lucheni, dealt a fatal stab to the queen's heart as she was boarding a boat on the quayside in Geneva. A wave of sympathy for the deceased monarch and public outrage at such a tragic and cold-blooded attack sent ripples of shock throughout the whole of Europe.

The Austrian press played a large part in Elisabeth's posthumous return to the public stage. For an unusually prolonged period after her death, the press focused their coverage on her, presenting her as a collective figure with whom the people could identify and as a symbol of the union between the nations of the Austro-Hungarian Empire. The background and the circumstances of her death were discussed in detail in articles and obituaries and slowly evolved into political rhetoric. Different groups appropriated the murder of the queen in order to support their own interests. Many of them focused on the question of an efficient fight against anarchy, calling on the European nations to work together to combat revolutionary groups. Conservative circles praised her as a saint, a benevolent Mother of Nations, even describing her as a martyr and a Mater Dolorosa.[2] From their perspective, her absence from court had been due to illness, her desire for privacy, and her grief over the suicide of her son Rudolf in 1889, after which she exclusively dressed in black and hid her face behind dense veils. More liberal newspapers exploited her sudden popularity to advance their own democratic convictions. They emphasized the empress's well-known anti-monarchist and anti-clerical attitudes. For example, Karl Kraus, the famous satirist and political commentator of the time, used her death to attack the monarchy and their preservation of an old feudal system that he believed was in need of change. He interpreted the decades of her retreat from public life as an escape from the established social order.[3]

One explanation for the endless discussions and heterogeneous opinions that surrounded Empress Elisabeth in the aftermath of her death could perhaps be attributed to her elusive character. Just as we are left with no trace of her physical image after the age of thirty (she refused to be photographed or portrayed to prevent any record of her aging), her character remains similarly undefined. What is clear is that she had an unusual and incomprehensible nature, bearing no relation to any preconceived notion of "empress," and, at the same time, it is evident that she exuded an inexplicable charm. These qualities invite many interpretations and render her an accommodating object for the personal and collective needs of projection.

After the catastrophic collapse of the old monarchies in 1918, and after the European disaster of World War II, Sisi's life and death might appear as an individual's anticipation of the tragic and confused ending of the old European world. Her extended and expensive travels throughout her empire and to other countries look like the "imperialistic" behavior of a privileged individual. The narcissistic addiction to her own beauty looks like a vain and hopeless unconscious attempt to conserve something of the old splendor of her empire. She must have felt that she was living in a prison, not only the prison of the court in Vienna that she hated so much but also the prison of a dying world she finally could not escape. The growing nationalism and emancipation of nations from patristic empires ultimately led to the collapse of what had been a universal pattern until then – an empire of states, the idea of which dated back to the notion of the Holy Roman Empire of the German Nation, which now also included other nations joined with the idea of Habsburg, a family of nations in Central Europe (*Pannonia*) under the pious leadership of a king whose rights were divinely ordained.[4] Sixteen years after Sisi's murder, a human earthquake shook the world in the form of the first global war, the emergence of a new Europe of democracies, militant nationalism, and genocides. Sisi's quest was already overshadowed by the twilight of gods.

Dream of a Better World

I want to touch briefly on some of the different representations of Elisabeth that mirror some of the major projections onto her. First, there is the picture of the naïve and youthful Elisabeth that emerges from the successful 1950s film trilogy, *Sissi*.

These films were produced at a time when the Austrian Second Republic was look-ing for a period in history with which their people could identify and use as a basis for forming a new national identity. *Sissi*, as Empress Elisabeth was widely known after the film was produced, was presented in such a personal and comprehensible way that the appropriation of her pet name seemed perfectly natural. The story is a simple romantic tale; people and events complicate her life, but these difficul-ties are happily resolved. Scenes were set in the Bavarian and Austrian country-side, presenting an idealized picture of the homeland. Interestingly, the story ends before Elisabeth starts to live independently, effectively whitewashing the more problematic events that occurred during her later years. This simplistic and roman-tic depiction, however, provided a useful historical counterweight to the first half of the twentieth century, which proved so difficult to integrate into Austria's image of itself. Indeed, these films were often understood as historical documentaries, especially by younger audiences whose educational experience, during the Hitler period, had been restricted to a much earlier period of German history. It was the time of whitewashing Austria from its Nazi history. Reaching back to an ideal of an imperial homeland gave Austrians a new and positive identity, untarnished by more recent and catastrophic events.

It was only during the 1980s that a contradictory portrayal of Empress Elisa-beth began to emerge, initiated by Brigitte Hamann's biography.[5] Since then, the deconstruction of the omnipresent stereotype of Sisi and the replacement of it with a historically grounded presentation of her "as she really was" is a recurring theme to be found in book editorials and exhibition catalogs. Now other aspects of her personality predominate, such as her extreme intelligence and her pioneering spirit. Throughout her life Sisi studied languages, and she spoke fluent Hungarian, Greek, French, and English. She was also an expert on Heinrich Heine's poetry and is reported to have had a great knowledge of art. Her understanding of politics is also well-documented, as is her clearly expressed sympathy for the democratic form of government (an unthinkable political view for a monarch, especially at the time). Another common theme that appears in more recent writing on the empress is her search for individual realization, which in contrast to previous images of her refutes the idea of her as a victim, running away from an overpowering force. This newer view presents her instead as a self-determining woman who was able to escape the constraints of court life and to take charge of her life according to her ambitions for freedom.

The aforementioned musical *Elisabeth* was born out of this movement of rewrit-ing the historical portrait of her character. The story is woven around a personality trait that has drawn quite a bit of interest from more recent biographers and which is evident in a book of Elisabeth's own poetry, published in 1984: namely, her fascination with death. In the musical, Elisabeth's real lover is the figure of Death. The play starts with a dance of Death, and as the story unfolds, Death reveals himself as her beloved friend from early childhood days. It is under his orders that Lucheni finally kills her on September 10, 1898. Elisabeth's life is presented as an inner conflict between a commitment to life and a greater pull toward Death. This interpretation undoubtedly resonates with the ancient Viennese pious and, at the same time, disrespectful familiarity with death.[6] The destiny of the empress is thus assimilated into a collective tendency of the Viennese character toward a casual, sometimes morbid, relationship with death. And this fits with the fate of Austria itself with its loss of empire, leaving Vienna today as a splendid city with imperial architecture in a very small country.

And What About My Image of Sisi?

Out of the multiple revelations about Empress Sisi's story and character, what I find most intriguing is the lengths she went to in order to liberate herself and real-ize her dreams. Having decided to leave Vienna and the royal court for long periods of the year, Elisabeth cut herself off from her husband and children. It was as if she had had enough of any responsibility to anything or anyone, even to those she loved. Her husband Franz Josef built her a castle in the Vienna Lainzer Tiergarten in an attempt to settle her closer to him, but she rarely used it. To ease her evasion of marital duties, Elisabeth found a mistress for him, Katharina Schratt. It was a match so well chosen that the liaison lasted beyond Sisi's own lifetime.

During her time in Vienna, Elisabeth tried to be an attentive mother, especially to her youngest daughter, Valérie. Indeed, it could be argued that Sisi's attachment to her bordered on the obsessive. When she left Vienna, however, the child was raised by court personnel, and Sisi made no efforts to maintain their relationship. It was as if her daughter had ceased to exist. Perhaps it could be argued that even her most personal relationships were essentially egocentric.

With so little to tether her, Sisi began to blend the unreal with the real, stepping sometimes into an imagined fairyland. She fantasized about herself as the charac-ter of Titania, Shakespeare's fairy queen from *A Midsummer Night's Dream*; she pictured her husband in the role of the donkey, Puck. This imagined world some-times felt more real to her than the tangible earthly one. She also experimented with outlandish religious beliefs. Having rejected Catholicism (being the religion of the Court, it was associated with everything she despised), Elisabeth dabbled in Spiritism and occult practices. She communicated with the dead. Her favorite poet Heinrich Heine became her spiritual lover from beyond the grave, and she spoke to her cousin Ludwig II of Bavaria after his death.

One can only be impressed by the inner strength Elisabeth must have possessed that allowed her to override and to free herself from the initial projections put upon her as the savior of the nation and to resist the centuries-old standards of courtly behavior. She truly achieved her goal of living as a person who was not subjected to any human law or obligation, but to what end?

Elisabeth had the power to gratify her most audacious desires. She built castles, learned languages, and traveled in order to forget Vienna. She wrote poetry. She was narcissistically obsessed with her body, training day and night to preserve its legendary beauty and regularly sleeping with a piece of raw calf meat across her breast to maintain the beauty of her décolletage.[7] She had no obligations to anyone or anything. Yet in spite of all this, one can sense the all-pervading presence of a great void within her. Her poetry clearly expresses this experience; she describes herself floundering in a melancholic, bored, meaningless, and world-weary mood.[8]

To my mind the freedom she enjoyed in her later years was not enough to create new and meaningful personal values. She stuck to an attitude of escaping and refusing, of passive opposition. For example, after the devastating battles that her husband fought (Solferino, Königgrätz, and so on), she became a declared opponent of war. Her pacifism developed soon after her marriage when she was asked to visit the wounded soldiers in order to strengthen the prestige of the imperial family. Sisi was deeply shocked at the suffering she witnessed. Her critical opinion toward the military was well-known in Vienna, but when Bertha von Suttner, a leading figure in the pacifist movement, asked her to support her novel *Die Waffennieder* (*Lay Down Your Arms*) through a sign of approval, she offered no support. Her liberated ideas lacked any committed action.

It seemed as if Elisabeth had stepped out of the Old but could not manifest the New. Thus she remained stuck in an intermediate zone, out of touch with reality, involved in nebulous spiritual relationships, seeking the fulfillment of eccentric wishes, more and more rejecting the commitments and responsibilities of real life, including her relationship with her three children. She retreated into her private sphere, absorbed in individual pleasure, dominated by weariness and dissatisfaction. Perhaps her life was a first and necessary step of disidentification from the Old, but she was unable to continue this process with more constructive steps toward individuation. She was caught in the cultural complex.

"The Old dies, but the New can't be born."[9] This famous diagnosis made by the Italian communist Antonio Gramsci about his time also describes the personal and collective complexes from which Sisi suffered – and finally died: she was killed by an anarchist. Anarchism was a pan-European movement at the dawn of the expected international socialist revolution. The "New" was not yet ready to be born; there was still no alternative hegemonial culture (as Gramsci would say) to replace the rotten "Old" system. All facets of Sisi's biography show the dilemma of being caught in unsolvable conflicts: be it as a mother who lost her children, be it as a political player in a system she hated. Sisi was both a leading figure and powerless at the same time; longing for escape, many women could project their situation onto her. And it touches the Austrian self-esteem: to have a grandiose international past with Vienna as the crown of an empire but actually to be a small European country among others on a quest for its identity.

Therefore, in spite of the conflicting interpretations that surround Sisi and her story, she remains accessible to us as a human being. Generations call her by her pet name. A broad public has the impression of being familiar with her life down to its intimate details. If her life seems like a myth, this is not only due to historical idealization or touristic promotion but also because she chose to live (and to die) with a mythical pathos, behind which one senses a familiar suffering and search for happiness. Perhaps this is one of the reasons why Sisi continues to touch us. She was an empress, and she was one of us.

Notes

1 B. Hamann, *Elisabeth. Kaiserin wider Willen* (München: Piper, 2002), p. 70.
2 "Wiener Abendpost, 10.9.1898," in E. Knappitsch (ed.), *(Nach-)Blicke auf die Kaiserin. Zur Konstruktion von "Sisi" – Bildern in der Wiener Presse um 1900* (Graz: Leykam, 2012), p. 33.
3 "Wiener Abendpost, 10.9.1898," p. 37ff.
4 Gerhard Burda, "Eine letzte Rede über Österreich," in *Seelenpolitik. Über die Seele und andere Selbst-Differenzen* (Wien: Passagen Verlag S, 2009), p. 79ff.
5 Hamann, *Elisabeth. Kaiserin wider Willen.*
6 C. Magris, *Donau. Biographie eines Flusses* (München: dtv, 2007).
7 M. Lindinger, "Mein Herz ist aus Stein," in *Die dunkle Seite der Kaiserin Elisabeth* (Wien: Almathea Signum, 2013).
8 B. Hamann (Hg.), *Kaiserin Elisabeth. Das poetische Tagebuch* (Wien: Österreichische Akademie der Wissenschaften, 1997).
9 Antonio Gramsci, *Gefängnishefte (1929)*, eds. Herausgegeben von Klaus Bochmann und Wolfgang Haug (Hamburg: Argument Verlag, 2012), Heft 3 §§ 34, 354.

Italy

The "Small Mother Complex" and the Royal Feminine

Marta Tibaldi

> We don't really know who woman is. She remains in that precise place within man where darkness begins. Talking about women means talking about the darkest part of ourselves, the undeveloped part, the true mystery within. . . . A man can't become whole or free until he has set woman free – his woman. It's his responsibility, not hers. He can't be complete, truly alive until he makes her his sexual companion, and not a slave of libidinous acts or a saint with a halo.
>
> – Federico Fellini

In this chapter, I reflect on some aspects of the cultural imagery of femininity in Italy, beginning with my personal experience and then approaching the topic in a more objective way. I am now sixty years old, and one of the advantages of my age is to have lived long enough to have a substantial historical memory. In fact, I came of age at a crucial time in the cultural evolution of Italy and the Western world. The revolution of the 1968 student movement ushered in a profound shift in gender roles and sexuality among men and women.

But let's begin this story with an actual recent event. A young patient told me that a twenty-four-year-old friend of hers had decided to remain a virgin until her wedding. The girl is from a Catholic family, and knowing the family, this news did not surprise me. It did give me pause to reflect on the image of femininity that probably shapes this girl's mind. It is an image that is far from the idea of femininity that has prevailed in Italy for the past twenty years – the image of the *bunga-bunga* girl.[1]

Unlike the feminine image associated with men's *bunga-bunga* fantasies, the girl who wants to remain a virgin until her wedding recalls the prevailing feminine image in Italy before the so-called 1968 Revolution. Before the revolution, I remember sitting in a church pew with uncrossed legs. I had been taught that sitting with crossed legs would have been a sign of indecency – unseemly behavior for a well-mannered girl. Girls were supposed to be modest, respectful, and as asexual in appearance and manner as possible. Girls were trained to answer to men's needs and requests, without attention to their own individual concerns. They were to be defined and enlightened by men, as the moon reflects the light from the

DOI: 10.4324/9781003609742-13

sun. Men's more unrestrained sexual fantasies toward women could find expression only with prostitutes in the protected spaces of brothels. There was not room for women's more unrestrained sexual fantasies toward men.

I remember my mother telling me that I was expected to remain a virgin until my marriage because "offering my virginity to my husband would be the greatest gift I could make to him" (*sic*). After so many years, looking at this statement now, I see how my mother's position was based on the male order of things and on the Catholic Church's image of women. It is unlikely that she felt critical of her era's gender/sexual rules, whose main purpose was to confirm men's power and to protect their psychic fragility with regard to the feminine. How satisfying it felt when I decided to lose my virginity to a tampon! My future husband had been replaced by a *Tampax*! Wow. That was my first personal feminine revolutionary act. I had only a vague awareness of its meaning, but it was my first act of rebellion against the male order and against the prevailing Italian cultural complex of the feminine at the time.

If today, more than fifty years after the 1968 Revolution, a young girl decides to remain a virgin until her wedding, it means an aspect of that complex remains alive and well in the Italian collective psyche, or at least in that part of the Italian psyche in which a Catholic point of view still prevails. In those under the influence of the Catholic Church, the highest representation of the feminine remains the image of the Madonna, the eternal virgin and mother who gave birth to her progeny without sexual intercourse.

In the city of Rome, which is rich with wonderful churches and sublime sacred paintings, the image of *Maria*, the Madonna, is familiar and widespread. When something unexpected and fearful happens to a Roman, they exclaim: "*Madonna mia!*" ("My Madonna!") or "*Mamma mia!*" ("My mom!") – as if to say that the images of the Madonna and mom are identical. Italians turn to "Mom Madonna" when they are afraid and in danger.[2] But when they are angry, they commonly and rudely exclaim, "*Porca puttana*" ("Slut whore"). This suggests the Italian cultural complex of the feminine equates women's sexuality with anger and aggression, whereas the asexual and reassuring image of the Virgin is associated with fear and weakness. Freud noted this in his formulation of the Madonna-Whore complex as early as 1912.[3]

The fact that before the 1968 sexual revolution most women were restricted to the role of virgin-mother is clearly indicated by the rules that shaped sexual behavior between husband and wife generations ago. For example, in the 1920s, young virgins prepared their *trousseaux*, sewing a special nightdress with an embroidered hole near the genitals, around which was written: "I do not do it [making love] for my pleasure, but to give a son to God." The new wife was not even expected to undress herself in front of her husband, much less take any pleasure or initiative in the sexual act, which was to be passively endured. A woman was to experience sexual intercourse as a duty of marriage above all. The law even stated that a woman could not refuse her husband's sexual requests. Sex for a woman was exclusively for the purpose of creating children and giving men pleasure.

In her book *Ave, Mary*, Michela Murgia notes that

> in *De bono coniugali* Saint Augustine clearly specified that the bride should
> be available to satisfy male lust, not for her pleasure, but only to prevent the
> husband from committing adultery with the wife of another, or from going [to]
> prostitutes, events that from the moral viewpoint appeared to the African bishop
> much worse of a coupling allowed by the spouse as *remedium concupiscentiae*,
> a remedy to the lust of her husband.[4]

Another typical Italian custom related to the wedding and a girl's transition from
being a virgin to a married woman was the tradition of hanging the wedding night's
blood-stained sheet from the window the next morning. This served the dual purpose of proving that the bride had been a virgin and that the husband had demonstrated his virility. Of course, there are funny stories of sheets being stained with
animal blood to testify to a man's sexual power in those cases where his impotence
did not allow him to consummate the marriage. In such cases, the girl was asked to
remain a virgin, but the man had to show that he was sexually powerful.

Men were expected to act out their sexual fantasies in so-called houses of pleasure or closed houses (*bordelli* in Italian), where "easy women" would do what
wives would never dream of doing. When did the collective sexual imagery of the
feminine previously linked to prostitutes become the new sexual standard that men
expected from women? How did the image of the Virgin Mary that was equated
with "mom" get replaced by the expectation that wives would become the sexual
objects of men's desires freed from the "closed houses"? Recently, a patient of mine
told me her husband asked her to perform oral and anal sex, which she refused. He
got very angry with her. The patient had grown up according to religious principles,
and her wedding was conducted in a traditional way. Her husband's sexual requests
were in direct conflict with the feminine image of her upbringing. Again, we can
ask when did the image of the wife/mother as virgin transform itself in the collective male imagination into wife as pleasure-giving sexual object liberated from the
"closed houses"?

******

Progressing forward from the 1960s, the 1980s saw the advent of Berlusconi's
commercial television and the birth of a different collective image of femininity,
the *bunga-bunga girls*, who were a far cry from the asexual virgin.

Commercial television stressed women's sexuality in its marketing appeal to
the public. The new images of young, sexy, and desirable girls were embodied in
the ranks of half-naked dancing girls featured in Berlusconi's variety shows. They
became the model for younger generations of girls and boys.

Television taught girls that being sexy was essential. They began to imitate the
new sexualized model of femininity. They learned to pose as only prostitutes had in
the past. Now, after twenty years of this kind of imagery, the streets of every Italian

city are filled with streams of young girls, looking as though they just jumped out of the television. The more provocative, the better. The more sexual, the better. The more like prostitutes, the better.

Lorella Zanardo, the author of the video and book *Il corpo delle donne* (*Women's Body*), presents a careful analysis of this change in the Italian cultural complex of femininity.[5] Zanardo describes the new reality of the feminine image in Italy that began in Berlusconi's era: "plastic bodies," all equal in shape and appearance, all responding to men's sexual fantasies. "The difference from before the advent of commercial television," writes Zanardo, "is this: you do not need to know how to do anything, it is enough . . . to be sexually provocative always, because the only form of entertainment is the sexual attraction."[6]

The implicit belief that seems to underline this new Italian collective image of femininity can be stated as this: "My sexy body is my weapon. As far as I embody men's sexual desire I am a precious good to be sold at the best price and to the highest bidder."[7] This movement suggests an ongoing oscillation in the cultural imagery of femininity between the Madonna-Whore poles. It is worth noting that the word "whore" is no longer used in Italy. They are now called "escorts" and function as high-class prostitutes that, unlike in the past, are light years away from those poor women forced to sell their bodies – as Pasolini portrayed them so vividly in his movie *Accattone*.[8] Nowadays they are seen as young girls who use their bodies to gain power over men and to gain advantages from them as long as they are young and comely.

But a new element has entered the mixture of the old collective complex of Madonna-Whore. Men who thought they would establish ultimate power over women by potentially turning all of them into free prostitutes at their disposal have discovered that their game is getting out of hand. They now risk getting trapped. There are gray zones that inextricably create relationships linked by destructive power. In her book *3096 Giorni*, Natasha Kampusch describes the ordeal of a ten-year-old-girl who was kidnapped in 1998 and held captive for eight years by a paranoid who forced her to act out his unconscious and perverted fantasies.[9] The story reveals indisputably that "the executioner is also the prisoner of his script." Men who imagine having complete power over women, shaping them according to their sexual desires, are now facing something quite unexpected: women are using their sexual body as an instrument of power against men.

This new collective reality is bringing about a slow and interesting shift in the Italian collective cultural complex: sexy girls are not only represented as desirable objects but are also being shown with scorn and humiliation.[10] Television programs and media advertising have begun to show "a hybrid figure of woman: erotic and available to the male, as for centuries, but often represented with an aggressive look and attitude, a slave-mistress."[11]

Men's collective difficulty and ambivalence toward this new image of women is well proven by a growing body of evidence from different sources. There is an increase in official misogynistic positions, such as the paradigmatic statement in 2012 by Don Piero Corsi, a priest of San Lerici, in which he accused women of causing the violence against them.[12] Even more disturbing, murders of women have been soaring, with femicide reaching epidemic proportions. In this sense, the cultural complex of Madonna-Whore seems to have reached a critical stage: are we witnessing the collapse of a male narrative that has lasted for centuries in the Italian cultural complex of femininity?

******

The 1968 Revolution was a turning point. In 1968, women and men enjoyed the sexual revolution for a while. They experienced their sexuality as a place of freedom, a new land to be discovered beyond the collective images that had previously shaped gender roles. This time of relatively innocent discovery lasted a short while – until a shadow of the sexual revolution emerged. What was initially experienced as a time of joy soon turned into one of unhappiness as well. Men quickly reverted to old habits, discovering that they could "fuck" a woman without buying her dinner. They could expect a woman "to put out" as if she were a prostitute but without spending any money. What a conquest!

And women? On one hand, some of them started organizing movements to raise self-awareness that, in time, turned into political action. On the other hand, many women entered a time of conflicting experiences that led both to greater compliance with men's requests and to a greater dependence on men.[13]

The women's movements in Italy began to coalesce, however, strongly expressing the desire to overcome the Madonna-Whore complex. A political slogan emerged over time: "Neither Madonna, nor whore, only woman." "Only woman": What did this mean in the early 1970s, and what does it mean today after so many years of women's movements? As women, are we really able to shape a "free" image of ourselves? Or have we, as Zanardo speculates, "internalized the male model so long and so deeply, that we are no longer able to recognize what we really want and what makes us happy"?[14] In summarizing the history of the feminist movement in Italy from the 1970s onward, Becalli puts it as follows:

Modern Italian feminism established itself in the early 1970s, expanding with remarkable strength and radicalism from its middle-class base to become a popular mobilization with an extensive network of activists throughout the organized labor movement. By the end of the decade, however, feminism was in decline; and the beginning of the 1980s saw it virtually disappear as a movement. It lost its visibility in political struggles and grew ever more fragmented and out of touch, as feminist activists increasingly committed their energies to private projects and experiences, whether of an individual or communal nature. Thus it was that the "new" feminist movement, following the example of other "new social movements" of the 1970s, evolved into just another form of lifestyle politics. At this time many attempted to account for the decline of these movements that had once aroused such optimism and political expectation, and in particular to question whether they had in fact disappeared or merely entered a period of inactivity.[15]

A new form of women's movement appeared on the social scene in 2010, especially through the action of *Se non ora, quando?* (If not now, when?). A group of women who wanted "to react to the degrading model flaunted by one of the highest positions in the State, detrimental to the dignity of women and institutions," initiated a season of civil awakening.[16] *Se non ora, quando?* developed a practical approach to gender problems, focusing, for example, on an equal division of quotas in politics (*pink quotas*, the compulsory number of women in politics). In 2012, the Italian Parliament approved the law that requires the boards of directors of companies quoted on the stock exchange and public companies to be comprised of one-fifth women. In 2015, the "pink quotas" rose to one-third.

As a depth psychologist, I was invited to reflect on the new women's movement in September 2012 at a Democratic Party meeting in Udine. I participated in a round table entitled "Women, ready!" in which I suggested a collective reflection on what psychology could add practically to the benefit of women's political engagement. I delivered a paper, *"Esercizi di democrazia psichica"* ("Exercises of Psychic Democracy"), in which I suggested we consider the inequality between women and men from the viewpoint of its negative emotional impact, even relapse, on women's view of themselves, on their personal and institutional relationships, and even more generally, on men and women to their common detriment.[17]

I proposed that we develop a more conscious synergy between education policy and emotional literacy that focuses our attention on the role that emotions and feelings play in our being women (and men) and our being women (and men) administrators. I advocated developing an "emotional economy" of women (and men) in politics that emphasizes taking responsibility for the emotional capital, or richness, of women (and men) administrators. Since we know that emotions are infectious, affecting our bodies and minds, as well as the collective, managing the emotional dimension within politics and in the social relations between men and women should be considered a public health issue.[18] We should limit as much as possible the contagion of destructive power relationships between men and women, developing protective strategies that promote the mental health of individuals and the community by increasing awareness of the cultural complex that affects gender identities and the relationships between men and women. This would be the first level of treatment for the cultural complex of femininity that "infects" the psyche of our population.[19]

******

I believe that as depth psychologists we have a responsibility to help citizens, and this is the focus of the fourth section of this chapter. As a woman and a depth psychologist, how can I contribute to the improvement of our personal and cultural consciousness of the Italian cultural complex of femininity and to the transformation of the relationships between women and men?

I suggest approaching the cultural complex by looking at it from the dual perspective of the personal and impersonal images that give shape to it, focusing on them as narratives of the complex itself. We could learn from observing the

unconscious stories of the complex as they are represented through dreams, spontaneous images, and active imaginations. How might these stories influence our
everyday lives as women and men in our reciprocal relationships? In this regard,
I briefly recall the dream of a lady who had a negative experience of men. She
was stuck in that experience and could not find any positive emotional indication for a transformation of her complex of masculinity. She was scared and mis-
trusting of men but also vacillated between a widespread devaluation and a risky
idealization of the male principle. In real life, she was unable to access positive
feelings toward men, making the possibility of a positive transformation of the
complex unlikely. A dream let her experience the complex in an unexpected way,
offering her a starting point to reflect on men and masculinity from a new and
never-before-experienced body-mind awareness:

> *I am in a car with an unknown man, who is driving; this man makes me feel
> calm and secure. The man takes me in a house where there are a lot of people, a
> vivacious and pleasant milieu; there is also another man; I speak with him with
> great serenity.*
>
> *Awakening, I notice that my feelings in the dream are very different from
> what I experience normally in my everyday life toward men.*

It is easy enough to say that the male-dominated culture devalues the feminine principle, leading to an imbalance in the feminine-masculine polarities both
in women and men in our personal and collective lives.[20] I think Italians are in a
different place psychologically than when Ernst Bernhard wrote in "The Task Confronting Analytical Psychology in Italy":[21]

> The mystery of the Italian psyche, with its light and shadow problems, is the
> recognition that in Italy the Mediterranean Great Mother rules, who, in spite of
> the many tides of culture that have swept over her throughout the ages, has still
> lost nothing of her power and influence. She is the archetypal precondition that
> comes to life in every individual Italian woman whenever her maternal quality
> is evoked.[22]

Federico Fellini, who was Bernhard's patient, added to Bernhard's notion when he
wrote about Rome in his book *Fare un film (Making a Movie)*[23]:

> Rome is a mother, and is the ideal mother, because indifferent. She is a mother
> who has too many children, and therefore cannot devote herself to you; she does
> not ask for anything; she does not expect anything. . . . She is a city of listless,
> skeptical and rude children, even a little deformed, mentally, because preventing
> the growth is unnatural.[24]

But in response to Bernhard's formulation, my questions today include these:
Are we still facing a collective Italian "Great Mother Complex," or, as I prefer to

say, are we experiencing a collective Italian "small mother complex"? Is it really the Mediterranean Great Mother as "the archetypal precondition that comes to life in every individual Italian woman," or rather is the contemporary "precondition that comes to life in every individual Italian woman" a devalued image of femininity? Are we confronting in contemporary society images of "small men" and "small women" – "small masculine" and "small feminine" – in both genders to the detriment of the individual and the collective?

Looking at the Italian complex from this perspective, I discover, for example, that one of woman's enemies is not only the "real" man outside her but also the masculine psychic image inside herself as a result of the internalization of the current male model.

> We have internalized the male model, or rather, the alleged male model. The colonization of our imagination has meant not knowing how to distinguish our deepest desire, and today we look at each other as we think we would be seen by a man.[25]

How many dreams of thieves, perpetrators, rapists, and so on do we see in our women patients, without asking ourselves *where do those presences act in our own personality*?

On the male unconscious side, things do not seem to be going any better. If we consider the inner feminine principle acting inside them, we discover that too often it is completely unrecognized. Men, too, are trapped in the male model, although in a different way: if women are supposed to be either "Madonna" or "whore," men can be only "macho" or "fag."

The following dream is an example:

> *A male patient dreams that he is in his parents' house at the seaside. He is in bed with his girlfriend. His parents enter the room with some people who want to rent it for the summer without asking the patient for permission. The patient is very irritated. He notices that his face is turning into that of a red-haired girl. The girl is very assertive, and she knows exactly how to behave with his parents. Noting his change in appearance, the patient wonders if he is becoming a fag.*

In working on the dream, he discovers that the red-haired girl gives shape to an assertive way to face and overcome difficult situations in which the patient would normally have behaved in a very ineffective and self-destructive way.

Considering the poor narratives that shape Italian women's and men's relationships that are trapped in the complex, it is clear that both women and men need other stories to survive. At a time in which we are not able to find new collective and cultural images to give shape to our deep needs as women and men, spontaneous unconscious imagery and its autonomous narratives represent a priceless resource. If we can become aware of the personal and cultural narratives inside ourselves, we can enter them and become active narrators of different stories.[26] For instance, the highest symbol of femininity is the archetypal image of the queen, and of masculinity, it is the king. I am not referring to intellectual notions of queens and kings, but to embodied and living images: "word-things, word-images, word-gestures," as Hillman describes them in *Alchemical Psychology*.[27]

To move from these theoretical speculations to actual experience, I will now recount the story of *The Montalcino's Princess*, a spontaneous narrative that came to me many years ago between wakefulness and sleep. At that time, I had just met a seductive and manipulative man, and *The Montalcino's Princess* was my unconscious response to this meeting: a deep warning that I took to heart. Over time it has become a point of reference for me by which to assess the dynamics of the Italian cultural complex of femininity.

Here is the story:

Once upon a time there was a princess who was about to be proclaimed queen. She lived in a beautiful kingdom, full of light and rich with wonderful wines. The princess would pass her days reflecting on the project that she would carry out for her kingdom. One day, after her usual walk through the town, she left the city, wanting to see the surrounding kingdom.

She passed through the city gates, looked around, and walked for a while until she reached a small wood near which an unknown man sat on the grass. His features were noble and handsome, though his clothes were ragged and his face was tired.

Her heart jumped in her chest. "Good morning foreigner," said the princess. "I do not know who you are, but from your appearance I see that you are tired, perhaps because of voyages and battles I do not know. Please enter the town with me, wash yourself, put on perfume and wear new clothes. I will wait for you in the banquet hall where we will eat a meal of friendship."

The foreigner gave the princess a perplexed look. Her invitation was sweet, and the princess was beautiful:

"It is too much for me to believe that she wants to share a meal of friendship with me," he thought doubtfully. Then they entered the town. The princess turned right, in the direction of her rooms, and the beggar turned left.

After a short time, they found themselves in the banquet hall where a rich table had been prepared, full of excellent and rare food.

"Sit down my Lord and take freely what the royal table offers to you. Your presence is sacred and sacred is my duty of hospitality," said the princess.

The unknown prince – for, in fact, the beggar was a prince under a wicked spell – could not hear the princess' words because of the spell that imprisoned his heart. Suddenly overwhelmed by an unexpected violent impulse, he destroyed the gold and silver plate on which the food lay, throwing it on the ground.

The princess looked at him and remained silent. But after a while she said: "Foreigner, I see that your heart betrays you. I offered you hospitality and now you offend this table with your anger. Do not let my guards drive you out of the town, shutting the city gates behind you. Instead, go away by yourself and leave the hall of friendship that your anger desecrates."

"But because I can see that a part of your heart is against you, let me offer you a present. Take this golden mirror, it is magic. Although at the moment it seems to reflect nothing, if you find the image that it has hidden inside it, you will be led on the road of destiny. Go, then, and look for the image. And I solemnly swear that if the image brings you back here, I will be your bride, and you will become the king of the realm. Go then and let this be my promise of love.[28]

If I wanted us to remain on a purely analytical level, we could work out this narrative in different ways, according to our various clinical or theoretical orientations. But my purpose in telling this story is to offer it as an example of how the personal and Italian cultural complex takes shape within us. It is a story that testifies to our need to overcome the imbalance between the male and female polarities that live inside us and in the culture that surrounds us. It is a story that aims toward totality or wholeness. It presents the possibility of bringing the unconscious forward by using imaginal techniques and then taking an ethical stand toward the story.[29] The narrative continues:

The princess came back to her rooms and reflected on what had happened. She was aware she had done all she could for the prince-beggar:

"I cannot undo the spell for you, prince-beggar," she said to herself. "Your task is to prove that you are a king and you deserve the kingdom. I will rule the kingdom with the pure image of the king in mind. The wisdom of the heart suggests to me the words to say: "I am a queen. Are you a king?"

When the words "I am a queen. Are you a king?" came to mind, I knew intuitively that they were my own deep way to answer the Italian complex of femininity. In fact, they summed up my personal, cultural, analytical, and professional confrontation with the complex and offered a simple and effective way to challenge it. Over time I have offered these words to my patients for their consideration. It has had a real effect on their awareness of the complex. Say these words out loud, and perhaps you will experience them directly.

******

I conclude this journey into the Italian cultural complex of femininity with the last words from my tale of *Montalcino's Princess*. These words summarize my *circumambulation* of the cultural complex, inviting it to move from a devalued image of femininity to that of the royal feminine.[30] As the myth of Europe's founding says, Europa, the beautiful princess from Asia, became a queen.

We know in our culture how much the relationships between men and women, between masculine and feminine, are marked strongly both by the dynamics of

*destructive power and by overwhelming idealizations. In such a culture, it is
a great risk that the reciprocal suspicions between women and men enforce a
vicious circle that makes women sterile in their capacity to love and men impo-
tent in their capacity to be fertile in the symbolic sense.*

*We recognize how much our souls and ours bodies suffer deeply the lack of a
propitious union between male and female, between human and divine, between
men and women. . . . We know that only the coming together of the masculine
with the feminine and the respect for mutual creativity, both physical and psychic, makes a human being the conscious author of reciprocal well-being.*[31]

*In the third millennium we need gestures and words of soul that tell, with pas-
sion and enjoyment, stories of love and friendship of men and women and our
common will to share creatively the pleasure of love.*[32]

I am a queen. Are you a king?

Notes

1 In Italy, the expression *bunga-bunga* girls refers to those young sexy girls who attended
   the "elegant dinners" held by ex–Prime Minister Berlusconi and who enacted the sexual
   fantasies of the participants.
2 "Mom Madonna" is the title of a song by Tonino Zurlo, a storyteller and folksinger from
   Puglia, who gives words and music to the popular Southern-Italian sensibility. "Mamma
   Madonna," *Jata Viende*, Circolo Gianni Bosio, Manifesto CD, 2003.
3 Sigmund Freud, "A Special Type of Choice of Object Made by Men (1910)," in *The
   Standard Edition of the Complete Psychological Works of Sigmund Freud*, Vol. 11 (London: Hogarth Press, 1957), pp. 165–175. Sigmund Freud, "On the Universal Tendency
   of Debasement in the Sphere of Love" (1912d), pp. 179–190.
4 Michela Murgia, *Ave, Mary. E la Chiesa inventò la donna* (Torino: Einaudi, 2011),
   p. 77.
5 Lorella Zanardo, *Il corpo delle donne* (Milano: Feltrinelli, 2010).
6 Zanardo, *Il corpo delle donne*, p. 25.
7 According to the anthropologist Amalia Signorelli, "Berlusconi has given to the old
   Italian machismo and prostitution a post-modern style, shifting it from the boast of
   achievements to the number of performances." From an interview given during the TV
   program *Ballarò*, Rai 2, aired May 7, 2012.
8 *Accattone* (1961) is the first movie by Pier Paolo Pasolini that he filmed in the Roman
   suburbs. It is the story of "Accattone" ("Beggar"), nicknamed Vittorio, a boy maintained
   by the prostitute Maddalena. Accattone meets Stella, and although he falls in love with
   her, he tries to prostitute her as well. Accattone will die tragically after an attempt to live
   in an honest way. Pier Paolo Pasolini, *Accattone*, directed by Pier Paolo Pasolini, 1961
   (Arco Film, Cine del Duca).
9 Natasha Kampusch, *3096 giorni* (Milano: Bompiani, 2011).
10 On May 7, 2012, in the TV show *Scherzi a parte*, the showgirl Nina Moric was hung
   "for a joke" on a hook and marked on her buttock as being a ham. Fatma Ruffina,
   Scherzi a parte, aired May 7, 2012 (Director, Massimo Fusi).
11 Zanardo, *Il corpo delle donne*, p. 35.
12 On Christmas 2012, Don Piero Corsi, a priest in the parish of Lerici (*La Spezia*), posted
   a leaflet on the door of the church, in which he accused women of causing male violence. He wrote, among other things: "Women and femicide. Women should ask themselves: how many times do they cause it?"

13 In 1985, Robin Norwood wrote *Women Who Love Too Much*: "A book written for women who are drawn to emotionally unavailable men and then become entrenched in trying to heal them and mold them into suitable partners. . . . According to Norwood, women who found themselves abused, neglected, or with too much responsibility as a child, try to reconstruct the relationships they had as children with their parents with their adult mates. She posits that by seeking out mates who will treat them in similarly painful ways, the women are trying to conquer the initial painful situation in which they grew up. While the women find the situations comfortable and familiar, they choose their men not because they consciously want to suffer, but with the desire to win over this parental representative and therefore correct all the emotional damage of a lifetime." Emily Green, Emily Green's Reviews, *Women Who Love Too Much*, Goodreads, May 26, 2013. Accessed October 10, 2014, at https://www.goodreads.com/review/show/625235922. Robin Norwood, *Women Who Love Too Much*: *When You Keep Wishing and Hoping He'll Change* (New York: Gallery Books, 2008).

14 Zanardo, *Il corpo delle donne*, p. 183.

15 Bianca Becalli, "The Modern Women's Movement in Italy," in Monica Threlfall (ed.), *Mapping the Women's Movement: Feminist Politics and Social Transformation in the North* (London: Verso, 1996), p. 152.

16 From the online presentation of the movement by its organizing committee, *Se non ora quando?* September 26, 2011. Accessed October 10, 2014, at http://www.senonoraquando.eu/.

17 Marta Tibaldi, *Esercizi di democrazia psichica* (Festa democratica "Diritto al futuro," Udine, Italy, Sept. 28–30, 2012); "Donne presenti! Soggetti, cittadine, amministratrici del bene commune," Maria Marion in dialogue with Marta Tibaldi, Tiziana Plebani, and Silvia Altran (round table, Udine, Italy, September 28–30, 2012, not published).

18 See Daniel Goleman, *Working with Emotional Intelligence* (New York: Bantham Dell, 1998).

19 In May 2013, the Italian Parliament ratified the Istanbul Convention on preventing and combating violence against women and domestic violence (opened for signature in 2011).

20 See Jennifer Barker Woogler and Roger J. Woogler, *The Goddess Within: A Guide to the Eternal Myths That Shape Women's Lives* (New York: Ballantine Books, 1987). See also Jean Shinoda Bolen, *Goddesses in Everywoman: Powerful Archetypes in Women's Lives* (San Francisco: Harper & Row, 1984).

21 Ernst Bernhard, "The Tasks Confronting Analytical Psychology in Italy," in Michael Fordham (ed.), *Contact with Jung: Essays on the Influence of His Work and Personality* (London: Tavistock Publications, 1963), pp. 97–110.

22 Bernhard, "The Tasks Confronting Analytical Psychology in Italy," p. 98.

23 Federico Fellini, *Fare un film. Con l'Autobiografia di uno spettatore di Italo Calvino* (Torino: Einaudi, 1980).

24 Fellini, *Fare un film*, pp. 144–145.

25 Zanardo, *Il corpo delle donne*, p. 144.

26 Again I recommend using the Jungian method of active imagination and developing the techniques of deep writing. Marta Tibaldi, "Hong Kong Seminars: From Dreamwork to Active Imagination – Parts I and II" (Seminar, Hong Kong, November 2012; Taipei [Taiwan], December 2012); "Hong Kong Seminars: Individual and Archetypal Experience in Clinical Practice – Parts I and II" (Seminar, Hong Kong, April 2013, not published).

27 James Hillman, *Alchemical Psychology*, Uniform Edition, Vol. 5 (*Psicologia alchemica*) (Milano: Adelphi, 2013), p. 19.

28 See Marta Tibaldi, "La passione narrativa. Appunti per una cura immaginale," in *Per nascosti sentieri* (a c. di F. Donfrancesco) (Bergamo: Moretti & Vitali, 2001),

pp. 191–206. I presented the English version of *The Montalcino's Princess* in the public workshop "Masculine and Feminine in Dreams, Men and Women in Awake Life," in Hong Kong on December 1, 2012, and in Taipei (Taiwan) on May 5, 2012.

29 I presented my technique of *Double Objectivation* in the seminars, "Hong Kong Seminars: The Technique of Double Objectivation: Making the Ego Complex and the Ego Style Visible, Parts I and II" (Seminar, Hong Kong, May 2–3, 2012). See also Marta Tibaldi, "Doppia oggettivazione e formazione dell'Io immaginale," in G. M. Cerbo, D. Palliccia, and A. M. Sassone (eds.), *Alchimie della formazione analitica* (Milano: Vivarium, 2004), pp. 329–338; Marta Tibaldi, "La pratica delle immagini," in *James Hillman. Verso il sapere dell'anima* (a c. di F. Donfrancesco), *Anima* 2012 (Bergamo: Moretti & Vitali, 2012), pp. 347–360. See also Marta Tibaldi, "Practicing Images: Clinical Implications of James Hillman's Theory in a Multicultural and a Changing World," in L. Huskinson and M. Stein (eds.), *Analytical Psychology in a Changing World: The Search for Self, Identity and Community* (New York-London: Routledge, 2014). See also Marta Tibaldi, "Practising Analytical Psychology in East Asia: A Post-Jungian Italian Perspective," in *Psychoanalysis and Psychotherapy in China*, Vol. 1 (London: Karnac, 2015), pp. 78–96.

30 See Riane Eisler, *The Chalice and the Blade: Our History, Our Future* (New York: Harper One, 1998).

31 See Marta Tibaldi, "Raping the Soul: An Experience of Active Imagination," in M. A. Mattoon (ed.), *Destruction and Creation: Personal and Cultural Transformation, Proceedings of the Fourteenth International Congress for Analytical Psychology, Florence 1998* (Einsiedeln, Switzerland: Daimon Verlag, 1999), pp. 208–219.

32 Tibaldi, "Raping the Soul," p. 218.

Part III

The Greater European Family: Cultural Complexes in All European Countries

Europe

North Sea Norway Finland

Sweden

North Sea Latvia Estonia

United Kingdom Denmark Lithuania

Baltic Sea

Ireland Netherlands Poland Belarus

Belgium Germany

Czech Republic Ukraine

Liechtenstein Slovakia

Atlantic Ocean France Austria Hungary Moldova

Switzerland Slovenia Romania

Crotia

Italy Serbia Kosovo

Bulgaria *Black Sea*

Spain Bosnia and Herzegovina

Portugal Montenego Albania Greece

Mediterranean Sea

Macedonia

Mediterranean Sea

The Jewish Anima

About the Christian-Jewish Complex in Europe

Jörg Rasche

When I was about fifteen years old, I received supplementary teaching in Latin from my grandfather Dr. Friedrich Pels Leusden. I was born in 1950 and grew up in Würzburg, an old town in Franken (Bavaria). In those years I was not the best student in the Gymnasium – partly because I preferred to play and study music. Every afternoon I went to my grandfather's house and was welcomed by him in Latin: "*Ave Jörg, tiro piger sed amatus!*"[1] In his later years my grandfather, an agnostic Lutheran Protestant, preferred to speak Latin instead of German. He used to say that he would have loved to live in the time of the Roman Emperor Antoninus Pius (86–161 CE) because during his reign no wars were fought in the entire (Roman) world. As a young man, he had been a Bavarian officer in World War I, and in the decades following he was the lawyer for a factory and lived in the old villa built by his father, who had been an engineer of printing machines. The house was full of wonderful antiquities and memories. Our teaching and conversation took place in Latin; not a single German word was allowed.

One day my grandfather told me the story of one of our ancestors who, in 1650, was teaching a scholar in the same way he was teaching me – by just speaking Latin. In exchange, the scholar spoke Hebrew with him, and both learned the language of the other. They had no money to pay for their studies, and so both gave to each other what they had to offer: their spoken language. This happened in Amsterdam in the Netherlands. The Latin teacher, Johannes Leusden, was a twenty-six-year-old Calvinist doctor of philosophy and Holy languages from Utrecht.[2] Before he took over the professorship in Utrecht, he went to Amsterdam to learn and study the living Hebrew of his time. At that time, Jews were not allowed to settle in Utrecht, but there were Jewish communities in Amsterdam. Sephardic Hebrew was said to be the wonderful, living language of King Salomon. My grandfather told me that the eighteen-year-old Jewish man was none other than the young Bento Despinosa, later known as the famous philosopher Spinoza (1632–1677)! I was told they became friends.

Many years later I came to understand the deep meaning of this encounter. It must have been a dangerous and secret friendship, especially after Spinoza was banned from the Jewish community as an atheist. He was also scorned by the reigning Calvinist Church in which my ancestor was a prominent figure. My ancestor,

DOI: 10.4324/9781003609742-15

Johannes Leusden (1624–1699), became the Christian specialist for Jewish matters of his time. He published many books, among them a famous edition of the Hebrew Bible as well as studies about the Mishna, the Talmud, and Jewish daily life. His first book, *Jonas Illustratus*, was a study of everything known about the Great Fish who swallowed the reluctant prophet Jonah. Leusden drew from works written in Latin, Hebrew, Greek, Aramaic, and Chaldean. He must have loved Jewish culture. As far as I know, this was the first encounter between Christianity and Judaism in the history of my family.

*****

During the following centuries one branch of the Pels Leusden family (now with the double name) settled in Germany and then in the town of Würzburg, where in 1924 my dear mother, Lieselotte Pels Leusden, was born. As I remember coming of age in the 1950s and 60s, I always had inside me a hidden relationship with Jewish culture, even though very few Jews lived in Würzburg following World War II. My great-grandfather on my mother's side, Dr. Josef Brod, looked like old father Abraham, but he was Catholic. He died when I was eight, but I remember well his serene, introverted, and wise attitude. He had been, as I was later told by his brother, a doctor to the Jewish community in Würzburg. He knew all of the Jewish families. In 1924, he assisted in the birth of a Jewish boy named Ludwig Pfeuffer, who in 1935 emigrated with his parents to Palestine where he changed his name and became the famous Israeli poet Yehuda Amichai. I was also told how Dr. Brod, then seventy years old, behaved on the night of November 9, 1938, when the Nazi pogrom against the Jewish population throughout the Third Reich erupted in Kristallnacht. The windows of synagogues, homes, and Jewish-owned businesses were shattered, and glass littered the streets, along with the furniture and other possessions that were thrown out of the broken windows. My great-grandfather closed the shutters of his home and sat behind his table crying and praying. He was already an old man and was much older after that night. The next day he went out, dressed in his most official habit, and went to where the Jewish men were being forced to clean the streets. The Nazis stood around. Lifting his cylinder hat, my great-grandfather greeted and honored the Jewish men by addressing them with their full names and titles: "Good morning, Herr Commerzienrat, Guten Morgen Herr Medizinalrat," and so on. They were his colleagues and friends. The Jewish people had been respected and integrated into Würzburg society before the Nazis took power and mobilized the preexisting, potent, and racist antisemitic underground.

There is another interesting connection to the Jews in Würzburg in my family's history. First a bit of background: Napoleon had brought full rights to the Jewish people living in Bavaria, and, after his defeat in 1815, the newly established Bavarian Monarchy followed more or less the new politics. Almost everywhere in Europe, the monarchs were, in principle, in favor of Jewish rights, often in opposition to many in the civilian population. But the new Bavarian kingdom (established in 1806) needed money, and so some Church property was taken over by the state to be sold. In Catholic regions such as Franken in Bavaria, many monasteries were disbanded and "secularized"; the monks had to leave, and the land and buildings were freed up for industrial development. Near Würzburg a large monastery named *Oberzell* was for sale. Only a Jewish company could afford it. They bought the property but sold it again after some years. A factory was established in the monastery, where my great-grandfather, August Pels Leusden, later constructed his printing machines. The nearby villages of Zell and Höchberg contained relatively big Jewish communities. The Rosenbaums from Zell, a Jewish clan, were famous for their influence. The Jungian psychoanalyst James Kirsch, who emigrated from Berlin in 1933 and eventually settled in Los Angeles, wrote a book about the Rabbi Hile Wechsler from Höchberg.[3] Rabbi Wechsler was a relative of the Rosenbaums. He was an orthodox mystic and published a book of his dreams. As Kirsch writes, the rabbi was a "reluctant prophet" who was terrorized by visions of a pending catastrophe for the Jews and argued that the Jews should leave Germany for Palestine as quickly as possible. This was in 1880. The "secularization" of Church property and its takeover by wealthy Jewish people fueled the anti-Jewish sentiments of the Catholic population.[4] This is just one example, and we will see more.

******

The issue of antisemitism is a difficult one for me and for many Germans who have to mourn what our people did from 1933 to 1945. Walking through this history is like walking through a mine field, with cultural complexes everywhere, ready to detonate with emotions of sadness and guilt, but also with prejudices, projections, and opinions filled with political correctness, the varying views of historians, and differing versions of oral history. There is also a connection between cultural complexes and religious convictions and traditions. In this chapter, I will develop a point of view based on my own personal memories and feelings. My religious background is Lutheran Protestant, and what I am going to explore is not simply antisemitism as a cultural complex in Europe but what I call the *Christian-Jewish complex.*

Contrary to widely held beliefs, antisemitism is actually a relatively young phenomenon. *Antisemitism* is a political-ideological term dating from approximately 1800; it has a racist meaning unknown and foreign to medieval thinking. *Race* is a biological term; it was created as a paradigm by the biological and physiognomic thinking of the nineteenth century. The scientific term *semitic* originally refers to a family of languages, including Arabian dialects and Hebrew, to differentiate them from the Arian or Hungarian branches of the tree of languages. But *anti-Judaism* was widespread in the late Roman Empire after 70 CE and in medieval Europe after the year 1000. In many European countries such as Spain, Portugal, France, and England, Jews were expelled or prohibited from settling for centuries. In fact, only in the German-speaking countries as well as in some Italian cities and eastward was a European Jewish population allowed to exist. Jewish life in Europe was almost synonymous with living in Germany. After 1933, when the Nazis destroyed Jewish culture in Germany, they destroyed the homeland where Jewish people had lived for centuries.

Medieval anti-Judaism was not "racist" but was motivated by religion and social and economic differences. Following statements of early Catholic Councils, Jews were not allowed to own and cultivate land but only to trade and to lend money. It was part of medieval Christian thinking that everyone could and should become a member of the redeemed human Christian community through baptism. This was not "racist" thinking. The Jewish psychology of the *Galuth* (exile) was, on the other hand, a psychology of an unchangeable identity. Ironically, to convert from Christianity to Judaism was seen on the part of Jews of the medieval era as much less of a problem than it is today. In addition to many other elements important to Jewish identity was the fact and idea of the exile following the destruction of the Second Temple in 70 CE. Exile became central to Jewish identity in the Diaspora. It was even given a special meaning in Jewish theology because it was seen as a precondition for the coming of the Messiah at the end of time. For instance, in 1655, the time of Spinoza, a chief rabbi of Amsterdam, Menasse ben Israel, traveled to London to beg Cromwell to allow a Jewish immigration to England. He argued that only if Jews spread everywhere in the world would the Messiah come.[5]

In medieval times, the city of Würzburg and its surrounding lands were in the hands of a duke who was also the Catholic bishop, the *Fürstbischof.* He served as both the political and spiritual lord and ruled over the souls and the bodies of the inhabitants with the same absolute power. It must not have been a pleasant atmosphere to be totally in the hands of such a lord! It was a totalitarian system, complete with the eruption of paranoia on the part of its citizens in critical times, for instance, when epidemics like the Black Death threatened the population. In the sixteenth century, Würzburg became a center of the Catholic Counterreformation and of the persecution and public burning of so-called witches. For decades the atmosphere must have been like a collective psychosis, even though Würzburg was freer and more tolerant than other places in Germany.

It was not until the Crusades (1095–1291) that Jews came to live in Würzburg. Before that, the main Jewish centers were in the Rhineland: Worms, Mainz, and Speyer, as well as other locales. Well-known Yeshivas and rabbis with a European-wide reputation were established in those areas. The Jewish and Christian communities lived near each other, and there were many mutual contacts and exchanges. To give an example, the use of wine and candles for the Jewish seder meal was adopted from the Christian ritual of the Holy Communion.[6] The Crusades changed everything.

In 1009, the fanatic Sultan Al-Hakim destroyed the Church of the Holy Sepulchre and many other churches in Jerusalem, which were among the most sacred and famous sites in the Christian world. Jews, too, suffered from the Sultan's intolerance. The destruction of the churches and monasteries in Jerusalem was a shock to Christian Europe, and the religious and political authorities finally proclaimed the First Crusade, an expedition to free the holy sites from the Muslims and to reconstruct the churches. On their way down the Rhine River in 1096, however, some Christian adventurers realized that they didn't have to travel so far to meet non-Christian people – and so began the anti-Jewish pogroms in the Rhineland, and as a result, some Jews fled to Würzburg.

There, the Jews again lived side-by-side with their Christian neighbors. There was no ghetto, and Jewish merchants assisted Christian trade with their lending money. Occupations other than trade, banking, and some handcrafts were forbidden to Jews, however. These restrictions were of pre-Christian origin, dating back to Roman times. After the Bar Kokhba uprising, the last attempt to reconstruct a Jewish kingdom in 135 CE, Roman Emperor Hadrian made strong rules against the Jews. Only his successor Antoninus Pius lifted these restrictions for a while. But in the medieval society of "The Holy Roman Empire of the German Nation," the Jews had a defined economic role. Each woman, each child, each Jew, and each merchant was under the special protection of the emperor. Nevertheless, the developing Christian companies and gilds tried repetitively to get rid of their competitors, and with the assistance of militant clergymen, anti-Jewish pogroms were instigated several times.

One of the darkest crises came in 1348 with the Black Death epidemic, when an estimated 75 to 200 million people died throughout Europe. Medieval Christianity remained superstitious with regard to infections and contagion. The epidemic became a psychic one, blamed on the Jewish population, and another round of pogroms began. Even in peaceful Würzburg, an anti-Jewish mob killed many Jews, burnt down their houses, and destroyed the synagogue. Later, on the spot of the temple, a church was erected and dedicated to St. Mary as an ambivalent sign of regret and atonement. The surviving Jews had no place to go other than eastward. Like them, many survivors of other medieval anti-Jewish pogroms escaped to Prague or Kraków in Poland. It was said that there, Jewish people were even invited to sit at the king's table![7] Galicia became a center of medieval Judaism; the people spoke Yiddish (a German-Hebrew dialect) and lived in small Chassid communities. After the divisions of Poland by Austria, Prussia, and Russia, many of these communities with their Jewish populations were overtaken by Russia, where again restrictions for settlement were imposed on the Jews, leading to a kind of closed greenhouse atmosphere in the Chassidic regions.

******

If we want to go deeper in analyzing the collective dynamic behind medieval anti-Judaism, we find a collusive dynamic of the cultural complexes of Christian and Jewish communities, having to do with the basic assumptions of both religions and their complementary meaning. In critical times, the complex behaves autonomously and can easily be abused and manipulated by interested groups such as economic competitors, profiteers, or religious fanatics.

The cultural complex has many features, including a strong emotional core. I have a personal memory: when I was about eight or nine years old, I traveled with my teacher to a medieval church in a village in the countryside of my beautiful homeland, Franken. In the center of the grandiose wooden altar were the carved statues of Mary and some saints. The wings on both sides of the shrine were painted. There, in lively colors that were painted around 1500, I could see the scene of Jesus's circumcision. Some strangely dressed men with long beards, turbans, and high hats, obviously Jews, stood around the naked little boy. One of them was cutting something off the boy's penis with huge black scissors. Clearly, it activated my own castration complex. And not only mine.

This image carried an important, not so subtle message with a strong anti-Jewish meaning. Circumcision, essential for Jewishness, is a horror for Christian children. Even though the Catholic calendar notes the Day of Jesus's circumcision (the eighth day after his birth), and even though some monasteries show a relic that they claim to be the Holy Præputium, the act itself was a taboo. In the many paintings of the naked baby Jesus with his mother Mary, seldom I have seen a circumcised penis! But behind these complicated, emotional reactions to circumcision, there is more than a Freudian castration complex.

Seen with medieval Christian eyes, it is about the complex of the body and the relationship between body and spirit, inner and outer reality, and how they may relate to each other. Embedded in these polarities, there was in the fifteenth and sixteenth centuries a highly loaded complex as we, for example, know from Jung's studies on alchemy in those times. In the Catholic mass, the bread (the *host*) is literally – or as an inner experience – transformed into the flesh of Christ. Protestants such as Luther, Zwingli, and Calvin emphasized that this was just a symbol, an "as if" we would say. C. G. Jung wrote about the archetypal meaning of the transubstantiation in his work on the Trinity symbol in the mass. It was a highly controversial issue. We should not forget that religious wars, like the Thirty Years' War (1618–1648) between Catholics and Protestants, destroyed many regions of Germany. That war was fought about the difference between "it is" and "it means." The Lutheran Protestants fought for the "modern" side (the *symbol*), whereas the Catholics fought for the real transformation of bread and wine into flesh and blood.

Anti-Jewish propaganda of the sixteenth century focused on that relationship between body and spirit. Jews were accused of cutting the consecrated host with a knife so that blood came out (*Hostienfrevel*). They were also accused of not believing in the mystery of the transformation in which the Christ is killed again when cutting his body (the sacred bread, the host) with a knife. This superstitious phantasm was a repetition of what happened in Golgotha where the Jews were accused of killing Jesus. (By the way, they forgot that the Romans, not the Jews, crucified Jesus.)

There was also another basic element active in the complementary relationship of the Christian and Jewish religions, which was about the nature of inner and outer reality.[8] In the New Testament Christ says, "My kingdom is not of this world" (John 18:36). Early Christianity took its persuasive power from this statement in that it offered the transcendence of earthly suffering and attachment into a non-material, spiritual dimension. Also the question of Israel's future (the pending destruction of the temple by the Romans) could be resolved by this shift of paradigm – for those who became Christians. Jesus was said to have proclaimed "his Torah" as a continuation and transformation of the old Torah of Moses and the prophets, to be accepted as the real Messiah, the son of God.[9] With the sanction of the new Christian confession as the official religion of Rome by Emperor Constantine after 325 CE, Christianity gained enormous political power. The Kingdom of the Lord could now be established on earth as well as in heaven. St. Augustine's (354–430 CE) *De Civitate Dei* became a manifesto of Christianity in its process of transformation into the leading paradigm of social and political structures. But at the core of Christianity the Lord's most profound vision was still alive like an underground stream, namely that the real Kingdom of God is not of this world. This was especially important around the first millennium – 1000 CE – when, following St. John's prophecy of the Apocalypse, Satan was to return to earth after 1000 years of imprisonment. The longing for a transcendent faith became urgent again during and after the passing of the first millennium. The movement of the *Spirituales* (Joachim da Fiore), the Christian mystics, the building of the Gothic cathedrals, the life and message of St. Francis – and, on the secular side, the Renaissance – were all answers to crises of faith in the following centuries.

The Jewish view has always presented a complementary orientation to an increasing secularized Christianity and its growing fixation on earthly, political power. James Kirsch, who was quite familiar with this Jewish tradition, wrote the following in 1931:

> The Jews were different. They had no place to settle.
> Through all lands they took their god with them, the god they conceived in the desert . . . Israel's god is a god of the wind, not originating from the earth, and from the very beginning he was grasped in spiritual form, as the Everlasting: I will be who I will be! As the Everlasting in Becoming, or as Becoming in the Everlasting. . . . The soul of the Jew was bound up with this single-singular principle; his soul was not permitted to open itself to the land where he traveled. The Jew's bride, the Jew's anima was Israel, the Jewish people, the Sabbath, the Torah. The Jew's emotional character, his psychic disposition was defined by the Sabbath. The Jew's homeland is the Torah, and the only content of his soul is God.[10]

Kirsch's text became quite important for Jung's own statements about Jewish psychology a few years later. Jung kept Kirsch's paper on his desk for a long time. As Ann Lammers points out, Kirsch helped modify Jung's 1927 and 1930 concept of the Jews as being not really earth-bounded.[11]

James Kirsch perceived that Jewish culture was opposite and complementary to Christian culture. Jews were not fixed on earth; they could let their soul be shaped by the image of God. As mentioned, this cultural and soul reality was a consequence of the 70 CE destruction of the Second Temple and the defeat and exile of the Jews by the Romans after the Bar Kokhba revolt from 132–136 CE. The Jews had no other choice than to arrange themselves and their culture in the *Galuth*. By the third century, rabbis interpreted the destruction of the Second Temple in Jerusalem and the exile as God's punishment for the sins of the Jewish people. This was also how the Christians framed it. It became a central argument in the discourse between Jewish and Christian theologians.[12] Step by step, the Jewish "other" was seen as the enemy who did not accept the Messiah.

Christians did not live in exile. But the idea of temporary "exile," or at least a journey away from home such as a pilgrimage to Rome or Jerusalem for the redeeming of sins, was activated on occasion in the Christian world. Even today the pilgrimage to Santiago de Compostela is a European journey and adventure, for some pilgrims comparable to the Jewish experience of the Exodus from Egypt. The established Church authorities were often skeptical about these undertakings. Jews certainly traveled to and sometimes migrated to Palestine to settle there, but this was not that common until the end of World War II and the founding of Israel. For Christians, Jerusalem was a holy site on this earth; for Jews, Jerusalem was identical with the Messiah and the end of time.

******

What sort of Jewish complex developed in relation to the Christian projections onto the Jewish people and religion? The seeds or precursors of such a complex were already in the Jewish psyche long before they encountered the Christians. Centuries before, the Jews had suffered their first exile at the hands of the Assyrians in 733 BCE. Later came the Babylonian Exile in 598/7 and 587/6 BCE, which formally ended in 538 BCE when Cyrus the Great of Persia conquered the Babylonians and gave the Jews the right to return to Palestine. The next great exile or Diaspora occurred after the catastrophic Bar Kokhba defeat of the Jews at the hands of the Romans in 132–136 CE. According to Cassius Dio, 580,000 Jews were killed at the time of the Bar Kokhba revolt. Fifty fortified towns and 985 villages were razed to the ground, with many more Jews dying of famine and disease.[13]

The surviving Jews had to leave their homeland in great numbers, and since that time they have been in exile, also known as the *Diaspora*. The Jews had to develop rules of behavior and an attitude that allowed them to endure and survive when living in hostile cultures. Meetings to frame how to approach living in exile occurred in Lydda (shortly before 135 CE) and also at the beginning of the third century at the Synhedrion in Uscha in Galilee. A *Mishnah* was developed to create a written record of the oral traditions by which in the past Judaism had always been transmitted from one generation to the next.

From that time on, as Jacob Neusner points out, the Jews cared less and less about earthly, political issues. It is as if they decided to live just for their religion and faith, more removed from the events of concrete history.[14] They lived in seclusion, and nobody knew what they really did in their homes, for example, on Shabbat. Their seclusion was sometimes perceived by Christians as a provocation. Isaac B. Singer gives an impressive example of the secluded Chassidic world in his classical novel *Satan in Goraj* and the hostile projections of the Russian farmers onto the Jews.[15]

As Gershom Scholem stated, the Messianic question became a crucial issue for the Jews.[16] Will the Messiah come, and when? James Kirsch called the "Christ Complex" the most important complex of the Jewish psyche.

> The rejection of Christ has, as it seems to me (Jews will never admit this), determined the fate of the Jews. From a Jewish viewpoint, Christianity is its shadow (and also vice versa, by the way, but that's the Christians' concern).[17]

As far as I understand Kirsch's point, the Jews' refusal to accept Jesus from Nazareth as the promised Messiah who would end the suffering of God's people became the defining event in the complex that developed between the Jews and Christians. Jacob Neusner gives examples of how close some rabbinic (*pharisaic*) positions around the time of Jesus were to Jesus's own sayings in the Sermon on the Mount.[18] Central to this belief are that love and forgiveness transcend the talionic law of the Old Testament and the Messianic vision that the Kingdom of God is not of this earth. The Jews hoped and believed that God's kingdom would be reestablished concretely at the end of time in Jerusalem. St. Paul understood that it scandalized the Jews to imagine that God had taken human form as a crucified criminal. "For indeed Jews ask for signs, and Greeks search for wisdom; but we preach Christ crucified, to Jews a stumbling block, and to Gentiles foolishness" (First Epistle to the Corinthians, 1:22). The exile, the *Galuth*, then became the frame and paradigm of Jewish life and thinking for centuries, from the third century on to the late Middle Ages.

James Kirsch wrote the following in his paper from 1931:

> And yet deep in every Jew is the yearning for oasis, for the earth. He longs to be like other peoples, yet this cannot be. Therein lays the paradox of Jewish psychology. It is a human being's eternally impossible attempt to direct the soul away from the earth, to adapt collective energy and its specific formation to his soul, and to turn the Eternally Becoming into the only content of his soul. Such attempts must almost always fail.[19]

During these many centuries, there were several Messianic figures arising in the Jewish world. The most famous was Sabbatai Zwi (1626–1676), a man from Smyrna who, in Spinoza's time, declared himself to be the Messiah. The chiliastic hope that the Messiah would come to reign on earth for 100 years arose among the Jews in Europe who followed Sabbatai Zwi; many sold their property and traveled to Palestine to witness the end of days. But Sabbatai was put in prison by the Sultan and forced to convert to Islam. His apostasy in 1666 was a great disappointment, but some said in his defense that the real Messiah had to go through the deepest humiliation – in this case, even the conversion to the confession of the enemy! Paradoxically, this is close to the Christian idea that the Messiah had to be crucified like a criminal! Nevertheless, as Scholem writes, the crucifixion of Jesus and the Apostasy of Sabbatai Zwi are not of the same dimension, but the pattern is similar.[20] The difference is, following Scholem, in the paradox that Sabbatai betrayed his belief whereas Jesus died in the name of his God. Interestingly, the Sabbatarian movement lived on in the Chassidic tradition. Scholem argues that after Sabbatai's conversion many *Marranes* (Sephardic Jews who were forced to be baptized) could identify their suffering with that of Sabbatai.[21]

In an interesting conversation between the Dalai Lama and rabbis from the United States, the Dalai Lama, himself in exile for decades, asked the Jewish wise men how their culture was able to survive during centuries of exile.[22] For Tibetans, this is an existential question. The point the rabbis emphasized most in their response to the Dalai Lama's question was the centrality of the Shabbat, the one day a week dedicated to the concentration on God's word in the frame and home of the family. The Shabbat is the living ritual of the Jews of the exile, which replaced the prayer in the temple of Jerusalem that no longer exists. The Shabbat became a potent symbolic ritual for transcendence and the transformation of inner reality. Instead of belief in the crucifixion and resurrection, the Jews found renewal and devotion in the Shabbat. In line with this thought, Scholem said that in the Kabalistic tradition the Shabbat is the Shekina, the residence of God in the world, in the inner dwellings of his people.[23] This also aligns with what James Kirsch wrote: "The Jew's bride, the Jew's anima was Israel, the Jewish people, the Sabbath, the Torah."[24] The Christian complement to the Shabbat is the Holy Communion.

******

The following questions arise: did the Jews have a "Christian element" in their collective unconscious, and did Christians have a "Jewish element" in their psyche? The longing for the Messiah may be an indication that both faiths have swum in the same waters. James Kirsch said that the Jewish anima is the Torah, the Shabbat; he didn't ask for a Christian anima for Jews, nor a Jewish anima for Christians. The point here is that a complementary dynamic existed between Jews and Christians as well as the much more familiar emphasis on the differences and tensions. The groundswell of complementarities and oppositions in the collective unconscious has risen and fallen over the centuries, which leads me to proceed with events in the lived history between Christians and Jews after medieval times.

In the Age of Enlightenment and the time following the 1789 French Revolution, two main developments emerged that affected the situation of Jews in Europe in an unforeseen way. On the one hand, there was the Napoleonic *Code Civil des Français* that established equal rights for all people, black or white, men or woman, Christians or Jews. And there was the American Constitution and its declaration of human rights. Following the Napoleonic Code, the Prussian and the Bavarian constitutions took steps on the way toward the emancipation or assimilation of Jews – *assimilation* in this context meaning the ability of the Jews to adapt to the cultural world around them and to become fully respected and privileged members of society with all rights and responsibilities. On the other hand, this was the period when antisemitism was invented as an ideological and racist category and slogan. The growing tide of antisemitism in any era is deeply disturbing, and we seem to be in a time when the tide is rising again. This was also true after the French Revolution and the following progressive century. Everywhere in Europe a kind of paranoid fever addled the brains of even the most distinguished thinkers and cultural leaders. Antisemitic pamphlets were printed throughout Europe and bloody pogroms proliferated. From around 1800 on, the cultural environment for most Jewish people in Europe was like living in an overheated prison in which the temperature reached critical and ultimately catastrophic levels in the Holocaust. There were few citizens who did not follow the mainstream of paranoid projections and scapegoat fantasies onto the Jewish population.

Psychologically, racism can be viewed as an unconscious paradigm that allows people to determine who is like "me" and who is not. In a kind of collective regression to archaic physiognomic perceptions, the psyche tries to define a system of inclusion and exclusion in a cultural situation when other paradigms of identifying individuals and groups have lost their value. Following the Enlightenment, the French Revolution, the rise of industrialization, and the replacement of the former prevailing God archetype by the Earth archetype, nearly all traditional patterns of emotional and social identity were undermined.[25]

C. G. Jung wrote in his late work *Aion*: "Since the stars fell from heaven, and our highest symbols became pale, a secret life is going on in the unconscious. Therefore today we have a Psychology, and therefore we are talking about an Unconscious."[26] This unconscious, as we know, contains powers and demons we never could imagine. Francisco Goya drew some in his famous etching *The Sleep of Reason Creates Monsters*. Prehistoric or archaic attitudes appear in the collective unconscious like dinosaurs.

Traditional social structures and roles lost their value. In rapidly industrializing societies, the traditional family was no longer the foundation of the culture. This was in striking contrast to the traditional Jewish emphasis on family. Envy and jealousy became strong psychodynamic drives differentiating one group from another, as if the rivalry between siblings became the model for cultural patterning. The old paradigms fell apart, and the unconscious (re-)construction of an enemy actually helped one cope with the disorientation and fundamental uncertainty by providing clues about who one was and wasn't. In addition, this was the time of the "Creation of Nations,"[27] when the collective Self was no longer projected onto and realized in God but onto the Nation, as so well-defined by Ernest Renan.[28] Basic questions arose: With whom do I want to live in my nation? Who are the mythological founders of my nation and its culture? Whose ancestors fought for my nation in previous times? Rarely were Jews imagined as being in the forefront of creating the nation, as being part of the mythological foundations of the nation. Perhaps it was for this reason that so many Jews gave their lives for the German Empire in WWI in the hope that this would lead to their acceptance as equal citizens with equal rights. Instead, following the defeat of Germany and the fateful Treaty of Versailles, the Jews were accused of having betrayed the emperor's army! Hitler used this as an argument in his 1925 *Mein Kampf* for why the Jews needed to be destroyed!

Another factor in the growing antisemitism following industrialization and the rise of capitalism centered on ownership: who owned the money needed for investment (what Karl Marx called the "original accumulation" of money that could be transformed into capital[29]) and who owned the land with its resources? Economic competition became fierce when increasing industrial production began to drive traditional products from the market.

The worst antisemitic pogroms in Würzburg in the nineteenth century were instigated by traditional button producers. The more well-connected Jewish merchants had access to cheaper industrial products from elsewhere, making them the first to market with less expensive industrialized button and hosiery goods. This became fuel for anti-Semitic excesses. For example, in Würzburg in 1819, Christian merchants joined forces with the unemployed and otherwise marginalized people such as alcoholics. On the evening of August 2, inspired by fanatic clergymen, they persecuted Jewish people on the streets. This continued for several days. Some were wounded, and Jewish houses were demolished. The mob cried "Hep, hep!" which means "*Hierosolyma Est Perdita*" ("Jerusalem is lost"). The slogan was obviously created by some priest who knew Latin. The city government stepped in to calm the people's emotions. The next pogroms in Würzburg happened in 1826. But there was a small Jewish establishment in the city; there were Jewish students at the university; and, in 1841, a great synagogue was built and opened in the presence of the president of the government.[30]

The fact is that the Jews were much more adept at arranging commercial networks. The long history of Jews having to live in different and changing exiles led to the severe handicap of being without a home of their own. At the same time, this very homelessness also led to a certain cosmopolitanism that was transformed into a business advantage, transcending the traditional business practices of non-Jews. Christians were, therefore, fearful about their own future as well as being envious of Jewish commercial acumen.

This was also the case when many impoverished Jews fled westward after pogroms in Russia and Poland around 1890. In medieval times, the Jews had fled from Western Europe to the relative safety of Eastern Europe. This later forced migration reversed the flight from West to East. Now Eastern European Jews headed to Berlin, Vienna, and America. The expanding non-Jewish national bourgeoisie in Russia and Poland drove out their competitors, and many thousands of poor Jews in their medieval *Stetl*-habit came to Vienna and Berlin in the 1890s. The *petit bourgeois* in these cities looked with horror at the impoverished immigrants who mirrored their own potential future in times of capital concentration, so they hated them and became ardent anti-Semites.[31] The antisemitic complex grew, replacing the former anti-Judaism with pseudo-biological, racist thinking. Further fueling that anti-Jewish sentiment was the fact that many of the young Eastern European

Jews had grown up in out-of-date, orthodox Chassidic families, such as in Galicia, and broke with their heritage to become ardent socialists and communists.

If I were to write much about the Nazi psychology, which demagogically abused all these trends, this would be another book. But it is important to note how effectively the German-Jewish population, assimilated or emancipated, had established itself. It created, in the second half of the nineteenth century and until 1933, an admirable cultural plateau and had made remarkable achievements that helped the German Reich to become the leading nation of science and arts in Europe, if not in the world. Martin Buber, after the fatal Reichs-pogrom in 1938, wrote in the *Jüdische Rundschau* (then edited in Paris and London) about the "unique symbiosis" that had developed in Germany over the previous hundred years. After 1918, this symbiosis had been overshadowed by growing antisemitism. "The break with this Symbiosis will damage Germany much more than it is aware of."[32] Perhaps the experience of the German-Jewish symbiosis was in Buber's mind as well when he emphasized later on the importance of a Jewish-Palestinian symbiosis in the new country.

******

C. G. Jung, the Swiss, wrote about the differences and unconscious interactions between Christian and Jewish psychology. His Jewish scholars and colleagues, Kirsch, Neumann, and Adler, had intensive correspondences about this issue with Jung. In an unpublished letter to his colleague W. Kranefeldt in Berlin in the 1930s, Jung asked a remarkable question: "How does it come about that a Christian doctor always falls in love with his Jewish Anima?" This may sound a bit sarcastic, but clearly the question revealed more than idle curiosity in Jung as he had his own deep experience with Sabina Spielrein. Jung invited Kranefeldt to write a paper about this question. We know that Kranefeldt (who trained with Jung, was a co-founder of the Berlin Jung Society in 1931, and acted as James Kirsch's supervisor before 1933) was active in the *Reichsinstitut* during the Nazi era.[33] Jung ended his contact with him in the early 1940s.

The question Jung brings up touches on the subject of this chapter about the Christian-Jewish complex. As already noted, the earliest Jewish anima projection we find evidence of in Jung's biography is Sabina Spielrein. The relationship between them and the memory of it lingered in Jung's psyche for decades, even when Sabina was already a member of Freud's circle in Vienna. Although conjecture, it may well be that Jung's experience with Spielrein contributed to the formation of his notion of the anima.

The "Jewish Question" was also a topic in Jung's family. Jung's grandfather Antistes Samuel Preiswerk, a professor of theology in Basel, had edited in 1860 a monthly magazine, *Das Morgenland*, where he argued that the Jews should return to their homeland and settle there. In his inaugural speech at the first Zionist Conference in Basel, Theodor Herzl honored Preiswerk as a "pioneer of Zionism."[34] Preiswerk was not the only one who endorsed the idea of a Jewish return to Palestine; there were many others, including the "reluctant prophet" Hile Wechsler whom I mentioned before. This endorsement occurred before the Balfour declaration supporting the establishment of a home for Jews in Palestine.[35]

The advocates for the Jewish return to Palestine undoubtedly saved the life of many Jewish people, although obviously not offsetting the millions who were killed in the Holocaust. But what, one may ask, happened with the Jewish anima after the foundation of the state of Israel in 1948? As you recall, Kirsch defined the Jewish anima as being identified with living in exile, with living in the Sabbath, with living in the Torah, but not as actually dwelling in Palestine. James Kirsch, a skeptic of political Zionism, wrote in 1931:

> And yet deep in every Jew is the yearning for oasis, for the earth. He longs to be like other peoples, yet this he cannot be. Therein lies the paradox of Jewish psychology. It is a human being's eternally impossible attempt to direct the soul away from the earth, to adapt collective energy and its specific formation to his soul, and to turn the Eternally Becoming into the only content of his soul. Such attempts must almost always fail. Then if money, socialism, or the belly take the place of god, the Jew turns away from his eternal task; he becomes inauthentic and his psychology is fraud. . . . This is the deepest ground for anti-Semitism. On the other hand, if the Jew lives according to his proper dynamic psychology, he is the salt of the earth. Theocracy is the basis of his endurance.[36]

******

To conclude I want to briefly mention some artists who have inspired my thinking about the issues I have raised in this chapter. The first is Felix Mendelssohn Bartholdy (1809–1847). He was the grandson of Moses Mendelssohn, who opened the way for Jewish humanism and assimilation. Moses (1729–1786) was honored by Gotthold Ephraim Lessing in 1779 in his famous play *Nathan the Wise* (*Nathan der Weise*). Moses's grandson Felix had been baptized as a child, but he had to fight all his life against antisemitic prejudices. Nevertheless he made his way and became the first and most important *explicitly Christian* composer after Johann Sebastian Bach. Goethe was his most famous admirer. Mendelssohn's music, often compared with Mozart, was, however, forbidden in the Third Reich.

The second is Marc Chagall (1887–1985), the famous Jewish painter and "Creator of Images" who was born in Wytebsk (Russia) and later lived in both the United States and France. Even in his early paintings such as the 1918 *Me and the Village*, Chagall had begun to work through and transform the Christian-Jewish complex. The inspired and luminous green man in the foreground of the painting wears a cross around his neck – the cross as a symbol of hope. During WWII, Chagall painted *White Crucifixion* (Figure 10.1) in which he identified Jesus with all the tortured and suffering Jewish people by having Jesus wear a Torah shawl.[37]

In his last years (1970–1978), Chagall made his famous glass windows in Zürich that featured the Green Christ. For Chagall, green was the transcendent color of inspiration and new life. There is deep hope in these paintings and glass

Figure 10.1 Marc Chagall, *White Crucifixion*, 1939. (Marc Chagall: © 2015 Artists
        Rights Society (ARS), New York/ADAGP, Paris.)

windows – emotion beyond words. Erich Neumann called Chagall a prophet.[38]
Jung once (in 1939) had a dream with a bright green Christ standing at his bed;
he learned from this dream that he should be more attentive to the living aspect of
incarnation. It was a big dream for him.[39]

    The last artists I want to call up are two poets. Else Lasker-Schüler (1869–1945)
was born in Elberfeld (Germany) and immigrated to Jerusalem in 1933. There, she
wrote a famous poem about her "Blue Piano," which I have translated here:

At home I have a blue piano
But I don't know any notes.

It stands in the dark behind the cellar door
Since the world became vulgarized and brutal.[40]

Lasker-Schüler, like many Jewish emigrants, suffered from the emigration. The blue piano reminds one of an earlier romantic vision of a better world, as prefigured by Novalis and the romantic symbol of the Blue Flower. But the time for dreaming and even for longing for a transcendent world is over.

Finally, I have translated the following quote from Yehuda Amichai, the former Ludwig Pfeuffer from Würzburg:

But through the wound in my breast God is looking into the world. I am the door to his dwelling.[41]

Notes

1 "Welcome, you lazy but beloved student."
2 The life of Johannes Leusden is described in the funeral speech by Gerard de Vries. Gerard de Vries, *Oratio funebris in obitum viri clarissimi et doctissimi Johannis Leusden (. . .)* (Utrecht: G. Van de Water, 1699).
3 James Kirsch, *The Reluctant Prophet. An Exploration of Prophecy and Dreams* (Los Angeles: Sherbourne Press, 1973).
4 For more on this period, see Roland Flacke, *Die Würzburger Juden. Ihre Geschichte vom Mittelalter bis zur Gegenwar* (Würzburg: Stürz, Verlag, 1987).
5 Theun De Vries, *Spinoza* (Reinbek: Rowohlt, 1970), p. 20. Menasse wrote about this in his book *Esperanca de Israel.*
6 Michael Hilton, *Wie es sich christelt, so jüdelt es sich: 2000 Jahre christlicher Einfluss auf das jüdische Leben* (Berlin: Jüdische Verlagsanstalt, 2000). Rabby Hilton shows how closely interconnected the medieval Christian and Jewish cultures were before the Crusades.
7 In fact, the position of Jews in Poland was better than in Germany at this time, perhaps because of the underdeveloped economy in eastern countries. See Isaak Leon, "Judenfrage und Kapitalismus" ("Kapitalism and Jewish Question") (private printing, 1970).
8 The polarity between inner and outer reality is still controversial today, even if we are not so possessed by it as our ancestors were 400 years ago. Quantum physics states that "at the bottom of matter there is no matter"; this is the same question.
9 See Joseph Ratzinger (Benedikt XVI), *Jesus von Nazareth I* (Freiburg im Breisgau: Herder, 2007), p. 152ff.
10 James Kirsch, summer 1931. In Ann Lammers (ed.), *The Jung-Kirsch Letters: The Correspondence of C. G. Jung and James Kirsch* (London: Routledge, 2011), p. 15f.
11 Lammers, *The Jung-Kirsch Letters*, p. 16.
12 Jakob Neusner, *Judaism in the Beginning of Christianity* (Philadelphia, PA: Fortress Press, 1984).
13 Cassius Dio, *Roman History*, book 69, trans. Earnest Cary (Cambridge, MA: Harvard University Press, 1914–1927), pp. 12.1–14.3. Online in LacusCurtius (http://penelope.uchicago.edu/Thayer/E/Roman/Texts/Cassius_Dio/69*.html#12) and livius.org (http://www.livius.org/ja-jn/jewish_wars/bk05.html). A scan of the book can be found at the Internet Archive (https://archive.org/stream/diosromanhistory08cassuoft#page/446/mode/2up).
14 Neusner, *Judaism in the Beginning of Christianity.*

15 Isaak Singer, *Satan in Goray* (New York: Farrar, Strauss and Giroux, 1955). The novel was originally published in Yiddish.

16 Gershom Scholem, *Die Jüdische Mystik in ihren Hauptströmungen* (Frankfurt am Main: Suhrkamp, 1980). See, in particular, Chapter 8, "Sabbatianism and Jewish heresy." Published in English as *The Jewish Mystic* in 1941.

17 Lammers, *The Jung-Kirsch Letters*, p. 50ff.

18 Neusner, *Judaism in the Beginning of Christianity*, p. 37ff.

19 Lammers, *The Jung-Kirsch Letters*, p. 16.

20 Scholem, *Die Jüdische Mystik*, p. 338.

21 Scholem, *Die Jüdische Mystik*, p. 339. The relevant chapter is about Sabbatianism and mystic heresy.

22 Rodger Kamenetz, *The Jew in the Lotus: A Poet's Rediscovery of Jewish Identity in Buddhist India* (San Francisco: Harper San Francisco, 1994).

23 Gershom Scholem, *Zur Kabbala und ihrer Symbolik* (Zürich: Rhein Verlag, 1960), p. 186ff.

24 James Kirsch, in Lammers, *The Jung-Kirsch letters*, p. 15.

25 See Erich Neumann, *Kunst und schöpferisches unbewusstes (1954)* (Zürich: Daimon Verlag, 1980), pp. 77ff.

26 C. G. Jung, "Aion (1951)," in G. Adler and R. F. C. Hull (eds.), *The Collected Works of C. G. Jung*, Vol. 9/1 (Princeton, NJ: Princeton University Press, 1968), § 50.

27 See Monika Flacke, *Mythen der Nationen. Ein europäisches Panorama* (Berlin: Koehler & Amelang, 1998).

28 Ernest Renan, "Qu'est-ce qu'une nation," in Henriëtte Psichari (ed.), *Oeuvres complétes d'Ernest Renan*, Vol. 1 (Paris: Calmann-Levy, 1947–1961), p. 892.

29 Karl Marx, *Das Kapital*, Vol. I (1867) (Berlin: Dietz Verlag, 1950). See "Die ursprüngliche Akkumulation."

30 For more details, see Roland Flade, *Die Würzburger Juden* (Würzburg: Stürz Verlag, 1987), p. 73ff. Before the opening of the great temple, there were seven small house-synagogues in Würzburg. The government wanted to have better control over the Jewish community, however, so it required the building of the temple for all Jews (p. 89).

31 Isaak Leon, *Judenfrage und Kapitalismus (Kapitalism and the Jewish Question)* (1942) (Private Printing, 1970).

32 Martin Buber, *Jüdische Welt-Rundschau Nr. 1* (1o. März, 1939). My translation.

33 Kranefeldt was not a Nazi; he was at least not a member of the National Socialist German Workers' Party, or NSDAP (information provided by Ann Lammers). Jung ended his contact with Kranefeldt in the 1940s.

34 Deirdre Bair, *C. G. Jung, eine Biographie (2003)* (München: Albrecht Knaus, 2005), pp. 26, 938.

35 The Balfour Declaration (November 2, 1917) was a letter from the United Kingdom's Foreign Secretary Arthur James Balfour to Baron Rothschild, a leader of the British Jewish community, for transmission to the Zionist Federation of Great Britain and Ireland, supporting the establishment of a national home for the Jewish people.

36 James Kirsch, in Lammers, *The Jung-Kirsch Letters*, p. 15.

37 "In 1939, Chagall painted a tour-de-force entitled, *The White Crucifixion*. In this work, the artist places the image of the suffering Christ on the cross in the midst of Nazi destruction. For his own personal safety and the safety of his family, this work was painted over and hidden several times by Chagall prior to being brought into public view. In this work, the central focus is the image of the crucified Christ. Chagall has replaced the traditional loin cloth with a tallis, the Jewish prayer shawl traditionally worn by men for morning prayers. Above Christ is the traditional INRI inscription, yet in the painting INRI is translated into Aramaic using Hebrew letters. At the base of the

cross is the menorah, an ancient and traditional symbol of Judaism. All of these symbols surround and identify the crucified Christ with his Judaism. The figures floating above him are three biblical patriarchs and Rachel, the matriarch, all in mourning for the death of their children. Amishai-Maisels explains, 'Their presence here stems from a popular Jewish legend that, after the destruction of the First Temple, god summoned Moses and the Patriarchs to share His grief, for they knew how to mourn' (143).

"Chagall has surrounded the Christ with pictures of Nazi destruction of a Jewish village and temple. As in the image of the Falling Angel, Chagall painted a Jewish man protecting the Torah as he runs away from the burning synagogue. The devastation of the world around the artist highlighted the terrible events that were occurring in Russia and Germany in the name of Christianity. Murder of innocents was not a part of the teachings of the biblical Christ. Murders were being committed in His name. The artist was expressing the distortion of Christianity that was occurring in their worlds."

Carol L. Rizzolo, "The Image of Crucifixion: A Exploration of the Relationship of Jewish Artists to the Passion of Christ," *ARAS Connections* (2011, 2). Accessed September 23, 2015, at https://aras.org/newsletter/newsletter11-02.htm#cultcom, pp. 15–16. Amishai-Maisels quote from Ziva Amishai-Maisels, "Chagall's 'White Crucifixion'," *Art Institute of Chicago Museum Studies* 17 (1991, 2): pp. 138–153, 180–181.

38 Erich Neumann, "Bemerkung zu Mark Chagall," in *Kunst und schöpferisches unbewusstes* (Einsiedeln: Daimon, 1980), p. 141.
39 C. G. Jung, *Erinnerungen, Träume, Gedanken (Memories, Dreams, Reflections)* (Olten: Walter Verlag, 1971), p. 214. I wrote about this dream in Jörg Rasche, *das Lied des Grünen Löwen. Music als Spiegel der Seele (The Song of the Green Lion: Music as a Mirror of the Soul)* (Düsseldorf: Walter/Patmos, 2004; and Gießen, Germany: Psychosozial Verlag, 2014), p. 394ff.
40 Author's translation of Else Lasker-Schüler, *Die Gedichte* (Frankfurt am Main: Suhrkamp 1997), p. 337.
41 Author's translation of Jehuda Amichai, "Ibn Gabirol," in *Wie schön sind deine Zelte* (München: Jakob, Piper, 1992).

Israel

Israel

My European Animus

Erel Shalit

I am grateful to the editors, Tom and Jörg, dear friends, for inviting me to add some reflections on Jörg's wonderful and moving chapter.

Jörg and I are the same age. Ever since we first met, I have always, for no obvious outward reason, felt a sense of affinity with him. I congratulated him when he managed *not* to get elected president of the International Association for Analytical Psychology, as he is better suited, I believe, to play music and create.

As children, would we have played in the same courtyard? Were it not for our respective introversion, which called upon Jörg to play the piano and compelled me to withdraw into the solitude of writing stories, we could easily, I am sure, have been playmates – a notion that pertains more to that affinity of soul than to physical reality.

What Jörg writes points so poignantly to is that mysterious communion of fate: Yehuda Amichai, the poet of Jerusalem, who Jörg tells us was born into this world by his grandfather, gives voice like no one else to the mortal burden of carrying the weight of Jerusalem:

I and Jerusalem are like a blind man and a cripple.
She sees for me
out to the Dead Sea, to the End of Days,
And I hoist her up on my shoulders
and walk blind in my darkness underneath.[1]

And on that fateful day when dignity, pride, and self-respect shattered like broken glass – November 10, 1938 – Jörg's grandfather Dr. Brod, wearing his best outfit, greets the humiliated Jew, while I myself wonder, cowardly, "If I had been a German, might I not have looked the other way, avoiding the shame and the guilt gazing back at me in the store owner's eyes of shattered glass?"[2]

Little wonder, then, that to me Jörg represents the best of Europe – its culture and enlightenment, as well as its depth, reflection, and integrity. But we live lives and worlds apart. "The times in which one lives," says Neumann, "and the phase of the supraordinate course of fate in which one's personal life span is embedded is not only individually fateful; *time* itself is fate and its course is what determines

DOI: 10.4324/9781003609742-16

humanity."[3] Likewise, the geography in which we dwell, the people and the tradition, the culture and the ancestry into which we are born, are our fate. They do shape the contours of our *psychography*.

My parents never met in Germany. At thirteen, my mother was thrown out of the illusion of enlightened Mosaic assimilation. The light was turned off, crashing into the black hole of shattered glass at Kristallnacht, walking through the night in the streets of her childhood's Hamburg. She never really arrived at morning's light, perhaps because she didn't meet Dr. Brod. For the rest of her life, she would wait for him, always prepared, dressed up for his arrival.

My father, a broken link in a long chain of rabbis, crossed Nazi Germany on his way to work on a farm. He was saved by an unknown, righteous officer at the Gestapo HQ, who shouted at him that German word, which otherwise evokes such horrendous connotations – *herauss*, get out! And so I learned that just like evil dwells in all of us, the spark of goodness may be found in evil's darkest cellar.

My father was a man who set out on his road but never arrived at his destination. Thrown into disarray by the losses, his mother turned into the ashes of Auschwitz, his grandmother dying in Theresienstadt's shadow of deception, he tried to create a life for his offspring. On his way to the kibbutz in the Land of Israel, his wings had lost their wind and his legs, stifled into clay, remained stuck in the charred earth of Europe.

In the Jewish and Israeli mind, Europe evokes contrasting images of kaleidoscopic complexity: sometimes the brightest colors and exquisite patterns, but, at other times, a chaotic conglomerate of broken, scattered shards, shattered hopes that the bonds of ancestral fate can be broken free, that there is enlightenment at the end of the tunnel – and then, hearts and bones trampled, again and again by the dark boots of perfect haughtiness. Europe is both the universality of individual enlightenment and the destruction of ancestral particularism. The Jewish craving for the layers of culture, protective against the harsh and bleeding Mother Earth in the Land of the Fathers, and the unmediated exposure to the blazing sun god, that desire, projected upon Europe, has all too often turned into disillusion, as civilization becomes a deceptive *Fata Morgana* and as the crystal prism of freedom throws its rays of projections on Judas, the traitor without whom there would be no Christ.[4]

While the heart is in the East, the mind craves for the West.[5] Two millennia already, in spite of pogroms and persecutions, Europe is the dream of a safe sanctuary. It provides a respite from the intensity and unmediated exposure to the archetypal forces that weigh heavily on the eastern Mediterranean. Europe, itself drifting westward from its birth in Phoenicia, along those same Mediterranean shores, lures herself like a white bull, tempts and promises a new life, cutting the suffocating strings to "the dust of the ruined sanctuary."[6] She promises a life detached from the swamps and the soil, from the spirit that inevitably sinks deep into matter that then falls into ruins; she promises air and wind – so much so that the breeze of freedom may turn into storms of shadowy projections and persecution. While sometimes Europe built walls around the ghettoes – sometimes enabling the comfort of life in seclusion and, at other times, tightening them into prisons of filth and suffocation – Europe bore in her bosom the hope for Jews of breaking out of those walls, either by assimilation or by lofty cosmopolitanism, so that the mind could turn toward the progress of humankind, whether in trade and merchandise or in "songs without words" and "imagination beyond knowledge."[7] As Amos Elon notes in *The Pity of it All*, within decades of his death, not one of the large number of offspring of the philosopher Moses Mendelssohn, father of Jewish enlightenment, remained Jewish.[8]

The dilemma and the conflict between particularism and universalism, between ancestral fate and individual destiny, between Jewish law and Jewish soul, between free spirit and fertile ground, between the Father's Commandments and the Mother's harsh Earth, are ever-present in the Jew. The birth of the God-image beats in the heart of Jerusalem, the one God born out of the gods and the goddesses, collecting the idols and the amulets into monotheistic worship. Everywhere you go, a hilltop here, a valley there, you tread the paths of the past. *Har Megiddo* is *Armageddon*, a little hilltop with an ancient fort along the important Via Maris Highway connecting Ancient Egypt with Mesopotamia. The location of ancient battles, it is, as well, the location of the projected War of "Gog and Magog," at the end of days.

Who can bear the archetypal burden, who does not want to shake off the weight of archetypal baggage?

The Hebrew God was born an old man, a Father without a childhood, a harsh and demanding, compassionate and sometimes righteous Spirit, full of promises, not a few of which he broke, such as promising Abraham he would multiply his seed into a great nation. If only God had spoken Yiddish, one would understand it was a joke. It took a son, a son of God, and a son of man to break the bonds of the religion of the Fathers, to preach what could then eventually break away and spread and become a much greater, larger nation.[9] In the Jew (as a collective generalization of a bundle of cultural complexes), there is a simultaneous envy of the freedom from carrying the burden of the ancestors and a fear of being pulled away from the roots.

Throughout the ages, Biblical history, agricultural festivals, social laws and codes of conduct, and the Hebrew language were cramped together in the luggage that the Jew carried from the Land, increasingly squeezed into the fold of Halachic confines and religious ritual.[10] Eventually it got abstracted into the spirit of the times as "German of Mosaic descent," with an as thin thread of ancestral link as possible, until finally cut off, whether by force or by will.

But then, at the other end, Hasidism served as a compensatory movement of rejuvenating the Jewish spirit and the soul of Jewish life. In fact, Erich Neumann saw Hasidism as the very basis of his own psychological formulations. In *Jacob and Esau: On the Collective Symbolism of the Brother Motif*, he describes the cycle from the ancestor's individual but prototypal experience, through the manifestations in tradition to modern man's need for the individually meaningful experience.[11] Neumann himself attempted to reinterpret the religious soul of the collective in the psychological experience of the individual.

The return to the ancestral soil was an attempt to unite the individual experience with both the particular ancestry and with universal principles. It was, and remains, an attempt to unite the maternal Earth with the paternal Spirit, returning the holy days to the living seasons, a return to the everyday soul that thrives in Hebrew as a living language, and not only as the often hardly understood holy tongue made soulless by repetition compulsion. The "ingathering of the exiles" aimed not only at physically bringing the Jews back to their ancient homeland to make the desert bloom, as the English translation of the Declaration of Independence says, but also "to make souls blossom," as the original Hebrew says, which so easily gets lost in translation, when uprooted from the soil.[12]

And yet, the moment of realization is also the moment of impurity. When the dream and the yearning, "if I forget thee, oh Jerusalem" turns into living reality, the wholeness of Heavenly Jerusalem becomes the strife and conflict of Terrestrial Jerusalem, and with the exiled soul, the shadows need to be gathered in as well.[13] But since reality is an ever-leaking vessel, the Jews, whether scattered in Europe or dispersed elsewhere, or in their own habitat, will continue to project, dream, and fantasize, and they will fear and despise – but the Jews will also remain the target, no less, of projected fear, hatred, and aversion, of admiration as well as rejection.

Notes

1 Yehuda Amichai, *Poems of Jerusalem and Love Poems* (New York: Sheep Meadow, 1992), p. 55. Also quoted in my chapter on Jerusalem, in Thomas Singer (ed.), *Psyche and the City: A Soul's Guide to the Modern Metropolis* (New Orleans: Spring Journal Books, 2010).
2 From Erel Shalit, *Requiem: A Tale of Exile and Return* (Cheyenne, WY: Fisher King Press, 2010).
3 Erich Neumann, "The Moon and Matriarchal Consciousness," in *The Fear of the Feminine and Other Essays on Feminine Psychology* (Princeton, NJ: Princeton University Press, 1994), p. 91.
4 Cf. Erel Shalit, *Enemy, Cripple, Beggar: Shadows in the Hero's Path* (Cheyenne, WY: Fisher King Press, 2008), for example, p. 148.
5 From a poem by Yehuda Halevy, ca. 1075–1141:

> My heart is in the East, and I in the uttermost West.
> My food has no taste. How can it be sweet?
> How can I fulfil my pledges and my vows,
> When Zion is in the power of Edom, and I in the fetters of Arabia?
> It will be nothing to me to leave all the goodness of Spain.
> So rich will it be to see the dust of the ruined sanctuary.

> From *The Jewish Poets of Spain 900–1250*, trans. and with an introduction by David Goldstein (Harmondsworth, Middlesex: Penguin Books, 1971), p. 128.

6 *The Jewish Poets of Spain 900–1250.*
7 Felix Mendelssohn and Albert Einstein, arts and science, respectively.
8 Amos Elon, *The Pity of It All: A Portrait of the German-Jewish Epoch, 1743–1933* (New York: Picador, 2002).
9 Mark 14:62: "And Jesus said, I am: and ye shall see the Son of man sitting on the right hand of power, and coming in the clouds of heaven." In Hebrew, "son of man" is "ben adam," which means "a human being," or, in Yiddish, simply a *mensch*.
10 The Land of Israel, *Haaretz* in Hebrew.
11 Erich Neumann, *Jacob and Esau: On the Collective Symbolism of the Brother Motif*, ed. and with an introduction by Erel Shalit (Asheville, OR: Chiron, 2016).
12 See Erel Shalit, *The Hero and His Shadow: Psychopolitical Aspects of Myth and Reality in Israel* (Cheyenne, WY: Fisher King Press, 2011).
13 Psalms 137:5.

A Very Narrow Bridge

Israel and Its Cultural Complexes

Henry Abramovitch

In this chapter, I want to speak of an Israel very different from the one portrayed on TV, in newspapers, or on social media focusing on war, conflict, or kidnappings. Israel is a land of polarities and contradictions. It is the realization of a 2000-year-old dream for the people of the Book; it is the *nakba* (the "catastrophe") for Palestinians. It is the land of oppression and terror, yet it is the only democracy in the entire Middle East. Feelings about Israel tend to bring out "recollectivization" of "group identity into an 'us versus them – for us or against us'" style of thinking. There is no other small country that attracts such intense projections of love and hate.

Nevertheless, it is difficult to make generalizations about Israel because there are so many different cultures and religions living side by side. There are very traditional villages of Circassians, whose origins are in Caucasus; Samaritans, who have lived here long before the time of Jesus; Druze, a unique people and religion that broke away from Islam in the twelfth century and that believe in reincarnation. There are Bedouins who were traditional nomads whose tradition goes back tens of thousands of years; there are Christian and Muslim Arabs; Palestinians, some of whom live alongside Jews in "mixed towns" like Jaffa, Ramle, or Lod, the burial place of St. George. The Jewish population is itself highly diversified. There are ultraorthodox Jews, who are themselves divided into hundreds of sects, or "courts," who follow a very restrictive lifestyles, where internet or even TV are strictly forbidden. There are Ashkenazi Jews whose roots are in Eastern Europe, and there are Sephardic Jews, descendants of those expelled from Spain in 1492, many of whom went to North Africa, the Balkans, or the Ottoman Empire. But there are also other Jews with unique traditions, such as Jews from Yemen, Italy, Ethiopia, Argentina, India, or Lithuania.

The country is deeply divided in their opinions about how to deal with the Occupied Territories in the West Bank. A strong group of nationalist Israeli Jews claim it as ancestral patrimony, seeing Palestinians there as second-class citizens at best. Many leftist peace-oriented groups oppose the occupation bitterly and are involved in activities to assist Palestinians in guarding their human rights or in joint therapeutic endeavors. The army plays a central role in Israeli life. The Israel Defense Force, as it is called in Hebrew, is more like a militia, in that everyone begins as a private in basic training and must work their way up by initiative and ability. It

DOI: 10.4324/9781003609742-17

serves as a rite of passage for young men and women, who take up high levels of responsibility from a young age. Reserve military duty goes on into a person's forties. It serves as a launching pad into politics, as most Israeli leaders were commandos if not generals. The army is also a unifying force for those who serve, which besides Jews includes Druze, Bedouin, Circassian, Christian Arabs, and others. There is great resentment against the ultraorthodox who do not serve but instead receive a stipend to study Talmud. Another tension is between those from richer urban centers and those from the poorer "development towns" on the periphery.

Living in the center of such dreadful tensions and war, one would expect Israelis to feel disheartened or depressed. However, according to 2023 Global Happiness Index, Israel is rated fourth in the world for overall happiness, ahead of Sweden and Switzerland. It has one of the longest life-spans in the world and the lowest rates in Europe for "despair deaths" from overdose, suicide, or alcohol-related deaths. Israelis have a strong sense of belonging, which combined with an open, honest, and friendly attitude, seems to make a difference. Another unifying secret is Shabbat, the Jewish Sabbath, which begins Friday at sunset. Although orthodox, traditional, and secular Jews observe the holy day differently, it is a time for family to gather and to eat a festive meal together with extended family. One observer said, it is "thanksgiving every week." Shabbat invites a different spirit and a different spirituality. To be in Jerusalem and see the sunset against the disappearing traffic is to enter into the Land of Shabbat. It can be understood as an active imagination in which you feel that everything you ever had to do is already done.

Culturally extraverted Israelis often talk to strangers on a bus and may end up inviting them home for dinner. Another reason may be culture. There are more museums in Israel per capita than in any other country, including the world-class Israel Museum with the Dead Sea Scrolls. Israel has more buildings designed in Bauhaus style than any other country in the world, including Germany. Its classical music, pop music, and modern dance are also at the highest level. Contemporary Hebrew literature includes Nobel Prize winner Shmuel Agnon and internationally renowned writers like Amos Oz, David Grossman, and the poet Yehuda Amichai.[1]

Certain Israeli cultural complexes contribute to this unreasonable happiness and its inevitable shadow. Cultural complexes are repetitive historical experiences that have taken root in the unconscious, and when activated, they take hold of the collective psyche of the group, function autonomously, organize group life, and facilitate functioning of the individual within the group. They may give members of a group a sense of identity, belonging, and historical continuity. Just as individuals may be traumatized, so too, may groups.

Language as Culture

It may surprise English speakers that Hebrew has no word for *mind* or *solitude* and uses the same words for *like* and *love* or for *home* and *house*. On the other hand, there are Israeli Hebrew terms that have no equivalent in other languages. One example is *dugri*, which is usually translated as "straight-talk." In the original

Arabic, *dugri* means "straight" as in "Go straight!" or "Speak the straight truth!" But in the Israeli cultural mode of speech, it means saying what you really think without consideration of the other person's feelings. In a sense, it is the opposite of politeness, yet it assumes that relationships are robust and can withstand conflict. *Dugri* implies that there is an enduring sense of equality so that one is allowed to speak directly. One commonly cited example concerns the situation when the boss of a tech company asks the new recruit how she is feeling in the new job. The new employee, instead of giving the expected polite response, might reply in the spirit of *dugri*, "Well, the computer is too slow and the food is lousy." And they would not get fired! In many cultures, such straight-talk is considered impolite, even rude. I use *dugri* in doing supervision with international router groups. I would often teach the group the meaning of *dugri* and then might ask the struggling supervisee, "Please, *dugri*, what do you mean to say?" It allowed for a directness in the supervision experience, even in cultures that favor indirectness.

Improvisation

Another central characteristic of contemporary Israel is improvisation. There is a joke that is commonly told: "In Germany, everything goes by the book, but in Israel there is no book." In countries like Germany, culture and personality are oriented toward following rules. Not to follow the rules is to invite disorder and even chaos. In Israel, the attitude toward rules is much more flexible and even reflects the cultural complex of questioning authority, which I discuss later. The positive aspect of such informality is that it allows Israelis to respond quickly and creatively to changing situations. This attitude served Israel well in the Six Days War, the Yom Kippur War, and other military operations that required creative flexibility. It may also be seen in niche areas like high tech where the ability to improvise provides a strong advantage. Israel, the Startup Nation, has helped to create an impressive list of innovations in technology, including the cellphone, voicemail, Waze, firewalls, Messenger, the Pentium chip, even elements of Windows were created with Israeli knowhow. This innovative, improvisational style has made Israel a world leader in agricultural technology, the creation of fresh drinking water from a desalination process, the use of solar energy, and the reuse of treated wastewater in agriculture. It is perhaps the only country that has more trees this century than the last. Israel is home to the lowest place on earth, the Dead Sea, and the lowest freshwater lake, the Sea of Galilee.

The origins of improvisation are also old and new. The new reflects the conditions under which pioneers struggled when living with the rigid rules of the British Mandate. An oft-heard phrase is, "Well, if we followed the rules, we would still be under British Mandate." One well-known example of this spirit is the so-called Wall and Tower kibbutzim, which were built overnight and therefore could not be torn down. Many leading kibbutzim were constructed this way. From the perspective of typology, Israel has an extraverted, intuitive orientation. Because of the intensity of Israeli life, the fast pace of shifting events, the collective seems to suffer from bipolar extremes of emotions, with extreme highs and lows.

The ethos of improvisation is connected to a strong tradition of questioning, including questioning authority. Another quick joke will set the tone:

Question: Why do Jews always answer a question with another question?
Answer: Why not?

This Jewish, sometimes irreverent, independence of thought may be contrasted with the catechism. Both Eastern and Western Christianity use a fixed set of questions and answers to teach about dogma and faith. Jews, in contrast, are encouraged to inquire and explore intellectually. The tradition is that a good question is valued highly above the answer. The Talmud, still the central text of orthodox and ultraorthodox Judaism, is based largely on building theory through the examination of examples, the opposite of traditional European philosophical traditions. A typical question might be this: "What if the opposite is true?" Encouraging freedom of thought, inquiry, and questioning makes Jews natural intellectuals. Symbolically, it was Einstein who was asked to be president of Israel.

Freier Syndrome

Israelis suffer from another, more shadowy cultural complex, called the *freier syndrome*. The origin of the German/Yiddish-sounding word is unclear. But to be a *freier* is to feel shamefully taken advantage of. It is like being a sucker, only a hundred times worse. A sucker may be a gullible, naïve innocent, but the sucker bears no moral responsibility for being victimized. No one wants to be a sucker, but the moral responsibility lies only with the exploiter. Not so with the freier syndrome. A freier feels morally culpable for being taken advantage of.

The freier syndrome, therefore, is based on the fear of being taken advantage of in a shameful way. In a defensive reaction, some Israelis, out of a paranoid fear of "being your freier," may unconsciously victimize and take advantage of others. The fear that "I will be a freier" blinds me to the fact that I am making the other person my "freier." One can see the impact of the freier in the free-spirited, dangerous way Israelis drive or in rudeness, the negative side of *dugri* "straight-talk." I believe the unconscious roots of the freier complex derive from the group trauma of the Holocaust, which still permeates the Israeli psyche. One cultural hint is found in the fact that youth used to refer to a weak, vulnerable child as *sabon*, "a piece of soap." A piece of soap references Auschwitz, where soap was made of human fats. The syndrome implies that if you let up your guard even for a minute, you may find yourself in the group trauma of the Holocaust.

Alte-Neuland, or Old-New Land

Another key metaphor for understanding Israel is as *Alte-Neuland*, or *Old-New Land*, to use the title of Theodore Herzl's prophetic book. The paradoxes of the old-new go far in explaining multiple and parallel realities in which Israelis live.

The dynamic between old and new is profoundly expressed in the archetypal rivalry between Tel Aviv, the first Jewish city, and Jerusalem, the Holy City. Tel Aviv, founded on the sand dunes in 1909, is open, relaxed, secular, leftwing, on the beach, by the sea. It is the gay and high-tech capital of the Middle East, the "24-hour city that never closes" for over four million citizens. It is not only a place but also a state of mind, the State of Tel Aviv.

The Old City of Jerusalem, with its massive stone walls and magnificent decorated gates, is a physical mandala at the center. The name *Jerusalem* itself means "peace" and is known as the place where heaven and earth meet. It includes the holiest places for Judaism, Christianity, and Islam: the remnant of the second Temple known as "the Wailing Wall"; the Church of the Holy Sepulchre, containing the tomb of Christ, built and maintained by the Russian Orthodox Church; and the Al Aqsa, or as it is called in the Qu'ran, the "Farthest Mosque" and the Dome of the Rock whence Mohammed went on his night journey to heaven. All of these holy places are within short walking distance of each other. It is place of pilgrimage, even if many, like Jung's strange visitors at the beginning of the *Septem Sermones*, said, "We have come back from Jerusalem where we found not what we sought." Over generations Jerusalem has been a natural symbol for the Self. At its best, Jerusalem holds together the opposites, pointing to something Higher. At Passover seder, Jews around the world, for 2000 years have said, "Next year in Jerusalem," even when they are living in Jerusalem. At its worst, it is gripped by violence committed in the name of a jealous God.

Jerusalem, over 3000 years old, is founded on tradition, with high walls, separate quarters (Armenian, Christian, Muslim, Jewish), and colonies (American, Greek, German), with a sanctity both in the imagination and in visible archaeological sites that reveal its history layer by layer. It has *Yad VaShem*, the world-renown Holocaust Museum and Memorial. The city has been attacked fifty-two times; it has been destroyed and rebuilt. It has the Knesset and Hebrew University. It has a unique architectural feature in that all buildings are cladded in white stone, which reflects in sunset and sunshine, giving a hidden archetypal unity to this city of many faiths. Older citizens claim you have to be in Jerusalem for ten generations before you can claim to be a Jerusalemite. There are shadows, of course. East Jerusalem is a dwelling place of Palestinians who make up a quarter of the population and who can vote in municipal elections but are notoriously underserved and discriminated against. The fans of the local football team are known for their brutality and racism. There are acts of terror but almost no street violence.

Tel Aviv and Jerusalem are only 50 kilometers apart geographically, but light years from each other in sanctity, ideology, and visions of looking forward versus looking back. There is also a unique Jerusalem syndrome, where pilgrims or tourists become seized by the Holy Spirit and enter a state of psychosis. I recall a Christian who was possessed by a Divine Voice and tried to circumcise himself in his hotel room. Another began speaking in tongues at the Wailing Wall. People from Tel Aviv will gladly agree that residents of Jerusalem are, by and large, "crazy." Tour guides are trained to identify the early phases of this geographical illness and seek help.

Jerusalem has another geographical versatility. It is, as the Psalms say, ringed by hills so that every step up or down gives you a new sightline. In one moment, you can see over to Jordan; in another moment, into the sheer valley or wadi where babies were sacrificed to Moloch and where Judas killed himself. Jerusalem is as heavy as Tel Aviv is light. No one sings for the welfare of Tel Aviv, but believers worldwide pray for the peace of Jerusalem, whose very name means peace. Somehow, Israel holds these opposites together in a dynamic tension.

Naming traditions is another area of clash between the "old-new." Traditionally, Jews name children for relatives. Ashkenazi Jews name for dead relatives exclusively, whereas Sephardi Jews may name children for both living and dead close kin, especially beloved grandparents. In "mixed" marriages, this itself can be the source of tension. Names of males can be feminized and given to a girl and vice versa. The key is that naming establishes ancestral continuity. However, in the case of serious or life-threatening illness, an additional name, such as *Chaim*, meaning "life," or *Alter*, meaning the "old one," would be added to their name. Here, the change of name is a way of changing the fate of the sick person, as if to confuse the Angel of Death. A child born after the death of their father might be called *Abba,* meaning "father," as in the case of illustrious poet Abba Kovner. Zionist pioneers looking toward a heroic future rejected the values of the Diaspora and with it the traditional Jewish family names. New chosen family names were often short, connected with nature or the Bible. In the 1950s, Israeli diplomats were forced to change their names to Hebrew ones. Naming tradition practices are widely upheld by ultraorthodox, mainstream religious, and traditional Israelis; whereas secular Israelis typically use short new names taken from nature, ones that are gender neutral like *Tal* (dew), or peripheral biblical names, like *Hagar* or *Omri*, or even made-up names, such as *Lior*, meaning "my light," chosen for their sound quality rather than for the meaning. Traditionally, the worst fate is not to have someone named for you and for no one to recite the *Kaddish* prayer at your funeral, traditionally the obligation of the eldest son. The tension between name as embodying destiny and name as a label is played out across generations within the same family.

Unity

Another important theme in Israel is unity. The theme of unity and oneness is expressed in the central prayer of Judaism, *Sh'ma*, which is said during daily prayers, on the Sabbath, at festivals, and by tradition in one's final breath. It refers to biblical text: "Hear, O, Israel, the Lord, our God, the Lord is One!" (Deuteronomy 6:4). Theologically, it is the profound expression of monotheism, the belief in one God, but it is much more. It reflects a unity in the world that He created. Togetherness is a strong historical element in Hebrew civilizations, which created a sense of unity between Jewish communities. A powerful Hebrew phrase (which loses much of its impact in translation) is *Am Israel Hai*, or "The People of Israel live!" This phrase of defiant existence is said in opposition to all efforts to destroy and exterminate the Hebrew nation. This central theme provides the background for many Jewish festivals, from Passover to Purim, Chanukah, Tisha b'Av, and so on. Another expression of this cultural solidarity and mutual responsibility is "All Israel are guarantors for one another," which was already well-known in Talmudic times (Talmud, Sh'vuot 39a). It highlights how each Jew is responsible for the other. In a negative sense, the actions of one Jewish person can lead to punishment of the entire Jewish community, as in blood libel. In its positive sense, it describes the deep kinship libido that individuals feel as members of the same tribe.

Despite almost a year of intense political protest against the anti-democratic judicial reforms, the phrase most used by media since October 7, 2023, is "Together we will win." After the Hamas attack of the "Black Shabbat," the theme of unity is the main rallying cry of Israelis concerning the war. The phrase "Together we will win" is displayed on buses, posters, buildings, telephone, poles, and so on. The call for unity is all the more poignant and ironic because it was preceded by the largest and most intense protest movement in Israeli history against Prime Minister Netanyahu and his government to undermine democracy through judicial reform, by undercutting the autonomy of the Supreme Court and other anti-democratic measures.

While the government and its agencies failed to respond to the shocking events of October 7, it was the protest movement itself that reacted by improvising immediate relief, social welfare, and emotional support for the bereaved and displaced. Indeed, the entire Israeli therapeutic community, including Jungian Institutes, quickly mobilized to provide trauma-related interventions to internal refugees from the North Border (under missile attack from Lebanon) or communities in the area that had been invaded. Rapid response volunteer teams of mental health professionals went out to treat individuals and groups in hotels at the Dead Sea, Eilat, or on the Mediterranean coast. Psychologically, however, it seems to me, writing in January 2024, that it is premature to reflect back on the atrocities of October 7 and their aftermath. As one of my patients put it, "How can I dream, when every day is a nightmare?!"

At the same time, even during the first weeks of the war, questions were being asked: Why were clear intelligence reports of Hamas training and intention ignored? Why was military help so long in coming? Why were there so many government failures in providing relief and assistance? The State Controller and Ombudsman have already published two damning reports about government failures. Another poignant experience of unity in modern Israel occurs during the collective moments of silence on Holocaust Memorial Day and then a week later, on Israel Memorial Day. Sirens go off, people stand in silence, even on the highway, next to their cars.

Friendship

Friendship is another crucial aspect of well-being in Israel in all its diverse communities. Friendship is seen as a deep, personal, almost sacred commitment that is at the center of social life. Expectations from friends are almost as high as for family.

The security and belonging that goes with true friendship has a therapeutic quality. When a friend knows all about you, there is no reason to hide or present a persona. Rather, true friendship dissolves persona anxiety entirely. In a metaphoric sense, a true friend functions like the Self, seeing all of us, accepting all of us.

The security that a true friend provides is illustrated in the phrase, "It is not so much our friends' help that helps us as it is, as the confidence of their help." This emotional security that friends provide is expressed poignantly in this phase: "It's the friends you can call up at 4 a.m. that matter." In Israel, I have had that 4 a.m. experience of friendship. It was the middle of the night, and I urgently needed to borrow a car. With trepidation, I called upon a friend. I was worried he might say that he never loans his car, that he would have to check with his insurance, that he would need his car back at 7 a.m., that he would agree but leave me terrified about what would happen if it received a scratch or a dent. Instead, when he heard my predicament, he said, "I will be outside in two minutes," and without a word, he gave me the keys with a smile. He said, "Good luck and bring it back when you can." This experience taught me a lot about what it means to be a friend in Israel.

True friendship has a timeless quality. It is timeless both in the moment of an actual meeting but also when, after a long break, true friends just effortlessly pick up where they left off. Friendship is, therefore, a never-ending conversation. Two other crucial aspects of the true friend are accompaniment and absence of hierarchy. Albert Camus gives a poetic expression of these qualities in his famous phrase: "Don't walk behind me; I may not lead. Don't walk in front of me; I may not follow. Just walk beside me and be my friend." Camus highlights how much friendship is a shared journey without "ahead" or "behind," but walking side by side in the long journey toward becoming ourselves. Israelis believe in the words of their Mediterranean neighbor, Pythagoras of Samos, "Friends are as companions on a journey, who ought to aid each other to persevere in the road to a happier life." True friends are not "yes men" but speak *dugri*. They do not tell us what we want to hear, but rather speak with refreshing directness. Friends give clear, focused, critical feedback that does not trigger a defensive ego reaction. They tell us what we need to hear, what no one else will tell us. Oscar Wilde put it succinctly: "A friend stabs you in the front."

In Israel, there are numerous times of passage where lifelong friendships grow and blossom. Friends are made in kindergarten, high school, youth movement, in the army, at university, or while trekking in South America, and some at least become "friends for life." Israel may have a big global presence, but, in fact, it is a very small country and over half is arid land or desert. The actual populated area of the country is about half the size of New Jersey, or the eastern quarter of Lake Michigan. The smallness of the country means that friends can easily stay in touch.

While individual friendships are very important, no less important are tight circles of friends, or *chevre*. These *chevre* are very characteristic of Israeli society where mixed groups meet to talk late into the night, on Shabbat or festivals, or to go hiking together with their children. One of my *chevre* were classmates of my wife at university with whom I formed a warm, intimate bond. We would meet throughout the year, but on the second day of Hebrew New Year, Rosh Hashana, we had a special ritual gathering. After a spectacular buffet banquet, each person would say something significant that happened to them during the past year. These were memorable, festive, but also reflective gatherings, in keeping with the spirit of the Hebrew New Year.

Like most Israelis, I have more than one *chevre*. One is a group of Jungian analysts, where each year we choose a theme and then each of us presents something personal, clinical, and theoretical on the topic. This "circle" has intimate space where sharing in individuation is highlighted. I have another *chevre,* which is closer to the original cultural meaning of the word, deriving from "friend," in the sense of "study partner," the main format for learning in the yeshiva world. In this *chevre*, we have been studying texts together every week for well over forty years. We have studied many Jewish books but also Gilgamesh, Dante, and Ovid. Many of the six of us are also close personal friends, on intimate terms with each other's wives and children. In the often turbulent Middle East, the group is an oasis of fellowship and inquiry.

The geography of Israel is noteworthy. It is the land bridge between three continents: Africa, Asia, and Europe. Many millions of birds pass through it twice a year in one of the greatest migrations of all. Archaeology has shown that early humans passed from Africa to Europe and beyond and there are, indeed, unique caves where Neanderthals and *Homo sapiens* lived at the same time. There are more than thirty distinct ecosystems in Israel; tiny Israel has more botanical variation than all of the United Kingdom.

It is also interesting to note changes in iconic self-images. From 1930s through the 1960s, the key Israeli myth and imagery was that of the *sabra*. The *sabra*, the tenacious, thorny prickly pear, provided a key image of the "new Israeli," rough on the outside but sweet on the inside. In those times, Israelis were seen and saw themselves as having a prickly persona. The cactus fruit was compared to native-born Israelis, who were considered tough on the outside but delicate and sweet, once one got to know them, on the inside. The term was implicitly contrasting the tough, stand your ground, ascetic style of native-born Israelis, such as Kibbutzniks, to weak, vulnerable diaspora Jews. Indeed, it was considered a compliment at that time to be called "a real sabra." Although the myth of the sabra played a key role in literature, arts, and presentation of self, it has almost entirely disappeared as a cultural icon. Instead, it retains only a literal meaning of a "native-born Israeli."

Death and Mourning

Another unique element in Israeli life concerns attitudes to death, funerals, and mourning customs, a topic in which I have a special interest. Significantly, Jews and Muslims share the same basic framework. In contrast to European societies, burial typically occurs within hours of death, almost always the same day. Coffins are not used, but the person is wrapped in burial garments with a winding sheet and carried to the graves. The only exception is Israeli military funerals, in which simple wood coffins draped with a flag are used. But even in these cases, the bottom of the coffin has special holes so that the dead body will be in contact with the purifying earth of the Great Mother. All funeral expenses, including the cost of burial plots, are covered by Israeli social security. Traditional Jewish funerals are carried out by "volunteers" in the *Hevra Kadisha,* or Holy Brotherhood. After a short graveside service, each one places a small stone on the grave. Flowers may also be left, but they are not traditionally used; as things that are wilting and dying, they signify impermanence, unlike the stone that is symbolically everlasting. Then mourners in the Jewish tradition pass between two lines of "comforters" and then proceed home to sit *shiva.* During these seven days, mourners receive visits and food from friends and relatives in what has been called "group psychotherapy." The tradition is not to speak until the mourner first speaks so that one may respond in dialogue. I believe it is likely that this tradition influenced Sigmund Freud in the construction of the structure of psychoanalysis. At the end of the *shiva*, mourners return to the grave and again at thirty days and at each yearly anniversary. Funerals of soldiers, or even those killed in tragic circumstances, are regularly shown on television. Ernst Becker's phrase *the denial of death*, so common in the West, is not characteristic of life in Israel.

Masada Complex

Perhaps the most dangerous cultural complex in Israel is the *Masada complex*. Today, Masada is a World Heritage Site, a flat-top mountain in the Judean Desert overlooking the Dead Sea, where King Herod built his sumptuous winter palace that was uncovered in one of Israel's most famous archaeological excavations. To hike up the mountain in the dark, in order to see the goldening dawn at the top, is truly a numinous experience. The psychological meaning of Masada in the Israeli psyche does not reside in its beauty but in its history. It is based on a famous description by Josephus, a Hebrew general turned Roman historian. The crucial historical setting is the brutal suppression of the Great Revolt of the Jews against the Roman legions, which began in 70 CE After a few short years of independence, the Jewish State was brutally and systematically crushed by the Roman legions. At the end, less than a thousand Jews held off an army of centurions, in the nearly impregnable fortress of Masada. Finally, they realized their position was without hope of victory or escape. Rather than become enslaved, these defenders decided to kill all men, women, and babies rather than fall into the hands of their enemy.

This "mass suicide" reflects the actions of desperate people who follow the motto of the American state of New Hampshire, "Live free or die!" This attitude proclaims that dignity, honor, and freedom are more important than life itself. Sadly, these sentiments are not unknown in Jewish history when, during pogroms, the Crusades, or the Black Death, desperate Jews felt it preferable to murder their own beloveds rather than let them be tortured, raped, and murdered by the mob.

But the modern meaning of Masada is darker still. The modern version began to take form when the Nazi armies threatened to conquer Egypt, Palestine, and beyond. Local fighters proposed that they would find a Masada-like location from which they would fight to the death, killing as many of the enemies as possible. Although Israel does not admit it officially, it is an open secret that it does possess nuclear weapons. If Israel were invaded and the situation desperate, it might use these nuclear weapons as a final stand, not only killing ourselves but also killing as many of the enemies as possible. This Masada complex recalls a similar gesture by Samson in the Book of Judges. Golda Meir told future President Biden, many decades ago, "Israel has a secret weapon. It has nowhere to go!" The Masada complex highlights an existential anxiety, or *angst*, expressed in the phrase, "When I go to sleep, I don't know if I will wake up to find my country." Such existential anxiety is perhaps unique to Israel and, paradoxically, is also the source of so much of its vitality.

A Very Narrow Bridge

I want to end with another cultural icon, which is a source of special courage. It comes from the words of one of the greatest Hasidic leaders, Rabbi Nachman of Bratzlav. The words, sung all together to a haunting melody are, "All the world is a very, narrow bridge, but the essence is not to fear at all." This beloved song might be a motto for Israel itself.

Bibliographic Essay

For more on the sources of Israel's resilience and happiness, see Dan Senor and Saul Singer, *The Genius of Israel: The Surprising Resilience of a Divided Nation in a Turbulent World* (New York: Simon & Schuster, 2023). Their previous book, *Start Up Nation: The Story of Israel's Economic Miracle* (2011), describes how Israel became a world center for new technology innovation.

J. D. Ziff discusses "Shabbat as Therapy," *Journal of Psychology and Judaism* 7 (2), pp. 118–134. The definitive study of *dugri* is Tamar Katriel, *Talking Straight: Dugri Speech in Israeli Sabra Culture* (Cambridge: Cambridge University Press, 1984).

For a discussion of the *freier complex,* see Linda Bloch, "Who's Afraid of Being a Freier?" *Communication Theory* 13 (2003, 2): pp. 25–59.

For examples of improvisation in different aspects of Israeli life, see Ira Sharkansky and Yair Zalmanovitch, "Improvisation in Public Administration and Policy Making in Israel," *Public Administration Review* 60 (2000, 4): pp. 321–339; and "Israel: Where Improvisation Usually Finds a Way," *Hospital Practice* 7 (1972, 11): pp. 145–174.

The most comprehensive study of the evolution of the sabra is Oz Almog, *The Sabra: The Creation of the New Jew* (Berkeley: University of California Press, 2000). The renowned biblical scholar and translator Robert Alter discusses "The Masada Complex," *Commentary Magazine*, July 1973, at commentary.org.

IAAP News Bulletin no. 24, January 2024, includes many examples of how Jungian analysts responded therapeutically and creatively to help victims of the October 7, 2023, invasion and atrocities, including joint Israeli-Palestinian projects. For more on Jewish funerals and mourning, see my, "The Jerusalem Funeral as a Microcosm of the 'Mismeeting' between Religious and Secular Israelis," in Zvi Sobol and Benjamin Beit-Hallachmi (eds.), *Tradition, Innovation, Conflict: Judaism and Jewishness in Contemporary Israel* (Albany: State University of New York Press, 1991); and " 'Good Death' and 'Bad Death': Therapeutic Implications of Cultural Conceptions of Death and Bereavement," in Ruth Malkinson, Simon Shimson Rubin, and Eliezer Witztum (eds.), *Traumatic and Nontraumatic Loss and Bereavement* (Madison, CT: Psychosocial Press, 2000), pp. 255–272.

For further discussion of the "Palestinian question" in Israel, see, Joseph Massad, "The Persistence of the Palestinian Question," *Cultural Critique* 59 (Winter 2005): pp. 1–23; and the recent video panel, *The Palestinian Question as a Jewish Question*, held at Harvard Divinity School, March 23, 2023, at https://rpl.hds.harvard.edu/news/video-palestinian-question-jewish-question.

Note

1 Yehuda Amichai was born in Würzburg, Germany. Jörg Rasche recounts in Chapter 10, "The Jewish Anima," the story of his birth. Before immigrating to Palestine his name was Ludwig Pfeuffer, and Rasche's grand-grandfather was the doctor who assisted in his birth.

Europe

The Ghosts of Two World Wars

Is the Replacement Child Part of a Cultural Complex in the European Psyche?

Kristina Schellinski

Two World Wars, ranking as the deadliest conflicts in history, originated in the heart of Europe and ravaged individuals and nations around the world. The seeds of war and destruction, loss and death are planted deep in the souls of many Europeans. When seeking analysis, older clients are often unaware that their suffering may be a consequence of a war that ended seven decades ago. Those born one, two, or three generations later may not even conceive of the fact that their psyche bears traces of transgenerationally transmitted trauma.

The psychological effects of trauma can be traced on the DNA up through the fourth generation.[1] In cases of massive, collective trauma, I have found that trauma can be recognized in dream images and in psychodynamic phenomena for more than four generations. For example, a female client has a dream early on in analysis: she escapes a deadly fire from the eighth-floor balcony; many years later she learns that her ancestors were killed – by fire – in a pogrom centuries ago. Another woman is haunted by nightmares; however, the images in her dreams stand in no connection to her life circumstances. She discovers that her great-great-grandmother and her descendants escaped persecution because she had married a member of another faith. Researchers on the Holocaust were the first to document how the trauma of previous generations is passed on to descendants who, although not having been exposed to the trauma of their ancestors, show similar symptoms as their survivor forebears.[2]

In this chapter, I examine to what extent individuals born in the aftermaths of two World Wars in Europe suffer because they have been born to *replace* someone who died or went missing during the war. In many cases, the "ghosts" of those who died are an element in the unconscious of those who were born to replace them, impinging on their sense of identity. Could elements of the *replacement child syndrome* reflect a cultural complex in the cultural unconscious of individual Europeans, regardless of which country they were born in? Are elements of such a European replacement child complex reflected at the collective level of the European psyche? My reflections and observations are based on my analytical work in Geneva, Switzerland, with clients from many European countries over the past fifteen years.

At the individual level, the person who is living a life that is meant to replace a *dead other* can discover his or her own true life force. Recognizing a

DOI: 10.4324/9781003609742-18

transgenerationally transmitted replacement child trauma brings relief and points to treatment options for the affected person. Collectively, becoming aware of a cultural replacement child complex handed on from generation to generation unconsciously can be a question of war or peace: if the replacement child elements are not rendered conscious, then the *dead other within* is at risk of being projected outward to the *other*. If such were to happen in many individuals in a post-war period, an unconscious predisposition toward acting out could be the seeds for another potential war – whereas recognizing this deadly potential and rediscovering the unique life force within the replacement child could tilt the unconscious drive, at the collective level, toward life. A post-war period extends thus to at least a hundred years – as traces on the DNA point to the transmission of trauma over four generations, it could be in the unconscious of people for centuries. Any warmaker, or nation engaging in war, and any peacemaker must envisage that the consequences for their own people and for their adversary are akin to psychic landmines lying explosively dormant for a very long time.

One can certainly question whether the "ghosts" of war dead may be viewed as unique to a supposed European cultural complex; large-scale death and destruction have wrought immeasurable suffering on human beings in many parts of the world throughout the centuries. As Thomas Singer points out, other war-torn countries, like Cambodia or Vietnam, may suffer from a similar cultural complex, even a "replacement generation syndrome" as a whole generation was killed under the terror regime of Pol Pot (personal communication, July 20, 2014).

What is specifically *European* then, to be examined from the point of view of a contemporary European cultural complex? After the massive loss of life during the two World Wars, Europeans' creative communal efforts were fueled by the desire to conceive a new political entity – the European Economic Community, which later became the European Union. It was conceived on a bed of ruins. The idea that gave rise to the first European endeavor, the European Coal and Steel Community in 1951, was to prevent France and Germany from waging yet another war against each other by fostering cooperation and community. This was followed by the European Economic Community (composed of six nations) in 1958, and finally by the European Union in 1993, which, as of July 1, 2024, counts twenty-seven member states.

The European Economic Community was created in the wake of unprecedented death and destruction, *replacing* a centuries-old structure of sovereign nations, with the goal of preventing future wars between European countries: in short, *giving* new life where death had *taken*. The effort was forward-looking; reconstruction was the rallying cry, not grieving and looking back at the horror of the past. French Philosopher Renan wrote in 1882[3]: "For, the essential element of a nation is that all its individuals must have many things in common but it must also have forgotten many things." The suffering and the forgetting of terrible events binds a nation together. But it is a dangerous binding material!

On an individual level, the replacement child born after a disaster comes into life with the desire to *forget*; the *replacement child* is conceived (or later on designated) to replace one who died. The parents seek to replace death with life and to forget what was taken from them. Such a constellation *can* lead to the replacement child syndrome, a specific psychological condition from which the replacement child as well as his or her descendants suffer, often unconsciously, for generations. Attachment and relational issues due to the absent "other," grief, survivor's guilt, and above all questions pertaining to identity, are telltale characteristics of a replacement child syndrome.[4]

World War II led to the deaths of some seventy-two million people.[5] This figure includes millions of children who were killed, starved, or went missing. More than one-and-a-half million Jewish children were murdered in the Nazi concentration camps.[6]

We do not have quantitative numbers of how many replacement children there are; in most cases, the replacement child may even ignore having been conceived for the purpose of replacing. Sometimes images in the unconscious will eventually point to such a condition surrounding the child's conception or birth. Whether it is an individual life or an entity such as the European Union that has risen from the ashes of previous entities – an existential and soul-searching quest for a new identity is to be expected, at individual and collective levels. I will explore whether elements of the replacement child syndrome are part of a cultural complex of individual Europeans and whether this replacement child syndrome can then be surmised to be part of the European cultural identity or collective psyche.

The Cultural Complex

Joseph Henderson was the first to reflect on the existence of the "cultural unconscious" in 1962.[7] He posited the cultural unconscious as positioned between the personal unconscious and the collective unconscious. To that we can add *another* layer – the layer of the *family unconscious*. Imagine these layers either as widening circles or, as shown in Figure 13.1, in pyramid form.

Emanating from the layer of the cultural unconscious identified by Henderson in 1962, the existence of a "cultural complex" was deduced in 2004 by Thomas Singer and Samuel L. Kimbles, two analysts from San Francisco.[8] Singer is continuing this research by engaging analysts from around the world to explore the concept. As of 2024, seven volumes have been published, including *Placing Psyche* from Australia, *Cultural Complexes of Latin America: Voices of the South*, *Cultural Complexes and the Soul of America*, *Cultural Complexes in China, Japan, Korea, and Taiwan,* and *Cultural Complexes and Europe's Many Souls: Jungian Perspectives on Brexit and the War in Ukraine*. The initial volume of this book, exploring European cultural complexes, was the third in the series.[9] The hallmark of the cultural complex is its "emotional core," its "unconsciousness," and the fact that it continuously collects "repetitive experiences" to validate its own point of view.[10] Rendering the cultural complex conscious is an important aspect in personal, group, and societal analysis, as unconscious *cultural complexes* can affect individuals, groups, peoples, and nations in their projections, perceptions, projects, and policy-making.

The layer of the cultural unconscious imagined as *between* the family and the collective unconscious

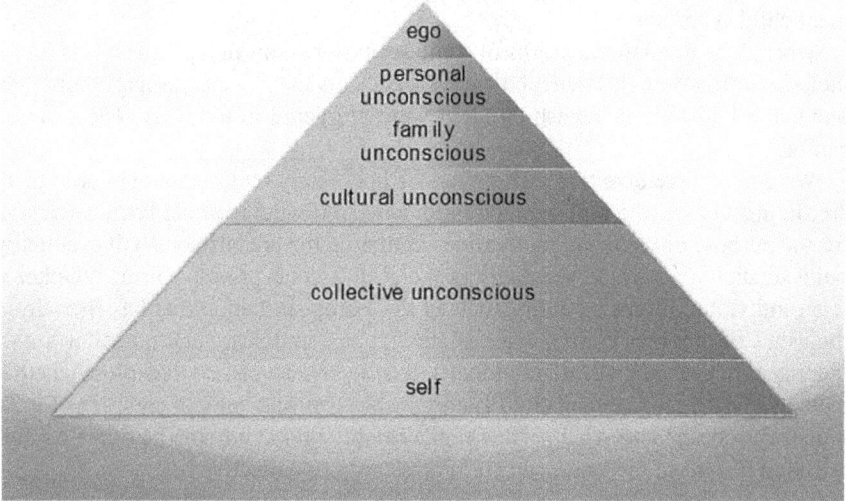

ego

personal
unconscious

family
unconscious

cultural unconscious

collective unconscious

self

Figure 13.1 Cultural unconscious' imagined layer

Freud pointed out the importance of rendering conscious the contents of the *personal unconscious*; Jung drew attention to the dimension of the *collective unconscious*. He also presumed the existence of a *family unconscious*. But he paid little attention to the influence of the unconscious dynamics of groups, large or small, as these led, in his view, to an *"abaissement du niveau mental,"* a lowering of the quality of consciousness that hindered the individual from pursuing a path of growth and responsibility.

In addition to the cultural complexes of different groups, peoples, and nations that make up Europe as a whole, I put forth the hypothesis of a *pan-European cultural complex*, a *European replacement child cultural complex*. I base this on the premise that millions of by-now adult replacement children were born to "make up" for the tens of millions of dead after the First and Second World Wars.

Many replacement children are unconscious well into their adulthood that they were born to *replace lost siblings*. They have little awareness of the psychological consequences of such a constellation, essentially giving rise to the following question: who am I?[11] Am I the dead other, returning, or am I me, my*self*? The true identity must often be unearthed from a heap of parental or wider family projections. The replacement child complex is informed at its core by the archetypes of death and life, with a propensity for repetitive experiences of the creative *or* the destructive poles, the latter potentially leading toward endangering the life of the individual or collective.

Replacement children are often on lifelong journeys searching for their true identity, carrying unprocessed parental (and/or sibling) grief and suffering from survivor's guilt, and looking for the "missing other," the one they replaced. If there is a *European replacement child cultural complex*, based on individual experiences and the collective psyche, what might this mean for Europe, its member states, and its citizens? A search for true identity and the missing other, mixed with guilt?

On a Personal Note

Sometimes when we talk among colleagues about cultural complexes, I have observed a tendency toward recalling historical material, referencing national myths, military victories and defeats, and religious confrontations of the past. Because my interests tend to lie beyond national boundaries, I asked whether a *European cultural complex* could be imagined and explored. Compared with the historical or mythological foundations of cultural complexes in different cultures in Europe, this would be a rather newish European cultural complex, the birth of the European Community dating back to 1951, some two generations ago.

Trying to be as conscious as possible in writing on this matter, I wondered whether my hypothesis of a *European cultural complex*, based on the experiences of two World Wars, might represent a personal defense against writing about the German cultural complex since I was born in Germany. Or my interest in the layer of the European cultural unconscious may reflect that my family roots take me back to several countries in Europe – an experience shared by many. In my family, World War II cast these long shadows: my maternal grandfather disappeared in Lithuania; the whereabouts of my East-Prussian paternal grandparents, last registered in Poland, remain unknown; two uncles, an aunt, and a cousin lost their lives. My parents and eldest brother, born during the war, survived, but the experience of World War II affected the physical and mental health of my parents and their capacity to relate to and bring up children. I was born eleven years after World War II, yet my birth was inextricably wound up with the death of another brother who died at the age of two when my mother was three months pregnant with me. Although I was not *conceived* to replace him, they hoped my birth would lessen the loss. Parental hopes and projections were transferred from my dead baby brother to me; I was literally bedded in the same pram. I often wondered what might have happened if my mother had been less dissociated due to her traumatic experiences in World War II? Would she *then* have noticed that her son was terminally ill with appendicitis? Might she have *seen* me? Lingering guilt feelings flooded my mother's psychic space and were transferred to my unconscious, culminating in the question: Do I live *because* another died? My mother felt guilty of neglect; although in the end the doctor was blamed, she suffered from a compulsive disorder: she kept washing her hands with a powerful disinfectant.

Growing up, I was unconsciously looking for my brother who had disappeared before I was born and left wondering "who am I?" Was I made to "carry" the projection of the missing sibling onto my budding self? My personal guilt feelings were compounded by the collective guilt of being born German. Early in my life, I appeared defended against the layer of collective guilt in the German psyche. When I learned with time to differentiate personal from collective guilt feelings, I was able to slowly let seep into consciousness the images of the crimes against humanity committed by the Germans.

Unaware of what being born as a replacement child in the aftermath of the Second World War meant for me and my identity, I left Germany at the age of twenty-six to live in the United States. I have spent more years in America, France, and Switzerland (my *home* now) than in the country where I was born. At times, my German-Lithuanian-Prussian-Polish ancestral cultural complexes appear *frozen* in time: Lithuanian folk music evokes feelings of yearning and *striving* for liberty, though the country has been independent since 1991. As if arrested in time, the process toward German-Polish reconciliation is engraved in my memory with an image: I can still see Chancellor Brandt falling to his knees in Warsaw on December 7, 1970.

My German cultural complex appears paradoxically more *intense* and more *watered down*: I had to face collective guilt individually and not as part of a German cultural complex-driven movement. On the other hand, it seems to me as if crossing the Atlantic Ocean back and forth twice allowed for an ethnological point of view, a distant and observant perspective.

I worked for fifteen years in international development at UNICEF, helping children in especially difficult circumstances and advocating for the Convention on the Rights of the Child. This work extended my views toward a more global, universal perspective, leading me to explore cultural complexes at another level, looking for commonalities rather than divisions, seeking reconciliation between conflicting parties, both in the world and at the level of my complexes. Training in Switzerland to become a Jungian analyst was an expression of a deeply felt need for reconnecting while transcending: I feel most at ease *coming from* Europe *and* being a resident of Switzerland, working as an analyst, soul-related on neutral territory. This led me to question whether in addition to long-standing, deep-running cultural complexes, new cultural complexes may emerge as regional entities are established, in other words, whether there is such a phenomenon as an emerging European cultural complex – one strand of which is the European replacement child complex.

Who Is a Replacement Child and What Are the Psychodynamic Consequences?

A replacement child is born to replace another human being, often (but not only) a child who has died. Well-meaning relatives, doctors, or counselors used to, unwittingly, recommend the conception of a new child in the wake of a death. The specific suffering of the replacement child was discovered after the Second World War, with the treatment of survivors of the Shoah and their descendants in the United States in 1945/6.[12] Weighing heavily on the (adult) replacement child's relationships, physical and psychological health, their intra-psychic representations and archetypal imagery, the symptoms of the replacement child range from low self-esteem to survivor's guilt, from relational difficulties to identity problems, from depression to pre-psychotic disorders. Adults who are conceived or born to replace a family member who has been killed, died, or disappeared may suffer from a specific replacement child syndrome or a handicap with important psychopathological risks.[13]

Albert Cain and Barbara Cain published "On Replacing a Child," a comprehensive basic reference article on understanding the psychology of the replacement child.[14] The authors identified "parents' inadequate or unresolved mourning," guilt feelings, and the fact that "parents grossly imposed the identity of the dead child upon his substitute, and unconsciously identified the two," leading to a pathological development and identification of the replacement child with the dead child.[15] These children were born into a family atmosphere of depression and sorrow; the dead child lived on in "hyper-idealization" because of the "parents' intense narcissistic investment in the children who had died."[16] "These children's identity problems (were such) they could barely breathe as individuals with their own characteristics and identity."[17]

Definitions

Cain and Cain define the replacement child as "a disturbed child who was conceived shortly after the death of another child, his parents' specific intention being to have this child as a replacement or substitute for their child who died."[18] Porot defines the replacement child as any child born after the death of another child in as far as it is invested with parental expectations and fantasies that were once projected onto the deceased child.[19] I use a wider definition: it is any child who is conceived or born to replace a child who died; or who was born shortly after a death, stillbirth, or abortion; or who "replaced" a sibling or another member of the family later on and *whose role* may have been reassigned to the "replacement child." Jungian analyst Henry Abramovitch (Tel Aviv) notes that "a replacement child is a living child who comes to take the place of a dead one."[20]

Not everyone born after World Wars I and II is a replacement child. On one hand, it depends on whether the parents intentionally conceived another child to replace one who died, and whether a parent transferred life projects and identity traits from one child to another, and whether feelings of guilt and grief (parental and/or sibling) were sufficiently processed before the new being came into the world so as not to burden the newborn. On the other hand, it depends on whether a conscious or unconscious identification between the lost and the living human being has taken root in the psyche of the replacement child – via projection from family members or by unconscious self-identification or archetypal dynamics.

If the child lives in his or her own right and is neither identified nor self-identifies, even unconsciously, with a dead other, the child may *not* necessarily suffer from the replacement child syndrome. But if the role of the new child is to cut short grief, to take the place of, or to embody the role of a dead child (or other family member), the psychological consequences may affect the individual unconsciously through-out his or her life.[21]

Archetypes of Death, Life, and Rebirth

From an archetypal perspective, the replacement child straddles the archetypal worlds of life, death, and rebirth or resurrection. The great opposites, the arche-types of death and life call each other forth. For the parents, the traumatic experi-ence of death may have given rise instinctually to increased sexual libido, possibly evoking feelings of shame. Salvador Dali was born nine months and ten days after the death of his brother, who was also named Salvador. Yet in his memory, Sal-vador Dali persistently put – incorrectly – *years* between his brother's death and his own birth. In the unconscious of the parents, death and life were joined. The same name was given to the new child; although it is a tradition in some cultures to pass on the name of ancestors, under certain conditions this can impact the forma-tion of identity. While the birth of a new human being may promise to cut short the parents' grief, this *can unconsciously* condemn *another* human being – the replacement child – to a life akin to death: the replacement child is not born to be; it is born to be a dead person. Eugene O'Neill, also a replacement child, states it like this: "As it is, I will always be a stranger who never feels at home, who does not really want and is not really wanted, who can never belong, who must always be a little in love with death!"[22] Often, a lifelong struggle ensues for replacement children to find a path back to life, to their *own* life. From before the child is born, the archetypal forces of death and life are joined in a fateful constellation; the soul of the replacement child bears the shadow of death from the very beginning of life. I believe hope for the replacement child lies in the emergence of a true self as the inalienable, original life force inherent in the soul of the replacement child searches for realizing the individual life force.

Jung: A Replacement Child

Jungian concepts lend themselves especially well to understanding the individual and collective significance of the psychological condition of replacement children. C. G. Jung was born after his parents mourned the stillbirths of two daughters and the death of a son who lived only five days. This was first published by Bair and confirmed in a personal communication by Andreas Jung, Jung's grandson (in a let-ter dated November 28, 2008).[23] Questions of life and death and of transcendence permeate Jung's work. In *The Red Book*, which he began at the age of thirty-eight, Jung extolls the importance of the legacy of the dead:

> These . . . are the dead, not just your dead, that is all the images of the shapes you took in the past, which your ongoing life has left behind, but also the thronging

dead of human history, the ghostly procession of the past, . . . I see behind you, behind the mirror of your eyes, the crush of dangerous shadows, the dead, who look greedily through empty sockets of your eyes, who moan and hope to gather up through you all the loose ends of the ages, which sigh in them. Your clueless-ness does not prove anything. Put your ear to that wall and you will hear the rustling of their procession.[24]

The focus of Jung's lifelong work rests on the process of individuation, with its emphasis on the essential role of the Self. In my view, the Self can help the replace-ment child find his or her path toward a new life, a life that is its own instead of resurrecting a dead other, the individuation process leading to a *rebirth* in the here and now. With its searching twists and turns, what Jung described as the *path of individuation*, guided by the self-healing quality of the psyche, can counter the replacement child's identification with the dead.[25] Jung believed in the capacity of the individual to proceed on a path of consciousness, to *individuate*, and to contrib-ute this consciousness toward the building of society. Whether facilitated by analy-sis or another creative process, by tapping into the deepest layers of the psyche and reconnecting to the life-giving force of the Self, the individuation process can lead the replacement child to a rediscovery of the original life force.

Whether the replacement child received the (parental or other) projection of a dead revenant or of a resurrected golden miracle child, either projection may have a significant impact on the personality development of the individual con-cerned – and also on the replacement child's descendants. If the replacement child complex has not been rendered conscious, it can be passed on from generation to generation. Volkan and Ast speak of "trans-generational transmission" and explain such a process through the "deposits of preformed self or object representation(s)"; other ways of transmission (of content or process) include attachment and relational patterns, patterns of behavior, modes of communication or noncommunication, and defense mechanisms such as denial, dissociation, or projective identification.[26]

The Replacement Child Complex at the Collective Level

If many individuals were conceived and born as replacement children in Europe in the aftermath of two World Wars, what is the cumulative effect for the col-lective? How many replacement children and their descendants are unconscious of their condition? How many are undertaking a conscious effort at individuat-ing, discovering their own identity, which means shaking off the *Tunic of Nes-sus*? The archetypal layer of such a condition is well described in the myth of Hercules, Deianira, and Nessus. Nessus, a centaur, is trying to abduct Hercules' wife Deianira; Hercules kills him with a poisoned arrow. Dying, the centaur gives Deianira his tunic, enticing her to put it over Hercules in order to protect him ("Keep this to strengthen waning love").[27] Instead the Tunic of Nessus (impreg-nated with his blood) kills Hercules. The metaphor of the Tunic of Nessus is a fitting symbol for the dying (or dead) person's fatal charm poisoning the life of the survivor. Only if the replacement child recognizes the deadly forces transferred from the dead onto his or her life can the forces of death and life be disentwined and individual life be truly born.

Are there equal forces that need to be recognized at the collective level? Were the archetypal forces of death and life also activated when efforts gave rise to the birth of the European Community? Might there be a Tunic of Nessus, a vestige of the old, abducting dying black or brown shirts (of the fascists), with the potential to poison the new union?

The European Union, as a new entity, has risen from the ashes of two World Wars. Not unlike individuals, born to replace the dead of two World Wars and who find themselves struggling to find their true identity amid the ghosts of millions of dead, the European Union was conceived in the wake of death and destruction and is struggling to find its true identity. How many of those who participated in the building of Europe, constructing a new entity, might have been affected by a replacement child complex that had plunged them, unconsciously, into the archetypal realms of life and death? How many had their self and object representations affected by the relational and attachment problems that are part of the replacement child syndrome and what may be the traces at the collective level in Europe?[28]

In the wake of such massive losses, how many individuals have been searching for ways to reestablish "missing links," rebuild lost attachments, reaching out to the "other," looking for life and new connections? Are there still unprocessed grief and guilt feelings hovering over Europe, impairing its development and the deepening of relations to the "other"? Are there elements of unconscious existential guilt and feelings of ambivalence, stemming from an unconscious replacement child cultural complex riddling Europe? Poets have well captured the existential anguish of the replacement child.

Victor Hugo described in haunting terms what can happen when a baby is born to a mother who thinks her dead child is returning in the newborn in his poem "Le Revenant" (in "Les Contemplations").

The One Who Returned

Mourning mothers, your cries are heard up above.
God, who holds all the lost birds in the palm of his hand,
Sometimes returns the same dove to the same nest.
. . .
Nestled in her arms, she heard
The newborn speak in a once-familiar voice,
And whisper softly: It is I. Tell no one.[29]

Rainer Maria Rilke and Hermann Hesse were born as replacement children; they tried to escape the archetypal energies of death nibbling at their heels by deploying their poetic wings of creativity. Vincent (II!) Van Gogh was also a replacement child; he was born, to the day, one year after his brother Vincent (I) had died.[30]

He created some the world's most beautiful paintings, yet he succumbed, in the end, to auto-destructive impulses. Although all forms of creativity can help counter destructive forces, in my view it is the *Self energies* that may be capable of *transcending* the opposites of the archetypes of life and death.

With respect to the European Union replacing old pre-war structures, we can assume a best-case and a worst-case scenario. The best-case scenario: one may ask whether Self energies have come to the rescue, compensating chaos and transcending death and destruction, individual by individual, helping in the collective effort of building postwar Europe, on the road toward a new collective identity. From such a perspective, we might be witnessing in Europe an unconsciously driven collective individuation process, with elements reminding us of the individual replacement child's path back to finding its own true life. *That* should be revealed to our discovering collective consciousness. Such consciousness is essential if a transgenerational transmission of the shadow sides of the replacement child complex to succeeding generations, often witnessed at the individual level, is to be avoided at the collective level. It is also vital, at the collective and individual levels, to be aware of the phenomenon of *enantiodromia*, a term used by Jung to define the "emergence of the unconscious opposite in the course of time."[31] While striving for peaceful postwar cooperation with the conception of the European Union, enantiodromia – the unconscious opposite – would, in the worst-case scenario, suggest a risk of a repetition of war and destruction: death feeding on itself. In the case of the replacement child, she or he who was born to replace the dead is *not born to be an alive person but to be a dead person* – unless, of course, consciousness intervenes and leads to a transcending of death into true new life. The state of *nonbeing* is, when remaining unconscious, at risk of being projectively passed on to the next generation. At the collective level, this could lead to a repetition of war and destruction or a displacement of this dynamic onto another theater of war.

Before I can attempt a tentative conclusion to these thoughts, I will now consider several of the elements of the replacement child syndrome. The individual may encounter several difficulties before the central creative force of the Self may be activated. Here, I experiment with transposing the following elements of the replacement child complex – questions of attachment, unprocessed grief, survivor's guilt – from the individual to the collective level.

A Question of Attachment, Identity, and Self-Worth

Mother and child research, especially attachment research, asserts that being born after a loss can have a significant impact on the bonding process, with ensuing developmental and attachment difficulties. Even if there is an attempt to short-circuit the grief by the birth of a new baby, grief and sadness will still be present in some form and may impair a mother's attachment to her other living children and/or to a new child, with consequences for attachment patterns and relational capacity.[32]

The replacement child often perceives a grieving mother as an absent mother. An absent mother is, intrapsychically, seen as a "dead mother."[33] Attachment patterns of replacement children reveal feelings of extreme ambivalence; rejection or "clinging" and periods of severe regression throughout the life-span may occur. The dependence such an absence can create may impact the quality of attachment and the relationships to self and others.

Whether the attachment experienced was secure, insecure, ambivalent, or avoidant will play a significant part – together with the degree of parental projection – as to whether the replacement child will suffer from attachment problems impacting its identity formation. If the replacement child constellation gives rise to a weakened identity, this may lead to identifications (with the *dead other*, the *murderer*, or *dead mother*), with the attendant risk of making the process of finding *true identity* more difficult; grave disturbances in self-esteem can be expected with a struggle to find true self-worth.

On a collective level, the European Union could, at different stages of its development, be seen as struggling with issues of attachment as well as with questions pertaining to its identity, which I view as intrinsic to the replacement child condition.[34] At times, it may even appear as if the European Union was suffering from low self-esteem – or its compensating opposite – inflation. Among some citizens of Europe, one can, at various periods, observe a tendency toward falling back into identification with nationalism, especially in times of crisis. In some member states, one may observe signs of ambivalent attachments or avoidant, if not outright rejecting, attachment in varying degrees among individuals or the collective.

While I am attempting to transpose clinical observations from individual cases to a theorized collective level, a one-to-one translation as such would be ridiculous! I am neither supposing that some of the European member states may have an attachment issue with regard to the European Union in proportion to the percentage of their citizens suffering from an unconscious replacement child complex – nor am I proposing that certain segments of society within member states that may exhibit more or less attachment to the European Union might do so because of their citizens' unidentified identity crisis due to an unrecognized replacement child condition – nor am I saying that the European Union may have been created by individuals suffering from an unconscious replacement child complex and, therefore, suffers from an endemic collective attachment problem. That is not what I am saying!

But with regard to the European Union suffering from a hypothetical replacement child syndrome, the collective psyche, as separate from the individual psyche, may function in similar ways; it stands in a mutually informative relationship with the individuals making up the collective, yet it also has a life of its own that may function in ways similar to the individual psyche. The "child" that died is the old order of European countries, and the replacement child is the new European Union. If the old order has not been mourned, like the "dead" child in a case of an individual suffering from the replacement child syndrome, the new order – the European Union – is plagued by the specter of the not fully mourned old order and can show similar symptoms at the level of the collective psyche that one sees in the individual psyche suffering from the replacement child syndrome. For instance, after the demise of the political structure of the Union of Soviet Socialist Republics

(USSR), one can observe, in some countries, a yearning for a *return* or a *replacement* of the old order, not a mourning of the loss of the old order opening the way to a new and unprecedented structure.[35]

From my clinical observations with adult replacement children from different European countries, I wonder whether questions of identity, unresolved feelings of grief,[36] unconscious survivor's guilt, and the feeling of "not being good enough" beset also the larger civic entity. Individually, these clients are searching for the "missing other"; they are trying, using more or less creative means, to overcome dependency symptoms, disturbances in self-esteem and relational disorders; struggling with shadow issues; and seeking to discover the inalienable Self energies that may lay dormant beneath the ashes of the dead other whom they came to replace in life. The individual replacement child also suffers from an absent, grieving, depressed mother, from the "dead mother" complex, in addition to impaired attachment.[37]

What would this look like at the collective level? Who is the dead mother? Who is the replacement mother? And what are the attachment issues? Could some of the apathetic or ambivalent attachment to the European Community be seen in relation to individuals who may once have latched onto the new European Collective while searching for a new sense to their identity after two World Wars with their tens of millions of dead? Have some since become more secure in their own identity, and might they no longer need the European collective identity? Or have some become even more insecure in their identity because of their attachment to the larger collective entity?

If a newborn who is meant to replace a dead human being is likely to experience mental (and possibly physical) suffering, might a new political entity replacing former ones be plagued by similar questions of attachment and identity? If many members in that entity suffer from such an unrecognized condition, what is the impact on the collective level? If many individuals have not become conscious of their condition and are not yet on the path of individuation toward rediscovering their own identity, what are the risks for identifications?

European identity cannot (yet?) substitute for or replace national identity, group identity, or individual identity; nor can European identity be ordained from the top down. Identity at the individual level is acquired in a slow maturing process while various identifications are sampled, but only those that fit with the authentic core, the self of the individual, are retained.

New levels of consciousness and identity formation need to rise up from the individual level, not trickle down from a supra level. Jung rightly emphasized that each individual's consciousness is a small but vital contribution to the larger whole; with respect to the question of a slowly developing European identity, each replacement child (or descendant born to a replacement child) can potentially contribute his or her consciousness and rising Self energies, which are vital for the replacement child's own life and that of the collective.

How much was the building of Europe invested with "parental" expectations and fantasies about replacing *death with new life* on the part of its initiators, early leaders, and citizens adhering to the idea of this new entity? The creation of the community was fueled by a desire for "no more war" – to foster cooperation and healthy competition *replacing* belligerent confrontation.

One central source of suffering in the replacement child is a feeling of "not good enough," a severe lack of healthy self-esteem, particularly in cases where the replacement child is compared with an invincible, since dead, rival. Rising sentiments of nationalism, noticeable among some groups of some member states, make me wonder whether the dead rival (the pre–European Union entities) is indeed defunct – or whether the new entity is subject to being unfavorably compared to what there was before. Dependent behavior (looking to the state for assured selfhood) or elements of narcissistic compensation for feeling "not good enough" could be afoot, with narcissistic rage besetting some of the confrontations.

On a speculative note, I wonder whether there is a component of narcissistic (hyper-) compensation for a lack of healthy self-esteem, with some traits of megalomaniac overspending. Many of the member states are highly indebted. Was the introduction of the euro meant to provide a sense of union, a feeling of oneness? Fifteen years later, the age of adolescence, we are witnessing some rebellion against the euro. Also that nasty, nagging feeling of not "being good enough," is that feeling – once again – being projected onto the *other*, the foreigner? Or is it she, Europe, who is made to carry the projection that *she* is "not good enough"?

The Issue of Grieving

The Europeans, aided by members of the Allied Forces – who also suffered millions of dead and wounded – reconstructed Europe after the war. The new political order was built on ruins and destruction, with their deadly traces in countless families and their descendants. Were these losses mourned sufficiently *before* new life was conceived?

"Grieving is a psychic process, in which the individual comes to term with loss. If the grieving process is disrupted, then relations, psychological development as well as creative capacities are impeded."[38] Instead of going toward the work of grieving and integrating loss, the energy of those who survived was understandably funneled into reconstruction and rebuilding, replacing old structures with new ones. When I look at this aspect of a European replacement child cultural complex, I wonder whether some unresolved grief may account for the difficult relations and impeded creative processes within the European Union and among its member states.

The individual replacement child suffers from grief that was not resolved, from a loss that was not mourned sufficiently before the conception of a new birth, burdening the newborn with parental grief. Might such unexpressed grief be plaguing the European Community from its inception and be part and parcel of a hypothesized European replacement child cultural complex? Mitscherlich noted nearly thirty years after World War II that the Germans were still unable to face the losses they had endured and were, therefore, unable to mourn the immeasurable losses their crimes against humanity had caused.[39] Almost two generations have been born since Mitscherlich's study. In some of my clinical cases, it is evident that the grieving work had not been done by the generation who lived through the war nor by the generation immediately following. This task has been handed down the generational ladder to descendants of the third and fourth generation. What the parents could not face was left to the children and often to the grandchildren.

I worked with a client, a man in his forties, who was *haunted* by the dead from two different wars. Both paternal and maternal grandparents had participated in the wars and family members had perished. Not only the dead in his own family weighed down his soul but also the collective deaths *caused* by the action or inaction of previous generations had led this client to a severe depression – and ultimately to the recognition that unconsciously he had carried the mirrored shadow image of a murderer in his own soul. The mourning work had been passed on to him – a task that summoned all his psychic forces and that he was motivated to undertake when he understood that if he were not to do it, it would be passed on to his children.

In cases in which the grieving process has been processed neither at the collective level nor at the individual or family levels, or in which a child has been conceived to make up for an entire family, feelings of loss and survivors' guilt pervade the life force – as is visible in dream images – of members two or even three generations later. If the suffering is not faced at one step on the generational ladder, there is a heightened risk for repetition compulsion, for risky auto- or hetero-aggressive behavior, or for passing on the suffering to "the other."

If the European Union was created before such mourning had taken place, or if the mourning process was not consciously integrated by those individuals who were conceived as replacement children, or by their descendants, one can expect to find at the collective level elements of dysphoria and depression or a passing on of this state to others, via projection, projective identification, or acting out. Could Europe be seen as *depressed* because second- and third-generation survivors and replacement child descendants are still struggling with grief and guilt feelings that were not faced? Must Europe, therefore, go through a phase of mourning to finally become itself?

Whether the *dead revenant* or the *golden miracle child*, whether *unresolved grief* or *survivor's guilt*, or even a *murderous shadow* that is projected onto the newborn "European Union" – all of these elements of the replacement child complex are deleterious and detract from this new entity coming into its true identity. What is important, in my view, is that there is increasing individual and collective consciousness of the elements of the replacement child complex, chiefly among them the questions of guilt and grief. We need to look at the collective European psyche with a critical examining eye for elements of a European replacement child complex as a layer in the European cultural unconscious.

Facing the Murderous Shadow and the Missing "Other"

On the path toward individuation, the replacement child will suffer from the memory of a dead child that is imposed onto the new living being. "It is this unwanted child who is most vulnerable to murderous and incestuous fantasies and action."[40] The replacement child is likely to have to face a murderous shadow, stemming from the erroneous but unconscious supposition that if one child is alive and the other is dead, then the living one caused the death of the other.[41] The replacement child will also seek to discover a living rather than dead image of an anima/animus within, a doubly difficult task for those born after another has died. Where there was a presence, there is now a gaping absence. The first inner representation of "other" is one of "missing other," "absent other," the "dead sibling," or the "dead mother."[42]

On one level, the shadow is the dead other child. That which he or she is not – yet is part of him or her. On another level, the confrontation with the shadow means coming face to face with a shattering, deeply unconscious shadow of a murderer, as the replacement child is made to feel responsible for the death of the other who disappeared even before she or he was born. To render such projections conscious is not easy nor to transform such deadly energies. Paradoxically, in order for the replacement child to live his or her own life, the replacement child must "kill" the dead child, the phantom identity of the dead sibling within him or herself.[43] The killing is, of course, a symbolic endeavor.[44]

If the replacement child complex were to stay unconscious, there is considerable danger not only for self but also for the "other." In working with many replacement children, I have come to ponder whether a self might put at risk an ego that does not incarnate it and thus "cause" or constellate life-endangering situations? If the innate self is not able to self-realize, but is in the service of an alien other that it is meant to replace, that is, if the ego does not incarnate the original self, then the self might put at risk or even annihilate the ego. In some cases, the replacement child suffers from unconscious hetero- or auto-aggression. This may amount to *soul murder* and may, in turn, create many victims, especially if others are made to carry the unconscious deadly shadow.

"[I]gnorance of the generational past can damage the individual psyche."[45] This applies especially to the replacement child and his or her descendants who may either be incessantly searching for the reason for being or be seduced by the forces of nonbeing, the destructive forces unconsciously harbored within. "This leads to looking for victims outside oneself, in order to access the pain one can not access inside."[46]

A human being without a sense of identity and who is not incarnating his or her own self energies, may be experiencing life as an unbearable void; this void may be filled with death. If this affects many individuals, it could have disintegrating, even terrifying consequences for society as well as the individual. If many were to be affected because of war, strife, or natural catastrophe, what would be the collective significance for a society? Is this how death and destruction may feed on itself? How do wars make victims long after the war is over? The dead, if replaced instead of mourned, may return to haunt the living many times over.

Understanding the replacement child (and his or her descendants) means helping these individuals find a livable path back toward living their own life and discovering the inalienable life force, their true self, within themselves. If the analyst can experience the *inner terror* of a replacement child, this inexpressible *not-me* feeling, of being in relation neither with *self* nor with the *other*, then the analyst can help the analysand to discover an intimate glimpse of the original *self*. This will not only reduce the risk of transgenerational transmission but is vital for rediscovering the original life force that was once smothered by the replacement child condition.

Re-creating Original Life

Europeans could benefit if each individual were able to contribute his or her own consciousness about whether they were born as replacement children or carry elements of the syndrome in their soul as part of a collective cultural complex. I have witnessed two types of development in adult replacement children. In some cases, a self is reconstructed with the aid of a mirroring, holding other and/or with the aid of archetypal Self energies rising to consciousness, helping the individuals gain a notion of themselves and leading to their individuation. In other cases, in which neither the Self with a capital *S*, nor the self with a lowercase *s*, can help secure a new, true identity, physical and/or psychic destruction can result.

In what ways may Europe with its member states and citizens *individuate?* How can this process be aided by self energies? I use the term *individuation* to refer to a developmental process toward wholeness or fullness that, according to Jung, includes all the deviations, detours, and wrong turns taken in the journey toward maturity. In the replacement child, the archetypes of life and death are called forth together; instead of there being life at the beginning and death at the end, the archetypes are constellated in *reverse* order: first there was death, giving rise to a new life, and the two were fused. Provided there is consciousness of such a condition, the individuation process can lead to a rediscovery of the *original life force* by looking to the deepest layers of psyche for the reasons for coming into existence and a reconnection to the life-giving force – the Self. I believe it is the Self, the central archetype for Jung, expressing the "wholeness of the personality" – "the Self [which] is the principle and archetype of orientation and meaning."[47] "The self compensates effectively chaos."[48]

For Europe, as for the individual, this would mean looking, after due grieving and a conscious look at the destructive energies, for the life-giving energies and making a conscious choice for *creative* self-realization. Creativity, in whatever form, is conducive to overcoming the destructive forces – and largely preferable to staying unconscious or seeking a return to a *status quo ante*.

A European Replacement Child Cultural Complex

There are traces of an unconscious replacement child cultural complex in many individuals in Europe and, as I speculate, also in the collective psyche of different European countries and the European Union as an entity. The elements of such a cultural complex can range from "dead revenant" to "never good enough," from a "phoenix rising from the ashes" to an unending search for the "missing other," or believing in being the "golden miracle child." If those who were born as replacement children face, as adults, existential questions – such as "Who am I?" "Why am I living and the 'other' is not?" "What is the meaning of my life?" – the collective psyche might be plagued with the same questions.

German angst could be a phenomenon stemming from such origins, considering the recurrent history of wars. During the Thirty-Years' War (1618–1648), some 25 to 40 percent of the German population died. A cultural complex analogous to the replacement child syndrome may have lain dormant in countless individuals and the collective psyche more than three-hundred years before the outbreak of the First World War. The dead from that devastating First World War, not fully mourned, left symptoms akin to the individual replacement child's suffering in the collective psyche, which, in turn, wrought massive deaths onto others in the Second World War. My hypothesis is that an unconscious replacement child complex may lead to an experience of life as a dead person, *at the levels of the individual and the collective psyche*, with the risk of being projected onto others if not rendered conscious.

Such a condition, akin to soul murder in an individual case, can lead, in the worst-case scenario to an unconscious transfer of the death pole (of the life-and-death pair of opposites) to the "other"; then the "other" is to be dead instead of "self." If such were to happen on a collective scale, in nations or member states, then one war breeds another, over generations.

A Tentative Conclusion

I set out to ask whether the replacement child cultural complex might represent a layer in the collective psyche, in the unconscious cultural complex of German or other peoples in Europe. To what extent does the European bear transgenerationally transmitted psychological traces of a replacement child cultural complex, be it death-dependent *or* death-defying, seeking tragic repetition *or* a triumph over loss and tragedy but circumventing grief and guilt feelings? How many individuals are left looking for the " 'missing other" and their true identity? In the absence of a statistical or other more "objective" study that would stretch over several generations, my reflections are based on clinical observations in individual cases but speculative with respect to the collective. I hope that those who find a resonance in my reflections will add their voice and observations, thus helping to render such a hypothetical complex, if it exists, conscious in order to transcend its potentially dangerous dynamics.

Those born to replace the war dead from the two World Wars are by now elderly, if still alive; but elements of this complex can be passed on to children, grandchildren, even great-grandchildren. Their soul and dream images echo the existential questions of their forebears:

Oh brother, oh sister, where are you?[49] Oh father, mother, uncle, aunt, and grandparents – where are you? Are you living still, with me or through me? Am I living to keep the memory alive of those who died?

Dina Wardi, who was one of the first in Israel to recognize and treat the transgenerational trauma of Shoah victims *and* their descendants, found that some children were designated as a "memorial candle," replacing entire generations of Jewish families murdered by the Nazis. This child was

> given the burden of participating in his parents' emotional world to a much greater extent than any of his brothers or sisters . . . serving as the link . . . [between] past, . . . present and the future.[50]

In working with clients from many European countries, I have observed traces of the tens of millions of human beings lost or wounded in the two World Wars, especially in those born as replacement children. How many of their descendants are aware that they may have inherited elements of a transmitted replacement child complex?

When archetypal death-and-life forces are joined and ravage the soul of an individual member of society or of many in a group or culture, this can lead to collective phenomena, such as mass projections and a passing onto others of guilt, grief, and tomb-like emotions. Projective identifications of this kind represent a potentially infectious and deadly cultural complex.

On the positive side, those born as replacement children, be it at the first, second, third, or fourth generation, can experience a conscious encounter with these potentially dark forces and transcend them, leading to a discovery of healing energies encountered deep within the soul. Individuals grappling *consciously* with the existential questions of a life conceived in the wake of death and discovering the deeper layers of human identity can become a source of life for themselves and for others. I have met in my practice many individuals who had a great potential for transcending death-dealing projections and discovering the inalienable original force of life, their innate source of creative being, the Self.

The full spectrum of potential reactions to a life conceived in the wake of death can be fathomed when we consider two quite different individuals. Jung was born after three dead children; he looked for the self-healing quality of the soul and charted a path to his true identity in life. Hitler was born after three dead children; he wrought death onto tens of millions of innocent victims.[51]

After a war, it may take a hundred years and countless individuals' conscious creative efforts to sort through and process the traces of massive collective and individual trauma. It is often the third or fourth generation who will become conscious of the passed-on trauma. Whoever does the conscious working through of the pain will make a contribution toward ridding European society of *death-scendants* and show a way toward a new life-based self-inspired society.

The analyst has the vital role of understanding replacement children and their descendants and is not only helping those individuals find a livable path back toward discovering and living their own life but also contributing to peace-making at the level of the individual and collective psyche. This valuable effort contributes to hopes of preventing larger disasters to come in the wake of the first ones. There is a collective significance to rendering the deadly legacy of a replacement child cultural complex conscious.

> The individual, suffering from a neurotic cycle of repeated self-destructive action, may need to be helped to reflect . . . his ancestral past . . . he may be carrying unconsciously . . . a past history that goes beyond the individual experience within the immediate family. This understanding might begin to free the individual from the unconscious chains of the past.[52]

Searching with compassion for a new identity is an important element in the treatment of the unconscious replacement cultural child complex, at both the individual level and the collective level of the European psyche deeply affected for more than four generations by the deadly legacy of two World Wars. The replacement children and their descendants are being called to transcend death, discover their own life force and identity from deadening ashes, and face the murderous shadows of the past and transform it, reaching out to the *other*, the discovery of the self *within* helping to overcome the *missing other (child or adult) without whom but with whose memory they have to live.*

The replacement child cultural complex in Europeans and in the European collective psyche affected by the two World Wars must be rendered conscious, at the personal and collective level of the cultural complex. Loss and grief, identity confusion, survivor's guilt, an ambivalent attachment dynamic due to the "dead mother" complex, and the "missing other" at the relational and transcendental levels need to be addressed at the individual and the collective level. The collective psyche when identified with the *dead* other instead of *being at one* with itself, can lead to auto- and hetero-destructive dynamics.

On the positive side, a conscious confrontation with the replacement child cultural complex can open a path of development. At the individual *and* collective level, this means working toward a new relationship between an authentic, not a replacement "I," and a new sense of self – not a borrowed self from the "other," thus allowing for an authentic sense of "we." When the grief and the guilt can be faced, when victim and aggressor parts can be made conscious and the projections recognized, a new sense of wholeness, an experience of the "self" ensues. It facilitates the birth of a new entity instead of a replacement structure. Those individuals who no longer suffer *unconsciously* from an inherited replacement child complex, it is hoped, will have different modes of attachment to Europe than their parents and grandparents. And the collective psyche may also find a way to mourn the loss of the old structures and wounds, thus opening the way toward a new European identity.

Perhaps the biggest unanswered question for Europe, in this era, is whether it is overcoming the legacy of its death-scendants and becoming a life-based society?

Notes

1 Yehuda Rahel, Nikolaos P. Daskalakis, Linda M. Bierer, Heather N. Bader, Torsten Klengel, Florian Holsboer, and Elisabeth B. Binder, "Holocaust Exposure Induced

Intergenerational Effects on *FKBP5* Methylation," *Biological Psychiatry* (2015): in press (published online August 12, 2015, at http://www.biologicalpsychiatryjournal. com/article/S0006-3223%2815%2900652-6/abstract); see also N. Perroud, A. Paoloni-Giacobino, P. Prada, E. Olié, A. Salzmann, R. Nicastro, S. Guillaume, D. Mouthon, C. Stouder, K. Dieben, P. Huguelet, P. Courtet, and A. Malafosse, "Increased Methylation of Glucocorticoid Receptor Gene (NR4C1) in Adults With a History of Childhood Maltreatment: A Link with the Severity and Type of Trauma," *Translational Psychiatry* 1 (2011): p. e59.

2 Ilany Kogan, *The Cry of the Mute Children* (London: Free Association Books, 1995); J. S. Kestenberg and M. Kestenberg, *Generations of the Holocaust* (New York: Basic Books, 1982).

3 This is twelve years after the Franco-German War of 1870 (July 19, 1870–May 10, 1871). E. Renan, "What is a Nation?" (Qu'est-ce qu'une nation?), Lecture at the Sorbonne, March 11, 1882, in *Discours et Conferences* (Paris: Caiman-Levy, 1887), pp. 277–310; also in Geoff Eley and Ronald Grigor Suny (eds.), *Becoming National: A Reader* (New York and Oxford: Oxford University Press, 1996), pp. 41–55.

4 A. C. Cain and B. S. Cain, "On Replacing a Child," *Journal of American Academy of Child Psychiatry* 3 (1964): pp. 443–456; Maurice Porot, *L'enfant de Remplacement* (Paris: Frison-Roche, 1993/1996).

5 Ryan Gibson, "World War 2," September 15, 2014. Accessed July 5, 2014, at http://worldwar2.org.uk/.

6 Yad Vashem, Holocaust Memorial, Jerusalem, Israel.

7 Joseph Henderson, "The Cultural Unconscious," in *Shadow and Self, Selected Papers in Analytical Psychology* (Wilmette, IL: Chiron, 1990); and "The Archetype of Culture," in A. Guggenbühl-Craig (ed.), *Der Archetyp, Proceedings of the 2nd International Congress for Analytical Psychology* (Basel and New York: S. Karger, 1962).

8 Thomas Singer and Samuel L. Kimbles, *The Cultural Complex: Contemporary Jungian Perspectives on Psyche and Society* (Hove and New York: Routledge, 2004).

9 Craig San Rogue, Amanda Dowd, and David Tacey (eds.), *Placing Psyche: Exploring Cultural Complexes in Australia*, series ed. Thomas Singer (New Orleans: Spring Journal Books, 2011); Pilar Amezaga, Gustavo Barcellos, Áxel Capriles, Jacqueline Gerson, and Denise Ramos (eds.), *Listening to Latin America: Exploring Cultural Complexes in Brazil, Chile, Colombia, Mexico, Uruguay, and Venezuela*, series ed. Thomas Singer (New Orleans: Spring Journal Books, 2012).

10 Thomas Singer, "On the Cultural Complex: Introductory Remarks to a 2013 IAAP Copenhagen Conference Panel," in Emilija Kiehl (ed.), *Copenhagen 2013, 100 Years On: Origins, Innovations and Controversies, Proceedings of the 19th Congress of the International Association for Analytical Psychology* (Einsiedeln: Daimon, 2014).

11 Kristina Schellinski, "Who Am I?" *Journal of Analytical Psychology* 59 (2014): pp. 189–211.

12 Streznzcka and Papanek, cited in Porot, p. 199.

13 Porot, *L'enfant de Remplacement*, pp. 215 and 218.

14 Cain and Cain, "On Replacing a Child."

15 Cain and Cain, "On Replacing a Child," p. 451.

16 Cain and Cain, "On Replacing a Child," p. 444.

17 Cain and Cain, "On Replacing a Child," p. 451.

18 Cain and Cain, "On Replacing a Child," p. 443.

19 Porot, *L'enfant de Remplacement*, p. 171.

20 Henry Abramovitch, *Brothers and Sisters: Myth and Reality* (College Station, TX: Texas A&M University Press, 2014), p. 3. Also delivered in 2013 as The Fay Series Lectures.

21 For a more extensive discussion, refer to Schellinski, "Who Am I?"

22 Eugene O'Neill, *Long Day's Journey into Night* (New York: Random House/Jonathan Cape Paperback, 46, 2011). Kindle Edition, p. 135.

23 Deidre Bair, *Jung: A Biography* (New York: Little, Brown, 2004), p. 18.
24 C. G. Jung, *The Red Book: Liber Novus*, ed. S. Shamdasani (New York: W. W. Norton & Co., 2009), p. 296.
25 C. G. Jung, "Rebirth," in *Four Archetypes* (1971), extracted from Gerhard Adler and R. F. C. Hull (eds. And trans.), *The Collected Works of C. G. Jung*, Vol. 9i (Princeton, NJ: Princeton University Press, 1973).
26 Vamik D. Volkan and Gabriele Ast, *Siblings in the Unconscious and Psychopathology* (Madison, WI: International Universities Press, 1997), p. 89.
27 Ovid, *Metamorphoses*, trans. Brookes More, Theoi E-Texts Library, 2000–2011. Accessed August 27, 2015, at http://www.theoi.com/Text/OvidMetamorphoses9.html.
28 Singer takes this thought to the global level when he asks: was the 1920 League of Nations born out of such a dynamic in the collective psyche after the First World War? (personal communication, July 20, 2014).
29 Victor Hugo, "Les Contemplations," in *Le Revenant* (Paris: Le Livre de Poche, 1965), my translation.
30 H. Nagera, *Vincent Van Gogh: A Psychological Study* (London: George, Hallen & Unwin, 1967).
31 C. G. Jung, "Psychological Types," in G. Adler and R. F. C. Hull (eds. and trans.), *The Collected Works of C. G. Jung*, Vol. 6 (Princeton, NJ: Princeton University Press, 1971), § 709.
32 John Bowlby, *Loss: Sadness and Depression* (London: Hogarth Press, 1980).
33 André Green, *Narcissisme de Vie, Narcissisme de Mort* (Paris: Minuit et Poche, 1983); and André Green, "The Dead Mother," in *Life Narcissism/Death Narcissism* (London, New York: Free Associations Books, 2011).
34 I thank Andrew Samuels for pointing out that other authors have noted the psychological dimension of the EU's shortcomings. To my knowledge I am the first to point to the replacement child dimension at the European collective level.
35 With grateful acknowledgment to Thomas Singer for this reflection.
36 E. O. Poznanski, "The 'Replacement Child': A Saga of an Unresolved Grief," *Journal of Behavioral Pediatrics* 81 (1972, 6): pp. 1190–1193.
37 Green, *Narcissisme de Vie, Narcissisme de Mort*; Bowlby, *Loss*.
38 Alexander Mitscherlich and Margarete Mitscherlich, *The Inability to Mourn: Principles of Collective Behavior* (New York: Random House, 1975), p. 9. My translation.
39 Mitscherlich and Mitscherlich, *The Inability to Mourn*.
40 Prophecy Coles, *The Uninvited Guest From the Unremembered Past* (London: Karnac, 2011), p. 17.
41 Cain and Cain, "On Replacing a Child."
42 Green, "The Dead Mother," p. 233.
43 A. Couvez, *Tuer le mort. Mémoire de Psychiatrie* (Fac. Méd. Lille, 1979), quoted in Porot, *L'enfant de Remplacement*, p. 125.
44 Jung was born after three dead children; the chapter "Sacrificial Murder" in *The Red Book* can be read as dealing with an unconscious murder shadow and how to come to terms with it.
45 Coles, *The Uninvited Guest*, p. 10.
46 Arno Gruen, *Der Fremde in uns* (Munich: Deutscher Taschenbuch Verlag, 2010), p. 58; and Arno Gruen, *The Insanity of Normality: Realism as Sickness: Toward Understanding Human Destructiveness* (New York: Grove Weidenfeld, 1992).
47 C. G. Jung, *Memories, Dreams, Reflections* (New York: Vintage Books, 1965), p. 196 and 199f.
48 C. G. Jung, "Transformation Symbolism in the Mass (1942/1954)," in G. Adler and R. F. C. Hull (eds. and trans.), *The Collected Works of C. G. Jung*, Vol. 11 (Princeton, NJ: Princeton University Press, 1988), § 444.

49 With grateful acknowledgment to Jörg Rasche.

50 Dina Wardi, *Memorial Candles: Children of the Holocaust* (New York: Routledge, 1992), p. 6.

51 Porot, *L'enfant de Remplacement*, p. 239. Porot mentions Hitler only briefly in the last paragraph of his book.

52 Coles, *The Uninvited Guest*, p. 7.

Europe and Islam

A Paradigm of Activated Cultural Complexes

Jörg Rasche

Pray for me, that God may reveal to me the religion which is most pleasant to him.
– Sultan Al Kamil to St. Francis in Damiette, 1219

How to Find an Imaginal Space?

Some cultural complexes are painful and touch our prejudices. A current crisis that concerns all of us is the terror and war in Syria, Iraq, and Gaza – and the question of how much we are part of the problem. It is extremely difficult to reflect on and to speak about the activated cultural complexes between the West and Islam with a clear mind and without stepping on the land mines that abound in such discussions. What is most dangerous – and most real – is the fear that many people from Western and Islamic countries feel in the face of the growing conflict's unfolding terror. In a quasi-paranoid state nobody can trust anybody. The videos of human decapitation by IS-Islamists activate the deepest level of horror and disgust. Europeans don't do this. Unfortunately, this is not totally true. Only seventy years after the end of the Holocaust, even German soldiers have assisted their allies in bombing and torturing in Afghanistan, Iraq, Syria, and Palestine. With the Universal Declaration of Human Rights (UDHR) in 1948, torture was banned "forever" from European and American civilization. In the last decades, however, all those moral and ethical principles that were established as a common and secure ground for Western civilization after the disaster of World War II have been undermined and removed. In addition, we must consider the structural violence of the current global economic system, which deprives approximately 70–80 percent of humankind of their basic rights for food, water, self-determination, and preservation of their culture.[1] The mass migrations that have resulted in untold numbers of immigrants and refugees represent the result of the ongoing destruction of older economies, natural resources, and indigenous and other long-established cultures.

Today many Islamic thinkers and writers say that the old, colorful Islamic world is gone forever. The fabulous world captured in *One Thousand and One Nights* was not a romantic fiction – it was a treasure of a culture's memory. The old spirit has vanished along with the destruction of many historical sites throughout much

DOI: 10.4324/9781003609742-19

of the Middle East, including those in Damascus and Baghdad. There is an inner degeneration, what Abdelwahab Meddeb calls "The Illness of Islam."[2] During this same time frame of profound upheaval in that region, there have been an increasing number of terrorist attacks in European countries, and a rising number of Middle Eastern refugees are fleeing to Europe. As a result, anti-Islamic movements are growing in European countries. The fear of Muslim immigrants, disseminated and fanned by news and mass media and promulgated by nationalistic ultras, have stirred up a hornet's nest of irrational feelings and statements. One woman in Dresden, Germany, in a December 2014 TV interview, when asked why she followed the neo-Nazi slogans of *Pegida* (Patriotic Europeans against the Islamization of Europe), gave expression to the fear and confusion surrounding these highly charged movements: "I am not really Christian, but I don't want to have to go to a mosque for Christmas."

The anti-Western attitudes of Islamist youth in European countries can often be traced back to social problems such as unemployment, disenfranchisement, and the loss of cultural roots and perspectives. The so-called Islam of the jihadists' promises a surrogate identity, especially to the descendants of immigrants. The propaganda campaigns of Islamist militant groups like Al Qaeda and IS have been financed by Wahhabist petrol-millionaires from Saudi Arabia. They want to export civil war to the countries of the enemy, the "evil" West, as a kind of a parallel to their exports of oil.[3] On the other side, Western drones and their bombs continue killing people in Islamic countries who are declared to be insurgents and terrorists. The management of these computerized killings is in the hands of US security services without any apparent democratic control, other than the general approval of the president and Congress. Many noncombatants have been killed in these attacks. The terrified become terrifying, in a never-ending vicious cycle.

In thinking about Islam, I am hard pressed to find an imaginal space for a measured reflection and meditation on the activated cultural complexes between the West and Islam. It's a bit like walking through a fog or, as Craig San Roque describes it in *Placing Psyche*, the temporarily lost or disoriented condition of living inside a cultural complex can be akin to living in

> a state where one is never quite sure if one is grasping what is real or not. Cultural complexes often place one in a borderland territory akin to being between dream and reality. The complex itself can be so disorienting that one becomes unsure of where and who one is.[4]

When writing about a cultural complex, I recognize that I both participate in it myself and am trying to keep in mind the audience I am addressing, which is assuredly equally mired in it, but often with quite different perspectives. Will the readers share my views and complexes, or will they scapegoat me and see me as a major part of the problem? Trying to understand what is happening in the midst of an activated cultural complex does not exonerate oneself of either personal or collective responsibility. One thing is certain: there is an undeclared war going on between Western and Middle Eastern or Islamic states, between democratic societies and religious fanatics who become terrorists, between opposing interest groups and cultures. In times of war, individuals have to decide where they stand. I remember a poem, which I've translated here, written in 1967 by the Polish Nobel Prize winner Wislawa Szymborska.[5]

Vietnam

What is your name, woman? I don't know.
Where were you born? I don't know.
Why do you hide in the ground? I don't know.
Since when did you dig in here? I don't know.
Why did you bite me in my forefinger? I don't know.
We don't mean you any harm, you know? I don't know.
On whose side are you? I don't know.
We have war now, you must choose. I don't know.
Does your village still exist? I don't know.

The poem ends with the following question and answer:

Are these your children? Yes.

For me, this poem says as clearly as possible where we can find an elemental common ground.

Contact Zones and Projection

Cultural complexes emerge, like all other complexes, out of the interaction of two psychic entities and in the space in between. There are *rhythms of internalized interactions that have been generalized* (also known as RIGs), which form the core of a complex as well as its surface and the contact zones between two entities.[6] This works for individuals and for communities and cultures. The mutual history of European-Christian and Middle Eastern-Islamic societies follow, if we look into the details, patterns of mutual influence, polarization, and complementarity.

For centuries Europeans did not know much about the Islamic world. When, for example, Goethe wrote his famous cycle of poems and reflections, *The West-Eastern Diwan*, he knew Islam only from translations of poems by Rumi, Hafis, and others. The mystic tradition and the erotic atmosphere of this Islam fascinated him, especially Iranian poetry with its highly developed philosophy. Regarding the Arabian mentality and the despotic attitudes of Islamic leaders such as Timur, he was skeptical. Goethe himself lived in a cultural field between, on one side, the revolutionary, egalitarian stream of the Enlightenment and the French Revolution and, on the other, the restorative system following Napoleon's defeat.

His "Diwan" can be seen as a beautiful, artistic compensation of his situation and the old poet's projection onto the imagined erotic community of his Islam. It is a fantasy of a possible paradise, in a coniunctio of East and West. In fact, Goethe had no real contact with the Islamic world. It was all his romantic imagination about "the poet's country."

Benedict Anderson, as mentioned by Peter Bishop in his paper "The Contact Zone as Imaginal Space," describes human communities as "imagined entities" with a lack of interaction.[7] Bishop quotes Thomas Singer: "Cultural complexes provide a simplistic certainty about a group's place in the world in the face of otherwise conflicting and ambiguous uncertainties."[8] Bishop then continues: "The idea of contact zones moves in the opposite direction by complicating 'notions of static, fixed, bounded socio-cultural wholes' and in so doing undermines simplistic certainties while providing a richer sensibility."[9]

The contact zone between two established cultures usually provides uncertainties about each culture's own values, especially if the contact becomes closer. This can occur when encounters multiply exponentially between the peoples of the two different cultures. A growing number of foreigners in a land tends to increase feelings of insecurity among the natives. Any kind of projection may seem to provide an unconscious feeling of orientation. Sometimes the projection focuses on a regression to some archaic aspect of physiognomy – for example, every man with a black beard being viewed as a potential terrorist. Powerful archetypal defenses of the group spirit and its physical identity tend to be activated.[10] Groups interested in exploiting the insecurities of different cultures become quite adept at manipulating the perceptions of what is happening in the contact zone.

Early Interreligious Dialogue

It is also not uncommon for the contact between different cultures to lead to unforeseen mutual enrichment. The history of encounters between Christianity and Islam provides astonishing examples of such positive outcomes. An impressive encounter of this kind occurred in 1219 when a fleet of crusaders was accompanied by the Italian mystic monk Francesco di Assisi (later St. Francis of Assisi), who went to Egypt with the intention of preaching to and possibly baptizing the sultan! This incredible attempt is well-documented by both Christian and Muslim historians. The crusaders besieged the harbor city of Damietta at the delta of the Nile River in Egypt, whereas the Muslims had their camp on the other side of the town. The beggar-saint crossed the battlefield and the demarcation line between opposing troops and cried loudly, "Sultan, Sultan" and was actually admitted to the sultan's tent. For several days, Francesco di Assisi engaged in a dialogue with Sultan Melek al Kamil, a nephew of the famous Saladin and a Sufi. One day a carpet in which crosses were woven into the pattern was laid before the Christian monk. The sultan watched to see if Francis would step on the crosses, the highest symbol of Christian belief. Francis stepped on the carpet without hesitating, saying, "We Christians have the real cross, and these on the carpet must be the crosses of the two criminals who were crucified together with Jesus."[11] The sultan was impressed. During his prayer, Francis always danced, which was his custom. He praised poverty and charity and said that all creatures were brothers and sisters. The Sufi Sultan may have perceived the strange and fearless Christian monk as a spiritual brother. When they said goodbye, he is said to have asked Francis: "Please, pray to your god, that he may reveal to me the religion which he likes most!"[12]

Unfortunately the story had a disastrous ending when some months later (November 5, 1219) the crusaders conquered Damietta and killed more than 70,000 people. Francis traveled on to Palestine and after some weeks back home to Italy, despondent.

The encounters between Christian and Islamic cultures in the eleventh, twelfth, and thirteenth centuries had a great impact on both sides. The Crusades were just the military side of a many faceted cross-cultural exchange. Francis was a representative of the highly developed Christian movement of mystic introversion and enthusiasm. He was happy to meet in the Muslim leader Melek al Kamil a Sufi with a similar religious imagination of the divine.

Others were more interested in the social and political dimensions of the cultural differences. For instance, the great Emperor Frederic (Friedrich) II (1194–1250), who resided in Sicily, spoke the Arabic language and was familiar with Islamic philosophy. A focus in his discussions with wise Muslims was the balance between religious authority and political power as developed in the Islamic world by the complementary system of the caliph (the spiritual leader) and the sultan (the political power). Frederic compared this structure with the European system in which the pope was the spiritual leader and the emperor held the political power. The pope hated and excommunicated Frederic. Others called Frederic "Stupor mundi" or astonishment/marvel of the world for the broad horizons of his interests and wisdom. And some regarded him as a Muslim. In 1229, he arranged the Treaty of Jaffa, which allowed Christian pilgrims free admittance to Jerusalem. The contact zone between the two cultures at that time was wide and intensively developed, adding enormously to the cultural growth of Europe in that time.

Love and the Hidden Core of a Culture

An interesting outcome of the encounters between Christianity and Islam during the Crusades (1096–1221) was the insight that one can only truly understand the deepest levels of one's own religion and culture. This insight is well developed in *Perceval*, the famous novel by Wolfram von Eschenbach (ca. 1170–1220).[13] The novel describes the quest of young Perceval for the Holy Grail. During his adventures, he comes across a man, a "black-and-white" knight. They start to fight, as knights are wont to do, but fortunately they don't kill one another. Rather, they make peace and then discover that they are half-brothers! Their father, Gahmuret, had been on a Crusade and was married to a Muslim princess before he returned home to marry Herzeloide, Perceval's mother. Feirefiz, the Muslim, was born from Gahmuret's first marriage. Feirefiz, on a quest himself, is looking for his brother.

The crucial scene comes when they finally find the castle of the Holy Grail (Perceval for the second time). When the Holy Grail is brought into the hall for the annual miracle, Perceval only has eyes for the cup that contains the blood of Christ, whereas Feirefiz only has eyes for the beautiful girl carrying the sacred vessel. Feirefiz and the beautiful girl fall in love with each other and marry! As Mohammed said in the Hadith, "Allah is beauty and loves beauty."

This fine story reveals an important difference between the Christian and Islam cultural complex of that time: the erotic, the body, female beauty, the joy of life, and nature were excluded from the Christian ideal. The Christian ascetic attitude had once been developed as a movement against the extroverted, hedonistic, and pagan culture of the ancient Roman world. What we now call the "anima" was able in its Christian context to emerge as the "soul" and later, in the modern spirit, as an inner function of the psyche.[14] But there had also been an emancipative aspect to early Christianity. In the Roman (and also the Jewish) world of this time, women had no rights of their own; their role in life was to marry and to bring up children. Fertility was the essence of their life. When the apostles declared that a woman did not necessarily have to marry, Christianity took a step toward opening up the possibility for women to explore wider aspects of their own spirituality. This message could especially be found in the Syrian church of Makarios and Nestor. The many female martyrs of early Christianity were women who refused to get married and wanted to pursue their own Christian spiritual path.[15] This created the opportunity for women to establish monasteries, which, in turn, became centers of a developed feminine culture.

In contrast to the Christian attitudes toward women and marriage, Islam permitted polygamy; concubines and divorce were also allowed. In Christian Europe, the role of Eros became more and more suspect, and the female body was stigmatized as a source of evil temptation that was countered in the Christian dogma with cruel fantasies of hell fire. Only in the mystic branch of medieval Christianity (as with Mechthild of Magdeburg or Clara of Assisi) did Eros find its (spiritualized) place. In stark contrast, Eros, beauty, and the care for the body were central elements of Islamic culture. The *Hammam*, the public bath, was an element of daily life; the beauty of the body was underlined by soft silk garments.

This has changed dramatically over the last century, and today we witness the opposite development: in the West, Eros, mostly reduced to sexuality and a cult of the athletic body, has become a leading paradigm, whereas in the "Islamized Islam" the former liberal attitude toward the body and Eros has been replaced by rigid repression. The burka is more than a symbol; in the hot and dry climate, Abdelwahab Meddeb says the burka is a prison and torture for women.[16] The burka also triggers a cultural complex among Westerners as it goes against the Western notion that an open, available face reflects an open-mindedness. A trustworthy person would not cover the face and entire body; the eyes peering through the slit of the black veil can be perceived as being as sinister and dangerous like the evil eye. Europeans want to see the face and its expressions, which can be taken in with our own eyes.[17] Other cultures are different. In many traditional societies, looking openly into another's face is regarded as impolite. What Westerners may experience as suspicious may be in different cultures a gesture of respect for the other.

The fact is that the veil in general has been part of feminine clothing since ancient times; it protects the female body, and it also protects the Self in a spiritual dimension. The ancient goddess Isis in Egypt claimed that nobody had ever lifted her veil.[18] The veil signifies female secrets and the mystery of life. But in today's Islamic societies – in Iraq, Iran, Syria, and Egypt, and also in the Islamic Diaspora (for example, in Berlin, Germany) – the obligatory and prescribed veil seems to be an emblem and instrument of an intolerant patriarchal society. Abdelwahab Meddeb further complains that inside the house women have lost their former domain.[19] If this is indeed true, it goes against common Western fantasies about a liberal erotic atmosphere in the homes of the Middle East. In Iran, before the Mullahs came, many women went out of their house without a veil.

Questions and Answers

Based on the stories of St. Francis, Frederic II, and Feirefiz, we can imagine the Islam of another era was quite different from the brutal face Islam shows us today in such aberrations as the IS videos. Both Islam and Christianity have a long history of vacillating between tolerance and intolerance, however. To understand the emergence of the interaction between European Christianity and Islam in their mutually tolerant and intolerant phases we have to go back to the beginning. As Robin Collingwood used to say, everything that happens is an answer to a question.[20] So the first question to explore goes back to the beginning of the relationship, to the origins of the encounter between the Christian and Islamic worlds and worldviews. When Islam sprang into being, Christianity was already 600 years old and had spread around the known world of Europe, the Mediterranean, and Africa, from Syria to Egypt to Maghreb and even to Arabia. There were Christian communities, cities, churches, and monasteries everywhere when Mohammed and his followers began to conquer this world.

The answer as to why and how the Islamic expansion after 622 CE was so successful in such a short period of time is controversial among historians and theologians. At the beginning of the expansion, Islam must have provided answers to underlying questions that Christianity had not successfully addressed. Christianity gained political power when Emperor Constantine embraced it and declared Christianity the official religion of the Roman Empire after 325 CE. All other religions (except the Jewish) were forbidden. Passionate discussions about the basics of the Christian confession took place in various councils, most important of which was the Council of Chalcedon in 451 CE that led to the expulsion and criminalization of so-called heretics. Christianity was not a unified movement.

For the Arabian Peninsula, the monotheistic religion of Mohammed provided a huge step forward in bringing together the different tribes and cultural centers under the umbrella of a unifying, rich vision that included age-old animistic traditions, elements of both Jewish and Christian narratives, and a practical sense for political action. Early Islam, for example, was not missionary; those who were conquered were not forced to convert but had to pay taxes in order to practice their own religious beliefs. There were exceptions, and often many generations of both Christians and Jews living in Islamic lands suffered harsh conditions. The relative tolerance of the Muslim conquerors may be explained by the fact that the early Muslims did not have such a highly developed philosophical and theological culture as both Christians and Jews. The respect shown by Mohammed to the "people of the book" may have also had political reasons. Nevertheless, the tolerance shown by Mohammed was different from the attitude of the Christian Roman Empire, especially of the dogmatic Roman Catholic Church. In contrast to this, Mohammed said, in questions of belief (faith) there is no pressure (no duress, no force, no violence, Sura 2, 256). The translation of this paragraph from the Qur'an is ambiguous, however, and today Wahhabi teachers argue that *Islam* (surrender) means that their mission should consist of more than just a gentle *Dawah* (invitation) to accept the right confession.

The early Islamic leaders and their troops were and behaved like kings and knights in the later medieval style. Some historians have argued that the people in the Christian countries of Palestine, Africa, and even Spain found it easier to live under Islamic governments than Christian states.[21] There was much insecurity during this era, and the Islamic conquerors were able to provide shelter. The rapid spread of Islam was also made possible by the struggles among the heirs of the Roman Empire, the new kingdoms, the empire of Constantinople/Byzantine, and the empire of the Sassanides in Iran. Later Sultans of Istanbul, such as Suleiman (1494–1566), regarded themselves as the successors to the Roman emperor and as a kind of "Holy Roman Emperor of the Islamic Nation."[22] The highly developed Islamic culture spread throughout Asia, India, and China. The original inferiority complex of the early followers of Mohammed was replaced by one of superiority.

But there is another, perhaps deeper answer to the question as to why Islam was so successful in its early expansion. The answer addresses the inner meaning of the Islamic experience and formulation of what we might call the "God complex." The early success of Islam can be viewed as a reaction and even an answer to basic developments and splits in the Christianity of that era. The Christian world of the fifth and sixth centuries was deeply troubled and divided. There was not only the Roman Catholic Church but also the older churches in Antiochia, Syria, Constantinople, and Alexandria. The main streams of Christianity other than the Roman Catholic Church were the Greek/Hellenistic tradition with its emphasis on philosophy (for example, the Gnostics) and the traditions of the Syrian church with its emphasis on asceticism. Makarios, a leading figure of the Syrian church, emphasized that the Christian way was one of poverty and pilgrimage. Central in these controversies were the core beliefs about the identity or nature of Jesus. Was he a man, as the Syrian Nestorians believed? Was he either divine or a synthesis of divine and human, as the Monophysitists said? Or was he both a man and a God? And depending on which theology one embraced, how did one understand the Holy Trinity? And the influential but heretical followers of Arius taught that Jesus was just a man and a prophet – a concept close to that of Mohammed (Sura 4/169).[23]

The visions and faith of Mohammed provided a clear, simple answer to these perplexing theological debates by avoiding altogether the questions of Jesus's nature, his cruel death, and the resurrection. He said that it was not Jesus who died on the cross but somebody else, and that Jesus was taken up into heaven alive (Sura 4/156). The image of a suffering God was not acceptable to Muhammed. Indeed, it must have been regarded as blasphemy, as it was also by the Jews. God had to be an absolute authority, not a man crucified like a criminal. The Christian God complex in its Catholic dogmatic version (*Credo*) contains the Creator of everything (*faith*), the Son as his incarnation as a suffering man (*love*), and the Holy Spirit as the source for an ongoing revelation of God's presence (*hope*).[24] The God of the Qur'an is the absolute and undivided authority and divinity – more like a principle.[25] He is beauty, and "Allah is beauty" does not fit with images of the crucified Jesus.[26]

Honor and dignity were other essential core values of Mohammed's culture. I suppose the roots of the emphasis on honor and dignity (and shame as the opposite pattern) date back to the elemental needs and realities of the clan structure of nomadic societies grounded in harsh natural conditions. Honor and dignity are old pre-Islamic values. Nomadic life has always existed close to the edge of survival, as the group constantly faces the danger of extinction. The clan was the only way to survive under such primitive conditions. Therefore, the inner rules governing the lives of its members had to be strict. Individuality was not valued, but rather the clan's honor and purity were the supreme values. "Rotten tomatoes" (for example, women who got pregnant by foreigners) had to be extinguished.[27] Allah was the highest symbol for this extremely strong inner law. The Christian distinction between a guilty act and the person committing the sinful action (*peccato* and *peccatore*), basic for the Christian system of confession, repentance, and forgiveness (*the redemption of sins*) had no place in the early Islamic tradition – and certainly not in the modern "Islamized Islam" of the Wahhabi ideology.[28]

Ambivalence and Ambiguity

I am writing this paragraph on the day (January 7, 2015) the world was shocked by the news that Islamist terrorists had killed twelve people in the *Charlie Hebdo* massacre in Paris. It was an attack against the editors of the satiric magazine that had published caricatures of the prophet Mohammed. The murder was carried out as an act of retribution or revenge for a satirical cartoon attack on the Islamic God complex – the untouchable holiness of Allah and his prophet. The barbaric act seems to be a further step in the escalation of a vicious cycle. It is quite painful to think that Western attitudes and behaviors, such as the *Charlie Hebdo* provocations, have contributed to the increase in violence and profound mutual disrespect. It is often asked whether the terror we see today is one side of the Islamic coin of vacillating between tolerance and intolerance, or whether this deeply embedded ambivalence is an essential feature of Islam in general. Perhaps less frequently asked in the West (in Europe and the United States) is whether the West's vacillation between tolerance and intolerance, as reflected in immigration policy, for example, is also contributing to the escalation of violence.

Following the scholarship of Abdelwahab Waddab and of Peter Scholl-Latour, the terror of Al Qaeda and IS has nothing to do with what Islam has been for more than 1000 years of its history.[29] Thomas Bauer, Professor of Arabic Studies in Muenster, Germany, also presents a different perspective on current developments.[30] He argues that the Islamic tradition was relatively tolerant for 1000 years. Even the modern term *Islamic world* doesn't adequately reflect the tremendous diversity that existed among all the different cultures in which Islam was the main religion – be it Egypt, Arabia, Mongolia, India, or Indonesia. There were different texts or versions of the Qur'an, with tremendous diversity and ambiguity in the readings of sayings, which were a source of ongoing discourse among the imams. Central to the history of Islam was the oral tradition (*Hadith*) about what Mohammed did. The openness to different versions and interpretations was signaled by the saying, "God knows it better," which served as the closing and opening to discourse about Mohammed and his faith. A famous scholar, Ibn al-Jazari (1350–1429), praised the ambiguity of the Qur'an, saying that the oral tradition was much more important than the written one. He mentioned seven possible ways (*harf*) of interpreting the Qur'an; others spoke of forty.[31] In the Islamic tradition, there was no dogma that was proclaimed as the truth as there was in the Christian tradition. We might, perhaps, put it this way: the Self, as projected and expressed in the Divine Self of Allah, was a flexible one, and it could work within many different traditions and cultures.[32]

This began to change in the nineteenth century, and that change accelerated in the twentieth century. Ibn Uthaimin (1929–2001), the Wahhabi-Salafist teacher, became the leading figure in the "Islamization of Islam" movement, eliminating as much as possible all the ambiguous and tolerant elements and declaring Islam a kind of state ideology.[33] The strangely dogmatic and brutal pseudo-Islam of IS shows this involution of Islam. It is not, in fact, a return to supposed "medieval origins" but a modern fiction. Also what they call sharia is mostly a modern invention. Following the Arabist Thomas Bauer, rarely was a woman stoned to death because of adultery in the 1000 years after Mohammed. The law about adultery was too ambiguous, making it extremely difficult to sentence a woman to stoning (not so far from what Jesus said in John 8:7: "Let him who is without sin among you be the first to throw a stone at her"). Also what we call sexuality (which often reduces sexuality, including homosexuality, exclusively to the physical act) was handled in the earlier Islamic faith in a much more tolerant way than we can imagine. Ambiguity, sometimes even in a playful manner, was essential to Islamic thinking, law, and culture. The dogmatic attitude of Roman Christianity with its councils and the absolute authority of the Pope has historically been just the opposite.

Old Traumas and the "Islamization of Islam"

The ugly face shown to Westerners by Islamized Islam reactivates age-old traumas among Europeans. Throughout its history, Europe felt it had to constantly defend itself against Muslim invaders. Before Mohammed's wars of conquest, Europe was Christian, and Christianity had hegemony everywhere in the known world. In the first generations after Mohammed, those who followed him conquered many Christian countries. The Iberian Peninsula also came under Islamic rule. Christian Europe was filled with religious conflicts and left in a state of helpless shock. Step by step, Christianity recovered in what has been called the *Reconquista* (711–1492), or the recovery of Spain.

In the middle of this period, in 1009, the Crusades began after the fanatic Fatimid Caliph Al-Hakim Allah B'Amr destroyed the famous Church of the Holy Sepulchre in Jerusalem, one of the most holy sites and cathedrals of Christianity. The Crusades, a reaction to this event, were intended to secure free access to Jerusalem for Christian pilgrims. With the fall of Byzantium in 1453, the capital of Eastern Europe and of the Eastern Christian church fell into Muslim hands under the Ottomans, and in 1683, the Ottomans besieged Vienna. The shocking invasions of Western Europe from the East are still potent symbols in the European psyche and its cultural complex of the danger and horror of Muslim barbarians. (The Russian army in World War II carried similar projections for Europeans, although without the Muslim attribute.)

The golden age of Islam ended in the sixteenth century. With the discovery of the Americas, the Islamic world lost its importance. International trade and economy took other routes in the following centuries, and military encounters with Europe's colonial powers led to humiliating disasters. Cultural and military colonization of Muslim lands went hand in hand. Medieval Islam was not able to recover. During this deep crisis within the Islamic world of the nineteenth and twentieth centuries, a fundamentalist Neo-Islam was created in response to this demoralization. Thomas Bauer and Abdelwahab Meddeb argue that the modern "Islamized Islam" became a copy of the more and more rigid European way of thinking.[34] The Enlightenment in Europe was reaction to religious wars such as the Thirty Years' War between Catholics and Protestants (1618–1648). It brought to an end the religious paranoia that had characterized much of the medieval world. But with the age of the *Cartesian cut* (to exclude everything from discourse that one cannot prove), with Newton's physics and its increasingly rigid scientific paradigm, any playful ambiguity was regarded as inaccurate, "medieval," silly, and chaotic. The modern Western way of thinking with its science, technology, and its military superiority brought even more humiliating experiences to the Arabian countries when the European states won colonial wars against them. Their reaction was to overcompensate by creating an "Islamized Islam," and in the process, they actually developed a parallel to and a mirror of European rigidity. The vision of the first leading Imam of this Islamized Islam, Sayyid Qutbs, is nihilistic and reads like a nightmare.[35] The involution of the traditional Islamic way, which originally had embraced ambiguity, resulted in increasing theological rigidities that became even stronger with the collapse of the Communist bloc, putting an end to the socialistic hopes of people in Islamic countries.

The West made many mistakes in its continuing humiliation of the culture of the Islamic states. The massive export of weapons to the Middle East by the United

States, its intensely ambivalent relationship with the Taliban in Afghanistan, and later with Saddam Hussein in Iraq, who was first a partner and then the "devil," ongoing human rights violations on both sides, and other social injustices inflicted on the Muslim people by their own leaders as well as foreign leaders, has driven people crazy. The cultural complex of the Muslim world has been fueled equally by the ongoing humiliation of its people and the demagogic statements of several leading figures such as Ibn Uthaimin and Osama bin Laden. The result has been the development of the increasingly rigid container of Islamic jihadism for the already profoundly scattered, fragmented cultural self of the Muslim people. George W. Bush's behavior became a perfect mirror in a disastrous symmetry with the fractured self-image of the Islamic world.

There is also an inner reason for paranoia among the Muslim population: the immense wealth generated by the oil of Saudi Arabia and its Middle Eastern neighbors, such as Iran and Iraq, seems to rarely be used for developing an infrastructure that would promote modern education and other social services for the general population. Autocratic governments such as in Saudi Arabia are selling the treasures of their earth to the "American devil." It seems schizophrenic to be selling the oil of the region to the West while simultaneously exporting the Wahhabi ideology, supported by oil-rich Saudis, which promotes everywhere in the Middle East a radical and narrow-minded "Islamized Islam." Saudi oil fuels the world, and Saudi Wahhabism fuels the black-and-white psychology of Islamist terrorism. The hypocritical attitude, nevertheless, is on both sides: of the consumer as well as of the seller.

Islamist Terrorism, Humiliation, Inflation, and the Paranoid State

We are confronted with activated cultural complexes on all sides of the split between the West and Islam. There is no resolution on the horizon. Israel is in the midst of an undeclared war with the Palestinians (as I wrote this in 2015; now we have open war in Gaza). Europeans are trying to live in a post-heroic age, desiring to do their business without confrontation. But European hopes seem to be vain when confronted with "heroic" suicide terrorists who fight an asymmetric war against the open societies of the West.

Hundreds of the terrorists in IS and other more or less informal terrorist groups are European immigrants who have given up their life in France, Belgium, or Germany and joined the jihad. They are psychologically in a desolate position and only a few find their way back home. "We have a terrible problem in France of disenfranchised young people, with no opportunities," said Oliver Roy. "Many of them start off in petty delinquency, but for some of them, radical Islam is a way to find a second life – not in society, but in terms of self-image and self-esteem."[36] It seems that they have no chance at all. Religion without a stabilizing culture is dangerous.

Of course, the specific social and cultural traditions are different in Syria and France, for instance, but the archetypal structural problem is similar. This shared archetypal pattern centers around the lost ability to tolerate ambiguity that would allow for the inner and outer psychic play of opposites. The ability to tolerate ambiguity does not yield to the rigid defenses of fixed positions. When the self of the collective and individual psyche is in real danger, the ego needs to take responsibility. This is an essential ego function at both the individual and collective level; there are far-reaching consequences if this doesn't occur. In this formulation, the ego, the "I," is far more than the persona. It is the ego – the inner hero – who fights the dragon, and normally this heroic ego complex functions as the carrier of ethics and morality. This is true in both individual and collective processes. But in critical times the ego complex is overwhelmed by primitive non-ego aggressive elements. Then a political or spiritual leader may arise to carry the projection and delegation of the ego complex of the many. Unfortunately such leaders are seldom aware of their responsibility for the psychic stability and lively well-being of the whole, of the collective psyche.

C. G. Jung wrote often about the consequences of the abaissement or lowering of consciousness into a collective mass psychology.[37] The individual loses his or her consciousness and forgets his or her moral responsibility, even for terrorist acts. The sociologist Philip Zimbardo gives many examples of this mechanism:[38] If people put on a uniform, or a black mask like the IS terrorists, and are then placed in an "extraordinary situation," they will follow the instructions of a leader who enables them to do the unthinkable. They lose their individuality, identify themselves with the collective, and become unconscious and inflated particles of their group. The IS terrorists, for example, project their need for redemption onto their faith and their commanders. They have nothing more to lose. Having lost their self, they are zombies, the walking dead.

Why Is the Complex So High Charged?

The contact zone between the modern or postmodern Western psyche and the neo-Islamic psyche seems to carry a highly explosive charge. On the Islamist side, there is psychic inflation and archaic destructivity. The suicide terrorist who wants to kill him- or herself in the murder of as many non-believers (Jews, Christians, and Americans) as possible is emblematic of a hopeless psychic situation within the collective. The bloody conflict between Shiites and Sunnis is suicidal and fatal for the Islamic world in general. It is a picture of despair and deadly aggression against everybody – a nightmare that calls to mind the end of time.

Muslim representatives in Europe usually declare that Islamist terror has nothing to do with the Islamic religion. This seems to mean that they don't feel responsibility for any terrorist attacks. In non-European countries, the position of most Islamic teachers is quite different. There, speakers propagate jihad against the West, the unbelievers, the Americans, the Israelis, and declare Fatwa against critics who should be killed. Even the traditionally moderate Al Azhar University in Cairo joins those advocating holy jihad. All parties, no matter how different their positions, claim to read the Qur'an in the proper way. The Shiites, Sunnis, and other groups declare their right to kill each other based on religious arguments. If a religion becomes ill (as Abdelwahab Meddeb calls the degeneration of Islam), it loses its moral authority.

On the other side of the Islam/West divide, European countries and the United States are trying to hinder the further expansion of IS and other radical Islamists. But they continue to sell weapons of every kind to governments like Egypt; the Kurds get the weapons for their fight against IS for gratis. The main military problem is that the new wars are quite different from the older ones like World War II. The combatants are mostly non-governmental armies and networks of terrorists – with the difference between soldiers and civilians becoming even more blurred. This results in an asymmetric war in which flexible partisans battle somewhat helpless dinosaurs who happen to be able to throw bombs as well.

About Ambivalence – a Personal Vignette From Berlin, Germany

In my work as a child psychiatrist and psychoanalyst in Berlin (the former Berlin-West) for over thirty years, I have seen many Islamic children and families, most of them from Türkiye. What I am writing here is based on my own experience, many discussions with social workers, and with my wife Beate who is a gynecologist caring for many patients from Middle Eastern countries, including Iran and Saudi Arabia. My observations do not fall into black-and-white patterns that can be placed into politically correct categories. I've tried to be as objective as possible, like an ethnologist in his own country.

At the beginning of the 1970s, the presence of oriental-looking Turkish families was regarded by many Berliners as a colorful addition to a multicultural society. Most of them were Alawites who might be described as belonging to a "soft"-Islamic faith. Their religion was inconspicuous and of little interest to others. "Islam" was not a topic. I learned about these people only because I had to arrange social work and psychotherapies for youngsters of these families. The problems grew over the years. The suicide rate of Turkish girls was (and still is) much higher than that of German-born children and adolescents. There was obviously a kind of collective depression among Turkish women, both the mothers and their daughters. They struggled between integrating into a Western lifestyle and maintaining the traditional role of women within their culture. The boys also suffered from role confusion; their fathers were often unemployed and had lost the authority they enjoyed in rural Anatolia. The patriarchal order became inadequate as a model for the education and socialization of boys in the modern city life of Berlin. Many of the Turkish boys found themselves in a cultural vacuum and acted out the resentments of their parents. They began to attack German boys on the streets and to take by force their mobile phones, sneakers, and money. A street war went on among schoolboys, often unknown to their naïve German parents. I frequently wondered why this did not appear in the official statistics of criminality. Obviously, it was a taboo subject. Later it was published that a high rate of youth crime in Berlin was committed by children of Islamic immigrants.[39]

In 2015, the third- and even fourth-generation of people with Turkish backgrounds are living in Germany. Their children are born here but often don't speak German fluently. Frequently, their mothers have come from rural, undeveloped parts of Türkiye through arranged marriages. They were forbidden by their husbands to learn German. Recep Tayyip Erdoğan, the nationalist Turkish president, visited Berlin in 2013 and warned its Turkish population not to integrate into a Western lifestyle. Insufficient education and language skills limit the Turkish population's opportunities on the job market. But there are also many Turkish families who are well-integrated into German life; their girls and women do not wear the veil and are keen on good education. They often risk conflicts with more traditional families. Among this more well-integrated population are many Iranian refugee families from an urban background who remain proud of their culture of origin.

In Berlin-West, there were also many people from Lebanon. In the 1990s, I sometimes had to take care of Lebanese boys whose fathers or uncles were absent and engaged in civil war, including terrorist activities. My job as a medical doctor was to treat the panic attacks or enuresis of the children. I remember one of these boys who obsessively drew exploding bombs in school and explained to me how to build an electronic detonator. With the increasing insecurity and civil wars in the Middle East, and after the Berlin Wall came down, more and more Sunnis and Shiites, also from countries other than Türkiye, came to Berlin. Germany's generous social welfare attracted them. This new immigrant population mixed with those who had come from Türkiye, and they began to establish ghetto-like structures in neighborhoods such as Neukoelln, Kreuzberg, and Moabit. The politicians ignored this development for years. Today, these neighborhoods include no-go areas, especially in the evening for non-veiled Western girls and women. In the Al-Nur Mosque, Salafist imams preach the inferiority of women and call for a jihad against Europeans. Arranged marriages and even murders (*Ehrenmorde*) based on old family and clan honor codes still occur.

Family, clan, and religious affiliations play a far more important role in the Middle Eastern immigrant community than we can imagine with our Western emphasis on individualism. I remember visiting a Lebanese family with a delinquent adolescent. On the wall was a portrait of a friendly looking man with a beard and a turban. I asked who he was, and they told me he was the leader of Hezbollah in Lebanon, Hassan Nasrallah. My patient's uncle was a close associate of Nasrallah. Later, the translator told me that everybody in the clan, including my young patient, had to be loyal to this group and their vow to kill all Jews and to extinguish Israel from the earth!

The first Salafists and Islamists, those who embrace a more literal, strict, and puritanical approach to Islam, appeared in Berlin about 2005. We have not yet had a major terrorist attack as in London or Paris. But even before September 11, 2001, terrorist attacks in the United States, a subliminal aversion against the growing number of Muslims in Berlin had emerged among many people. This created an inner conflict for many Berliners who did not want to be racist and sought to live in peace with immigrants from other cultures. But, over time, this aversion became less a matter of private disquiet.

Lurking behind the mainstream emphasis on tolerance is a deeper level of defiance (*Trotz*) or intolerance. The cultural complexes of Islamic societies have met and triggered complementary complexes in the German "natives" as well. Both sides are ambivalent: On the Islamic side, there is often the basic wish to live in peace and social security, which is rarely possible in their own countries. At the same time, immigrants wish to affirm their identities in a way that is, at times, offensive to the German population, triggering a vicious cycle of further exclusion and reinforcing the Muslim identification with Islamist beliefs as unwelcome, alienated "foreigners." A good example of how this vicious cycle is intensified is the symbolic matter of wearing the veil. Many Muslim women now consider it obligatory to wear the veil, which affirms their group identity. But the veil is regarded by many Germans, both female and male, as representative of a sexist, foreign psychology that they have left behind over the centuries. The veil symbolizes an attack on the progress that many women have long fought for, beginning with the early suffragettes in the late 1800s and early 1900s. In Germany, for instance, the feminist movement of the 1970s and 1980s was essential for female emancipation with rights equal to men. Muslim women with their black veils are perceived as submissive victims of a reactionary, patriarchal society. In fact, not all Muslim women wear the veil, and some of those who do say that it protects them from indiscrete aggression from young men of their own culture![40]

There is a fragile balance between the tolerance that is fostered by economic well-being and a wish for nonviolent conflict resolution on the one hand, and a growing animosity, grudges, and built-up fears and resentments on the other hand. The role of the media is critical in maintaining the fragile balance, but it, too, can fall into fueling the *Trotz* and inflaming the ever-ready cultural complexes on both sides to erupt in a destructive fury.

Children of Abraham

I want to close this chapter by going a step deeper into the dynamics of humiliation, rigid defenses, and the formation of a cultural complex. How does one find a sense of inner security in a culture?[41] This leads to a further complicating aspect of the West and Islam that I have not yet mentioned: the relationship between the Muslim and Jewish cultures. Both Islamic and Jewish traditions originate in the same common ancestor, Abraham. From Hagar, Ishmael was born as the first son of Abraham; and from Sarah, Isaac was born as the second son of Abraham. Both traditions claim to have the ancestor who was closest to God's heart, the real one who carried the promise of becoming a people as flourishing as the stars in heaven. But love is unpredictable and arbitrary. As the Jewish philosopher Jacob Taubes writes, "Nothing but the fairness of law is able to moderate the arbitrariness of love."[42] The sibling rivalry of Ishmael's Muslim people and Isaac's Jewish people runs through history to this very day. Jesus was born a Jew; he could never be the Messiah for Muslims, the descendants of Ishmael. There are two completely different narratives of God's and Abraham's preferences. There are even two different versions of the temptation of Abraham: whether Ishmael or Isaac was to be sacrificed for God on Mount Moriah, which was both the site of the later Temple of Jerusalem and of the Muslim sanctuary of the Dome of the Rock and the Al Aqsa Mosque. This site is an eternal symbol for the love-hate of siblings. Mohammed, interestingly, in Sura 2/135 refers to father Abraham who was neither Jew nor Christian.

Both religions, Jewish and Islam, are based on the law. Living daily life according to the law made the interpretation of its provisions fundamental in the Jewish Mishna and the Islamic Hadith; both traditions required continuous reflections through educated dialogue on the meaning of the law and the ambiguities of its interpretation. With Christians claiming to be the beloved and true children of God, a third applicant and candidate for divine love joined the family. We know that the ability to play freely with inner realities is essential for mental health. Preserving a "free and protected inner space" is essential for the development of the child as well as for the development of a culture.[43] C. G. Jung calls this the "transcendent function."[44] If living according to the law is the only way to moderate the arbitrary unfairness of divine love or rejection, one can better understand the value that was given to its discourse. If a culture feels humiliated, the question of divine justice will arise. The law may appear in quite rigid and pathological forms, as we see in the contemporary Salafist-Wahhabist system. To reduce the pressure and to release positive energies, one should support and strengthen the side of trust and self-confidence. To redeem the destructive collusion of the activated complex between Islam and Europe (and also between Islam and Jewish culture), it seems necessary to reflect on the origins of the mutual humiliations, rivalries, defeats, and threats, and to change our attitudes. Lessing, in his famous theater piece *Nathan der Weise* (1779), wrote that there were three rings, given by the father to his sons, and nobody could say which the right one was. Sultan Al Kamil's response to Saint Francis is wise: "Pray for me, that God may reveal to me the religion that is most pleasant to him."

I will end with a joke: An imam, a Christian priest, and a rabbi were asked if God exists. The Imam said: Of course, Allah, blessed be his name! The Christian said: O Yes, it's Jesus. Then the rabbi said: I don't know, but if he exists, then he is three.

Notes

1 Of course, the numbers differ. Compare Le Monde, *Atlas der Globalisierung 2012* (Paris: Le Monde, 2012). See also Johan Galtung, *Menschenrechte-einmal anders* (Berlin: Suhrkamp, 2012).

2 Abdelwahab Meddeb, *Die Krankheit des Islam* (Zürich: Unionsverlag, 2007). Also published as *La Maladie de l'Islam* (Paris: Édition du Seuil, 2002).

3 Meanwhile the IS and other Islamistic armies have found other sources, especially oil and extortion.

4 Craig San Roque, *Placing Psyche: Exploring Cultural Complexes in Australia*, series ed. Thomas Singer (New Orleans: Spring Journal Books, 2011), p. 11.

5 Wislawa Szymborska, *Gedichte, übersetzt von Karl Dedecius* (Krakow: Wydanie Czwarte, 1997), p. 122 (my translation).

6 Representation of Interactions that have been Generalized (RIG), a concept by D. N. Stern, *The Interpersonal World of the Infant* (New York: Basic Books, 1985).

7 Peter Bishop, "The Contact Zone as Imaginal Space," in Thomas Singer (ed.), *Placing Psyche: Exploring Cultural Complexes in Australia* (New Orleans: Spring Journal Books, 2011).

8 Thomas Singer, "The Cultural Complex and Archetypal Defenses of the Group Spirit," in T. Singer and S. Kimbles (eds.), *The Cultural Complex: Contemporary Jungian Perspectives on Psyche and Society* (London and New York: Routledge, 2004), p. 21.

9 Bishop, "The Contact Zone as Imaginal Space," p. 27.

10 Singer, "The Cultural Complex and Archetypal Defenses of the Group Spirit."

11 Adolf Holl, *Der letzte Christ. Franz von Assisi* (Frankfurt/Main & Berlin: Ullstein Verlag, DVA, 1979/1989), p. 213ff. The original documents are from St. Francis' biographers Bonaventura and Celano.

12 Holl, *Der letzte Christ*, § 224.

13 Wolfram von Eschenbach, *Parzival*, several editions. My colleague Sylvester Wojtkowski (New York) referred me to the story of Feirefiz.

14 See C. G. Jung, "Psychological Types (1921)," in G. Adler and R. F. C. Hull (eds. and trans.), *The Collected Works of C. G. Jung*, Vol. 6 (Princeton, NJ: Princeton University Press, 1971), about the early Christian ascetics. Regarding the development of the Christian anima, see also Jörg Rasche, *das Lied des Grünen Löwen: Music als Spiegel der Seele (The Song of the Green Lion: Music as a Mirror of the Soul)* (Gießen: Psychosozial Verlag, 2004/2014), Chapter 3.

15 See Marie-Louise von Franz, *Passio Perpetuae* (Zürich: Daimon Verlag, 1982) and Alan Posener, *Maria* (Reinbeck bei Hamburg: Rowohlt tb, 1999), p. 82. See also G. Quispel, *Makarius. Das Thomasevangelium und das Lied von der Perle* (Leiden: Brill, 1967), passim.

16 Meddeb, *Die Krankheit des Islam*, p. 153 ff.

17 Ethnologists and philosophers such as Michel Foucault have written about the different cultural meanings of the eye and the power of looking. See Michel Foucault, *Überwachen und Strafen (Surveiller et punir)* (Frankfurt am Main: Suhrkamp, 1975).

18 "I am what exists, what has been and will be, and no mortal human has ever lifted my veil." Plutarch in *De Idide and Osiris*, quoted in Adolf Weis, *Die Madonna Platytera, Die blauen Bücher* (Königstein/Taunus: Karl Robert Langewiesche, 1985).

19 Meddeb, *Die Krankheit des Islam*.

20 Quotation after Cathy Urwin and John Hood-Williams, *Child Psychotherapy, War, and the Normal Child: Selected Papers of Margaret Lowenfeld* (London: Free Association, 1988), p. 80ff. Important writings of Collingwood (a close friend of Lowenfeld) include "An Essay on Philosophical Method" (1933) and "The Idea of History" (1947).

21 Walter Kaegi, "Le fulgurantes victoires des conquerants arabes," in *Chretiens-Musulmans* (Paris: Premiere Rencontres, La Croix-Le Monde de la Bible, 2010), p. 29ff.

22 Alexander Von Gleichen-Russwurm, "Die Kulturwelt des Orients," in *Kultur-und Sittengeschichte* (Wien: Gutenberg Verlag, 1928), p. 277.

23 Von Gleichen-Russwurm, "Die Kulturwelt des Orients," p. 229.

24 See David Steindl-Rast, OSB, *Credo* (Freiburg: Herder, 2010).

25 Verena Tobler, personal communication, 2015.

26 *Allah Is Beauty* is the title of a book by Navid Khermani, *Gott ist schön: das aesthetische Erleben des Koran* (Muenchen: Beck, 1999). Khermani says that the Qur'an is music and should be recited in a musical manner.

27 Bert Meltzer and Rokaya Marzouk Abu-Rekayek, "Sandspieltherapie als psychosozial-politischer Vermittler in der Veränderung der traditionellen Beduinenkultur," *Zeitschrift für Sandspieltherapie* 37 (December 2014).

28 See Johan Galtung, *Konflikte und Konfliktlösung* (Berlin: Homilius Verlag, 2007), p. 181.

29 See Meddeb, *Die Krankheit des Islam*, p. 191ff. He discusses the legends of the Assassines and Ismailites. Peter Scholl-Latour, *Der Fluch der bösen Tat: Das Scheitern des Westens im Orient* (Berlin: Propyläen/Ullstein, 2014).
30 Thomas Bauer, *Die Kultur der Ambiguität. Eine andere Geschichte des Islam* (Insel, Berlin: Verlag der Weltreligionen, 2011). I have to thank Dr. Sepp Grässner, Berlin, for the reference to this important book.
31 Bauer, *Die Kultur der Ambiguität*, p. 86ff.
32 Bauer doesn't speak about the conflicts between the Shiite and Sunni traditions. Still today in Iran, there are respected minorities like Zoroastrians, Alevites, and Syrian Christians.
33 A term coined by Thomas Bauer.
34 Bauer, *Die Kultur der Ambiguität*, p. 192ff; Meddeb, *Die Krankheit des Islam*, p. 125ff.
35 Meddeb, *Die Krankheit des Islam*, p. 137.
36 Oliver Roy, interview in *Le Monde*. See Oliver Roy, *Holy Ignorance: When Religion and Culture Part Ways* (New York: Columbia, 2011).
37 C. G. Jung, "Civilization in Transition," in G. Adler and R. H. C. Hull (eds. and trans.), *The Collected Works of C. G. Jung*, Vol. 10 (Princeton, NJ: Princeton University Press, 1968).
38 Philip Zimbardo, *Der Luzifer-Effekt. Die Macht der umstände und die Psychologie des Bösen* (Berlin-Heidelberg: Springer, 2012). Published in English as *The Lucifer Effect: How Good People Turn Evil* (New York: Random House, 2007).
39 For the criminality statistics, see *Bundeskriminalamt*, at http://www.bka.de/pks2004/index.html.
40 Some feminists show sympathy with the veil of their Islamic sisters, as a sign of female culture.
41 I am referring in general to Charles Taylor, *Multiculturalism and "The Politics of Recognition"* (Princeton, NJ: Princeton University Press, 1992).
42 Jacob Taubes, "Die Streitfrage zwischen Judentum und Christentum," in *Vom Kult zur Kultur, Bausteine zu einer Kritik der historischen Vernunft* (München: Fink Verlag, 1996), p. 98.
43 As described by Donald Winnicott or Dora Kalff.
44 C. G. Jung, "The Structure and Dynamics of the Psyche," in G. Adler and R. H. C. Hull (eds. and trans.), *The Collected Works of C. G. Jung*, Vol. 8 (Princeton, NJ: Princeton University Press, 1969).

Index

Note: Page numbers in *italics* indicate a figure on the corresponding page.

For Product Safety Concerns and Information please contact our EU
representative GPSR@taylorandfrancis.com
Taylor & Francis Verlag GmbH, Kaufingerstraße 24, 80331 München, Germany

www.ingramcontent.com/pod-product-compliance
Lightning Source LLC
Chambersburg PA
CBHW050337270326
41926CB00016B/3503